KHOMEINI'S GHOST

Con Coughlin is the executive foreign editor of
the *Daily Telegraph* and a world-renowned expert on the
Middle East. He is the critically acclaimed author of several
books, including the best-selling *Saddam: The Secret Life*.
He appears regularly on television and radio in
Britain and America to comment on
international security issues.

CON COUGHLIN

KHOMEINI'S GHOST

PAN BOOKS

First published 2009 by Macmillan

First published in paperback 2010 by Pan Books
an imprint of Pan Macmillan, a division of Macmillan Publishers Limited
Pan Macmillan, 20 New Wharf Road, London N1 9RR
Basingstoke and Oxford
Associated companies throughout the world
www.panmacmillan.com

ISBN 978-0-230-71455-7

Typeset by Setsystems Limted, Saffron Walden, Essex
Printed in the UK by CPI Mackays, Chatham ME5 8TD

Visit **www.panmacmillan.com** to read more about all our books
and to buy them. You will also find features, author interviews and
news of any author events, and you can sign up for e-newsletters
so that you're always first to hear about our new releases.

For Katherine

Picture Acknowledgements

Getty Images: 5 (Roger Viollet), 7 (Gabriel Duval/AFP),
8 (Rolls Press/Popperfoto), 9 (Kaveh Kazemi), 12 (Central Press),
16 (H. Kotilainen/AFP), 19 (Kaveh Kazemi/Keystone), 20 (STF/AFP),
24 (AFP), 26 (Mike Nelson/AFP), 27 (Kaveh Kazemi), 28 (Georges DeKeerle),
29 (SIMO/AFP), 30 (Thomas Hartwell/Time Life Pictures),
31 (Georges DeKeerle), 43 (Behrouz Mehri/AFP).

PA Photos: 4, 6 (Campion), 10, 11, 13, 14, 15, 17, 18, 21 (Ron Edmonds),
22 (USMC), 23, 32 (Adam Butler), 33, 34 (Behrouz Mehri), 35 (Ali Mohammed),
36, (Mohammed Zaatari), 37 (Jacob Silberberg), 38 (Hasan Sarbakhshian),
39 (Alaa Al-Marjani), 40 (Mehr News Agency, Sajjad Safari),
41 (Mohammed Zaatari), 42 (Parspix).

Every effort has been made to contact copyright holders of photographs
reproduced in this book. If any have been inadvertently overlooked,
the publishers will be pleased to make restitution
at the earliest opportunity.

Contents

Introduction

My first encounter with the forces of revolutionary Iran took place on a grey, wet morning in Beirut at the height of the Lebanese civil war in February 1984. For several days, in common with the rest of the civilian population of West Beirut, I had been forced to take shelter in a basement while rival militias battled for control of the city. The Lebanese government had all but ceased to function, and the American-led multinational peacekeeping force that had been deployed two years previously was preparing to undertake an ignominious retreat, its morale eviscerated by a sequence of deadly suicide bomb attacks. During the course of the war I had become well acquainted with the various factions fighting for supremacy, from the Christian Phalangists and their Israeli backers who dominated East Beirut, to the various Muslim, Palestinian and Druze factions that occupied the city's western and southern districts. But that morning, as I made my way tentatively through the familiar streets of West Beirut to examine the damage caused by the recent fighting, I came across an ominous new arrival on the scene – groups of heavily armed young Muslim militiamen bearing the Iranian flag and posters of Ayatollah Ruhollah Khomeini, the founder of Iran's Islamic revolution.

I knew that a small contingent of Iran's Revolutionary Guards had deployed to Lebanon soon after the Israeli invasion of 1982, but had mainly confined their activities to their base in the Bekaa Valley in the east of the country. There were plenty of rumours circulating about their involvement in the suicide truck-bomb attacks against the Americans and French the previous year, but until this moment they had not made their presence felt on the war-ravaged streets of the country's capital. Nor did they make any attempt to conceal their true allegiance when I approached them. 'I am a Khomeini Muslim,' declared one seventeen-year-old youth who was standing beneath a picture of the Iranian leader and clutching a Kalashnikov rifle. 'Khomeini is our strength and our power.' It later transpired that these young men were members of Hizbollah, the newly created Shia Muslim militia set up by Iran to defend the interests of Lebanon's 1.5 million Shias.

Within days of their arrival on Beirut's streets the city's atmosphere took a dramatic turn for the worse. Even in the midst of a brutal conflict Beirut had managed to retain some of its pre-war glamour, when it was known as the Paris of the Levant. But within days of the arrival of pro-Khomeini militiamen young women in Western dress were roughly instructed to dress more modestly, and several bars, restaurants and hotels were attacked for refusing to dispose of their stocks of alcohol. This was the start of a campaign of intimidation that would have a dramatic impact on the city. By the end of the year, pro-Iranian militiamen had begun kidnapping Westerners as part of a deliberate campaign to drive the last remnants of Western influence from Lebanon. One morning I would be sitting in the hotel restaurant having breakfast next to Terry Anderson, the Associated Press bureau chief; hours later he had been kidnapped by pro-Khomeini gunmen, and would not be released for another six years. On another occasion I had dinner with the British journalist John McCarthy: two days later he, was abducted. Through the simple expedient of kidnapping Western citizens and holding them hostage for an indefinite period, Iran's Lebanese allies succeeded in driving the remaining Westerners out of the city.

A few years later I saw another side to the devotion of

Khomeini's supporters for the Islamic revolution when I accompanied a unit of Revolutionary Guards to the front line of Iran's long-running war with Iraq. It was January 1987, and Iran had just launched a massive offensive on the southern front in an effort to capture Basra, Iraq's second largest city, which lies in the heart of some of the country's largest oilfields. This was during the period when Iran was using 'human wave' attacks against Iraqi positions, whereby thousands of young volunteers – many of them teenagers – would literally run across Iraqi minefields to clear the way for the main Iranian assault. I met some of these volunteers as they prepared to face certain death, and I was struck by their utter fearlessness. 'There is no need to be afraid,' one young Iranian soldier told me as we settled down for what would probably be his last meal on earth. 'If I die, I know my reward will be in heaven.' The following morning, when we toured the front line, the commanders of the Revolutionary Guards displayed the same courage when we came under heavy-machine-gun fire and mortar attack. At one point the Iraqi bombardment was so intense that we were forced to seek refuge in a former Iraqi trench full of dead Iraqi soldiers, so close were we to the Iraqi front line. 'Don't worry, you have nothing to be afraid of,' one of the commanders tried to reassure me. 'Allah will look after us, either in this world or the next. If I die I will go straight to heaven, and why should I be afraid of going to heaven?'

These are just some of the experiences of the past two decades that have aroused my interest in the profound effect that the Islamic revolution, launched by Ayatollah Khomeini on a largely unsuspecting Iranian nation, has had on defining the shape of the Middle East. From the radicalization of Lebanon's Shia population to support for the anti-coalition insurgency in modern-day Iraq, the legacy of Khomeini's revolution is as powerful today as it was when he came to power in February 1979. At the heart of Iran's revolution lies the charismatic figure of Khomeini himself, who started life as an orphan in a remote region of Persia and became one of the most influential leaders of the late twentieth century. Following his death in 1989 Khomeini bequeathed to his heirs a legacy of militant Islam that is the cause of so many of the challenges the world faces today, whether it is the potential threat posed by Iran's nuclear programme or Iranian funded and trained Islamist groups in Iraq and Afghanistan, Lebanon and Gaza. In writing this book I have sought to examine and explore the influences that made Khomeini one of the towering figures of modern Islam, and the contribution that his doctrine has made to the radicalization of the Muslim world.

I have drawn on a wide range of sources, including many former supporters of the Iranian revolution who have often been the targets of assassination attempts, which they survived despite suffering severe injuries. During the past thirty years thousands of opponents of Iran's Islamic revolution have been killed for their political beliefs and opinions, so it is hardly surprising that many of those I have interviewed do not want their identities revealed. Similarly, most of the senior government officials and military officers I have interviewed in Britain, America, Europe and the Middle East have requested that their names not be made public. To all of those who helped this book come to fruition I give my heartfelt thanks. I am grateful to my colleagues, past and present, at the Telegraph Media Group, firstly for giving me the opportunity to cover these momentous events and then for encouraging me to pursue my interest in the subject. I am indebted to Georgina Morley at Macmillan in London, and to Dan Halpern at Ecco in New York, for the commitment and support they have provided to this most challenging of projects, and to my redoubtable agent Gill Coleridge for making it all happen.

PART ONE

ORIGINS

1

Stealing the Revolution

Only a few days had passed since Ayatollah Ruhollah Khomeini had staged his triumphant return to Tehran on 1 February 1979, and the crowds were still out in force on the city streets celebrating the fall of the Shah. But the delirious atmosphere that had accompanied the 76-year-old ayatollah's homecoming was slowly changing, and the millions of Iranians who had supported Khomeini's return were now starting to turn their attention to how the country would be run in the future. For months the country had lived on a knife-edge as the cancer-ridden Shah had battled to save his throne, but Khomeini's return to Iran meant that the Pahlavi dynasty's rule had been brought to an end. It was a testament to the widespread unpopularity of the Pahlavis that hardly a tear was shed when Mohammed Reza Shah and Empress Farah left Tehran for Egypt on 16 January. Instead their departure was greeted with paroxysms of joy and relief throughout the country; jubilant crowds took to the streets and immediately began pulling down statues of the Shah and his father, the founder of the Pahlavi dynasty. After decades of brutal repression at the hands of the Shah's SAVAK security police, Iranians were more than ready to embrace the revolutionary ideals of 'freedom, independence and an Islamic Republic' that had been espoused by the returning ayatollah. Now they wanted to know precisely what these inspirational words meant in practice.

Under the Shah, Iran had been a monarchical dictatorship, with all political power and the nation's wealth concentrated

3

in the hands of a small clique of loyal royalists. Political dissent was fiercely suppressed, and the state media was, for the most part, rigorously controlled. With Khomeini's return, both Iran's liberal intelligentsia and the public at large looked forward to a new era where freedom of expression was enshrined in law, and the nation's vast oil wealth was used for the benefit of the entire nation, not an unelected elite. Khomeini himself had promised as much when, writing from exile, he had vowed to set the people free from the cruel despotism that blighted their lives.

But even as the crowds continued to proclaim their unequivocal support for Khomeini's revolution, the ayatollah was already hard at work on a very different political agenda. Ever since the early 1960s, when he had first emerged as a vociferous critic of the Shah, Khomeini's burning ambition had been to establish an Islamic state in Iran in which supreme authority was vested in the country's religious leaders, and the country was governed on the basis of Sharia, or Islamic, law.

To Khomeini's mind, politicians and other representatives of the state were subservient to the wishes of the clergy, who derived their authority directly from God. Khomeini had developed his unorthodox personal philosophy during his time as a student and teacher at the ancient holy cities of Qom and Najaf, where he was drawn to an obscure interpretation of Shia Islam, which held that all power should ultimately derive from the will of a divinely appointed religious leader. Khomeini had drawn up his manifesto for an Islamic state in a pamphlet entitled *velayat-e faqih*, 'the regency of the theologian', and he regarded this as the prefect model for Islamic government. As Khomeini would later write with marked understatement about his proposed new system of government, 'Islamic government does not correspond to any of the existing forms of government.'[1]

When he was still an unknown cleric at Qom, not even

Khomeini's own students paid much attention to his idiosyncratic interpretation of Islamic jurisprudence. 'People looked up to Khomeini because of his political opposition to the Shah, not because of his religious teachings,' recalled a former pupil who studied under Khomeini at Qom. 'When we went to his classes he was talking about things that happened 1,000 years ago, which were of no interest to us. Little did we realize he was looking for a path that would give him so much power.'[2]

Now that he was safely back in Tehran as the undisputed figurehead of the Iranian revolution, Khomeini was determined to implement the radical agenda he had championed for more than twenty years. It was of no concern to him that his programme bore little relation to the wishes of the majority of the Iranian people, and was firmly at odds with the desire of most Iranians for the establishment of a constitutional democracy to replace the Shah's highly dictatorial system of government. If he were to ignore the democratic aspirations of the Iranian people, Khomeini would need to rely on far more than personal charisma to achieve his ambition, particularly as the power vacuum created by the Shah's removal was being hotly contested in Tehran by a variety of factions, from nationalists on the right to Marxists on the left.

Khomeini convened a meeting of the close-knit group of followers who had stayed with him during the long years of exile, and had accompanied him on his return journey to Iran. He had set up his temporary headquarters at a disused girl's high school in the city centre. While still in exile, he had appointed a small group of trusted supporters – some based in Iran, others exiled abroad – to form a revolutionary committee responsible for organizing grass-roots opposition to the Shah and to plan for Khomeini's eventual return. From early January 1979, when it became clear Khomeini would soon be returning home, this motley collection of clerics, politicians and activists was formally constituted as the Revolutionary Council, and one of its first tasks was to acquire a suitable location for Khomeini to use as his provisional headquarters.

The Refah School in Tehran was the ideal choice. Built in 1968, it was an institution devoted to traditional religious training, a refuge from the secular education then being championed by the Shah. Its founders included two Shia clerics who later became key figures in Khomeini's Islamic revolution; Ali Akbar Hashemi Rafsanjani, the future Iranian president, and Ali Khamenei, who was Khomeini's successor as Iran's spiritual leader.[3] Apart from having the right ideological credentials, the school was situated between two of Tehran's most significant buildings. On one side was the Sepah Salar Mosque, a grand religious monument that fulfilled a role similar to that of Westminster Abbey in London. For more than half a century the mosque had hosted every important official event in the capital, from state funerals to key religious festivals. And on the other side of the school stood the Majlis building, the home of the Iranian parliament, which was expected to play a more active role in the political life of the country following the demise of the Shah's autocratic regime.

A few weeks before Khomeini's return the Revolutionary Council had commandeered the school for its own clandestine meetings, and this modest, mud-brick building replaced the Shah's palace as the main focus of political activity once Khomeini was back in Tehran. Almost immediately the school became a hive of political activity, with followers and loyalists flocking to the school compound to pledge their allegiance. The school was Khomeini's home as well as his headquarters, and to start with he lived in a room overlooking the schoolyard, from whence he could keep a beady eye on the chaotic scenes taking place below. Scores of young revolutionaries – many of them Communists and left-wing activists who had little interest in radical Islam – enthusiastically chanted their devotion to the new regime, and their hatred for the old, before dutifully filing out.

In the turbulent atmosphere that prevailed in the nation's capital during those first heady days of the revolution, Khomeini's aides were rightly concerned that their leader might be the target of an assassination attempt. They broke down the walls between the school and neighbouring houses to give Khomeini a variety of escape routes if the compound came under attack, and Khomeini was obliged to sleep in a different building each night. He insisted that all members of his immediate family – including his fourteen grandchildren – should be housed in the same part of the building, away from the main road, so as not to face any direct danger. All the streets and alleys leading to Refah were sealed off by an estimated eight hundred heavily armed supporters, many of them Lebanese and Iraqi Shia who had arrived in Tehran to support Khomeini's Islamic revolution.

Once he and his family were settled at Refah, Khomeini turned his mind to safeguarding the revolution, rather than himself. Khomeini understood that if the revolution were to succeed he had to maintain the momentum for change his arrival had generated. On 5 February Khomeini appointed Mehdi Bazargan as the country's new prime minister. A few days later he organized a nationwide boycott of a curfew that had been imposed by the Shah's government, which was still clinging to office even though the Shah had fled abroad. Khomeini's boycott had the desired effect, and within two days the final collapse of the regime had been accomplished, as the political, administrative and military organs of government ceased to function.

But Khomeini was concerned lest the revolution developed a momentum of its own, and he was determined not to lose control. For him, protecting the purity of the Islamic identity of the revolution was of paramount importance. He worried that the brave new world of Islamic rule that he intended for Iran might become compromised by the participation of Left-ists, Nationalists and the various other anti-Shah groups who, for the moment at least, blindly supported Khomeini's leader-ship without fully comprehending what he stood for. The enthusiasm among the Iranian masses for opposing the Shah and his supporters was so infectious that few people bothered to consider the implications of Khomeini's controversial agenda, which the ayatollah, it should be said, had taken great care to conceal from the ordinary populace. Khomeini understood better than anyone else that he would face stiff opposition, particularly from Iranian secularists, once the full scale of his master plan for a religious dictatorship became better known. For the most part he kept his radical Islamic agenda to himself, and only a small group of his closest followers understood the full implications of what he sought to achieve.

In speeches made in exile Khomeini had referred on several occasions to the necessity of creating an 'Islamic Army', although he did not explain precisely what he meant by the phrase. As a predominantly Muslim country, the Iranian armed forces that had served the Shah could be said to constitute an Islamic army. But after the Shah and his family fled the country, many senior officers followed suit, and those who remained were either sympathetic to the revolution or bitterly opposed to it. Whatever the political affiliations might be of those who remained to serve Iran's armed forces, Khomeini and his close advisers did not feel any great confidence in the ability of the Iranian military to protect them, particularly as Khomeini intended to overturn the entire constitutional basis upon which the country had been governed for much of the past century. So Khomeini took the first decisive steps towards creating a body that would come to define the tenets of the Iranian Revolution for decades to come.

It was amid this feverish atmosphere that Khomeini sum-moned the meeting of the Revolutionary Council at the Refah

School that would have a lasting and dramatic impact on the future course of the Iranian Revolution, which hereafter would become Khomeini's revolution, rather than the revolution of the Iranian people. This was the meeting at which the formation of the Iranian Revolutionary Guard Corps (IRGC), the storm troops of the Iranian revolution, was first proposed. It was held on 24 February 1979, less than two weeks after the Shah's regime had formally ceased to exist. Khomeini's first request to the Revolutionary Council was to draw up lists of names of dedicated young Iranians who might be suitable for recruitment to such a body. The Revolutionary Council, which had been active as an underground movement in Iran during the reign of the Shah, had an extensive network of contacts with Islamic militants both inside Iran and beyond. Some of them, like Mostafa Chamran, who was one of the IRGC's founding fathers, had fought with Palestinian groups in the Lebanese civil war, while others, such as the wealthy Tehran merchant Mohsen Rafiqdost, had concentrated their energies on trying to overthrow the Shah's regime. But at this stage Khomeini was not too particular about who should be allowed to join the Guards. So long as the recruits were prepared to swear undying loyalty to the supreme leader and the Islamic revolution, they would be eligible for membership. Only later, when the Guards were better established, would the leadership set more onerous standards for entry.

As the Refah School meeting drew to a close, Khomeini made it clear that he would brook no opposition to his plans to transform Iran into an Islamic republic. 'This is not going to be an ordinary government,' Khomeini told Revolutionary Council members. 'This will be a government based on the Sharia. Opposing this government means opposing the Sharia of Islam . . . Revolt against God's government is a revolt against God, and revolt against God is blasphemy.'[4] The formation of the Revolutionary Guards would mark the start of one of the bloodiest periods in the recent history of the Middle East as

Islamic zealots launched a bloody purge to rid the country of its middle-class professionals who, whilst welcoming the overthrow of the monarchy, had little enthusiasm for religious bigotry.

Even at this early stage of Khomeini's revolution, the ayatollah had his sights set on expanding his Islamic agenda well beyond Iran's borders. The Guards' first priority was to protect the revolution against any counter-revolutionary opposition the new regime might encounter. But their role was not limited to internal Iranian affairs. Another important responsibility assigned to the Guards was to support foreign groups that were committed to establishing Islamic governments in other parts of the world. Khomeini's vision of leading a truly Islamic government lay far beyond Iran: the ayatollah was looking to extend the principles of Islamic rule throughout the entire Muslim world. As one of his former students explained, 'Khomeini did not just want to be the supreme leader of Iran; he wanted to be the supreme leader of the entire Islamic world. He wanted to export his revolution throughout the world, and he needed an organization like the Revolutionary Guards to defend and promote the Islamic revolution.'[5]

The formation of the Revolutionary Guards so soon after Khomeini's return to Tehran demonstrated his determination to assume absolute control over Iran's new government. The established pillars of the state were collapsing all around him, and Khomeini's priority was to gather together a trusted cadre of revolutionary activists who were wholly committed to the ayatollah's vision of creating an Islamic republic, and who would defend the new regime against both domestic and foreign opponents. But by authorizing the Revolutionary Council to set up a Revolutionary Guard Corps, Khomeini was effectively declaring war on many of those whose support he had relied upon to get him back to Iran in the first place. Many Iranians recognized Khomeini as a great Islamic leader, but that did not mean they wanted him to be the undisputed leader of an authoritarian Islamic state. They had just rid themselves of one dictatorship, and had no desire to have it replaced by another. They had no objection to Iran being an Islamic state – the majority of the population was, after all, Shia Muslim. But what they wanted more than anything else was some semblance of democracy that would allow them a say in the running of their affairs, an aspiration that would be firmly denied to them once Khomeini had established his vice-like grip on power. Khomeini was about to steal the revolution from beneath the noses of the very people who had brought him to power.

*

Khomeini's Islamic revolution will be remembered as one of the epoch-making events of the twentieth century. The collapse of the Iron Curtain in 1989 had ended the Cold War divisions between Communism and capitalism. But Iran's Islamic revolution the previous decade heralded the start of a far deeper clash between the forces of radical Islam and the liberal, secular values of the West. Before the Iranian revolution most conflicts in the region had been defined by the struggle between Arab nationalist groups, such as Yasser Arafat's Palestine Liberation Organisation and Saddam Hussein's Baath party, and the Western powers that sought to protect the regional status quo. Before 1979, these conflicts were primarily political in nature. The PLO sought to create a Palestinian homeland, while the Baathists and other Arab nationalist groups sought to change the colonialist settlement that had been imposed on the Middle East following the collapse of the Ottoman Empire at the start of the century. But after Khomeini's revolution, these conflicts would acquire a distinctly religious character, and the banner of radical Islam would be unfurled as a potent symbol to challenge the supremacy of Western influence throughout the region and beyond.

Khomeini had waited patiently during the fifteen long years

of his exile for the moment when he could return to his homeland, and having waited for so long he was determined that he would only do so when the conditions were right. After his expulsion from Iran in 1964 for his vociferous opposition to the Shah's secularization programme, Khomeini had spent much of his exile in obscurity, denied access to the various underground movements active in Iran by the ruthless efficiency of the Shah's SAVAK intelligence apparatus. First in Turkey, and later in the Shia holy city of Najaf in southern Iraq, Khomeini devoted his time to his religious studies and to consolidating his standing among the senior Shia clergy. It was only after he arrived in Paris in the autumn of 1978 that Khomeini began to contemplate seriously the prospect of returning home.

The event that had the most profound effect on changing Iran's internal political situation in the ayatollah's favour was Jimmy Carter's election as American president in late 1976. One of Carter's campaign commitments was that his administration would be devoted to the pursuit of the highest moral ideals, and that the protection of human rights would be high on the new president's agenda. Carter's idealism was far removed from the pragmatic realpolitik worldview espoused by Dr Henry Kissinger, who had served as US Secretary of State under the previous Republican administrations of Presidents Nixon and Ford. The Shah had been a particular beneficiary of Kissinger's policy, with teams of American military and intelligence specialists providing the Shah's all-pervasive security apparatus with help and guidance on suppressing opposition groups. Given Iran's crucial geographical location between the Soviet Union and the oil-rich Gulf states, Washington regarded the country's stability as the bedrock of its policy of maintaining influence throughout the region. President Carter, too, recognized Iran's strategic importance to American interests, but was less than happy with the repressive methods employed by the Shah to maintain his regime in power. When Carter entered the White House in January 1977 his new foreign policy outlook immediately had an impact on the Shah, who came under pressure to ease the country's draconian restrictions on political dissent.

By the time Khomeini arrived in Paris in 1978, Carter's human rights policy was having a considerable effect on Iran's political landscape, and the release from prison of many leading dissidents had emboldened opposition groups to intensify their attacks on the Shah's autocratic style of government. Within Iran the main vanguard of opposition to the Shah was formed by Iranian nationalists who, soon after Carter's election, wrote an open letter to the Shah calling on him to 'observe the principles of the constitution and of the Universal Declaration of Human Rights, abolish the one-party system, allow freedom of the press and freedom of association, release all political prisoners, allow the return of political exiles and establish a government based on the representation of the majority.'

The main Iranian opposition parties at this time, the Freedom Movement and the National Front, were secular in outlook, and the main thrust of their campaign was to persuade the Shah to return the country to democratic government. Although he was far-removed from the action, Khomeini gave the impression he was sympathetic to the secularists' campaign, even though his own agenda was very different to the one being advanced in Iran. Khomeini's immediate concern was to introduce a religious dimension to the opposition campaign, and to position himself as a radical leader who was committed to changing the system of government within Iran. Before he moved to Paris Khomeini had signalled his willingness to act as a figurehead for the opposition movement. In an interview with *Le Monde*, he surprised hard-line opposition leaders in Iran by calling for the overthrow of the Shah's regime and the establishment of an Islamic state in its place, making himself the first prominent Iranian leader to demand the Shah's removal as a means of resolving the country's political crisis.[6]

In Iraq, Khomeini had developed close links with a number

of Iranian student bodies based in Europe and America that were campaigning for the Shah to undertake radical political reforms. Many of these groups were leftist in their outlook, but had been encouraged by Khomeini's followers to accept the ayatollah as their figurehead because of his staunch opposition to the Shah. Most of them had little appreciation of Khomeini's obscure interpretation of the role of the clergy in Iranian society. But the fact that Khomeini had been prepared to go much further than the secular leaders in Iran, and call for the Shah's overthrow, had made a deep impression on the young activists, and they readily adopted Khomeini as a revolutionary icon.

Prominent among the left-wing intellectuals campaigning against the Shah from exile was Abol Hassan Bani-Sadr, a well-educated, middle-class Iranian who had the advantage of coming from a prominent Iranian religious family while receiving a secular education at some of Iran's leading academic institutions. Khomeini knew Bani-Sadr's father, who had been an ayatollah in the ancient Persian city of Hamadan in western Iran, and by the time he arrived in Paris, Bani-Sadr had been studying in the French capital for more than a decade. Like many impressionable young students of his generation, Bani-Sadr had fallen under the influence of French Left-Bank intellectuals, and had been particularly affected by *Les Evénements* in Paris during the summer of 1968, when French students joined with trade unionists in an attempt to bring down the government of President Charles de Gaulle. Bani-Sadr had written a number of books which set out an alternative system of government to the Shah's autocratic rule, one based on Islamic principles under which freedom, national independence, social justice and prosperity would be realized. When Iranians began to march and demonstrate against the Shah in 1978, Bani-Sadr regarded the protest movement as a replication of the Paris protests, in which the 'popular effervescence' of the Iranian people sought a higher stage in the nation's political development.[7]

Khomeini's own views about the nature of a future Iranian government were significantly different from those of Bani-Sadr. But that did not prevent him from accepting Bani-Sadr's hospitality when he first arrived in Paris on 12 October 1978, and stayed with him at his modest fourth-floor flat in Cachan on the outskirts of Paris. Almost immediately Khomeini found himself under siege from a host of admirers and sycophants of various political persuasions who, having been unable to meet with the ayatollah when he was living in Iraq, now sought to take full advantage of his presence on European soil. The attention Khomeini attracted did not go down well with his Parisian neighbours, and after complaints were made to the police his aides arranged for him to move to a more spacious house with a garden in the nearby village of Neauphle-le-Château. Khomeini himself gave the impression that he was not much concerned about where he stayed, and worried that Paris was too far removed from the action unfolding in Iran. He asked his aides whether he might be better off staying in Syria, although he went off the idea when he learnt that there were no direct phone lines between Damascus and Tehran.

In Paris Khomeini gathered around him a group of close confidants, many of whom played leading roles in the Iranian revolution and the formation of the Revolutionary Guards. Khomeini's inner circle consisted mainly of his immediate family – his wife, his sole surviving son, Ahmad, his son-in-law Ayatollah Mohammad Eshraqi, and some fourteen grandchildren. Both Ahmad and Eshraqi were highly active in Khomeini's *nehzat*, or movement, and were responsible for maintaining links with the ayatollah's close friends and supporters, and passing sensitive messages and information to them.

Khomeini drew on the support of a group of three, largely

self-appointed, *viziers*, who maintained the ayatollah's links with the outside world. Of these Bani-Sadr was the most prominent, playing the role of the ideologue and engaging in heated discussions with visiting journalists, on one occasion even reassuring them that he had persuaded Khomeini not to set up an Islamic state that would be run solely by the clergy. Another important member of Khomeini's group of advisers was Ibrahim Yazdi, a naturalized American physician of Iranian origin who had originally joined Khomeini at Najaf. Yazdi was a wily operator who, despite Bani-Sadr's protestations, regarded himself as Khomeini's official spokesman, and he was the main conduit for passing messages between Khomeini and the underground revolutionary movement in Iran. He was one of the founders of the Revolutionary Guards when Khomeini returned to Iran. The third member of this triumvirate was Sadeq Qotbzadeh, another student who later became Khomeini's foreign minister. Qotbzadeh's primary role in Paris, where he earned himself something of a reputation for being Khomeini's court jester, was to keep the ayatollah informed about Western media coverage of the unfolding situation in Iran.

Khomeini set himself a punishing daily schedule at Neauphle-le-Château, which often began at 3 a.m. when he would read through the briefing papers he had received the previous day but not had time to read. He read translations of foreign press reports prepared for him by his aides before taking his breakfast at seven. For the next three hours he would then deal with the latest news from Iran and his personal affairs. From ten to twelve he prayed and ate lunch before taking a one-hour siesta at two. From three onwards he would resume work relating to his political campaign, breaking off at five to perform the evening prayer. If he found time during the day he would go for a walk in the countryside around Neauphle-le-Château, although the permanent police protection provided by the French government meant that he was rarely alone. His day would finish at nine when he would have dinner with his family and listen to recordings of the day's broadcasts in Persian or foreign radio stations, particularly the BBC. His son Ahmad later wrote of his father's stay in Paris that he was happiest when playing with his grandchildren. 'He argued with the children, played with them, talked to them and made them laugh. At breakfast-time, when the table was laid on the floor, he would place himself near the samovar and serve the family.'[8]

But behind this cosy family facade Khomeini and his aides were working frantically to link up with the burgeoning opposition movement to the Shah that was gaining momentum in Iran. Khomeini was kept abreast of developments by the constant stream of visitors making their way to the modest villa at Neauphle-le-Château. Some of the visitors were former students who had studied under him at Qom, but Khomeini's main interest was in meeting the leaders of his own Islamic underground movement in Iran. Two of his most important, and frequent visitors at this time were two ayatollahs, Hossein Ali Montazeri and Morteza Motahhari, who were key figures in building up the Islamic resistance movement in Iran. Their efforts were so successful that, while left-wing and nationalist groups generally dominated the industrial and urban parts of the country, Khomeini's movement, led by the clergy, had taken control of most of the countryside.

Thanks to the efforts of Khomeini's well-organized underground movement, cassettes containing Khomeini's speeches condemning the Shah's government circulated deep in rural Iran, and demonstrations in support of those killed in clashes with the Shah's security services were now regular events in most villages and towns. This mass mobilization of Iran's predominantly rural population was unheard of in Iran, and gave the impression that Khomeini was the undisputed leader of the anti-Shah movement. He further developed the notion that he was controlling the revolutionary movement in Iran by starting a network of 'Imam committees', which sprang up in November as the nation faced paralysis from an oil strike. Ali Akbar Hashemi Rafsanjani, a former student of Khomeini's who had been jailed by the Shah for his anti-government activities, was appointed Representative of the Imam and sent to the oilfields to persuade the workers to produce enough oil for the country's domestic needs.

With so much at stake Khomeini took care to conceal the true nature of the Islamic revolution he was planning. In one of the cassettes distributed throughout the country in November Khomeini spoke of a 'progressive Islam' in which even a woman might one day become the country's president.

'Khomeini was an opportunist,' recalled a left-wing activist who participated in the anti-Shah campaigns in late 1978. 'He realized there was a different political climate taking root in Iran from the one that he championed, and he was determined to take advantage of it, even if it meant keeping quiet about what he really wanted.'[9]

Khomeini used his network of intermediaries to put out feelers to key figures within the Iranian political establishment to reassure them that he could work with them if he were to replace the Shah. They had talks with General Abbas-Karim Gharabaghi, the Shah's Chief of Staff of the Armed Forces, who had come to the conclusion that the chaos enveloping his country was none of the military's concern. He regarded the events as a political struggle that could only be resolved by the warring factions themselves. Perhaps the most intriguing of the contacts Khomeini made at this time was with the head of the Shah's dreaded SAVAK security service. General Nasser Moqaddam, who had been personally involved in persecuting Khomeini's supporters for more than a decade, was so convinced that Khomeini's movement was on the brink of replacing the Shah that he offered to fly to Paris to meet the ayatollah and discuss terms for his return. 'In principle SAVAK did not have any problem about working with Khomeini,' explained one of the ayatollah's former advisers. 'Like all good intelligence agencies, they wanted to make sure they ended up on the right side, and by then it was clear Khomeini was in the ascendent.'[10]

The Shah's position was becoming increasingly desperate, and in November he took the drastic step of appointing a senior army general, Gholam-Reza Azhari, as his new prime minister. But even the Shah seemed to realize the game was up, and in what would turn out to be his valedictory television address to the nation, he made the astonishing admission that much of his rule had been marred by 'corruption and cruelty' and asked for the nation's forgiveness. The Shah became the first person to describe what was happening in Iran as a revolution rather than a 'movement', as Khomeini insisted on calling it. 'As the Shah of Iran as well as an Iranian citizen, I cannot but approve your revolution,' he told his astounded audience. But the intervention of the military did little to restore order, not least because the military had little stomach for turning its guns on its own people. Azhari did little to inspire confidence among the beleaguered government officials still in Tehran when he ordered the arrest of Amir-Abbas Hoveyda, the Shah's loyal and diligent former prime minister, together with 132 other high-ranking officials. Azhari's attempts to impose his authority came to an abrupt end in late November when he was carried out of his office after suffering a stroke. With government officials deserting their posts and fleeing the country in their droves, the Shah realized he had lost all control of the civil service and was on the point of losing whatever control he still retained over the armed forces. He now concluded he must leave the country.

Before the Shah could take his leave it was first necessary for him to appoint a new prime minister who could run the country in his absence. Few figures of any weight were prepared to accept such a poisoned chalice. After scouring Tehran's political establishment the only candidate of stature who could be found to accept the position was Shapour Bakhtiar, a veteran nationalist politician who opposed both the Shah's autocratic style of government and Khomeini's fundamentalist Islamic agenda. Bakhtiar agreed to take the position on condition that the Shah left the country while he attempted to restore order, which was music to the Shah's ears. But within days of Bakhtiar's appointment, Khomeini publicly denounced the arrangement, which meant that Iran had lost its last realistic opportunity to resolve its political differences by peaceful means.

By now an irresistible momentum was driving Khomeini's movement, and the ayatollah wasted no opportunity in capitalizing on his burgeoning popularity. At the end of November he published a poem that promised all the hardship being suffered by the Iranian people would end the moment the ayatollah returned home. His standing among the uneducated masses was further strengthened by a portentous episode in which a pious old lady living in Qom claimed to have found a hair from the Prophet's beard in the pages of her Koran. The same evening an apparition had informed the woman that the faithful would be able to see the face of Khomeini in the full moon due on 27 November. Within days the rumour of the woman's 'prophecy' had spread throughout the entire country, and on the 27th millions of people gathered on their rooftops to wait for the full moon, and catch a glimpse of their saviour. A carnival atmosphere enveloped the country's major cities, with devout worshippers pointing out that criminals and bastards would not be able to see Khomeini's face in the moon. Throughout the country tears of joy were shed and huge quantities of fruit and sweets consumed as millions of Iranians celebrated the apparition. Even the leaders of Iran's Communist party celebrated the event, with an editorial in their newspaper *Navid* declaring, 'Our toiling masses . . . have seen the face of the beloved Imam and leader, Khomeini the Breaker of Idols, in the moon. A few pipsqueaks cannot deny what a whole nation has seen with its own eyes.'[11] The majesty of the Shah of Iran was about to be replaced by the superstitions of ignorant peasants.

Khomeini's 'moon trick', as it was disparagingly called, was not well received by Iran's Grand Ayatollahs who still commanded considerable respect within the country's religious establishment. They telephoned Khomeini in Paris asking him to issue a denial. But Khomeini refused, declaring that he would not act against 'the spontaneous initiatives of the people'. When a crowd of pro-Khomeini sympathizers pulled down a statue of the Shah at the Iranian holy city of Mashhad, one of Khomeini's activists had the statue removed immediately and smashed to pieces so that it could no longer be restored. From this moment on Iran's religious establishment realized they were no match for Khomeini's superior organization and support.

The Shah and the Empress finally departed the country on 16 January 1979, having tried, and failed, to establish a Regency Council to administer the country in his absence. The Shah had succeeded in appointing an 82-year-old astronomer, Jalal Tehrani, to run the Council in conjunction with Prime Minister Bakhtiar only to see Tehrani fly to Paris immediately after his appointment to offer Khomeini his resignation. The Shah, whose health was rapidly deteriorating through cancer, was thrown into deep despair. 'Everything is at an end,' he confided to one visitor. 'Even if I return to Iran one day as Shah, nothing will be the same again. It is like a beautiful crystal vase that is broken for good; repair it and it will still show its cracks.'[12]

With the Shah gone the only question that remained was whether Bakhtiar would be able to form a credible government that could prevent Khomeini's return. Bakhtiar's position was not helped by the vacillation of the Carter administration in Washington, which could not decide whether it would be better to allow Khomeini to return or to support a military coup led by Bakhtiar. Carter's official position was that it was 'up to the people of Iran to decide' the Shah's fate. At the same time Carter dispatched one of his most senior generals, Robert C. Huyser, the deputy commander of NATO, to Tehran to advise the Iranian military. Some senior Iranian generals were in favour of staging a coup d'état, but Washington decided against the idea, believing that it would undermine the Bakhtiar government's chances of success. Even so senior Iranian air force commanders wanted to shoot down any aircraft bringing Khomeini to Iran, and tried to contact the Shah, who had taken refuge in Egypt, for the authorization to attack any aircraft entering Iranian air space without proper permission. But the Shah refused to respond to the request, and any hopes the Bakhtiar government still entertained of preventing Khomeini's return evaporated at the end of January when Tehran's Mehrabad airport fell under the control of armed members of Khomeini's revolutionary committees. The way was now open for the ayatollah to return.

The moment Khomeini's aides heard that Bakhtiar had given the order for Iran's airports to reopen, they set to work organizing transport. Attempts to charter an Air France jumbo jet proved problematic. French officials wanted guarantees that their aircraft would not be put at risk, as the consequences of a French government-owned civilian airliner being shot down over Iran were too horrific to contemplate. Having received direct assurances from the Iranian government, and imposed punitive insurance terms, the airline agreed to charter the jet on the strict condition that it flew with sufficient fuel to make a return flight to Paris if it were refused landing permission in Tehran. Even so Khomeini's entourage still feared the aircraft might be sabotaged, and ordered that no women or children be allowed on the flight. Khomeini's wife, daughter, daughter-in-law and grandchildren would follow the ayatollah by commercial airliner once he was safely back in Tehran.

Shortly before the flight left on the evening of 31 January,

Khomeini sought to reassure those who would not be accompanying him when they joined him for evening prayers. 'The important thing is not that you be at my side on the plane but that you continue the struggle with me.' He thanked the French government and its people for its hospitality and the French people 'who have followed with interest the struggle for freedom of conscience and the way of democracy desired by all clear-minded Iranians.' The sentiments were not reciprocated by the French government, which felt let down that the ayatollah had ignored their pleas not to use French soil to foment revolution in Iran.

After take-off, Khomeini climbed the spiral staircase to the aircraft's lounge section, removed his turban and sandals, curled up under several Air France blankets and slept for two and a half hours. His personal bodyguard, who was suffering from a bad toothache and numb from taking several aspirins, sat at the bottom of the steps barring entry to curious passengers. As the sun began to rise when the aircraft entered Turkish air space, Khomeini awoke, said his prayers and ate an omelette for breakfast. Sometime later, when the captain announced that the aircraft had entered Iranian air space and would land in Tehran in half an hour, Khomeini craned his neck to look down at the magnificent spectacle of the snow-covered Zagros Mountains. 'The ayatollah,' one of his aides dramatically announced, 'is back in his home country.'[13]

The aircraft circled three times over Tehran and the Elburz Mountains to the north of the city while the pilot sought assurances from air traffic control that he was cleared to land. Finally the jumbo jet made its approach and at 9.30 a.m. on the morning of 1 February 1979 settled down gently on the tarmac of Mehrabad airport. An expectant crowd of officials, wellwishers and journalists milled around the aircraft, before the doors swung open and a frail old man, wearing a black turban and ankle-length robes, stepped through the door into the chill

February morning. His back hunched, he clutched the arm of an Air France purser as he walked down the portable ramp to touch Iranian soil for the first time in fifteen years.

After all the violence and demonstrations that had attended the Shah's last year in power, the nation appeared to erupt spontaneously in wild celebrations of joy. Millions of people thronged into the capital from all across the country, encouraged by the continuing stream of *Elamiehs*, Khomeini's messages, urging them to support the revolution. The organization put in place to make sure Khomeini's return was properly handled revealed the strength and effectiveness of his support. The 'welcoming committee' set up by the Islamic Revolutionary Council was on hand to receive the ayatollah the moment he had departed the aircraft. Headed by Ayatollah Morteza Motahhari, Khomeini's chief field officer in Iran who had worked tirelessly for months to undermine the Shah's attempts to prop up his regime, they moved quickly to keep at bay anyone whose Islamic credentials were not considered to be of the highest order. The last thing the revolution needed was for Khomeini to be photographed with those not directly committed to the Islamic revolution. Several prominent Iranian politicians were asked to leave, and even Khomeini's *viziers* in Paris, Bani-Sadr, Yazdi and Qotbzadeh, were lost in the sea of turbans that surrounded the ayatollah. As Bani-Sadr was later to comment wryly of the day's events, 'It seemed that the duty of the intellectuals was to bring Khomeini to Tehran and hand him over to the mullahs.'[14]

Khomeini might have spoken in Paris of his desire to return Iran to democracy, but from the moment he set foot back on home soil the whole focus of his effort was concentrated on establishing an Islamic fundamentalist state. Following the clash with the country's religious establishment over the incident of the moon apparition, all but one of Iran's Grand Ayatollahs turned up at the airport to greet him, and they paid him their full respect, which Khomeini graciously acknowledged. They knew this was no time to pick a quarrel with the undisputed master of the Iranian revolution. Once inside the airport terminal building, Khomeini addressed the 1,000 or so members of the welcoming committee who were gathered to greet him, and he immediately lashed out at the Shah and his foreign backers who had 'destroyed our culture and turned it into a colonial culture'. And he gave a warning that the struggle was far from over. 'We are only victorious when we can cut the hands of the foreigners from our lands. I pray to God for you for glory and good health, and I pray to God to help us cut off the hands of the foreigners.' To which the crowd exploded with rapturous chants of 'Allahu Akbar', God is great.

Previously the ayatollah had supported the activities of the various secular groups opposing the Shah. He now made it clear that he had no desire to be associated with them once back in Iran. To mark his return, the country's leading liberal politicians and intellectuals organized a rally at Tehran University where they hoped to celebrate the Shah's demise in Khomeini's presence. But Khomeini was not prepared to share his moment of triumph with any other group. Instead he decided, with the Revolutionary Council's help, to embark on a victory procession through the centre of Tehran and pay homage to the victims of the Shah's repression who had been laid to rest at the Behesht-e Zahra cemetery.

Khomeini's supporters arranged for more than 1 million of his supporters to stage a vigil in the form of a human chain stretching several miles from the city centre to the cemetery. Having completed the formalities at the airport, Khomeini was led to a waiting blue-and-white Chevrolet, where his driver for the day was Mohsen Rafiqdost, a key figure in the ayatollah's underground movement in Iran who would soon become the minister responsible for running the Revolutionary Guards. Accompanied by his son Ahmad, Khomeini constantly asked the names of the streets as they passed by, for Tehran had changed considerably during his fifteen-year absence.

This was the first time most Iranians had caught a glimpse of Khomeini in the flesh, and his supporters ensured the whole event was carefully choreographed to give him the appearance of a deity. Since December 1977, Khomeini had openly referred to himself as 'the Imam', a title that conferred upon him divine-like status and one which had not been used in mainstream Shia Islam for hundreds of years. The title suggested, particularly among Iran's ill-educated and superstitious peasantry, that Khomeini was himself the 'Twelfth Imam', a reference to the twelfth and last imam of the Shia branch of Islam who disappeared in the tenth century. According to Islamic tradition, the Twelfth Imam has been hidden by God and will only reappear at the end of history to lead an era of Islamic justice. The clerical establishment in Iran never accepted the use of this title, and even those senior clerics who supported Khomeini's Islamic movement shied away from it. But now that Khomeini was back in Iran his followers had no such inhibitions, and encouraged the use of the title, giving the clear impression that Khomeini was the long-awaited Hidden Imam. Consequently the crowds who lined the route to the cemetery chanted 'Khomeini, O Imam.' Other supporters equated Khomeini's flight from Paris to Tehran with the Prophet Mohammed's flight from Mecca to Medina in AD 622, yet another indication that the ayatollah was an important prophet.

The crowds that gathered to greet Khomeini were so dense that it became impossible for his motorcade to proceed any further, and a helicopter of the Imperial Air Force was dispatched to enable him to complete his journey. The cemetery was of particular significance for Khomeini, as it was the place where many of his supporters, killed during clashes with the Shah's security forces, had been buried. Once there Khomeini launched a bitter attack against the Shah, and against the government of Shapour Bakhtiar, the prime minister, whom he accused of seeking to restore the Shah to power. 'These people are trying to bring back the regime of the late Shah . . . I will strike with my fists at the mouths of this government. From now on it is I who will name the government.' Bakhtiar himself appeared unconcerned by this outburst, and reassured his aides, 'Don't worry about this kind of speech. That is Khomeini. He is free to speak but he is not free to act.'[15]

Having cleared the way for Khomeini's return, Bakhtiar was still hoping that he would be able to reach a political accommodation with the ayatollah, even if Khomeini had made it clear he regarded Bakhtiar's government as illegitimate, and a remnant of the monarchy. But Khomeini's appointment of Mehdi Bazargan, the leader of Iran's Freedom Movement, as the country's provisional prime minister on 5 February effectively signalled the end of Bakhtiar's government. In theory there was nothing to prevent the two men working together, particularly as they had both been imprisoned by the Shah for championing democracy. Although Bakhtiar refused to share his administration with Bazargan, he was prepared to tolerate Khomeini's 'shadow' government so long as it did not interfere with the running of the country. But Khomeini was not prepared to tolerate any link to the Shah's former regime, and his supporters organized large rallies in support of Bazargan, while Bakhtiar's office was besieged with politicians and officials tendering their resignations.

The death knell for Bakhtiar's administration was finally sounded a few days after Bazargan's appointment when the Imperial Guard, the so-called 'Immortals' who had dedicated their lives to defending the Shah, launched an attack on air force bases around Tehran to punish hundreds of air force technicians who had descended on the Refah School to pledge their allegiance to Khomeini. Incensed by what they regarded as an act of treachery, the Guard felt obliged to intervene, but their impulsive action only served to strengthen Khomeini's cause, as thousands of left-wing activists, many of whom had just returned from exile abroad, took to the streets to defend the revolution. The leftists, who were joined by a number of junior officers from the regular armed forces, raided army and police arsenals and even succeeded in stealing tanks, anti-aircraft guns and rocket launchers. They also raided a number of banks, and substantial sums were 'confiscated' in the name of the revolution. Khomeini gave his unequivocal backing to the leftists, whose cause was helped immeasurably when the final meeting of the country's military command held on the morning of 11 February announced that the army would remain neutral in the power struggle. By the end of the day the left-wing guerrillas had taken control of the city, and Bakhtiar went into hiding. Many of the generals who had participated in the fighting were rounded up and shot, but Bakhtiar was saved from suffering a similar fate by Bazargan's intervention, who provided him with a safe house until he was able to leave the country on an Air France commercial flight disguised as a French businessman.

Although Khomeini claimed leadership of the campaign that led to the collapse of the Bakhtiar government, it was actually brought about by the concerted efforts of left-wing guerrilla groups, such as the People's Fedayeen and Mujahideen-e Khalq (Warriors of the People), which, had they been better organ-ized, would have been in a strong position to take control of the country following the final collapse of the Shah's regime. All Khomeini could do was to give speeches in support of the fighters, and he was careful to use extreme language to ensure that no one should appear more radical than himself.

Amid the turmoil that followed the collapse of Bakhtiar's government, Khomeini realized he needed to make a gesture to reassert his standing as the undisputed leader of the revolution, and he now turned his attention to punishing key members of the Shah's regime who had been captured since his return. While still in Paris, Khomeini had often declared his intention to put a number of the Shah's officials on trial. Bazargan, who still hoped to oversee a peaceful transition to democracy, was against taking reprisals, which he thought would only deepen divisions within the country, and wanted to abolish the death penalty. But Khomeini was keen both to exert his own authority and to introduce the concept of Sharia law. At his first press conference he had made it clear that 'revolt against the government of the Sharia has its punishment in our law . . . it is a heavy punishment in Islamic jurisprudence. Revolt against God's law is a revolt against God. Revolt against God is blasphemy.'

Khomeini regarded the Shah and his aides as 'satanic' because they had tried to exclude Islam from having a central position in the affairs of the state. And he regarded the Shah's close ties with the United States as part of a 'Jewish plot to destroy Islam'. From now on he wanted the clergy to have the final say in the running of the state, and for the rules of Islam to be strictly applied. To set an example, Khomeini ordered the execution of a number of high-ranking military officers who had been captured by the left-wing guerrilla groups, and were detained rather than being shot on the spot. The executions were a blatant attempt by Khomeini to reclaim the limelight after the left-wing fighters' success in bringing down the Bakhtiar government, and to reassure the country that there was no possibility of the Shah returning to power. Among those selected for execution was the former head of the Shah's SAVAK intelligence service, General Nematollah Nassiri, and four other senior military officials. By the time they were brought to Refah School, where Khomeini had decreed the executions would take place, all of them had been badly beaten. One of the condemned men had his arm broken by the butt of a rifle for slapping Khomeini's son Ahmad on the face after he had insulted him.

Khomeini's first difficulty was to find someone to preside over the country's inaugural Islamic 'trial'. Several mullahs were approached, but politely declined the invitation, concerned that the proposed trials and executions had no basis in Iranian law. Eventually Khomeini appointed Sadeq Khalkhali, a radical cleric who had visited him frequently in Paris, to conduct the hearings. Khalkhali's enthusiasm for sentencing to death former regime members would later earn him the nickname 'judge blood', but on this occasion he was simply following the orders he received directly from Khomeini. 'These people are guilty in any case,' said Khomeini after persuading Khalkhali to take the job. 'So hear what they say and then send them to hell.'[16] Khalkhali converted one of the classrooms at Refah School into a makeshift courtroom. The hearing itself was over in a matter of minutes. After a brief recitation of the Koran by Khalkhali, and some terse exchanges between the judge and the accused, he duly followed Khomeini's orders and sentenced the five generals to death.

Having appointed a judge, Khomeini needed to find an executioner. He now turned to Mostafa Chamran, one of the founder members of the Revolutionary Guards who had spent several years fighting with Shia Muslim militias in Lebanon. Chamran was one of the few members of Khomeini's inner circle with any direct experience of combat, and the ayatollah was insistent his own movement carried out the executions rather than one of the left-wing groups, even though they had far more experience. Executing the Shah's generals would be the first public act of the men who would become the founder members of Iran's feared Revolutionary Guards.

The generals were made to wait eighteen hours while Chamran put together a makeshift firing squad, as few of Khomeini's supporters had any experience of such matters. Finally an execution party was assembled on the morning of 16 February. The generals were blindfolded and taken to the roof of Refah School, where they were then shot one by one. When Khomeini heard that the executions had been carried out, he climbed the narrow, winding steps to the terraced roof where he spent a minute inspecting the naked, still bleeding corpses. 'Allah gave them their just desserts,' he remarked, before returning to his private quarters. The bodies were then filmed by a television crew, and the pictures broadcast on Iranian television that night to prove that Khomeini's rudimentary form of Islamic justice had now been introduced to Iran.

The executions were the first of many that would take place at Refah School on an almost daily basis, and they revealed Khomeini's true colours, not as a champion of democracy he had portrayed himself to be when in exile, but as a ruthless tyrant who would stop at nothing to achieve his ambition of turning Iran into an Islamic dictatorship. And slowly it was beginning to dawn on some of the naive young Iranians who had campaigned so enthusiastically for the ayatollah's return that his view of the revolution was very different from their campaign for the restoration of democracy and the rule of law. A few days after the executions, when a young pro-democracy activist attended a rally at Tehran University, he found a teenage girl student sitting on the steps crying. When he asked her what was the matter, she replied, 'I thought Khomeini was going to bring us democracy, but now I realize that all that is going to happen is that we are simply going to replace one dictator with another.'[17]

2

Child of the Revolution

The roots of Khomeini's rise to become one of the world's most notorious revolutionary leaders can be traced to his childhood in a remote and harsh area of provincial Iran. The entire course of the twentieth century was a period of immense political and social upheaval in Iran and would have a deep and profound effect on the development of Khomeini's character. From the year of his birth in 1902 until his death eighty-seven years later, Khomeini knew nothing but political turmoil in his country as different factions fought over the type of government Iran should have, and what role the religious establishment would play within it. On one side were what could broadly be described as the patriotic nationalists who sought a government that would truly reflect the wishes of the people, work to protect their interests and defend them from the unwelcome attention of foreign powers. On the other were the unelected autocrats who believed it was their destiny to govern the country in what they thought of as the people's best interests. These two powerful, yet irreconcilable, forces would be in conflict for the better part of a century until, with the country exhausted by decades of bitter feuding and internal dissent, Khomeini was able to mould the country to his own ideas.

In common with many of the twentieth century's more notorious dictators, the young Khomeini's origins were both humble and obscure. He was born on 24 September 1902 in the Iranian oasis town of Khomein, which lies deep in the heart of the vast semi-arid plateau of central Iran about 180 miles (290km) south-east of Tehran. The newly born infant was actually named Ruhollah Musavi, and only took the name Khomeini in later life, because of the custom in Iran for leading ayatollahs to take the name of their home town. Ruhollah, a rare name in Iran, means 'the soul of God', and many of his followers would later claim that Mostafa had received divine guidance in naming his son. Ruhollah was the sixth and youngest child of Mostafa Musavi, a prominent local cleric in Khomein, who had previously had two sons and three daughters.

Ruhollah was born in a two-storey house standing in a large garden on the eastern edge of the town. Today the house has been transformed into a museum called Beit al Nour, the house of light, covering some 46,000 square feet, which thousands of Iranians visit each year to pay homage to the founder of the Islamic revolution. A large sign directing visitors to the museum declares, 'Ayatollah Khomeini, peace be upon him, was the reviver of religious government in the contemporary world.' This once unremarkable dwelling has been transformed into an attractive place of pilgrimage, where visitors are greeted by a banner proclaiming in Persian, 'The House of the Revered Imam Khomeini'. The house where the young Khomeini spent the early years of his life is at the side of a large courtyard with a circular pond at its centre. The rooms are filled with large portraits of Khomeini and his two sons, and the room in which he was born bears the inscription, 'Imam Khomeini first opened his eyes to the world and illuminated the Islamic world with his radiance and splendour in 1902.' Inside the exhibition contains a framed copy of the identity document that was later issued to Khomeini when he reached adulthood by the Interior Ministry of the Islamic Republic of Iran: 'Number A/12/514514. Sayyid Ruhollah Musavi born in 1279 (Iranian year) . . . Issued by Ali Akbar Rahmani on 20.11.1358.' Across the street from the museum airy, well-stocked shops sell pictures, audiotapes and videotapes of the late ayatollah's speeches.[1]

Khomein is now a thriving town of about 130,000 people, but when Ruhollah was born it was a remote and nondescript place of about 3,000 inhabitants. Iranians refer to such places as *akhar-e-khat*, the end of the line. The town is so lacking in distinction that it hardly merits a mention in any of the great histories of Persia. The town's name derives from *Khom*, the Persian work for 'jar', and its literal translation means 'two jars'. The town's name is said to owe its origins to the seventh century AD when an Arab army then attempting to conquer Persia camped at the site of the town for a few weeks. According to legend, while his troops rested, the Arab commander set up two large jars, one filled with pomegranate juice, the other with the essence of a spirit distilled from local grain and perfumed with the essence of a wild plant, which is better known to Arabs today as *Arak*.[2] The Arab soldiers who had arrived after months of bitter fighting in the cold mountain regions of the Iranian plateau were able to refresh themselves before proceeding with their campaign of conquest to the larger cities in the north-east of the country.

At the time of Khomeini's birth one of the town's few distinguishing features was a solitary plane tree on the outskirts of the town that provided the local inhabitants with shade on hot, dusty afternoons. The only other significant feature, the local mosque, was in a sorry state of repair. A brick building built around a courtyard, which contained a rectangular pond of green, stagnant water, the mosque was semi-derelict, and its dome had lost many of its turquoise-blue tiles, and the only form of life consisted of half a dozen pigeons who had built themselves a nest on the mud-covered roof of the main prayer chamber. On Thursday evenings local women would come to the mosque to pay their respects to deceased family members. They would tie pieces of cloth to the long-dead tree standing by the pond, and would weep and pray for their lost ones. On Fridays the menfolk would gather in the mosque for the weekly communal prayer ritual, and recall the glorious days of Islam.

Not surprisingly Khomeini had little enthusiasm for returning to the place of his birth following his return from exile, even though both his mother and father are buried there. His memories of the skinny goats and sheep roaming the dust-blown streets in search of fodder were sufficient to persuade him to stay in more salubrious surroundings.[3]

In 1902 Ruhollah's family home was spacious and comfortable compared with the majority of unremarkable mud and brick buildings that abounded in Khomein. Ruhollah was born into a relatively wealthy family, one of considerable social stature, as the Musavis could trace their ancestry directly back to the Prophet. The Musavi family is said to have come from Neishabur, a town near the Iranian holy city of Mashhad in north-eastern Iran. By the eighteenth century the family had migrated to India where they settled in the predominantly Muslim town of Kintur, close to the regional capital Lucknow in what was then the Kingdom of Oudh. Rulers and inhabitants of Oudh were followers of Twelver Shi'ism, who believe in the twelve divinely ordained leaders of Shia Islam, which today is the Islamic tradition to which most Iranians adhere.

Khomeini's family were themselves Shia Muslims, the dominant faith in the country then known as Persia. The Shia are a minority within the wider Muslim community, and are mainly found in Iran, southern Iraq and southern Lebanon. The origins of the Shia faith go back to the earliest days of Islam when a schism developed over the appointment of a successor to the Caliph, the position created by the Prophet to oversee the Islamic faith after his death. In early Islamic history the Shia were a political faction, known as the 'party of Ali', that supported Ali, the son-in-law of the Prophet Mohammed, who became the fourth Caliph of the Muslim community. But Ali's appointment was challenged by other members of the Prophet's descendants, who believed they had a better claim. Ali was murdered in AD 661 by his chief rival, Muawiya, and buried in Najaf, in southern Iraq, today regarded as one of the most important Islamic shrines and visited by millions of devout Shia every year. After Ali's death, Muawiya became Caliph, but when he died Ali's son Hussein refused to accept the legitimacy of Muawiya's son Yazid, and fighting ensued between the two rival camps. Hussein and his followers were later massacred in battle near Karbala in AD 680, another site deemed holy to devout Shia. The Shia believe that all this suffering would have been avoided if Ali had been appointed Caliph at the time of the Prophet's death. Instead a Shia cult of martyrdom has developed around the deaths of Ali and Hussein, and led to a sense of betrayal among the Shia community, and the belief that they are destined to struggle against injustice, oppression and tyranny.

The Musavi family came from a long line of Islamic teachers and clerics. Ruhollah's grandfather, Ahmad Musavi Hindi (his last name was taken from the Indian region the family settled in), had left India in about 1830 to make a pilgrimage to the Shia holy city of Najaf in south-eastern Iraq, where many years later his grandson would languish in exile. Having spent some time in Najaf studying in one of the seminaries, Ahmad was persuaded to return to Iran by a landowner he met who came from a village not far from Khomein. According to Khomeini's own family's account of their origins,[4] Ahmad returned to Iran in about 1834, and five years later bought a house and a large tract of land in Khomein where the family would remain for a century and a half – until it was turned into a museum after Khomeini's death. By the standards of the time, Ahmad was relatively wealthy, and had already taken two wives by the time he married his third wife, Sakineh. Although Ahmad had only one son by his first two wives, Sakineh bore him three daughters and a son, Mostafa, Khomeini's father, who was born in 1856. Ahmad continued to prosper in Khomein and bought land in some of the surrounding local villages, while in Khomein itself he bought an orchard. When he died in 1869 he instructed his family to have him buried in the holy Iraqi city of Karbala.

Khomeini's father, Mostafa Musavi, was just thirteen when his father died, and his relatives arranged for him to train for the clergy, which by that time had become established as a family tradition. Like many young men of his age and background, Mostafa first attended a seminary at nearby Isfahan, the former capital of Persia and one of modern Iran's most beautiful cities, before moving on to complete his studies in Najaf and Karbala in southern Iraq. In the nineteenth and early twentieth centuries it was not considered unusual for Shia Muslims in Iraq and Iran to move freely between the two countries' main Shia shrines and cities, even though they were keen to maintain their distinct Arab and Persian cultural identities. According to Khomeini's family history, his father probably arrived in Najaf around 1891 with his first wife Hajieh, who was the daughter of a distinguished Iranian cleric.

Mostafa arrived in Najaf at a time of great political turmoil. To improve both his own financial standing and his relations with the West, the then Shah had granted British Imperial Tobacco a monopoly over the country's large tobacco business for an annual payment of £15,000. The agreement provoked outrage among Iran's mercantile classes, who succeeded in winning the support of the country's clerical leadership, many of whom were resident in Najaf. They responded to the Shah's trade deal by issuing a fatwa, a religious ruling, banning the use of tobacco by the faithful, with the result that even the royal harem obeyed the edict, forcing the Shah to back down and cancel the concession. The tobacco controversy was one of the first documented instances where Iran's religious establishment had colluded with the mercantile classes to challenge the authority of the Shah, and it greatly increased the standing of the clergy and marked the start of their active involvement in Iranian politics.

Khomeini's father continued his studies at Najaf and other Shia academies in Iraq before returning to Khomein in 1894. The 39-year-old Mostafa qualified as a senior member of the Shia clergy and was given the right to publish his own interpretations of religious law and principle. His first child was born in Najaf, and five others followed after he returned to Khomein, three sons and two daughters. His eldest son, Morteza, was born in 1896, and lived to be 101; the second, Nureddin, would become a lawyer; the third, Ruhollah, would be Mostafa's sixth and last child.

But Ruhollah would never get to know his father, for on a cold day in March 1903, less than six months after the birth of his youngest son, Mostafa was shot and mortally wounded while travelling on the road from Khomein to the nearby provincial capital of Arak. Many fanciful tales have arisen about the circumstances surrounding Mostafa's murder, of which the most compelling is the suggestion that his niece was having an illicit affair with one of the assassins. According to this version, the Shah had ordered Mostafa, who was clearly a figure of considerable standing in Khomein, to attend him in Arak. Fearing for Mostafa's safety, his sister urged him to take a bodyguard, but he declined and travelled on his own, and paid for his stubbornness with his life.

When news of the murder reached Mostafa's sister, she immediately sent out a search party to track down the killers. But her efforts were hampered by the fact that her daughter – the infant Khomeini's cousin – was in love with one of the assassins, and tried on several occasions to warn him of his imminent arrest. When the men were eventually arrested and sent to Tehran for interrogation, Mostafa's niece pleaded for their lives to be spared. But her entreaties were in vain. The assassins were duly condemned and executed, and for many months later the niece dressed in black, officially out of respect for her Uncle Mostafa, but she was really mourning the loss of her lover and her uncle's assassin.[5]

The more likely explanation for Mostafa's untimely demise, however, is that he became involved in a feud with a group of rival landowners, who were harassing the local population in Khomein and the surrounding villages. According to Khomeini's eldest brother Morteza, who was eight years old at the time of his father's death, Mostafa had become so concerned about the activities of some local noblemen that he set out for Arak to make an official complaint to the provincial governor, who happened to be the Shah's son. But the nobles got to hear of Mostafa's plan, and when he was about two days' ride from Khomein he was attacked and shot. 'The bullet went clean through the Koran my father had put in his shirt pocket and pierced his heart,' Morteza recounted many years later. 'He fell from his horse and died instantly.'[6]

Eventually two of the nobles held responsible for the murder were rounded up. One of them died in prison, but the other, Jafar Qoli Khan, who had close family ties with the Shah, made a spirited plea for clemency. To ensure that justice was done, Morteza and his brother Nureddin were taken to Tehran by their aunts and uncles to lobby the Shah. Ruhollah, who was precisely four months and twenty-two days old when his father was murdered, was left behind in Khomein with his two sisters. The family lobbied the prime minister and a number of government ministers, and their entreaties were ultimately successful: the nobleman was condemned to death. Morteza recalls that he and his brother were introduced to the Crown Prince amid the marbled splendour of the Golestan Palace. Having received assurances that justice would be done, they ran into Khan as they left the palace grounds. He begged the two young boys for mercy, but they ignored his pleas, and on the morning of 9 May 1905 Khan was beheaded in Baharestan Square, where all public executions were held in Tehran at that time. Afterwards, Morteza later wrote, 'the executioner took his head to the bazaar where he showed it to the merchants and shopkeepers who offered him tips.'[7]

Although orphaned at such a tender age, the family's wealth meant that the infant Ruhollah would be well cared for. Apart from the land he had purchased in Khomein and the surrounding area, Mostafa left his family an annual income of 100 to 200 tomans, the local currency of the time and a considerable sum given that it was calculated an individual required just one toman a month to survive. The young infant was now cared for by his mother, his aunt and his wet nurse, and by all accounts he had a happy and boisterous childhood. As a boy Ruhollah was physically strong and good at sport, and his family recall that he would spend all day playing in Khomein's dusty streets and come home with his clothes dirty and torn. He could beat most of the other boys in the town at wrestling, and his favourite game was leapfrog, at which he was considered something of a local champion.

At the age of four Ruhollah was enrolled at the local *maktab*, a religious school, to commence his religious education. In a backward, provincial town like Khomein in the early twentieth century, a religious education was the only kind of schooling available, and Ruhollah could count himself lucky to be receiving any sort of education at all as only about 10 per cent of boys and 5 per cent of girls were admitted to the *maktabs*. The schools were financed by a mixture of parental donations and religious endowments.

The syllabus, taught by a local mullah, was limited to learning verses from the Koran by rote. Each child would take some food and a blanket to sit on, and the younger pupils would be entertained by popular religious stories. But the education, such as it was, consisted of the teacher giving the children a few lines, which they were then expected to repeat. Apart from learning the Koran they would be taught the Persian alphabet, calligraphy and build up a small but vital Koranic vocabulary, as well as a few phrases and words in Arabic about the Prophet and the Imams. Once the pupils had mastered this, they would progress to studying selected suras,

verses from the Koran that could most easily be learnt by
heart, which would be read, chanted and copied out again
repeatedly for two years until they were inscribed on their
impressionable young minds forever. This element of traditional *maktab* schooling forms an important part of the
modern Iranian educational syllabus today.

Discipline was strictly and harshly enforced, and the
slightest mispronunciation of a Koranic word frequently
merited a severe beating, with the children being hit on the
back of their legs with cherry-tree branches until they bled.
Boys and girls were strictly segregated and while girls were
only expected to attend until the age of nine, boys could
continue their education until they were sixteen – so long as
their parents could afford it. As life expectancy at this time
was around thirty years, most boys had finished their education
at twelve, and left school to begin work at their family's
business or farm. The Musavi family had the resources to keep
Ruhollah and his brothers at the *maktab* until they were
sixteen, and all three boys appear to have flourished, as they
all enjoyed successful professional careers in later life.

Ruhollah was, by all accounts, a talented and diligent pupil,
and by the age of six had learnt the whole of the Koran by
heart and was developing his talents to discuss and question
important doctrinal issues. His family also arranged for Ruhollah and his brothers to have private tuition to broaden their
education beyond the narrow syllabus of the *maktab*, and
they received elementary training in subjects such as arith-
metic, history, geography and basic science. Throughout his
education Ruhollah maintained a close bond with his older
brothers. His brother Morteza, who helped Ruhollah to learn
Arabic grammar, recalled how their calligraphy became so alike
that he would start a letter, and then leave it to Ruhollah to
complete to see if anyone could tell the difference.

The *maktab*, however, remained the focal point of Ruhollah's academic endeavours. There were no formal examinations

as such, but the pupils were subjected to frequent tests to demonstrate the progress they had made in calligraphy, the recitation of the Koran and the meaning of specific Koranic phrases. Ruhollah clearly excelled, for many years later, after he had established himself as a teacher at Qom, a fellow scholar who met him in the early 1960s recalled that when he recited a Koranic verse with Khomeini, he would recite the next without any hesitation.[8]

In 1918, when Ruhollah reached the age of sixteen, the teacher at his local *maktab* concluded that he had learnt all that the school could offer, and that if he wished to continue his education, he would need to move to another institution. 'I have taught you all the things that I know, except one,' his teacher remarked enigmatically, 'and that one thing you must go and seek elsewhere.'[9] The teacher wanted Ruhollah to become a *talebeh*, a 'seeker' who studies theology with the aim of entering the clergy. To do this Ruhollah would need to travel to the nearest local theological college at Arak, which necessitated making the same perilous journey his father had taken sixteen years before. Whatever reservations the teenage Ruhollah might have had about placing himself similarly at risk were overtaken by the deaths of his mother and aunt. They both perished within months of each other in the great flu epidemic that swept through the region in the aftermath of the First World War. These two women had cared for, raised and loved Ruhollah in the years following his father's death. But after their passing there were no longer any strong family ties to detain Ruhollah in Khomein. His aunt, who had been impressed with the progress he had already made in his schooling, had set aside a small sum to finance his further education, and so, armed with a modest income and a basic religious education, Ruhollah set off from Khomein in search of his destiny, never to return.

*

The young Khomeini's education took place against a backdrop of tumultuous political upheaval in Iran, the consequences of which had a direct bearing on the Islamic revolution he was to lead many decades later. By the early twentieth century the same strong nationalist forces that had changed the complexion of nineteenth-century Europe were stirring in the Middle East. In Iran this was to have a dramatic effect both on the way the country was governed and who governed it. And the occasionally violent struggle over the country's future political destiny that took place at the turn of the century laid the foundations for the far more traumatic upheavals that erupted towards the century's end.

By the close of the nineteenth century, in the decades directly preceding Khomeini's birth, the fortunes of the once great ancient kingdom of Persia, were at a low ebb. A country that, at the height of its powers under King Darius in 522 BC, had stretched from Greece to Afghanistan, from the Black Sea to the Blue Nile, was crippled with debt and fighting off the unwelcome attentions of two of the nineteenth century's most formidable imperial powers, Russia and Britain. The ruling Qajar dynasty – a Turkic tribe that had migrated to Iran from Central Asia in the fourteenth century – had governed the country since claiming the throne in 1795, but a combination of their personal greed and their predilection for making disadvantageous trade deals with foreign powers had resulted in a gradual erosion of their popular support. In 1814, after the Qajars signed an agreement with Britain – The Definitive Treaty – to protect them from the grasping hands of Russia's imperial ambitions in the Caucasus, British officers and businessmen were particularly favoured at the Qajar court. And the more the corrupt and incompetent shahs got themselves into debt, the more they were tempted to bail themselves out by selling lucrative manufacturing and trade concessions to wealthy foreigners.

The British were the main beneficiaries of this largesse, a fact that did not endear the British Empire to ordinary Persians, who were none too pleased to see their precious wealth and resources being handed over to a foreign power. Britain's unpopularity deepened when the British military, which was then fighting alongside the Russians against the Turks in the War of Greek Independence, failed to come to the aid of the Shah when he provoked the second Russo-Persian War in 1826. The Persian armies were no match for the Russians, and by 1828 had been so badly mauled that they were forced to sign the humiliating Treaty of Turkmanchai, by which Tehran ceded all its territories in the Caucasus to Russia and granted economic concessions to Russian citizens. This resentment came to a head in 1872 when the Shah, Nasir ed-Din, demonstrated his enthusiasm for doing deals with the British by granting Baron Paul Julius von Reuter, the founder of Reuters news agency, a monopoly over virtually all of Iran's economic and financial resources. Lord Curzon, the British Foreign Secretary, described the Reuter Concession, as it became known, as 'the most complete and extraordinary surrender of the entire industrial resources of a Kingdom into foreign hands that has probably ever been dreamt or, much less accomplished, in history.'[10]

The Reuter Concession revealed the growing influence within Persia of a powerful coalition of interests that were highly critical both of the Shah's incompetent government and the nation's constant humiliation at the hands of foreign powers. Throughout the nineteenth century the influence of the ulema, the country's leading Islamic scholars, had grown exponentially as a rallying point for opposition to the Shah. The views of the ulema were sought, though not always acted upon, when a new shah was appointed. Relations between the clergy and the royal court became strained in 1851 when Qajar ministers attempted to introduce a secular school system. The more ostracized the clergy became from the government the more they linked up with the *bazaaris*, the influential mercantile classes that controlled the country's commercial activity.

Most *bazaaris* were Shia, and inevitably had close family ties to the clerical establishment. Mullahs and *bazaaris* often came from the same family, with one son entering business and another joining the clergy (just like Khomeini and his own brothers). Much of the clergy's income derived from the *bazaaris* who, according to Shia tradition, would donate 20 per cent of their income to the mosque. In return the mullahs would officiate at religious and social ceremonies, and would help the *bazaaris* – many of whom were illiterate – in drawing up petitions and other documents for government business.[11]

By the time the Shah agreed the Reuter Concession these two powerful interest groups had formed a formidable opposition front, one that dominated the country's political landscape until the Islamic revolution a century later. The Shah's prime minister, Mirza Hosain Khan Moshir-al-Dowleh, was determined to Westernize the country, and believed that the only way to achieve this was by handing over the entire economy to the British. The clergy were bitterly opposed on the grounds that any Westernization of Persia would undermine their influence and standing in the country, while the *bazaaris* were outraged at the surrender of the country's vital interests to a foreign power. Their combined opposition became so intense that the following year the Shah had no alternative other than to cancel the concession. The humiliating climbdown by the Shah marked the emergence of the clergy and the *bazaaris* as a coalition with the power to shape the course of the country's political development.

The abrogation of the Reuter Concession did not curb the Shah's predilection for handing over vital national assets to foreign control, nor the opposition's vociferous criticism of such arrangements. By 1890 the Shah's indebtedness led him to offer a fifty-year monopoly of purchase, sale and manufacture of the entire tobacco crop of Iran to Major G.F. Talbot of the British-owned Imperial Tobacco Company for a personal gift of £25,000. Again, religious and business leaders combined to oppose the agreement, which was eventually cancelled in 1892, but not before a mob had attacked the royal palace and the government had ordered its troops to open fire on demonstrators. But cancellation of the agreement only deepened the Shah's problems, as he was now obliged to pay £500,000 in compensation to the Imperial Tobacco Company, and the only way he could do this was by raising a loan with Reuter's Imperial Bank of Persia, which was to be paid back by the bank's agents collecting customs duties in the Gulf. Not surprisingly this arrangement provoked yet more hostility, and the new anti-Shah campaign reached an intensity that ultimately culminated in the Shah's assassination at a Tehran mosque in May 1896.

The new Shah, Muzzafar ed-Din, seemed incapable of avoiding the mistakes of his predecessor. In 1901 he raised a series of loans from the British and Russians by awarding British entrepreneur William Knox D'Arcy a sixty-year concession for oil exploration rights throughout most of Iran, and two years later he eased tariffs on Russian imports, allowed the Russians to flood the country with wines and spirits, which are forbidden in Islam and only served to infuriate the clergy, which dutifully reminded the faithful of their obligation to forgo alcohol. The Shah's position was further weakened by the deepening economic crisis that afflicted Persia at the beginning of the twentieth century.

The profligacy of the Qajar dynasty meant the country was burdened with a massive national debt, and the impact of the Russo-Japanese war of 1905 led to a drastic reduction in trade with Russia, resulting in sugar prices rising by 33 per cent and wheat by 90 per cent.[12] The Shah's various attempts to raise funds had saddled the country with a massive national debt – Persia owed Britain £800,000 and another £3,250,000 to Russia.[13] It has been estimated that at the turn of the twentieth century Persia was one of the four least-developed countries in the world.[14]

A popular poem from the period aptly summarized the educated Persian's hatred of their quasi-colonial status:

> Ne'er may that evil-omened day befall
> When Iran shall become the stranger's thrall!
> Ne'er may I see that virgin fair and pure
> Fall victim to some Russian gallant's lure!
> And ne'er may Fate this angel-bride award
> As serving-maiden to some English lord![15]

Relations between the Shah and the country's mercantile classes were further strained by the appointment of an officious Belgian director of the Customs Administration, Monsieur Naus, whose arrogant demeanour prompted a number of protests from Tehran's merchants in the autumn of 1905. He also succeeded in upsetting the clerical establishment when a photograph of Naus dressed in mullah's robes for a fancy dress ball was circulated throughout Tehran. Once again the outraged mullahs linked up with the outraged *bazaaris* to demand the Shah mend his ways. The prevailing mood of political instability was complicated by the formation of a number of 'national societies' in the country's major cities which campaigned for radical government reform, and led to the creation a national consensus within Persia that the Shah's autocratic powers should be curbed.

Two completely unrelated events led to the Constitutional Crisis of 1905–6 which set the parameters of the country's long-running political struggle for the rest of the century. The first was the 1905 rebellion in neighbouring Russia, which forced Czar Nicholas to agree the establishment in Moscow of a parliament with its own legislative powers, and which would curb the authority of the Czar. Many Iranian intellectuals and reformers were encouraged by the success of the first Bolshevik revolution in Russia, even if they had little sympathy for its underlying Communist agenda. If the Czar's powers could be curbed in Moscow, why not the Shah's in Tehran? The other event that marked a turning point in relations between the Qajars and the country's mercantile classes came in December 1905 when Tehran's governor ordered the public beating of two elderly, respected sugar wholesalers for overcharging. The two *bazaaris* were subjected to the excruciating punishment of being bastinadoed (beaten on the soles of their feet) for failing to comply with an order to lower the price of sugar.

This callous act of violence, imposed against two men who were themselves the victims of the government's economic mismanagement, succeeded in uniting the country's leading mullahs and *bazaaris* against the Shah. The merchants responded by closing the bazaar, thereby bringing all commerce in the nation's capital to a standstill, while two of the country's leading ayatollahs, Abdullah Behbahani and Mohammad Tabatabai, led a 2,000-strong demonstration of mullahs and *baazaris* against the Shah, who then sought sanctuary inside Tehran's Abdul Azim mosque. It was left to the mullahs, as was the custom, to articulate the protesters' demands, which ranged from the enforcement of Sharia law to the establishment of a House of Justice, which would have the authority to draft laws. After a month-long general strike, the Shah agreed to concede to the demands. But the rebels were not convinced, and a stand-off between the demonstrators and the government continued throughout the winter and spring of 1905.

The protests had by now spread far beyond the confines of the capital, with the religious leaders in Qom allying themselves with the merchant leaders. Matters came to a head when the Shah ordered his security forces to detain the leading opposition figures. More than twenty demonstrators were shot dead when the Shah's elite Cossack Brigade opened fire, prompting 14,000 merchants and mullahs to seek sanctuary in the spacious grounds of the British embassy. (The British were suspected of tacitly supporting the protest movement over concerns that the Shah was pursuing pro-Russia policies.)

Faced with a national strike orchestrated by the country's mullahs and merchants, the Shah, whose health was starting to fail him, finally capitulated on 5 August, when he issued a *firman*, a decree, ordering the establishment of a national consultative *Majlis-e Melli*, which literally means 'the sitting place', but is Persian for parliament. The decree authorized that 'an Assembly of delegates elected by the Princes, the Doctors of Divinity (ulema), the Qajar family, the nobles and notables, the landowners, the merchants and the guilds' be set up in Tehran to consider 'important affairs of the State and Empire'.[16] The decree had the desired effect of bringing the political agitation to an end, and the first session of the Iranian Majlis convened on 7 October.

The representatives of the first Majlis represented a broad range of Persian society. The constitutional movement had the backing of the country's propertied classes, as well as religious and intellectual leaders. The former, which consisted of land-owners, merchants, administrators and craftsmen, looked forward to an era where they could develop their own potential, unfettered by the constant interference of the European powers in their affairs. Among them were mullahs who embraced Western political ideals, and had cast away their turbans in favour of fashionable European hats. Another substantial constituency was the religious establishment who believed that by reducing the authority of the Shah they would inevitably benefit from an increase in their power and prestige. As the *bazaaris* who ran the guilds reverted to their traditional practice of electing clerics to represent their interests, the first Majlis was not surprisingly dominated by the ulema, which enjoyed a majority of 106.

A photograph taken of the members of the new Majlis provides an intriguing snapshot of the divide taking root in Persia at the turn of the twentieth century between the traditional clergy and the Westernizing mercantile classes, a division that persisted until Khomeini's Islamic revolution seventy-three years later. The photograph shows sixty ulema wearing turbans while forty other newly elected Majlis members are wearing fez caps, the favoured dress of Western-oriented Persian intellectuals.

But strains were starting to appear between those who sought genuine, Western-style reform and the traditional Shia clergy, who wanted the country run on Islamic principles. The reformers, who were backed by Tehran's emerging mercantile middle classes, were intoxicated by Western concepts of national sovereignty, the separation of Church and State and individual rights. The first task of the new national assembly would be to draft a constitution, something that was unheard of in the Islamic world where all government strictly adhered to the laws and traditions set out in the Koran. Such concepts were anathema to conventional Shia theologians, who were appalled by the notion that elected representatives of the people could assemble to pass legislation. For them all laws derived directly from the Holy Book, and laws were made by God, not mere mortals. Islam was not a mere concept to be accommodated into the government of the nation: Islam controlled and directed every aspect of an individual's life from the cradle to the grave.

In the early stages of the constitutional revolution these tensions were not so apparent, as the main focus of the Majlis was to consolidate its position. Tehran's two leading ayatollahs, Behbahani and Tabatabai, took a pragmatic view and sought to work with the constitutionalists, even if they were personally uncomfortable with some of aspects of the constitutionalists' political agenda. The main priority, so far as they were concerned, was to curb the power of the Shah, and to this end they supported the new constitution, which contained, in Article Thirty-Five, the decidedly secularist declaration that 'Sovereignty is a trust confided by the People to the person of the King.'[17] The Shah, who was by now mortally ill, ratified the collection of Fundamental Laws which formed the basis of the new constitution on 30 December 1906. But five days later the political achievements of the past year were placed in jeopardy when the Shah died and was replaced by his son, Muhammad Ali, who immediately set about undermining the country's new constitutional arrangements.

At first the new Shah led the Majlis to believe he would be cooperative, but when they presented a revised set of Fundamental Laws, including a bill of rights for all citizens and a parliamentary form of government, he initially refused to sign them. This provoked another bout of anti-government demonstrations, culminating with the assassination of the prime minister, Amin al-Sultan. The Shah was taken aback by the ferocity of the opposition, and in October 1907 agreed to sign the new laws which, taken together with those ratified by his father, formed the basis of the new Iranian constitution. This should have augured a new epoch in Iranian history, but the Shah had no intention of keeping to his word. He was encouraged in his opposition both by the British, who worried that such similar progressive political ideas would spread to India, and by the Russian Czar, who was determined to undermine the authority of Russia's Duma. Under the Anglo-Russian Entente of 1907, Persia was divided into British and Russian 'spheres of influence', with the British taking the south-eastern region, adjoining British India and Afghanistan, and the Russians the north, close to their territories in the Caucasus.

When news of the agreement became public in 1908, it was deeply unpopular with the constitutionalists, who, suspecting the government was involved in yet another deal to surrender national sovereignty to foreign interests, directed their ire at the Shah, who was himself the target of an assassination attempt in mid-June. In scenes reminiscent of Khomeini's revolution, the Shah responded by ordering the Cossack Brigade, the Russian-trained imperial guard, to attack the Majlis building in Tehran, which was defended by 7,000 lightly armed constitutionalists, and in the ensuing fighting more than

250 were killed, and much of the Majlis building was reduced to rubble. Many of the pro-reform leaders were rounded up and executed. But the Shah's response did not succeed in crushing the opposition leaders' spirits, and full-scale civil war now erupted. But the Shah's efforts to suppress the constitutionalists foundered when royalist forces encountered stiff resistance from well-organized local tribes in the north of the south of the country, and by the summer of 1909 the Shah's forces had been roundly defeated, and the Shah himself forced to seek sanctuary in the Russian embassy. His abdication a few days later in favour of his twelve-year-old son, Ahmed, signalled the collapse of the royalist counter-revolution.

Reprisals against those who had supported the Shah's attempt to overturn the Constitutional Revolution quickly followed, and among those put on trial was an elderly cleric whom Khomeini would later hail as his personal hero from this turbulent period in his early childhood. Sheikh Fazlollah Nuri was a prominent Shia cleric who, in common with most of the Shia clergy, had initially supported the nationwide campaign to curb the Shah's powers and limit the interference of imperial powers such as Britain and Russia in Persian affairs. But once it became clear that the participants in the first Majlis were pursuing a secular, rather than an Islamic, agenda, Nuri turned on the constitutionalists with a vengeance. Echoing many of the sentiments Khomeini himself would use in his campaign to overthrow the Shah in the late 1970s, Nuri launched a vitriolic propaganda war against the constitutionalists, preaching that they would bring vice to Iran. He issued a fatwa, accused them of being 'apostates', 'atheists' and *koffar al-harbi* (warlike pagans) whose blood should be shed by the faithful.[18]

The violence of the rhetoric Nuri directed against the reformers was to some extent the result of his own, initially enthusiastic support for the movement, which itself was the result of a fundamental misunderstanding of what they were seeking to achieve. Coming from the cloistered confines of the mosque, Nuri was not familiar with the Western political ideologies that were attracting such interest among young Persians, and believed that the reformers' campaign to curb the power of the Shah was aimed at increasing that of the mullahs in pursuit of Persia's re-Islamification. He did not discover his error until he attended the first few sessions of the Majlis, where he was horrified to discover that its function was to make laws. So far as Nuri was concerned, it was not for mere mortals to make law. In his view the role of parliament should only be to ratify and enforce Sharia-based laws. In fact Nuri went a lot further than most of his contemporary Shia theologians, concluding that in the absence of the Hidden Imam, an absolutist government which applied Islamic law was the best form of government.[19]

Having initially supported the constitutionalists, he reverted to supporting the Shah. Unlike the more pragmatic ayatollahs, Nuri dedicated himself with such force to opposing the movement that the constitutionalists nicknamed him 'the Perfect Ass' (*Gav-e-Mojassam*). His attacks on the reformists were deemed to be so extreme by other Shia leaders that most of them disowned him. The only mullah of any distinction who supported Nuri was Ayatollah Sheikh Mohsen Araki, who would later become Khomeini's personal tutor.[20]

Nuri supported the Shah after he declared war on the Majlis, and in their support he declared *jihad*, holy war, against all the groups that supported the Constitutional Revolution. When the constitutionalist forces finally entered Tehran in July 1909, Nuri refused to flee, but stayed with the royalist forces while they made one last, doomed stand. But they were quickly overwhelmed, and Nuri was arrested. The constitutionalists were in no mood to show Nuri any mercy after he had sided with the Qajar despots and their Russian protectors. A special Islamic court was convened on the morning of 31 July, and he was tried for treason before a ten-man tribunal headed by a reformist Ayatollah, Ibrahim Zanjani. In a matter of hours Nuri was found guilty of treason, and condemned to death.

The seventy-one-year-old cleric was taken straight from the courtroom to Toopkhaneh Square, where a crowd of several thousand had been waiting since long before sunrise. Dancing bears and playful monkeys had been brought into the square for the crowd's amusement before the main spectacle took place, and fruits and sweets were distributed among the spectators by the triumphant supporters of the revolution. There was little sympathy among the crowd for the fate awaiting the aged cleric who, apart from committing treason, had vociferously opposed the reforms that would have improved the lot of the poor. Most of the Shia clergy also approved of the verdict, issuing fatwas against Nuri, denouncing him as a 'Corrupter on Earth' (*Mufsed fel-Ardh*). The old mullah refused to be blindfolded and, as his guards led him to the scaffold, he managed to make one last sermon before the noose was fixed around his neck. The constitutional system, he declared, was designed to destroy Islam. 'Either this system must go or Islam will perish.'[21]

With the exception of Khomeini's future teacher, Sheikh Mohsen Araki, few of those present at Nuri's hanging mourned his passing. He had betrayed his country, and he had shown utter disregard for the plight of ordinary Iranians. But his final words on the gallows in Toopkhaneh Square could almost be taken as a rallying cry for the Islamic revolution that was to follow seven decades later. Khomeini was only a young boy of seven when Nuri was hanged, but in later life he would hold up the maverick cleric as his personal idol. From 1979 onwards, Nuri has been hailed a national hero by the country's leading ayatollahs, and Khomeini personally ordered that one of Tehran's main roads be renamed the Sheikh Fazlollah Highway, which is what it is called today. 'Khomeini always used to say that the reason the Shia hierarchy was defeated in the Constitutional Revolution was because the mullahs had not been following the lead of Sheikh Nuri,' explained a senior Iranian cleric who was formerly one of Khomeini's pupils. 'Khomeini taught us to admire Nuri, and would take us to his shrine at Qom, where he is hailed as a martyr. For Khomeini Nuri was a national hero, and had pictures of him on the walls of his study. Khomeini made no secret of the fact that he admired Nuri and the form of Islamic despotism that he preached.'[22]

The tumultuous events surrounding the Constitutional Revolution did not directly impinge on the young Khomeini's childhood in a remote outpost like Khomein, though he and his family were caught up in the national mood of excitement generated by this defining moment in the creation of modern Iran. The weakness of the central government in Tehran – never strong at the best of times – meant that its ability to exert its authority in the provinces was severely diminished, and led to an increase in banditry and raids by marauding tribesmen, who were a perennial threat in the more remote regions of Persia. Despite his religious status, Khomeini's father had always kept a number of rifles and employed local gunmen to protect his land from the unwelcome attention of rogue princes and bandits. After his murder the family looked to other members of the town for protection. Morteza, Khomeini's elder brother, recalled an incident in the spring of 1907, when the Shah's government was in total disarray, and a large assembly of bandits on horseback attacked Khomein. The family had been visiting friends to celebrate the Iranian New Year (which falls on the spring solstice) when the alarm was raised. 'We got up and returned to our homes,' said Morteza. 'When we got home we found that the gendarmerie had taken over our house and were shooting from the watch tower. I went up the tower and saw the tribesmen on their horses . . . but the attack was repulsed.'[23]

This hair-raising existence was replicated in thousands of villages across Persia as the rival royalist and constitutionalist

factions battled for control of the country. The overthrow of
the Shah in July 1909, and his replacement by his twelve-year-
old son, finally put the constitutionalists in a strong position,
and they set about implementing the reform agenda that they
had initially proposed before the Shah launched his counter-
revolution. Their greatest challenge was to restore the authority
of the central government and to deal with the massive mountain of debt that had been accumulated by the Shahs. They
realized they needed outside help, but could not stomach the
idea of inviting the rapacious British and Russians to meddle
in their affairs. So they turned to the Swedes, who helped
to train and equip the Gendarmerie, and to the Americans,
whose innate anti-colonialism struck a resonant chord with the
imperialist-wary Persians.

It was not long before Persia's brave experiment with
parliamentary democracy ran into trouble. The appointment of
an American, William Morgan Shuster, as the constitutionalists'
economic adviser upset the British and Russians who, regardless of the Persians' strong desire for self-government, still
regarded the country as being within their sphere of influence.
Shuster harboured the same strong anti-imperial sentiments of
many of his countrymen, and his high-handed manner did not
win him much support in Tehran. So when Shuster made the
cardinal error of trying to play the British against the Russians
– by appointing a British tax official to collect taxes in territory
technically under Russian control – the old imperial powers
combined to devastating effect.

Citing the 1907 Anglo-Russian agreement (which the Persians had never ratified), the Russians, with tacit British support, invaded northern Persia and occupied two cities – Rasht
and Anzali. The Russians demanded Shuster's dismissal, and
issued an ultimatum that the Persian government did not hire
any additional foreign advisers without Russian and British
consent, and reimburse Moscow for the cost of the invasion. In
Tehran the regency government of Shah Ahmed pressed the

Majlis to accept the Russians' terms, and when it refused, it was forcibly disbanded in December 1911, thereby bringing Persia's first experiment in democratic government to an ignominious end.

Apart from the profound effect Persia's Constitutional Revolution of 1905 to 1911 had on the development of modern Iran, it also raised the awareness of the country's clerical establishment about its potential role in shaping the nation's destiny. In the past the Shia hierarchy had always sought to influence the deliberations of the royal court, but their position was mainly advisory as the government under the Shah dynasties was in essence an Islamic autocracy. While the Shah might enjoy the secular trappings of office, his rule was based firmly on Islamic principles and the teachings of the Koran. But the Constitutional Revolution for the first time introduced the notion of modern, unIslamic, modes of government where the will of the people took precedence over the will of God.

The revolutionary politics that consumed Persia in the early twentieth century made a deep impression on the country's clerical establishment, and caused a serious rift between those who cautiously supported measures that curbed the Shah's dictatorial powers and those, like Ayatollah Nuri, who viscerally opposed any government structure that was not divinely inspired. Nuri's vehement objection to the introduction of democratic government not only led to him becoming the first Ayatollah in the country's history to be executed; it created lasting divisions within the clergy over the fundamental relationship between Islam and government. Furthermore, the clergy's close involvement – by virtue of their close association with the merchants – in the revolutionary currents that swept the country gave them a taste for power that would endure for the rest of the century, and would provide Khomeini with the political platform from which to launch his own brand of Islamic revolutionary ideology.

3

To Be a Mullah

When the time came for the teenage Khomeini to leave the family home to further his education, Persia was struggling to come to terms with the catastrophic consequences of the First World War. It was not just the appalling flu epidemic that swept the country – as it did through most of Europe – at the war's end, claiming the lives of the two people most responsible for Khomeini's upbringing, his mother and his aunt. The outbreak of hostilities between the Great Powers in 1914 had been used as yet another excuse by Britain and Russia to reignite their neo-colonialist interest in a country that was still struggling to come to terms with the failure of the Constitutional Revolution.

At the start of the conflict the Shah had publicly declared Persia to be neutral, but the moment the Ottoman Empire declared its support for Germany it was inevitable that Persia would become embroiled. Persia shared a 1,000-mile border with the Ottomans along the territories that today comprise modern Iraq, and its geographical location alone meant Britain and Russia felt compelled to reassert their traditional spheres of influence in the north and south of the country.

British interest in Persia had been heightened before the outbreak of hostilities after William D'Arcy, whom the Shah had granted a sixty-year exploration concession, struck oil in the south-west of the country in 1908. For the British government, which had just ordered the Royal Navy to convert from coal-burning to oil-burning ships, the pressing priority was to secure access to the oil for British warships, which led to London buying a 51 per cent stake in the newly created Anglo-Persian Oil Company. In 1915, when Winston Churchill was pursuing his bold Dardanelles strategy to link up with the Russians in the Black Sea, the British even went so far as to offer Moscow control of Istanbul and the Turkish Strait after the war in return for expanding Britain's sphere of influence to Persia's 'neutral' zone, where the vast Persian oilfields were located.[1] Persia, which provided a gateway to India, became a key strategic asset for the British, and it was from Persia that the British launched their invasion of southern Iraq at the end of 1915 in their ill-fated attempt to capture Baghdad.

By the end of the war a succession of Ottoman, British, Russian and local military forces had been involved in a series of military confrontations on Persian soil. Initially the main area of activity was in the north, where Russian and Turkish troops fought several skirmishes in Iranian Azerbaijan. But after the 1917 Bolshevik Revolution, the focus changed, with the British, who were concerned about the import of Bolshevik ideology to India, using their bases in Persia to mount expeditions against the Communists and provide safe havens for White Russians in northern Iran. Not surprisingly the war took a devastating toll on the Iranian economy. The north of the country, which boasted the most fertile agricultural land, lay in ruins, with crops and livestock destroyed and left to rot. The presence of large numbers of troops placed unsustainable pressure on the nation's food resources, with the result that the country was afflicted by widespread famine which, together with the flu epidemic, claimed the lives of an estimated 2 million Iranians out of a total population of about 10 million. The presence of so many foreign armies, coming so soon after the upheaval of the Constitutional Revolution, also saw the government's authority diminish to the extent that a number of tribal sheikhs became so powerful that they were able to carve out their own autonomous states.[2]

For Khomeini, who left Khomein in the autumn of 1918, these cataclysmic events severely limited his options in terms of where he could pursue the next level in his studies. Although he was an orphan, he nevertheless came from a respectable family that was relatively wealthy. In normal circumstances a student of Khomeini's educational promise and social standing would have applied for a place at one of the main Shia shrines. Khomeini's personal preference may well have been to study at Najaf, where his grandfather Ahmad had resided for many years in the mid-nineteenth century. But the collapse of the Ottoman Empire at the end of the First World War made this unfeasible, as travel to war-torn southern Iraq was considered too dangerous, and so he had to settle for a seminary closer to home. After long consultations with his elder brother Morteza, Ruhollah firstly decided to go to Isfahan, the nearest city of consequence to Khomein and a renowned centre of Shia learning. But soon after he arrived at Isfahan he learnt that a new theological college had been established at Arak, formerly the Persian city of Sultanabad, and he decided to relocate there.

By all accounts the teenage Ruhollah had grown into a handsome and quite striking young man. At 5ft 9ins (1.76 metres), he was tall by the Iranian standards of the day. He was slim, but heavily boned, and had the gait of a potential athlete. Although just sixteen years old, he had already grown a beard, which he kept neatly trimmed. His contemporaries recall that his face had regular, almost feminine features, which were dominated by a pair of deeply penetrating eyes, which would later be described as 'fathomless oceans' by those who knew him well. At the college he quickly acquired a reputation as a hard-working student and a talented debater, and as a headstrong person who was not afraid to speak his mind. Khomeini's son, Ahmad, would later recall how one day, when his father was hard at work studying Arabic grammar in the college courtyard, he was disturbed by the noise of the principal teaching another class nearby. Khomeini approached the teacher and, politely but firmly, asked him to speak more softly.[3]

Khomeini's choice of college was important in terms of the influence it was to have on his personal and religious development. Its main benefactor was Mohsen Araki, who had been the only Persian cleric of distinction to have supported Ayatollah Nuri's uncompromising campaign for an Islamic state during the Constitutional Revolution. Araki had attended Nuri's execution in Tehran, where he was moved to tears by the indignity of the elderly cleric being hanged in public before a jeering crowd. He left Tehran soon afterwards, disgusted at the way the state had treated a deeply committed and devout guardian of Islam. He returned to Arak to set up his new theological college convinced that the country's inexorable slide towards a Western style of government would destroy Islam's role and purpose in society. Araki dreamed of launching a counter-revolution against the country's secularization, but he had neither Nuri's courage nor charisma. So he settled for a quiet life of teaching and preaching, and also producing some of the region's finest grapes on his farm.[4]

The standing of the clerical establishment had been much diminished because of its involvement in the political turmoil created by the Constitutional Revolution, and remained so for the following decade, not least because the country found itself at the mercy of the political and military vicissitudes of the First World War. But the clergy's status was also weakened by the deep doctrinal splits that the revolution had provoked. In scenes reminiscent of the Reformation in sixteenth-century Europe, the schism was so deep that, with the hanging of Ayatollah Nuri, the clergy found itself in the unique position where one ayatollah had sentenced another to death, which was unheard of in the Islamic world. Nuri's death symbolized the triumph of the pragmatic clergy over the radicals, but the violent manner in which the dispute was resolved did little to enhance the clergy's standing with the public at large. For many years the mullahs would be divided into two camps, the constitutionalists *(mashruteh)* and the theocrats *(mashru'eh)*. But it was the latter group which took control of the next stage in Khomeini's education.

Khomeini formally entered the theological college established by Araki and chose as his main tutor a peripatetic Shia scholar who nurtured ambitions of uniting the divided Shia clergy behind his leadership. Sheikh Abdul-Karim Ha'eri, who had spent many years studying in the major shrine cities of Iraq, such as Najaf and Karbala, had first settled in Arak in 1900. At the time of the Constitutional Revolution he moved to Najaf in southern Iraq, where he found himself at odds with the traditional clergy because of his strongly held view that mullahs should not become involved in politics. The Shia establishment in Najaf broadly supported the aims of the Constitutional Revolution, but there were those who opposed the clergy becoming involved in politics, and in one ugly incident a group of anti-constitutionalists attacked their rivals in the streets of Najaf, killing many religious students. Soon afterwards Ha'eri left Najaf and made his way back to Arak, where he became a teacher at Araki's college.

Araki and Ha'eri may both best be described as Islamic purists, and their combined experience in opposing the Westernization of Persia made a profound impression on the seventeen-year-old Ruhollah, who quickly established himself as a star pupil at the seminary. Khomeini strictly adhered to one of the Prophet Mohammed's most popular quotations: 'Search for knowledge from the cradle to the grave', one which he would observe closely for the rest of his life. Within a year Khomeini's hard work was rewarded by his appointment as Ha'eri's personal companion and scribe, although this may have well been more a case of Ha'eri, who was sixty, acting as a father-figure to his young, orphaned student. Khomeini was clearly very fond of Ha'eri, whom he later described as 'a true father and guide to all his pupils', and some of Khomeini's early attempts at poetry were dedicated to Ha'eri.[5]

Khomeini had taken to wearing a turban, a sign that he was a fully fledged *talebeh*, or seeker, who had committed himself to a life of religious devotion, rather like a novice monk who is admitted to join a holy order. This was hardly surprising in view of his background. Khomeini's family, the Musavis, had a distinguished lineage as *sayyids* – those who claim direct descent from the Prophet. Consequently Khomeini was entitled to wear a black turban, while non-*sayyids*, those who do not trace their ancestry to the Prophet, wear white turbans and are called sheikhs. Khomeini, as a student, would initially have worn a skullcap and short jacket when he was first admitted to the college. Having proved his academic capabilities, and indicated a desire to make a lasting commitment to the study of Islam, he would then have received his turban in a formal ceremony conducted by Ha'eri. Apart from the turban, Khomeini was also given a long black cloak to be worn at all times when he left his abode. From now on the young student would be addressed by his full title, Sayyid Ruhollah Musavi Khomeini.[6]

The strong bond between master and pupil was such that when, in the early 1920s, Ha'eri decided to move on from Arak in pursuit of his own ambitions, Khomeini felt obliged to follow him. Qom, an important Shia shrine city, had fallen into a state of neglect after its most famous theologian had died in 1815. It was a great compliment to Ha'eri's rising stature as a Shia teacher of distinction that leading members of the clergy in Qom should invite him to move from Arak. Qom was once more becoming a major centre of Shia religious activity after the British, in their attempts to control the newly created state of Iraq, had expelled the Shia leadership from Najaf in southern Iraq for their refusal to accept the new government London had just set up under King Faisal. At first Ha'eri hesitated, but when he realized that a move to Qom would further his hopes of becoming a dominant figure within the Shia clergy, he relented. An indication of the high esteem in which Ha'eri was already held throughout the country was reflected in the fact that, when he finally arrived at Qom towards the end of 1921, the Shah personally travelled to Qom to greet him. Once Ha'eri had established himself in the holy city, most of the other leading members of his circle in Arak – including Khomeini – travelled to Qom to join him.

Khomeini moved into a semi-derelict former hospital which had been built in the nineteenth century, and although it was being used as a madrasa, a religious establishment, no funds were available to convert it to its new use. Conditions were spartan, and the daily routine demanding. In common with the other students Ruhollah would begin his day before dawn, when he would perform the ritual ablutions with the other *talebeh*, after which they would attend morning prayers. This would immediately be followed by the first lecture of the day, which could last for up to two hours, before the students would be allowed to have their breakfast, which would consist of tea, bread, some white cheese and fruit. They would then attend lectures and take part in discussions in the main hall of the madrasa, or a nearby mosque, with the lecturer sitting on the floor or a low stool and the students sitting cross-legged around him in a semi-circle. Apart from studying the Koran, students were encouraged to read history, poetry, mysticism and philosophy. One subject that aroused Khomeini's interest was Darwin's theory of evolution, which was considered to be deeply unIslamic by devout Muslims, and he read many Persian religious works that sought to refute Darwin's theory.[7]

After a light lunch, the students continued with their studies, and were given spare time to tend to their personal affairs, such as shopping and washing their clothes (self-sufficiency is an important aspect of training for madrasa students). In the evening the group would gather together for their evening meal, and for the final prayer session of the day.

They were then allowed free time, and some of the more adventurous students would head off to Qom for the night in search of a woman they could 'marry' for the night. Shia Islam recognizes two different sorts of marriage, the permanent and temporary. And while Islam encourages permanent marriage, those devoting their lives to religious study are given an exemption, and are allowed to arrange a temporary marriage for a specified period.

Many Persian theological colleges consequently attracted large numbers of women – some of them retired prostitutes – who made themselves available for temporary marriages in return for food, lodging or small donations. The practice of temporary marriages was particularly popular in Qom, where there were men who specialized in marrying divorcees for just one night. It is unlikely that Khomeini himself indulged in this custom, especially as his wife later said he was virgin when he married her and that she remained the only woman in his life.[8] But it would certainly have made for a lively college atmosphere with the constant interchange of 'wives' taking up their temporary residence for the night at the seminary.

Khomeini occupied his time with other pursuits, and it was as a student in Qom that he developed his lifelong interest in poetry. He had learnt most of the major Persian poems in Khomein, and in Qom he had the opportunity to study the main Arabic texts and to try his own hand at writing verse. His early poems show that he had a sense of humour, and there are references to pretty girls in Qom winking at him from beneath their veils. But like most adolescent poetry, Khomeini's style was clumsy and awkward, and it was not until he was much older that his writing became more readable. He also made a number of friends, and would go for walks with them to a nearby river where they would make tea and sit discussing the texts that they were studying. Ruhollah and his friends would sometimes venture on trips to other cities, and it was around this time that he made his first visit to Tehran where, to celebrate the occasion, he had a photograph of himself and his companions taken in their full clerical dress.

He demonstrated an early aptitude for learning, and was soon ear-marked to undertake the lengthy and gruelling course that would make him a *faqih*, an interpreter of religious law and the highest position to which the madrasa student can aspire. In Shia Islam, the course generally divides into three basic levels: stage one consists of learning Arabic grammar, logic and rudimentary theology; stage two focuses on the basic principles and application of Sharia law; and in the third stage students who have demonstrated a mastery of the first two levels work on developing their own opinions as to how religious laws should be interpreted. If successful, the student is then authorized by his teacher – in Khomeini's case Ha'eri – to practise as an Islamic judge, making judgements on every aspect of Islamic law and human activity. Khomeini had completed most of the first stage by the time he arrived at Qom, and completed the next two stages during the course of the next decade. He most likely completed the course's second stage in the mid-1920s, and finally received his 'permission' to practise as an Islamic jurist a decade later when he was about thirty-two years old.

Only a small percentage of the students who enter a madrasa complete the full course, which in Khomeini's case took about fifteen years. The successful candidates acquire the honorific title 'hojjat al-Islam' (proof of Islam), and can then either remain as a teacher at one of the main seminaries or become a preacher at a leading mosque, where one of their main functions would be to deliver the weekly sermon at the midday Friday prayer service. After the Constitutional Revolution the government introduced the title 'ayatollah' (which translates as 'sign of God') as a tribute to those clerics who had accepted the new constitution, and the title soon became commonplace to denote those mullahs who had acquired a reputation for outstanding learning and piety.

Khomeini was already an established teacher by the time he became an hojjat al-Islam, probably in 1936, the year his mentor Ha'eri died. While still studying at Qom on the third stage of his course, Khomeini started teaching his own classes, as do many postgraduates in Western universities, and quickly developed a reputation as an impressive and challenging jurist. Ayatollah Jafar Sobhani, one of his students from this period, recalls that Khomeini would 'put forward a topic in a decisive manner, first explaining other opinions and then his own before looking for arguments. He never introduced issues that were unclear in his own mind, preferring to do his homework and reflect upon topics before discussing them.'[9] Khomeini always appeared smart and neatly dressed for his classes, and eschewed the custom of many of his contemporaries who demonstrated their lack of interest in worldly goods and their piety by dressing in torn old clothes. While some considered this a mark of holiness, Khomeini saw no reason for clergymen to dress like beggars.

The young mullah's regard for his appearance may well have had something to do with the fact that in 1929, at the age of twenty-seven, he married. The idea of marriage was first put into Khomeini's head by Mohammed Lavasani, whom he had befriended at the Qom madrasa. Khomeini, with his family money and growing academic reputation, was regarded as an eligible bachelor, and Lavasani introduced him to Batoul Saqafi, the daughter of a wealthy Tehran mullah. When Lavasani had originally asked Khomeini, 'Why don't you want to get married?' Khomeini had replied, 'I have no one in mind and don't want to marry a girl from Khomein.' But his mind changed when he was introduced to Batoul, and soon afterwards he requested her hand. At first Batoul, who was then a fifteen-year-old schoolgirl, declined the offer. But, according to an interview Batoul gave after the 1979 Revolution, she changed her mind after dreaming about her future husband. 'The night after I refused Ruhollah's hand I saw the Prophet

Mohammed's daughter, Fatima, in my dream. She told me to marry him so the next day I told my parents that I had changed my mind. When we married . . . his only request was that I should observe the rules of Islam.'[10]

*

Sequestered in his quarters at the Dar al-Shafa seminary in Qom, Khomeini and his fellow students were shut off from the normal lives of ordinary citizens. Most of their day was spent in intensive study, and in their spare time they socialized with each other. Khomeini was deeply committed to his studies to become a religious jurist, but he nevertheless managed to take a close interest in the epoch-making political events in the aftermath of the First World War which would ultimately lead to the creation of modern Iran.

The end of the First World War left the British as the undisputed masters of Persia, especially as Russia's October Revolution had severely diminished Moscow's attempts to maintain its own sphere of influence. Britain's dominance, which meant that it was ultimately responsible for military training, tax collection and all the other main administrative functions of government, was enshrined in the Anglo-Persian Agreement of 1919. But a combination of fierce local opposition to foreign interference, and the British government's desire to reduce its overseas expenditure, resulted in London withdrawing all its troops two years later, leaving the Qajar government in Tehran to assert its authority.

The inherent weakness of the Qajars, together with the continuing corruption of the court, meant that the stage was set for the emergence of a new generation of political leadership. This was provided by the charismatic figure of Reza Khan, a tall, accomplished military officer and protégé of the British who had taken command of the Shah's elite Cossack Brigade. Encouraged by his British sponsors, Khan used his military power base to great effect, gradually removing all his political opponents in Tehran until he was in a position to challenge the Shah himself. By 1923 Khan, who had already had himself named Minister of War, had become so powerful that the Shah had no alternative but to appoint him prime minister. Another two years passed until the newly revived Majlis finally lost patience with the Qajar dynasty, and forced them into exile in Switzerland. Khan was installed as the new Shah, and announced that he would in future be addressed as Reza Shah Pahlavi, thereby founding the Pahlavi[11] dynasty that would rule Iran from 1925 until Khomeini's revolution fifty-five years later.[12]

Reza Shah I was very much a man of his time and was determined to transform Persia, with its antiquated system of government that was regularly subjected to the clergy's reactionary influence, into a modern state. From the moment he was confirmed in power he set about implementing his radical reform agenda. Such was the unpopularity of the Qajars and the impotent clique officials that propped them up that Khan was almost swept into power on a wave of popular support. Even though his accession to power had been aided by the British, Khan managed to appeal to ardent nationalists who wanted to see an end to the decades-long interference of foreign powers in Iranian affairs. He appealed to the merchants who believed his modernization programme would breathe new life into the country's moribund economy. And he even had the support of the clergy, to whom he paid due deference until well after he was safely on the Peacock Throne.

Like many Iranian post-war modernizers, Khan had been deeply impressed by the secularist reform programme undertaken by Kemal Ataturk in neighbouring Turkey, who had sought to create a modern, Westernized state from the rubble of the Ottoman Empire. After he was crowned King of Kings at the Golestan Palace in April 1926 the newly installed Shahan-shah (Shah of Shahs) set about destroying all the traditional centres of power – including the clergy – in order to reassert the government's authority throughout the entire country. His first target was the tribal chiefs and provincial emirs who had taken advantage of the Qajars' weakness to establish semi-independent states. A brief edict was issued cancelling all aristocratic honours and titles, and the highly disciplined and effective army that he had assembled during his rise to power was dispatched to the country's furthest reaches to ensure the government's writ was enforced and respected. He embarked on a whirlwind programme of modernizing every aspect of the country's economic and social infrastructure, undertaking a massive road-building programme, setting up a modern education system, reforming the judiciary, introducing a metric system, instituting the wearing of 'modern' dress and even banning camel caravans from entering the country's main cities.

The rush to modernization, though, came at a price. Although he claimed to support democratic government, Reza Shah was at heart – in common with the previous dynasty he had deposed – an autocrat, and his regime was intolerant of any suggestion of criticism or opposition. Elections were rigged, newspapers censored or shut down, trades unions banned and political gatherings violently disrupted. His all-pervasive secret police network – the forerunner of SAVAK – intimidated, arrested, tortured and even murdered opponents. Rather like Oliver Cromwell's treatment of parliament during the seventeenth-century English Revolution, in 1928 Reza Shah placed the Majlis under direct army control, so that it could do nothing more that comply with his legislative demands.

For all his talk of reform and modernization, by the 1930s Reza Shah had turned the country into a police state, as the British travel writer Robert Byron discovered in the course of writing *The Road to Oxiana* when he visited Iran in 1932. Just as foreigners travelling in Soviet Russia would, in private conversation, refer to Joseph Stalin as 'Mr Brown' to avoid attracting the unwelcome attention of Moscow's all-pervasive secret police, so Byron and his companions, with typical English eccentricity, called Reza Shah 'Marjoribanks'. When they got to Iran Byron's party learned that a leading political agitator had died in prison 'having been denied of all comforts, including his bed,' wrote Byron. 'Justice here is royal and personal; he might well have been kicked to death in public. Marjoribanks rules this country by fear, and the ultimate fear is that of the royal boot.'[13] A less colourful, but nonetheless critical, assessment of the regime was provided by an American Embassy official in 1934, who described Reza Shah's Iran as 'strongly reminiscent of Soviet Russia in the period of militant Communism, 1917–1921.'[14]

Reza Shah's drive to make Iran a modern, twentieth-century country alienated many powerful groups, not least the large percentage of religious Muslims who, while enjoying the economic benefits, loathed the effects secularization had on their traditional customs and way of life. It was not just that the Shah required men to wear the European-style, broad-brimmed Pahlavi hat that was specifically designed to make it difficult for a devout Muslim to pray, as he could not touch his head to the prayer mat. Having opened the nation's new schools to girls and women teachers, the Shah undermined the appeal of universal education by insisting that all teachers and school-girls be unveiled. The Shah's assault on the status of the clergy was even more direct. Much of the mullahs' status and influence was severely diminished by the judicial reforms of the late 1920s that disbanded the Sharia courts, standardized civil marriage and divorce ceremonies, and imposed government supervision over all religious endowments.

The Shah made no secret of his contempt for the clergy, the majority of whom he dismissed as 'charlatans'. Tensions between the mullahs and the government intensified over new conscription laws that made it compulsory for all seminarians and young clerics to undertake two years military service, thereby ending their traditional exemption from state activity.

The Shah was convinced that military conscription would help to erase the ethnic and tribal differences and generate loyalty and respect for a strong national government. But the mullahs regarded this as an attack on their autonomous status, and serious disturbances broke out in many of the major religious cities, such as Isfahan and Qom. A brief truce was negotiated, but the Shah provoked further agitation in late 1928 when he issued rigid restrictions on the wearing of clerical attire and the forcible removal of turbans as part of his campaign to enforce the laws on the adoption of European clothes and hats. The final straw for the mullahs came when the government authorized the licensing of liquor stores in Qom. Undeterred by the protests, the Shah made a personal visit to the holy city where he publicly humiliated a local ayatollah by beating him in front of a Shia shrine and having him dragged by his beard through the square.[15]

The Shah's anti-clerical drive spread throughout the country. In towns and villages huge bonfires were built to burn thousands of turbans and traditional tribal hats. Some of the more enthusiastic army officers insisted that all beards should be shaved, and in some instances mullahs were prevented from wearing their traditional slippers. After the Shah completed a state visit to Turkey in 1934, where he marvelled at the progress being made by Kemal Ataturk in secularizing the country, he declared his intention to eradicate religious superstition from Iran during his reign. The teaching of the Koran and religious instruction in state schools was banned and in March 1935 the police were ordered to remove veils worn by women in the streets by force. The Shah's unrelenting assault on the clergy culminated with the gathering of large numbers of devout clergy at the shrine of Imam Ali Reza in Mashhad in July, where they refused point-blank to don the Shah's anti-Islamic brimmed hats. After a stand-off lasting two days, government troops summoned from Azerbaijan attacked the shrine, killing about a hundred people, including women and children. Although the Shah later executed the commander responsible for the massacre, the incident nevertheless served to demonstrate the state's dominance over the clergy, and confirmed the separation of religious and political power in the running of the state. So long as the Shah remained in power, the clergy would have no influence.

Throughout this turbulent period Khomeini, who was too junior a member of the clergy to play any significant leadership role, mainly confined himself to his studies, although he was not afraid of criticizing the Shah's policy. In 1924, when Reza Khan was still positioning himself as the standard-bearer of Iranian nationalism, Khomeini published an essay in which he took issue with the Shah's promise to return Iran to the glory days of the pre-Islamic Persian Empire. 'Before Islam,' wrote Khomeini, 'the lands now blessed by our True Faith suffered miserably because of ignorance and cruelty. There is nothing in that past that is worth glorification.'[16] But Khomeini was lucky that, during the early years of Reza Shah's reform programme, the holy city of Qom was left in relative peace, allowing him to concentrate on his education.

It was not until 1928, when the Shah promulgated his edict banning the wearing of turbans and beards, that the secularization policy intruded upon Khomeini's personal circumstances. Khomeini was attending a funeral at Arak when he learned of the Shah's edict, and while his immediate response was outrage at this assault on traditional society, his primary concern was to get back to Qom with his turban and beard intact. Khomeini was very proud of his beard, which he referred to in one of his poems as 'the cherished friend of my face.'[17] His black turban was even more important, as its colour denoted direct descent from the Prophet; to suffer the indignity of having it removed by a soldier would constitute a grave insult to the Messenger of Allah himself. Khomeini returned to Qom by taking a circuitous route through the mountainous region of Khamseh to avoid encountering the Shah's officious security forces. He safely made his way back to Qom where, to ensure he steered clear of the unwelcome attention of the pro-secularization authorities, he rented a small house with a group of friends a few hundred yards away from the seminary. Years later, referring to this period, Khomeini would write of those 'days of terror' when every footstep heard in the narrow alleys of the neighbourhood in the moonless night was dreaded as belonging to the Shah's agents searching for more beards to shave and more turbans to burn.[18]

For the most part Khomeini kept a low profile during this turbulent period in the formation of modern Iran, and instead concentrated his energy on his academic studies at the seminary, where he developed a deep interest in the more mystical traditions of Islam, which would profoundly affect the development of his religious and political persona. He was particularly attracted to the teachings of twelfth-century Islamic theologians who, like many Saints in the Christian tradition, claimed to have had direct experience with the Almighty and his prophets. For these mystics the strict discipline required to achieve a deep understanding of religious law and the teachings of the Prophet were the basis for achieving a transcendental state, in which direct knowledge of God is achieved. Such illumination was considered to be a God-given gift, and only the chosen few would be the happy beneficiaries of this ultimate spiritual reward for their religious endeavours and their piety. Like the Christian saints, many of these theologians were accused of heresy, and suffered brutal persecution. Some were hanged or crucified, and in one particularly savage execution, a twelfth-century mystic who lived in a town not far from Khomein was hanged, and his body burnt with oil and marsh reed.

Khomeini, who was appalled at the Shah's assault on the clergy but realized that he could do nothing about it, sought solace in mysticism, which also led him to develop a life-long interest in Persian mystical poetry. In Qom he sought out teachers who specialized in teaching the works of the great mystical theologians, and in 1929, at the age of twenty-seven, he published a book, *The Dawn Supplication*, in which he provided a detailed commentary on an important Shia prayer which is often said during the Muslim holy month of Ramadan. The book demonstrates Khomeini's familiarity with the major sources of Islamic mysticism in Arabic and Persian in both poetry and prose. But although he was known within Qom's religious circles for his devotion to the pursuit of mystical knowledge, Khomeini was careful to keep his mysticism to himself, as he was well aware that to claim special knowledge of God carried the risk of excommunication, exile or worse. In public he conducted himself as a typical student of the time, confining his studies to jurisprudence and the Koran, rather than suspicious subjects like philosophy or mysticism. Khomeini liked to present his personal relationship with God as something of an enigma to the outside world, although his own family were well aware of his mystical yearnings. His son Ahmad later wrote that his father 'believed he had a special relationship with God, with whom he was at one, often speaking with frightening enthusiasm about his beloved Lord.'[19]

By the early 1930s Khomeini's personal circumstances were showing signs of improvement, not least because of his marriage. By marrying Batoul he had been taken into a wealthy, highly respected family which had provided the newly-weds with a substantial dowry. Added to Khomeini's own inherited family wealth, the young couple were relatively prosperous compared to all the other young clerics and, apart from furnishing their new home in Qom, were able to use the dowry to purchase a share of a farm close to Khomein. It was somewhat ironic that Khomeini should be a beneficiary of the Shah's economic reforms, for as the farm prospered he was able to buy even more land, joining the ranks of Iran's emerging middle class. His marriage to Batoul also proved to be happy and, unlike many men of the time, he did not treat his wife as his

personal servant. In an interview with an Iranian magazine
many years later the couple's daughter Farideh recalled that
her father 'never even asked our mother to bring him a glass
of water.'[20] After initially suffering a miscarriage, in 1932
Batoul became pregnant again and bore the couple their first
son, whom Ruhollah named Mostafa after his own father.

As the Shah continued his assault on the clergy's status and
privileges, Khomeini became more inclined to speak his mind
about what he regarded as the moral degeneration the government's secularization policy was causing Iranian society. At
Qom, and at the country's other leading shrine cities, most
senior mullahs took the path of least resistance to the Shah's
purges, believing that the anti-clerical storm would eventually
subside. Their pacifism was encouraged by the knowledge that
the Shah dealt harshly with his opponents, with imprisonment
and death often the reward for those who crossed him. But
there were nonetheless some mullahs, including some of those
who taught Khomeini, who were prepared openly to criticize
the regime, and were on occasion forced to seek sanctuary at
local mosques for their trouble.

As a senior student at the seminary Khomeini began to
teach ethics, and in his lectures he was critical of the Shah's
policies. His lectures soon attracted a popular following, with
people travelling from neighbouring towns and villages to hear
him speak. Khomeini's criticism inevitably attracted the attention of the police, who visited him and tried to dissuade him
from lecturing. But, according to the accounts of his supporters
provided many years later, Khomeini was defiant and refused
to comply with their wishes. 'I am duty-bound to continue
with these lectures,' he declared. 'If the police want to stop
them, they will have to come themselves and physically prevent them from taking place.'[21] Whether Khomeini, who ran
the risk of imprisonment or worse, was quite so forthright with
the Shah's security forces is open to question, but there is no
doubt that he was implacably opposed to the Shah's seculari-

zation policies. He would later write how, during this period, the people 'were selfish, feeble and sluggish', so that 'they were unable to resist the dictatorship of Reza Shah'. So far as Khomeini was concerned, the Iranian people lacked the moral fibre to combat this decay, 'and Iran, as a nation, thus lay dormant'.[22]

*

Reza Shah's bold attempt to turn Iran into a modern, Western-style state came to an abrupt halt at the end of the 1930s with the outbreak of the Second World War. Although Tehran once more declared its neutrality in the conflict, its geographical importance meant that it was unlikely that its territorial integrity would be observed, particularly as the Shah had established a warm rapport with Berlin following Adolf Hitler's rise to power in 1933. In an attempt to use Germany as a counterweight to British and Russian interests in the region, the Shah, who admired Hitler's autocratic style of government and ultra-nationalism, had strengthened ties between Berlin and Tehran to the extent that, when war broke out, Germany accounted for nearly half of Iran's foreign trade. German officials and engineers were engaged in the construction of Iranian roads, railways and docks – as well as organizing the Shah's peace corps.

At the start of the war the British confined their displeasure about Germany's growing influence in Iran to a formal protest about the presence of an estimated 2,000 German advisers working in the country. But after Germany invaded Russia in June 1941, the Soviet Union was obliged to side with the Allies, and London and Moscow were no longer prepared to tolerate the possibility that the Shah might form an official military alliance with Berlin. On 25 August 1941, Soviet and British troops invaded Iran on five fronts. Within two days Iranian resistance had collapsed, and a ceasefire was signed on 28 August, giving the Russians control of the traditional sphere of influence in the north, while the British took control of the south, thereby protecting their precious Indian colony. Unable to withstand the strain of having his country re-occupied, Reza Shah abdicated in favour of his 22-year-old son, Mohammed Reza Shah. He left immediately for Mauritius, then a British colony, before relocating to South Africa, where he died a broken man in 1944.

The end of Reza Shah's fifteen-year dictatorship brought relief to many in Iran, not least the clergy, who were given a respite from the unremitting assault on their traditions and status. After its occupation by Russian and British forces Iran suffered nowhere near as badly in the 1939–45 war as it had done during 1914–18. Its main value to the Allies was as a 'Bridge to Victory' that enabled Britain and America to ship billions of dollars of military equipment to support the Red Army's war effort (by the end of the war two-thirds of the Red Army's trucks were American). The new Shah, a nervous young man who had been terrorized during his childhood by his overbearing father, was certainly in no position to object to the conduct of the Allies. And Khomeini's family, which had established a small road transportation business before the war, was one of the beneficiaries of this lucrative trade. Khomeini invested his share of the profits in purchasing a house in Qom's Gozar-Qazee district, which he needed to accommodate his growing family. Khomeini's second son, Ahmad, was born in 1936 and two daughters, Farideh and Sadiqeh, followed soon after within a year of each other.

Apart from its role as a major military supply route, Iran was also a convenient location for planning war strategy, most famously hosting the Tehran Conference in December 1943, at which Joseph Stalin, Franklin D. Roosevelt and Winston Churchill, the wartime leaders of Russia, America and Britain, discussed opening a second front in Europe to defeat the Nazis. The three leaders also signed a separate protocol pledging their commitment to honour Iran's independence once the war was over. The Allies staggered their withdrawal from Iran, with the Americans and British complying with their undertakings and withdrawing their troops in early 1946, and the Russians hanging on until May 1946 when they were finally shamed into withdrawing by the newly created United Nations.

The Shah, who had hardly had an opportunity to exert his authority since assuming the throne from his father, found himself in a very weak position when the Allies left. With the country suffering from rampant inflation and the general dislocation caused by the war, he was not able to resist internal pressure, and eased some of the more oppressive measures his father had imposed against devout Muslims, such as allowing urban women to wear veils in public. There was a revival in the ideals of the Constitutional Revolution, with intellectuals, clergymen and merchants once again uniting in their desire for more influence in the running of the country. Newspapers appeared and it was possible to criticize the Pahlavi dynasty without being thrown in jail. Clergymen were able to wear turbans without fear of assault by the police, and many long-standing political detainees were released from prison. The end of the war also saw the emergence of a new player on Iran's political scene in the form of the Marxist Tudeh party, whose founding members had drawn inspiration and support from their recently departed Russian occupiers.

The old divisions that had afflicted the clergy during the Constitutional Revolution also resurfaced, between those of the quiest tendency who believed the clergy should not be involved in day-to-day politics and those who believed it was their duty to campaign against the pernicious legacy of Reza Shah's secularization policy. Matters came to a head in January 1948 when a group of mullahs issued a fatwa decreeing that all women must wear a veil while shopping. The Shah's advisers referred the matter to the country's leading clerics, including Ayatollah Mohammed Borujerdi, the country's supreme spirit-ual leader, who decreed the clergy had no business interfering in government affairs. This more conventional approach was opposed by militant clerics such as Ayatollah Abolqassem Kashani, who demanded the cancellation of all secular laws, the application of Sharia and the reintroduction of the veil. Kashani had already been jailed twice for his militant activities – once by the British for expressing pro-Nazi sympathies, and then by the Shah. After the war he was involved in the foundation of Iran's first Islamic fundamentalist terrorist group, the Fedayeen-e Islam (Fighters of Islam), which was heavily implicated in a failed assassination attempt on the Shah at Tehran University in February 1949. Kashani was arrested a third time and exiled to Lebanon whilst the Shah persuaded the newly reconstituted Majlis to pass a law restricting the participation of the clergy in the nation's politics. The moderate Shia leaders rallied round the Shah, and a conference of 2,000 clergy called by Borujerdi at Qom at the end of February – which Khomeini attended – concluded they should play no part in political activism, and threatened to discipline any cleric who defied the ruling.

Khomeini's personal loyalties were split as to which faction he should back. He supported Borujerdi, and had helped with his appointment as the country's spiritual leader, and for a time during the 1940s acted as the grand ayatollah's adviser. But there was much in Kashani's agenda that appealed to Khomeini's gut instinct, particularly the restoration of Sharia law and the campaign to rid the country of secularism. Khomeini's political sophistication had developed considerably during the past decade, and he took the abdication of Reza Shah as an opportunity to write a short pamphlet, *Kashf al-Asrar* (The Discovery of Secrets), in which he launched a full-bloodied attack on the evils of secularism. He denounced Reza Shah as 'that illiterate soldier who knew that if he did not suffocate the clergy with the force of bayonets, they would oppose what he was doing to the country and religion.' Khomeini lamented the fact that the status of the clergy had sunk to such a low ebb that no one was even prepared to give a mullah a lift in their cars. And he was incensed that, with Reza Shah's overthrow, the faithful had not done anything to reverse 'their darkest days of exploitation' and stand up for their legitimate rights. This allowed the government to continue with its secularist policy of 'challenging religion and belief itself and trampling the rules of the Koran so that they can get on with the implementation of their corrupt and poisonous intentions'.[23]

One particular target of Khomeini's invective was Ahmad Kasravi, a former mullah who had swapped his turban for a Pahlavi hat and become a fierce critic of the clergy. Kasravi enthusiastically supported the Shah's reform programme and denounced the advent of Islam as a 'historical setback'. Kasravi's pro-Westernism went so far that he openly advocated the adoption of the Latin alphabet, a step that had already been undertaken by Ataturk in neighbouring Turkey. Khomeini was incensed by Kasravi's betrayal of his faith and his country and, without naming him directly, denounced him as *mahdur addamm*, one whose blood should be shed by the faithful, which practically constituted a death sentence against Kasravi.[24] That was certainly how the Fedayeen followers of Ayatollah Kashani interpreted Khomeini's tirade, and in 1946 a Muslim radical murdered Kasravi. The assassin was promptly arrested and sentenced to death. Kasravi's murder shocked Tehran's intelligentsia, and nationalists and Communists united in calling for the mullahs to be taught a lesson. Ayatollah Borujerdi, the country's spiritual leader, was alarmed that Islam was becoming associated with acts of terrorism.

Most of the Shia establishment would have been more than happy to see the assassin hanged for his crime, but Khomeini managed to persuade the grand ayatollah that to allow a man of religion (the assassin was himself a mullah) to be tried by a civilian court was a tacit recognition that the Shah's government had primacy over the Islamic hierarchy. Borujerdi reluctantly agreed to intervene, and charged Khomeini with the task of seeking a pardon from the Shah. Khomeini himself had doubts about approaching the Shah on such a mission, as it would legitimize the Shah's authority in such matters. But Khomeini was still too junior to challenge the grand ayatollah's will, and set off to Tehran for an audience with the Shah with a delegation of five sympathetic mullahs, including Morteza Motahhari, who later became one of Khomeini's closest aides in the 1979 Islamic revolution.

The meeting between the young Shah and Khomeini, whose status in the mid-1940s as one the country's leading Islamic figures was already attracting interest, would set the tone of their relationship for the next thirty years, when Khomeini replaced the deposed Shah as the country's leader. On arrival in Tehran, Khomeini's party was kept waiting for ten days while the Shah and his officials deliberated over whether they should even grant the visitors an audience. It was decided that only one of the Qom party would be granted an interview, and Khomeini was selected for the task. On arrival at the palace, Khomeini was shown into the Shah's office and told to stand until His Imperial Majesty arrived. Khomeini, as was the clergy's custom, sat down on the floor and waited. When the Shah, who was extremely shy, finally arrived he did not know how to respond to finding Khomeini sitting on the floor, so simply sat down beside him. Khomeini may have been observing tradition, but his failure to rise was interpreted by the Shah as a deliberate act of arrogance. The audience only lasted ten minutes, during which Khomeini delivered his message with force, and succeeded in securing a pardon for the assassin, whose death sentence was commuted to life imprisonment. But during that brief meeting the two men took an almost instant dislike to each other. 'This was hate at first sight,' one of the mullahs who accompanied Khomeini on the Tehran trip later recalled.[25]

Khomeini had another meeting with the Shah the following year, when he joined a delegation of mullahs seeking the Shah's financial support for renovating an important Shia shrine. But

Khomeini's increasingly close association with the Fedayeen-e Islam terror group, which continued with its campaign of assassinating prominent public figures – including the failed 1949 attack on the Shah – resulted in Borujerdi dropping his support. The grand ayatollah did not approve of the Fedayeen's violent methods, and at the same time did not want to provoke a schism within the ranks of the Shia clergy. He therefore decided to remain aloof. Whenever Khomeini went to visit him at Qom, he was told that the grand ayatollah was unwell and would not be receiving visitors.

The violent campaign instigated by the radical mullahs against the Shah was completely overshadowed in the 1950s by the far more emotive subject of oil nationalization, an issue that succeeded in arousing Iran's latent nationalism like no other. The wilful disregard for Iranian interests by the British-owned Anglo-Iranian Oil Company, which creamed off 90 per cent of the profits while paying its Iranian employees a pittance, led to the creation of the National Front, whose leader, Mohammed Mosaddeq, established himself at the undisputed leader of Iranian nationalists of all political and religious persuasions. Mosaddeq was an elder statesman of Iranian politics with a long history of opposing foreign oil companies and the Pahlavis (he was one of only four Iranian parliamentarians to oppose Reza Shah's appointment in 1926). Kashani, whose father had been killed fighting the British in southern Iraq in the First World War, had no hesitation in lending his support on behalf of Iran's Muslims after the Shah had allowed him to return from exile in Lebanon. Many other powerful interest groups backed Mosaddeq, and the British government's refusal to negotiate a fairer deal on the distribution of the profits from Iranian oil production meant that, when Mosaddeq proposed the wholesale nationalization of Iran's oilfields to the Majlis in April 1951, hardly a dissenting voice was to be heard. After the bill was passed by an overwhelming majority, the Shah obediently added his name to it two days later.

The nationalization of Iran's oil provoked the biggest international crisis in the country's short history since its creation by Reza Shah. The British immediately referred the 'illegal' nationalization to the United Nations and, in what would have been a forerunner to the 1956 Suez invasion, drew up plans to invade Iran and secure the southern oilfields with a force of 70,000 troops. Mosaddeq had taken a calculated gamble that the United States would protect Iran from any British sabre-rattling, as Washington's primary strategic concern at the time was to prevent Iran from falling under Soviet influence, rather than defending Britain's commercial avarice. But even though American President Harry Truman was sympathetic to Iran's point of view with regard to oil nationalization, Washington's first loyalty was to Britain, its old war-time ally, whose military support it was counting on following the outbreak of the Korean War. The Truman administration persuaded the British to drop their invasion plans in return for negotiating a compromise. But it proved impossible to negotiate a deal between the British and Mosaddeq, and the Iranian prime minister's standing in Washington diminished further when he was accused of rigging elections for the new Majlis in 1952 to stay in power.

Mosaddeq's virulent demonstration of Iranian nationalism nevertheless won him almost universal support, to the extent that he was able to manoeuvre himself into such a strong position that he became more powerful than the Shah, prompting His Imperial Majesty seriously to consider tendering his resignation. But while Mosaddeq remained popular at home, his standing was on the wane in Washington where the new American president, Dwight Eisenhower, was concerned about Mosaddeq's increasingly quixotic behaviour. When Mosaddeq turned down a deal with Britain that the Americans thought was perfectly reasonable – Anglo-Persian's profits were split fifty–fifty between London and Tehran – Eisenhower lent his tacit approval to a British intelligence-led operation to destabilize Mosaddeq's government with a view to removing him from office. Mosaddeq had gambled on Washington's support against Britain, but the Eisenhower administration effectively sealed the Iranian prime minister's fate when it refused to provide economic assistance to alleviate the effects of the British trade embargo. The CIA was encouraged to support British intelligence efforts to mount a coup against Mosaddeq – code-named Operation Ajax – which was eventually launched in August 1953, and very nearly came close to disaster.

Mosaddeq had received forewarning that the Shah, acting under pressure from Washington, had signed two *firmans*, deposing him as prime minister and appointing an American-backed Iranian general in his place. When the military delegation arrived at his house in the middle of the night, Mosaddeq had them arrested and the following morning informed the entire nation that he had been the victim of a coup, and that the culprits were being rounded up. The Shah, displaying a lack of nerve that would later hamper his epic power struggle with Khomeini, fled the country for Rome. But Kermit Roosevelt, the CIA station chief in Tehran, prevailed upon the Shah to abide by the coup plan, and details of his decree deposing Mosaddeq were published on the front pages of Iranian newspapers. Slowly army units loyal to the Shah were persuaded to enforce the royal decree. They received welcome support from militant Islamic followers of Ayatollah Kashani, who had switched his support from Mosaddeq under pressure from other ayatollahs, who were wary of the prime minister's secularist outlook. The struggle culminated in an all-out battle outside Mosaddeq's house in Tehran where army units loyal to the different sides fought pitched battles with tanks and artillery. Eventually the forces loyal to the Shah prevailed, and although Mosaddeq escaped over the roof of his house, he was later caught and arrested. The Shah was dining in Rome with the Empress when news of Mosaddeq's fall eventually reached him, and is said to have exclaimed, 'I knew it, I knew it. They love me!'[26]

Khomeini, who had become a close ally of Ayatollah Kashani, was a somewhat anonymous figure during the great upsurge in militant anti-colonialism that swept Iran in the aftermath of the Second World War, which was primarily directed against Britain. He supported Kashani when the ayatollah energetically backed Mosaddeq in the first flourish of his oil nationalization campaign, and he supported Kashani when he fell out with Mosaddeq and switched his allegiance to the Shah. Khomeini's non-committal attitude to Mosaddeq's brief moment of glory was reflected in a comment he made many years later in his memoirs. 'Mosaddeq meant well and wanted to serve the nation, but his main mistake was not to have got rid of the Shah when he was strong and the Shah was weak.'[27]

During this period Khomeini was still drawn to the more militant wing of the Islamic movement and supported the Fedayeen terrorist group, which had suspended its assassination campaign against mainstream Iranian politicians while its leaders worked out whether they could lend their support to Mosaddeq. But the Islamic agenda proposed by Navab Safavi, a young theological student who ran the militia, was far too radical for the secular-minded Mossadeq. Safavi demanded the wholesale application of Sharia law, such as cutting off the hands of convicted thieves, and demanded a ban on alcohol, tobacco, cinema, opium, gambling, the wearing of foreign dress and the re-introduction of the veil for Iranian women. When Mosaddeq refused to accommodate any of their demands, the Fedayeen resumed their murderous attacks against government ministers, and Safavi and other Fedayeen leaders were arrested. Mosaddeq later released them after Kashani personally intervened on their behalf, but after the coup of August 1953 the Fedayeen resumed their terrorist activities. A failed assassination attempt on the prime minister in November 1955 resulted in the Shah ordering a nationwide clampdown against the Fedayeen, and Safavi and the rest of the leadership were again detained, as was Ayatollah Kashani. The ayatollah was soon released after he publicly disassociated himself from the organization, and promised not to protest against the expected executions of the main Fedayeen leaders.

Khomeini took a different view. Although he had not been implicated in the Fedayeen's activities, Khomeini launched a personal campaign to save Navab Safavi from the gallows after he received the death sentence for his participation in the attempted assassination of two government ministers. While the rest of the country's leading clergy, including Grand Ayatollah Borujerdi, sought to distance themselves from the extremists, Khomeini stood apart as he mounted a spirited campaign to save Safavi's life. He personally lobbied Borujerdi, who turned down his entreaties to petition the Shah for Safavi's release. And when that failed he wrote to several leading members of the Shah's court appealing for clemency. But Khomeini's efforts were to no avail, and in January 1956 Safavi and three other Fedayeen leaders went to the gallows.

The limits of Khomeini's authority and status within the hierarchy of Iran's Islamic establishment had been amply demonstrated by his peripheral role in the turbulent events of the oil nationalization crisis. While most of the country's leading religious figures had contributed in some way, Khomeini's voice was rarely heard, and his views were of little consequence. He found himself caught between two opposing ideologies. He remained loyal to Grand Ayatollah Borujerdi, who thought the more distance the clergy kept between themselves and the government, the better. But he felt a deep attachment to the uncompromising Islamic agenda espoused by Kashani and Safavi's Fedayeen. It was at around this time that Khomeini realized that if he were ever to exercise real influence over how the country was run, he would need to have a more effective power base and far broader support.

4

Living in Exile

The event that contributed most to Khomeini's transformation from being a bit player on the fringes of Iran's Islamic leadership to becoming the chief protagonist in the campaign to make the country an Islamic state occurred not in Tehran, but in Washington. John F. Kennedy's arrival at the White House in January 1961 not only heralded the dawn of a new era for American politics; its repercussions would soon be felt throughout the world as the new administration undertook a radical review of its relations with its key allies. As a senator, Kennedy had been a tireless campaigner for human rights and civil liberties, and once in office he determined to make these issues central to his foreign policy. For a country like Iran, which under the Shah had scant regard for even the most basic human rights, such as freedom of speech, Kennedy's election would require His Imperial Highness to undertake fundamental changes in the way the country was run. These changes, which the Shah called the 'White Revolution', provided Khomeini with the freedom to attack the very foundations of the state.

After the turmoil of the oil nationalization crisis, the Eisenhower administration moved quickly to shore up the Shah's power base to ensure that there would be no repetition. Consequently relations between Washington and Tehran reached a high point of diplomatic cooperation, where Iran's strategic importance became a crucial factor in America's regional outlook, and the Shah a key White House ally. Iran's geographical location alone, as a buffer to the Soviet Union's expansionist drive towards the oil-rich Gulf states, meant that Tehran was central to Washington's effort to thwart Moscow's ambitions. The Cold War between the West and the Soviet bloc was the defining conflict of the 1950s, and the Middle East one of the key battlegrounds. In all the main regional capitals – Cairo, Baghdad, Damascus and Tehran – Washington detected the insidious influence of Communist agitators attempting to undermine the regional status quo. This sense of paranoia deepened after Gamal Abdul Nasser became Egypt's president and warmly embraced Moscow, securing the new alliance with a massive arms deal with the Soviet Union in 1955. Similar pro-Soviet movements sought the overthrow of pro-Western governments in Jordan, Syria and Iraq.

Encouraged by this success, the Russians intensified their efforts in other regional capitals. They were especially encouraged by the gains they had made in Tehran, where the Tudeh party, the local Communist organization, actively participated in the street agitation that had brought Mosaddeq to power. Although the Tudeh had been a peripheral force during the Mosaddeq-inspired upheaval, it was the biggest casualty of the post-Shah restoration. Both the CIA and MI6 believed the Tudeh leadership was conniving with Moscow for a Communist takeover of the country, and the Shah, whose natural support base came from Iran's wealthy landowners, had no hesitation in purging the Communists. Mosaddeq himself, who gave a spirited defence of his actions at his trial, was jailed for three years, followed by permanent house arrest, where he died of old age in 1964. After the trial more than 2,000 Communists were arrested and imprisoned in a purge that lasted well into 1954.

The Shah's security forces were ably supported by the CIA, which sent a number of experienced military and intelligence advisers to help root out Communist sympathizers. On his return to power, the Shah had remarked to Kermit Roosevelt, the CIA's station chief in Tehran, 'I owe my throne to God, my people, my army and you,' and the CIA took full advantage of their favoured intelligence service status to consolidate their influence over the Peacock Throne. The Americans set up a highly effective intelligence operation, which in 1957 became SAVAK, the Iranian acronym for the National Intelligence and Security Organisation.[1] The United States established its largest military aid mission in the world in Tehran, and between 1953 and 1961 the United States assisted with the rapid expansion of the Shah's military forces from 120,00 to 200,000.[2] American aid and expertise also helped transform the Iranian economy, particularly its oil industry. American firms were active in exploring and developing new oilfields, and the new investment saw Tehran's oil revenues increase fivefold between 1955 and 1964 to $482 million. The oil revenues were boosted by generous economic aid packages, which substantially added to the financial resources available to the Shah.[3] For his part, the Shah demonstrated his commitment to Washington by fully subscribing to the Eisenhower doctrine, which the president set out in January 1957, whereby the United States promised to support any Middle East government against 'overt armed aggression from any nation controlled by international Communism'.

These were the wilderness years for Khomeini, a period when he was overshadowed, if not marginalized, by the more senior figures within the Islamic establishment who were keen to maintain a modus vivendi with the Shah's regime after the disturbances of the early 1950s. Having backed the Shah's restoration, the clergy were the beneficiaries of a marked improvement in relations with the court, which were put on a more traditional footing. Under the leadership of Grand Ayatollah Borujerdi, who strongly opposed the militant antics of the Fedayeen, the clergy sought to remove themselves from the business of day-to-day politics. But the Shah was assured of their tacit support, and responded by easing some of the concessions that had been made during his father's attempts to suppress the clergy's role in Iranian society. Borujerdi and the rest of the Islamic hierarchy had been genuinely shocked to discover the extent of Communist penetration of the country's armed forces and political establishment under Mosaddeq, and actively backed the Shah's anti-Communist purge of the Tudeh party. So keen was Borujerdi to demonstrate his support for the Shah that he sent him a cable saying he would pray for the monarch's good health and success in 'serving the people of Islam'. The Shah responded by making regular visits to the Shia shrines at Mashhad and Qom, and even kissed the grand ayatollah's hand in public, a gesture that would have had Reza Shah spinning in his grave.

Khomeini's involvement with the Fedayeen, though peripheral, had marked him out as a radical, as had his abortive campaign to save the lives of Safavi and the other Fedayeen leaders. Khomeini always seemed to be more comfortable with the more fanatical elements of the Islamic movement. Borujerdi wanted to normalize relations with the Shah, not confront him, and militant clergy like Khomeini found themselves excluded from his inner circle. Likewise Ayatollah Kashani, whose virulent anti-colonialism and support for an Islamic state had attracted Khomeini's support, moved to distance himself from his former protégé. Kashani's brief imprisonment with the Fedayeen during the Shah's crackdown had taught him the perils of overstepping the mark in opposing the Shah's will, and he had no desire to martyr himself for the Islamic cause. Khomeini, who had been a frequent visitor to Kashani's home, objected to the ayatollah lending his full support to the Shah, which provoked a parting of the ways between the two clerics. Khomeini's more austere and uncompromising outlook was at odds with Kashani's urbane and populist approach, and Kashani made it clear that Khomeini was no longer welcome in his home, describing him to his friends as a *sholugh*, or busybody.[4]

Shunned by the mainstream Islamic hierarchy, Khomeini

concentrated his energies on his teaching and on building up his own network of devoted followers within the Shia community. Khomeini's explanation for remaining silent during this period was that 'he did not feel duty-bound to talk while Borujerdi was in charge of the theological centres'.[5] But that did not mean to say Khomeini was above ridiculing the grand ayatollah, whom he referred to disparagingly as 'the Red-Bearded One'. Borujerdi had recently taken a new wife aged only fourteen, and started dyeing his beard with henna to make himself look younger. Ribald lyrics – some of them said to have been penned by Khomeini himself – about the grand ayatollah's prowess in the marital chamber caused great mirth among the students of Qom, and reduced Borujerdi's standing among the Shia clergy to that of caricature.

Khomeini's primary focus, though, was concerned with building his reputation as an Islamic authority and scholar. One Iranian religious historian has described Khomeini during the 1950s as 'one of the great teachers and prominent figures of Qom's theological centres'.[6] Khomeini taught ethics, theology and philosophy, and developed a devoted following among his students, who travelled from all over the country to attend his lectures. He became a centre of attention for many students and residents in Qom, and his lectures on ethics were particularly popular. He acquired his own circle of *talebehs*, devout young men who had dedicated their lives to Islam and the pursuit of enlightenment. When they completed their studies, many of them returned to their homes, thereby providing Khomeini with a network of supporters scattered throughout the country. He wrote several books and pamphlets during this period which were primarily commentaries on specific verses of the Koran. His scholarly reputation was further enhanced by the growing number of devout Muslims who wrote to him seeking guidance on key religious issues. Khomeini would respond to each query in writing, always keeping a copy of his judgement for himself, which were published many years later as a collection of essays.

Students who were taught by Khomeini in Qom during this period recall that by the late 1950s his classes were attracting the biggest audiences. 'He was incredibly popular with the students,' recalled one former student whom Khomeini taught at Qom. 'This was the period after Mosaddeq and everyone was very excited about changing the country for the better. Khomeini seemed different to the other teachers and said repeatedly that he was in favour of changing the system.'[7]

Many of the more radical young students were concerned about the corruption that was endemic throughout the clergy. In the Shia system the faithful are obliged to give 20 per cent of their earnings in donations to the mullahs, and the money is then used to fund charitable institutions, such as schools and care for the sick and elderly. But Qom was in such disarray after decades of unrest that much of the money stayed with the mullahs, and never reached the organizations for which it had been intended. Grand Ayatollah Borujerdi was inclined to turn a blind eye to such malpractice, but Khomeini positioned himself as one of the few leading clergymen who wanted reform. For Khomeini, the corruption of the clergy was just one example of the general decay of Islam, together with the clergy's acquiescent attitude towards secularism.

'Khomeini was something of a hero for us,' recalled another student who later became an ayatollah in his own right. 'His main focus at that time was to rid the clergy of corruption and make it a stronger force. We all thought Khomeini was the man to sort things out. What the students wanted was a system with more order and which provided better education.' On occasion the students would interrupt Khomeini during his classes and ask him how he expected the clergy to run the world when they were so corrupt? 'Khomeini would always answer, "God willing there will one day be good clergy capable of doing this."' For Khomeini's agenda was not just confined to reforming the clergy; he still harboured dreams of creating an Islamic state that was governed by devout clerics. 'Khomeini taught us that the reason the mullahs had been defeated during the Constitutional Revolution was because they were corrupt and divided,' said Khomeini's former student. 'If the clergy were ever to gain power they needed to be united in their goals and had to get rid of all the corruption that made them weak.'[8]

In public Khomeini was already acquiring a reputation as a radical cleric, but his students were surprised to discover that his lessons on Islamic theology were very traditional. 'He was always talking about obscure things that happened hundreds of years before. He would lecture us about obscure Persian clerics who had devoted their lives to the establishment of an Islamic state. We found it baffling, because all we were interested in was improving the country we were living in, not the past,' Khomeini's student recalled. The students were also struck by the fact that Khomeini, despite his growing reputation, led a humble home life. Unlike many of the other teachers he did not indulge in luxuries, such as expensive carpets, and even had to be persuaded to buy a telephone so that he could communicate with other teachers. His students recall that he appeared to have a happy family life and sometimes, when Khomeini was telling his children a joke, he would laugh so loud that 'everyone in the street could hear him'.[9]

Khomeini enjoyed a significant increase in his personal wealth during this period, which he needed to care for his growing family. He engaged in a number of land deals, which included selling land to the government for the construction of a sugar refinery near Qom, which in the event was never built. But the Khomeini family enjoyed the proceeds of the sale. His elder brother and guardian, Morteza, was now firmly established as a lawyer in Qom, and helped Khomeini with his investment portfolio. Having benefited from his previous land transactions, Khomeini's main interest was the purchase of agricultural land, which proved a shrewd purchase, and the inflation that affected Iran in the late 1950s greatly increased the family's private wealth. By 1960 it has been estimated that as many as 3,000 families were working on land belonging to Khomeini and his brothers.[10] The family were, by all accounts, good landlords, and Khomeini was popular with the shareholders who worked for him. Having taken care of his household expenses, Khomeini used the profits from his land transactions to fund his educational activities, for in the Shia system the teacher pays the pupils, not the other way around. The healthy returns he enjoyed from his farms meant that his classes grew in size, which was an important factor in his drive to become an ayatollah, the symbol of Allah on earth.

The only overt political activity Khomeini was involved in concerned a favourite pastime of the Shia clergy – persecuting the Baha'i. The Baha'i are the followers of a Shia leader who proclaimed himself a prophet in the nineteenth century, thereby causing a major schism within the Shia hierarchy, the majority of whom regarded the proclamation as heresy. The proselytizing tendencies of the Baha'i, together with the fact their pro-secular and modernist outlook fitted in with the political climate of mid-twentieth-century Iran, provoked feelings of deep animosity within the traditional Shia establishment. Shia leaders complained that the Baha'i had prospered during the upheavals of the Mosaddeq period, and had taken advantage of the chaos to advance their commercial interests. After his restoration the Shah granted the clerical establishment a free hand to counter the growing influence of the Baha'i, and a group of radical mullahs orchestrated a sustained anti-Baha'i propaganda campaign that resulted in the destruction of a Baha'i temple and unruly mobs attacking Baha'i families.

Khomeini was in constant contact with the leaders of this somewhat unedifying assault on a defenceless, minority sect, whom he personally detested because of their close links to the newly created state of Israel (Baha'ollah, the sect's founder, is buried in Acre, and its main administrative centre is located in Haifa). Khomeini's role in the anti-Baha'i campaign was instrumental in organizing a nationwide boycott of Pepsi Cola after it was discovered a Baha'i businessman had acquired the franchise to market the drink in Iran. In 1957 Khomeini declared that Muslims who drank Pepsi would 'roast in the fires of hell', and his comments, which were the most extreme uttered by any religious figure within the mainstream Shia hierarchy, resulted in an overnight slump in demand for the beverage. The only practical consequence of Khomeini's action, however, was that the boycott enable Pepsi's bitter rival, Coca-Cola, to make inroads to the Iranian market after the company appointed a non-Baha'i to administer their franchise.

Khomeini's prominent role in the Pepsi saga confirmed his emergence as one of the country's leading, and most radical, religious leaders. He was now generally regarded as being among the country's top twelve clerics, although he was still some way from challenging for outright leadership of the Shia, not least because his militant tendencies alienated many important backers, including the Shah himself. But Khomeini was gradually accumulating an impressive collection of loyal and capable followers in Qom who would play a crucial role in assisting him in achieving his ultimate goal during the Islamic revolution, such as Hossein-Ali Montazeri and Sheikh Sadeq Khalkhali, who would become notorious as 'judge blood'. All Khomeini needed now was an opportunity to allow him to present himself as the undisputed leader of the Shia.

*

By a stroke of luck two events coincided that provided Khomeini with just the opportunity he sought. While President Kennedy's arrival at the White House in January 1961 prompted a dramatic change in Tehran's political climate, the death of Grand Ayatollah Borujerdi in Qom the following

March threw the Shia leadership wide open. Kennedy's election forced the Shah to undertake a fundamental reassessment of how he ran the country, and Borujerdi's death put him in the difficult position, in his capacity as Protector of the Shia faith, of having to choose a successor who commanded sufficient respect to lead the faithful and who was well disposed towards the Shah's regime. Khomeini, who was in his fifty-ninth year, was still regarded as being too young and lacking in stature to claim the position of Marja Taqleed, which literally means 'source of imitation' and is the highest position attained by the Shia clergy. Originating in nineteenth-century Iran, Marja Taqleed is bestowed on an individual who is regarded as so learned and so perfect that it is incumbent upon the faithful to follow his decisions. A *marja* is appointed by his Shia peers, rather as the Pope is elected by the cardinals, and receives the honour after the most senior members of the clergy have deliberated in private. But what Khomeini lacked in religious stature was more than compensated for by his militant political agenda, which came to the fore once more as he locked horns with the Shah over his proposed reform programme.

Tensions between the turban and the crown began to resurface in 1961 when the Shah, reacting to pressure from the Kennedy administration, decided to launch a land reform programme that would distribute land among the peasants and seriously undermine the wealth and status of large landowners. This included the religious establishment which, like Khomeini's family, relied heavily on the incomes they derived from their holdings to fund their foundations and institutions. Even Borujerdi, shortly before he died, broke his rule of non-interference in politics to lodge a formal protest with the Shah. But the Shah could not be persuaded to change his mind, not least because the Kennedy administration was pressuring him. Kennedy's attitude to underdeveloped countries such as Iran was summed up in a speech he made at the White House in 1962. 'Those who make peaceful revolution impossible will make violent revolution inevitable.' The Shah also had to be aware of Moscow's continuing vulture-like interest in its near neighbour, particularly after Soviet Prime Minister Nikita Khrushchev informed the American journalist Walter Lippmann that Iran was a country heading for revolution because of the misery of its people and the corruption of its government. On another occasion Khrushchev referred to Iran as a 'rotten plum' about to fall.

The mood of political discontent deepened as the country's economic fortunes suffered a severe reverse in the early 1960s, mainly through the Shah's economic mismanagement. The oil wealth and American aid were squandered in a self-indulgent spending spree, so that by 1960 the country was suffering from a huge budget deficit, growing inflation and a runaway import bill. The stabilization programme initiated by the International Monetary Fund created a severe recession which lasted for three years, and the Shah's rapidly declining popularity was not helped by his blatant rigging of the Majlis elections. But it was not until the Shah proposed a bill to allow women and non-Muslims to vote in local elections that Khomeini decided to make his move. 'The son of Reza Khan,' Khomeini informed one of his Qom colleagues, 'has embarked on the destruction of Islam in Iran. I will oppose this as long as the blood circulates in my veins.'[11]

Most of the clerical establishment opposed the changes to the local election law, but it was Khomeini who stole the limelight, and the fierce rhetoric he used to denounce the reforms helped to transform his status from that of a relatively obscure Qom cleric to one of the country's leading anti-Shah agitators. He condemned the proposal to allow non-Muslims the vote on the grounds that it 'was perhaps drawn up by the spies of the Jews and the Zionists . . . the Koran and Islam are in danger. The independence of the state and the economy are threatened by a takeover by the Zionists, who in Iran have appeared in the guise of Baha'is.'[12] Khomeini and many other

Shias readily equated the Baha'is with Zionists simply because their leader was buried in a town that had subsequently become part of Israel. And Khomeini considered allowing women the vote as a violation of Islamic principles and an attempt 'to corrupt our chaste women'.[13]

He adopted a high-handed attitude in his dealings with both the government and the Shah over the issue. During a meeting with the prime minister, Asadollah Alam, which took place after the government had agreed to remove the offending clauses, Khomeini lectured him 'to take care that such things do not happen again'. And he made no attempt to conceal his contempt for the Shah. He delighted in telling other clerics, 'He [the Shah] says, "I have no business with the clerics. Sir. The clerics have business with you." '[14] The government finally agreed to concede to Khomeini's demands after he organized demonstrations and petitions throughout the country, which culminated in nationwide meetings of protest and prayer. Khomeini was gradually learning the art of mass political demonstration, and in so doing he was becoming a national figure.

Khomeini's emergence as a political mullah was greatly helped by Borujerdi's death. So long as the grand ayatollah was alive, Khomeini, in keeping with the rest of the senior clergy, was obliged to observe Borujerdi's general policy of non-interference in government affairs. But without Borujerdi's restraining influence, Khomeini was free to act according to his conscience. To Khomeini's mind there was no distinction between the religious and the political sphere. All human activity on earth was subjected to the will and laws of God, and, as a leading Shia jurist, he saw it as his personal duty to ensure that God's will was observed, and not in any way compromised. 'Khomeini was in a very strong position after Borujerdi's death,' recalled one of his former students who took part in the anti-Shah protests in Qom. 'Through his teaching he had built up the largest classes in the city, and this gave him great authority, even if he did not have the recognition of the Shia leadership.'[15]

Khomeini's antipathy towards the Shah strengthened when he learnt that he was the only one among all the leading Shia clergy in Qom who did not receive a cable from the royal palace offering His Majesty's condolences after Borujerdi's death. If Khomeini held the Shah in contempt, the sentiment was reciprocated by the Shah. So far as the Shah was concerned, Khomeini was never in the running to replace Borujerdi as *marja*: that honour went to Grand Ayatollah Tabataba'i. It was rumoured that Borujerdi had personally ruled Khomeini out of the succession by warning, on his deathbed, 'Follow anyone you like, anyone except Khomeini. For following Khomeini shall lead you knee-deep in blood.' Khomeini's ostracism from the mainstream Shia leadership simply strengthened his resolve to achieve his goals by other means. Khomeini had discovered he had the power to organize mass public protests, and was deeply encouraged by the large numbers of people who wrote to him expressing their support for his stand and offering to lay down their lives in the cause of Islam. As Khomeini later recalled in his memoirs of this period, 'If one word had been said there would have been an explosion.'[16]

The voting rights dispute was the prelude to a far greater battle of wills between Khomeini and the Shah over a more wide-ranging reform programme the government had drawn up in response to continuing pressure from the Kennedy administration. The Shah's frustration at Washington's constant prompting to modernize at a pace faster than he thought prudent caused him to remark to one American diplomat, 'I can start a revolution for you, but you won't like the end result.'[17] In January 1963 the Shah presented a reworked version of the land reform proposals, together with five other ambitious legislative measures setting out the nationalization of forests and pasture land, profit sharing for workers, the privatization of state factories, reform of the electoral laws that gave

greater representation to workers and farmers, and the foundation of a Literacy Corps, whereby the government would
arrange for recent college graduates to travel around the
countryside teaching reading and writing to the peasantry. The
measures, which were collectively called 'The Revolution of
the Shah and the People', but became more colloquially known
as the White Revolution, were put to a national referendum,
which recorded a hardly credible 99.9 per cent vote in favour.
Although the referendum was clearly rigged, the measures
nonetheless enjoyed popular support, particularly among the
working and peasant classes, who were being enfranchised for
the first time in the country's history.

The Shah, who seemed always to be trying to shake off
the overbearing shadow of his father, Reza Khan, genuinely
believed his revolution was an opportunity to cement the
bond between the Peacock Throne and the people, even if
the process had been motivated by the need to placate Washington. Throughout the 1950s the Shah had sold off modest
plots of his own land to peasants at reduced rates, and liked
to regard himself as a modern leader who genuinely had the
interests of his people at heart. But Mohammed Reza Shah
lacked his father's natural confidence and authority, and was
beset by self-doubt, and saw plots to unseat him everywhere,
which was hardly surprising in view of the fact that his father
had been driven into exile, and he had himself come close to
suffering a similar fate during the Mosaddeq era. Henry Kissinger, who befriended the Shah in the 1970s, concluded the Shah
'was not by nature a domineering personality. Indeed, he was
rather shy and withdrawn. I could never escape the impression
that he was a gentle, even sentimental man who had schooled
himself in the maxim that the ruler must be aloof and hard,
but had never succeeded in making it come naturally.'[18]

The Shah was pleased with the results of the referendum,
and proceeded to implement his ambitious plan to modernize
both Iranian society and the economy. He received a telegram

of congratulations from President Kennedy, who wished him well in guiding the Iranian nation towards progress and prosperity. His reforms were undoubtedly popular with significant sections of the population. Impoverished peasants were enthusiastic supporters of land reform, better literacy and a fairer judicial system. Many women were pleased that they could at last vote, and profit sharing appealed to the growing ranks of industrial workers. But more powerful and traditional interests within Iranian society, such as the landowners, were less than happy at the prospect of having to break up their vast estates. Old National Front sympathies again rose to the surface, as the middle classes and intelligentsia saw the reforms as a sop to foreign interests. As one of the country's largest landowners, the clergy was particularly opposed to the White Revolution which, apart from threatening the wealth of the nation's religious establishments, heralded a new age of secularism in Iran.

Khomeini was uncompromising in his opposition to the White Revolution, which he warned other clerics would weaken their role and that of Islam in society. Being a large landowner himself, he had a vested interest in opposing the land reform agenda. After the success of the local election stand-off, he worked hard to consolidate his ties with wealthy bazaar merchants who saw the reforms as usurping their commercial viability. A group of Tehran *bazaaris* visited Khomeini at Qom to offer him their services. They said they were willing to do whatever Khomeini wanted. 'If you give the order we are prepared to attach bombs to ourselves and throw ourselves at the Shah's car to blow him up,' one of them offered.[19] This led to the creation of an organization known as 'The Coalition of Islamic Societies', which Khomeini helped to establish and which comprised a mixture of religious activists and merchants who were committed to the defence of Islam.

The White Revolution provided Khomeini with the opportunity to test the strength of his new-found popularity against the Shah. He gave his backing to the reformed National Front, which campaigned under the slogan, 'reform yes, dictatorship no'. He condemned the Shah's programme as a fraud and refused to let his followers participate in the referendum. On 21 March, the eve of the Iranian New Year, Khomeini issued a declaration to the effect that the New Year was 'a time for mourning, not celebration'. He repeated the populist accusation that the reforms were being undertaken in the interests of foreign forces – America and Israel had replaced Britain and Russia as the bogeymen of popular demonology – to destroy Islam and the religious classes. 'In the interests of the Jews, America and Israel, we must be jailed and killed. We must be sacrificed to the evil intentions of foreigners.'[20] Khomeini repeated these sentiments at the well-attended sermons he gave in Qom to mark the New Year.

Khomeini maintained his verbal offensive against the government while unrest grew among Islamic students, leading to frequent protests. The Shah was incensed by this open challenge to his authority and the blatant attempt to impede what he described as his 'bloodless revolution'. He denounced the protesting clergy, during an address to his senior military officers, as 'numb and dispirited snakes and lice who float in their own dirt. If these vile and sordid elements with their reactionary friends do not awake from their sleep of ignorance, the fist of justice, like thunder will . . . terminate their filthy and shameful life.' The Shah's 'fist' manifested itself on 22 March when an elite unit of the Imperial Guard, some of whom wore civilian dress, devastated the Feizeyeh, one of Qom's leading seminaries where Khomeini frequently preached. The soldiers roughed up the students, pushing them off balconies and terraces and generally going on the rampage through the seminary. Several students were killed and many others injured. The soldiers smashed furniture, destroyed books and manuscripts and generally laid waste to everything they could lay their hands on. All the turbans and cloaks they found were placed in the middle of the courtyard and set alight. The Shah was showing an altogether different side to his regime from the reformist zeal of the White Revolution.

But Khomeini would not be intimidated by the brutality of the Shah's tactics. After much private reflection – during which his supporters said Khomeini was in communion with the Almighty – Khomeini concluded that the faithful should willingly sacrifice their lives in defence of Islam. The more the Shah threatened Khomeini's followers, the more he urged his followers to 'prepare themselves for death, imprisonment, compulsory drafting, and maltreatment'.[21] After the destruction of the Feizeyeh, Khomeini said the attack was 'no cause for anxiety, and even beneficial' because it showed the Shah's government in its true light. 'With this crime the regime has revealed itself as the successor of Genghis Khan and has made its defeat and destruction inevitable,' Khomeini told his loyal followers after the soldiers had departed the ruined Feizeyeh. 'The son of Reza Khan has dug his own grave and disgraced himself.' A forty-day period of mourning was observed to mark the desecration of the seminary, after which Khomeini launched into yet another spirited denunciation of the Shah and his policies. 'Love of the Shah means rapine, violation of the rights of Muslims and violation of the commandments of Islam,' Khomeini declared, and referred to the Shah as a 'usurper' who had to be removed. He depicted the government as the agent of Israel and said the Iranian army 'is not prepared to see the country crushed beneath the Jewish boot'.[22]

The Shah was in no mood to back down in his confrontation with Khomeini, and sent a delegation of senior police and security officers to Qom to negotiate with him. Khomeini refused to see them because they worked for the Shah, so they saw one of the city's leading ayatollahs and told him in no uncertain terms that if the anti-government unrest persisted, 'commandos and whores will be set upon you; you will be killed, your honour will be defiled and your homes pillaged.' Fearing Khomeini's campaign might indeed result in a blood bath, the senior Shia leaders based in southern Iraq suggested it might be a good idea if their Qom colleagues decamped to Najaf, and continue their anti-government protest at a safe distance from the Shah's security forces. After consulting his fellow clerics in Qom, Khomeini rejected the offer, saying he could not abandon Qom to 'unbelievers and infidels'.[23] The Shah intensified the pressure on the clerics by forcibly conscripting young seminarians into the armed forces. One of those dispatched for military training was the 29-year-old Ali Akbar Hashemi Rafsanjani, a loyal student of Khomeini's who was a key figure in the 1979 Revolution. Rafsanjani was seized as he walked past the local police station and sent to a military barracks in Tehran for training. 'We began to learn useful things from our military instructors, and we also taught them a few useful things,' recalled Rafsanjani.

Something had to give, and the event that sealed Khomeini's emergence as the undisputed leader of radical Islam was a sermon he delivered at Qom on 3 June to mark *ashura*, the religious festival that commemorates the martyrdom of Hussein, the grandson of the Prophet Mohammed. *Ashura* is particularly poignant for Shia Muslims, who believe that Hussein was unfairly deprived of becoming Caliph. Throughout Iran the faithful enact passion plays of Hussein's death, and the festival is memorable for the willingness of young Shia Muslim men to flagellate themselves with chains or cutting their foreheads until their bodies stream with blood. With emotions already running high, Khomeini chose this moment to deliver his most incendiary speech to date against the Shah's regime, in which he launched a devastating attack on the Shah himself, Israel and the United States. He publicly denounced a warning he had received from SAVAK not to criticize the Shah, mention Israel, or claim Islam was under threat. In the speech Khomeini came close to suggesting that Iran's head of state was an Israeli agent. Addressing the Shah contemptuously as 'you wretched, miserable man', he demanded, 'What connection is there between the Shah and Israel? Mr Shah, perhaps they want to depict you as a Jew, so that I should declare you an infidel and they [the people] should throw you out of Iran.' He concluded by declaring, 'We have come to the conclusion that this regime also has a more basic aim: they are fundamentally opposed to Islam itself and the existence of a religious class.'

As Khomeini spoke, a network of SAVAK informers who had infiltrated the audience noted down every sentence of his speech and passed it to the police waiting outside. By now senior SAVAK officials had arrived in Qom, and on hearing the tone of Khomeini's comments, they felt compelled to act after reading details of the most insulting speech that had ever been delivered against the Shah. Two days later, in the early hours of 5 June, a team of SAVAK security officials arrived at Khomeini's house and arrested him. He was bundled into the back of a black Volkswagen Beetle and taken to the local police station. Word quickly spread throughout Qom of Khomeini's arrest, and an angry crowd started to gather outside the police station. When the crowd started to attack, the police opened fire, killing an estimated twenty-eight demonstrators. Within hours rioting had spread throughout the country, as pro-Khomeini loyalists took to the streets to protest against the government's action. The Coalition of Islamic Societies that Khomeini had helped to set up alerted supporters in Tehran, where by 9.30 a.m. some 2,000 youths had gathered in the bazaar shouting 'Death or Khomeini'. Rioting quickly spread throughout the country, proving the effectiveness of Khomeini's underground network, and there were violent clashes in Shiraz, Isfahan and Mashhad. On the outskirts of Tehran, several hundred men wearing death shrouds, signifying their readiness for martyrdom, marched on the capital. The Shah ordered the army to put the demonstrations down by force, and violent clashes continued for several days, claiming the lives of more than 200 demonstrators.

Scores of other senior clerics were detained along with Khomeini as the Shah imposed a widespread clampdown against anti-government activity, but most of them were soon released. The government's anger with Khomeini, though, ran so deep that senior figures within the Shah's inner circle publicly stated that they were in favour of having the troublesome cleric executed. It was only after a delegation of senior clergy intervened on Khomeini's behalf that the Shah concluded that executing Khomeini would only serve to make him a martyr, and stir up even stronger anti-Shah sentiments. Khomeini was eventually released from prison in early July with a warning not to meddle in politics. He was visited in prison by General Hasan Pakravan, the then head of SAVAK. According to Khomeini, Pakravan told him, 'Politics is lies, deception, shame and meanness. Leave politics to us.' To which Khomeini replied, 'All of Islam is politics.'[24] Khomeini was allowed to move into the house of a prominent bazaar merchant who lived in north Tehran, where he was placed under twenty-four-hour surveillance by SAVAK to prevent him causing further trouble.

One of the arguments used by the clerics who supported Khomeini to secure his release was that he had now attained the level of *marja*, the highest level of learning and piety to which a Shia cleric can aspire. Khomeini's opponents disputed that a man who was so committed to undertaking acts of violence could be worthy of such an honour. But Khomeini's nationwide popularity gave him the upper hand, and at the very least he could now present himself as one of the country's leading ayatollahs, even if his claim to supremacy over all the clergy was still a matter of dispute. The important factor from Khomeini's point of view was that his ayatollah status provided him with immunity from prosecution by the civil courts. The state had set the precedent of prosecuting senior clergy by executing Khomeini's hero Ayatollah Nuri, who went to the gallows for his part in the revolt against the Constitutional Revolution. But this was an extreme measure taken in extreme circumstances, and the Shah had no desire to provoke an irreversible rupture with the clerical establishment, which Khomeini's execution would undoubtedly have caused.

As a consequence Khomeini emerged stronger from his confrontation with the Shah. He now had his status as a *marja* confirmed by his clerical peers, and the nationwide demonstrations that had erupted in his support revealed the popularity of his radical and uncompromising interpretation of Islam. Many of those who supported Khomeini, particularly those linked to the bazaar, did so because they opposed the Shah's attempts to impose foreign practices, such as universal suffrage and the distribution of wealth, on their traditional way of life. They supported Khomeini because he was the most articulate and steadfast opponent of the Shah's policies, which Khomeini proved as adept at exploiting in 1963 as he would in 1979.

Khomeini's standing within the Shia community rose considerably after he became an ayatollah. But the fundamental difference between Khomeini and other senior Shia clergy who attained the same level was that he had achieved this status through political activity, rather than through religious endeavour. 'The biggest mistake the senior clerics made at this time was to acknowledge Khomeini's rank as an ayatollah to save him from the gallows,' said a religious student from the period who initially supported Khomeini, but later switched allegiance. 'This placed Khomeini above the law and made it impossible for the Shah to curb his activities.'[25] But for others Khomeini's stand, and his steadfast refusal to be cowed by the Shah's intimidatory tactics, was a source of great inspiration. Rafsanjani, who became Iran's president after Khomeini's death, described the impact on his generation of Khomeini's political militancy. 'Mr Khomeini was in the vanguard, and struggled more firmly than many others in this cause. I, who was with him, was his student and found his approach more to my liking, and drew closer to him.'[26]

The authorities finally freed Khomeini from house arrest and allowed him to return to Qom in April 1964, where his homecoming was turned into a major festival. The Feizeyeh school, which had been renovated in his absence, organized three days of celebrations and the bazaar was festooned with lights. The government believed it had obtained an undertaking from Khomeini that he would refrain from involvement in politics. But Khomeini denied this, and within ten days was delivering sermons at Qom that were every bit as incendiary as the one of the previous year that had led to his detention. If anything, Khomeini's confinement had had the effect of boosting his personal confidence, and he now had the self-belief to make certain demands of the Shah, such as granting the clergy responsibility for the administration of education and religious endowments. The Shah was in no mood to make concessions to him on any level, but the fact that Khomeini was suggesting that the clergy might contribute to the business of government was putting down a marker for the future – that the clergy was just as capable of running the country as the politicians.

The final straw, so far as the Shah was concerned, came the following autumn when the Majlis, which was filled with pro-Shah supporters, was asked to approve a new law that provided all American military personnel and their dependants with full diplomatic immunity. Although the law was narrowly passed by the Majlis, it was unpopular with the people, who saw in it overtones of the humiliating concessions imposed on Iran by the British and Russians earlier in the century. The government's handling of the measure was not exactly tactful, for twelve days after the Majlis vote it approved a $200-million loan from a consortium of American banks to allow the Shah to purchase military weapons. The loan confirmed the worst suspicions of many Iranians, who concluded that the Shah was up to his old tricks of selling the country to the highest foreign bidder.

Khomeini once more mustered the anti-Shah offensive. In a speech to a packed audience in Qom on 26 October, Khomeini was at his rhetorical best as he laid into the Shah. 'I cannot express the sorrow I feel in my heart,' he began. 'If some American's servant, some American's cook, assassinates your Marja in the middle of the bazaar, or runs over him, the Iranian police do not have the right to apprehend him! Iranian courts do not have the right to judge him! The dossier must be sent to America, so that our masters there can decide what is to be done! . . . They have reduced the Iranian people to a level lower than that of an American dog. If someone runs over a dog belonging to an American, he will be prosecuted. But if an American cook runs over the Shah, the head of state, no one will have the right to interfere with him. Why? Because they wanted a loan, and America demanded this in return.'[27]

This time the Shah did not hesitate in responding to Khomeini's outburst, which made no attempt to disguise its crude appeal to populist sentiment. On 4 November, Khomeini was re-arrested by SAVAK officers and driven straight to Tehran airport where an official handed him his passport and informed him he was being sent into exile to Turkey, where he would soon be joined by his family. His departure was later broadcast in a short statement on Tehran Radio. 'Since Mr Khomeini's behaviour and his agitation are against the interests of the people and the security, sovereignty and independence of the country, he has been sent into exile.'[28] On this occasion, while there was much support for Khomeini's views, there was no great appetite among his supporters for a repetition of the street violence that had claimed so many lives the previous year. They might have admired Khomeini, but they were not yet prepared to die for him.

*

Khomeini was led aboard a Hercules transport plane of the Imperial Iranian Air Force by a SAVAK officer who had been deputed to ensure the cleric was safely delivered to his new home. Turkey was an unusual location for Khomeini's exile. By tradition Irianian Shia clerics who fell foul of the authorities in Tehran usually decamped to the major shrine city of Najaf in southern Iraq. But the Shah's security officials had good contacts with their Turkish counterparts, who agreed to assist with monitoring Khomeini's movements, which was not possible to the same degree in Iraq. For Khomeini, though, the choice of Turkey could not have been worse. As his younger son Ahmad later remarked, his father felt like 'a fish out of water'.[29] It was a country where the secularism of Kemal Ataturk had completely subjugated the role of Islam to the state, a complete reverse from the glory of the Ottoman Empire where the Caliphate had ruled the Muslim world. Khomeini had built his entire career on his visceral opposition to Iran becoming another Turkey, and frequently confided to his friends that he regarded the collapse of the Ottoman Empire at the end of the First World War as 'one of the greatest disasters in world history'.[30] It was Khomeini's ultimate ambition to re-establish the Caliphate under his leadership, but now he found himself languishing in a country that gloried in its apostasy, and never missed the opportunity to remind him of the fact. When, after he had been in Ankara for three days, Khomeini demanded that he be allowed out of the hotel to see the city, his guards banned him from wearing his clerical attire, a gross insult to a cleric of his stature.

In January 1965 Khomeini was joined in Turkey by his eldest son Mostafa, who had developed into a portly young man. He had also been dispatched into exile for anti-Shah activities and arrived bearing nuts and coffee and other items that his father had requested, including a number of religious books. In the summer the Shah gave permission for a group of leading mullahs to visit Khomeini, who was taken to Istanbul in civilian clothes for the occasion, which prompted some of his visitors, seeing him without his clerical robes, to burst into tears. Khomeini and his followers struggled to adapt to Turkey's secular culture. The party of mullahs was taken to visit a nearby resort, where he found himself confronted by the sight of hundreds of bikini-clad Muslim women disporting themselves on the beach. Khomeini deliberately averted his gaze, but when Mostafa set off for a swim wearing his long underpants to protect his modesty, he was surrounded by angry Turks and chased off the beach.

With Khomeini languishing in exile, the more extreme elements among his supporters continued with their anti-Shah activities. On 21 January the Shah's prime minister, Hassan Ali Mansur, was killed after his motorcade was sprayed with bullets as he made his way to the parliament building in central Tehran. The assassin was caught, and revealed to his SAVAK interrogators that the murder was the work of the Coalition of Islamic Societies that Khomeini had helped to set up with the support of *bazaari* loyalists. The Coalition had acquired an armed wing called Hizbollah, the party of God, which was mainly made up of former members of the Fedayeen that had masterminded the anti-government terrorist campaign in the 1950s, which Khomeini had also supported. Before going into exile Khomeini had entrusted several of his most loyal followers with the responsibility for running the Coalition. After Khomeini's deportation to Turkey, the Hizbollah wing of the Coalition drew up an extensive list of government officials who it had targeted for assassination, including the Shah himself. 'Khomeini was very impressed with the work of Hizbollah,' recalled one of his former followers. 'This was a group that believed in assassination and armed resistance in the name of Islam. All Hizbollah achieved in the 1960s was the murder of Mansur, but Khomeini supported everything that they did.'[31]

Khomeini liked to portray himself as a man of God, but he associated himself more and more closely with radical Islamic groups that regarded terrorism as a legitimate course of action for achieving their political goals. He had begun his career by supporting Sheikh Fazlollah Nuri, the ayatollah executed in 1909 for his violent opposition to the pro-Western reforms of the Constitutional Revolution. In the 1950s he had associated himself with Navab Safavi, another Islamic radical who went to the gallows after his Fedayeen terror group conducted an assassination campaign against the Shah's government in the 1950s. Ten years later, after he had positioned himself as the undisputed champion of the radical Islamic cause in Iran, Khomeini lent his support to the creation of yet another Islamic group that fully embraced the tactics of terrorism. This latest group was to become the prototype for the foundation of the Revolutionary Guards following the 1979 Islamic Revolution, and also for the creation of the radical Islamic group Hizbollah in Lebanon in the 1980s, which would develop into two of the world's most deadly Islamic terrorist organizations.

Khomeini had developed into a fanatic, a leader who believed that any action, no matter how violent or destructive, was justified so long as it helped to achieve his ultimate objective of creating an Islamic state run with his uncompromising interpretation of Islamic law. Khomeini's closest supporters fully embraced his militant ideology, which defined the doctrine of Islamic fundamentalism for the entire Muslim world. Many of Khomeini's followers who were involved in Mansur's assassination in 1965 became key figures in the 1979 Islamic Revolution. Hashemi Rafsanjani, who was arrested and tortured by SAVAK for his involvement in the assassination plot, became Iran's president under Khomeini. Another detainee, Mohammed Beheshti, was a founder member of Khomeini's Revolutionary Council and later became the Islamic Republic's first chief justice.

The assassination of Prime Minister Mansur led to the destruction of the Coalition's terror network in Iran after SAVAK launched a nationwide crackdown on Islamic radicals. Mansur's assassin, Mohammed Bokhara'i was tried and executed, along with three of his accomplices. Twelve other members of the assassin's group were imprisoned. The measures taken by SAVAK against the Coalition, and its armed wing, Hizbollah, severely curtailed Khomeini's ability to influence events in Iran. By the summer of 1965 SAVAK had been so successful in destroying the radical Islamic organizations that it no longer regarded Khomeini as posing a significant threat to state security, and agreed to allow him to move from Turkey, where he felt completely out of place, to the more familiar surroundings of Najaf in southern Iraq, where he would be surrounded by fellow Shia clerics. Although Khomeini's ability to influence events in Iran had been much diminished, he still managed to maintain contact with his supporters, who supplied him with donations to finance his anti-Shah campaign. His Turkish minders estimated that Khomeini, who had arrived in exile with hardly a penny to his name, had received so much money while in exile in Turkey that he had become a millionaire by the time he left for Iraq.

5

The Ayatollah Returns

Najaf is one of the holiest cities in Islam and a major centre of Shia learning and study. Located almost equidistant between Baghdad and the Iranian border, it is renowned as the site of the tomb of Imam Ali, whom the Shia believe to be their founder and first Imam, and was the cause of the original split between Sunni and Shia Muslims in the seventh century AD. Before Qom's emergence in the nineteenth century as the principal centre of Shi'ism, Najaf had for centuries enjoyed the reputation for being the religious epicentre of the Shia world. Even in the nineteenth century the city attracted leading Shia scholars and divines. Both Khomeini's grandfather and father had studied at Najaf and, as a young man, Khomeini himself had seriously considered going to Najaf to further his religious education, but had been prevented from doing so by the First World War. So the Shah's decision to allow Khomeini to move from Turkey to Najaf in October 1965 was almost like a homecoming for the itinerant ayatollah.

He began his exile in Najaf, where he would reside for the next thirteen years, in some style. As news of his arrival spread, visitors from every theological school in Iraq travelled to Najaf to meet him. The Iraqi government sent a minister to afford an official welcome, and Khomeini spent several days visiting the surrounding important shrines at places such as Karbala, where the descendants of Imam Ali were massacred in AD 680, and Samarra, where the Hidden Imam of the Shia, the Mahdi, is said to have gone into occultation – to have removed himself from the world – in 874.

Khomeini's arrival in southern Iraq assumed the appearance of a magisterial procession among the Shia shrines, as his enthusiastic supporters carefully choreographed his visits to generate maximum publicity. The tour concluded with Khomeini's stage-managed arrival at the tomb of Imam Ali, where he prayed at the spiritual home of Shia Islam. But while Khomeini's presence generated much excitement among the faithful, he was regarded with suspicion, if not downright hostility, by the more conservative-minded leaders of Iraq's Shia community, who viewed him as a rival and a threat. 'This Sayyid [holy man] has created havoc in Qom. We must be careful not to let him do the same in Najaf,' commented one senior cleric after Khomeini had set up home in a small rented house close by the Imam Ali shrine.

Relations between Khomeini, with his background of radical teaching and supporting violence, and Najaf's clerical establishment, which eschewed both, were frosty from the outset. He was visited by two of the city's grand ayatollahs, Khoei and Shahrudi, who bade him the traditional welcome, but the overall head of Iraq's Shia community, Grand Ayatollah Hakim, waited several days before paying a visit, and then it lasted only five minutes, which was seen as a mark of disrespect by Khomeini's supporters. When Khomeini repaid the compliment by visiting Hakim, he lectured the grand ayatollah about the 'atrocities' being committed in Iran by the Shah's security forces, and decried the fact that the persecution of the clergy in Iran had generated so little support from their Shia brethren in neighbouring Iraq. But Khomeini got short shrift when he suggested that Hakim declare that all Shia Muslims participate in an uprising to overthrow the Shah. Hakim simply smiled and made no reply.[1]

Khomeini had always regarded Najaf as a 'den of snakes' because of the reputation of the city's clerical establishment for political intrigue, and he soon realized that he could not rely on the local clergy to support his anti-Shah activities. This was partly because the Iraqi Shia, who comprised the majority of Iraq's 12 million population, had experienced great domestic political turbulence of their own, with a succession of American-backed governments taking power in Baghdad amid much bloodshed. The military coup of 1963 that brought President Abdul Salam Arif to office resulted in the Pinochet-style slaughter of tens of thousands of Iraqi Communists in the space of just one week. The clerical leaders in Najaf had managed to keep out of harm's way by issuing a fatwa forbidding the Shia from joining the Communist Party. But the brutality with which the military dictatorship, with Washington's backing, had suppressed the Communists had persuaded Shia leaders of the folly of getting involved in politics, and made them utterly disinclined to support any similar such action in neighbouring Iran.

This meant Khomeini and his committed group of followers were largely left to their own devices. Lack of support from Najaf's clerical elite did not dampen Khomeini's enthusiasm for attacking the Shah and Tehran's secular regime. The Shah and his advisers had hoped that by sending Khomeini into exile they had found an elegant way of ending his career as a political activist. Khomeini was, after all, sixty-three by the time he arrived in Najaf, a time when most people are turning their attention towards a contented retirement. But Khomeini confounded these expectations by embarking on what proved to be a highly productive period in his development as a religious and political leader. He channelled his energies into teaching, writing, speaking and issuing declarations, all of which were based on the central theme of exposing the 'crimes' of the Shah's government and warning of the threat posed to Islam and Iran by the regime of 'tyranny and unbelief' that held sway at the Golestan Palace. He argued persuasively that Islam should be used as an instrument for mobilizing and forging a united opposition, and teaching his followers to gird themselves for resistance to a ruler who had turned himself into 'a servant of the dollar'.[2]

Khomeini's exile provided him with a highly effective platform from which he could direct an almost constant volley of invective against the Shah. He commemorated important state occasions in his home country – such as the Shah's coronation in 1967 and the twenty-fifth centennial celebrations of the Iranian monarchy in 1971 – by issuing public declarations just as inflammatory as the speeches that had led to his expulsion in the first place. He condemned the imprisonment of religious figures, university students and other opposition groups, the practice of 'medieval torture' and execution in the Shah's prisons, and the suppression of basic freedoms. He criticized the Shah for violating Islamic law and the constitution, and spoke up on behalf of the downtrodden and dispossessed. He championed the interests of ordinary shopkeepers and bazaar merchants while denigrating the lifestyle of the ruling classes and the royal family as 'corrupt, the pursuit of animal pleasures'.[3]

This period helped to consolidate Khomeini's stature as the Shah's most potent and uncompromising opponent. His frenetic political activity in Najaf resulted in a marked increase in the size of his circle of students. He managed, despite the ever-watchful scrutiny of SAVAK security agents, to maintain contact with the network of supporters he had left behind in Iran which, even allowing for the clampdown that followed Mansur's assassination, continued with its underground activities. There was a constant flow of Shia clerical traffic crossing between Najaf and Qom, and Khomeini continued to receive a plentiful supply of donations from his supporters within the clergy and the bazaars to fund his movement, in return for which he would send messages and pamphlets articulating his latest views on developments in Iran. SAVAK agents did their best to disrupt the traffic, and a small army of agents was sent to Najaf as cooks and servants to report back to Tehran on the constant procession of visitors to Khomeini's home.

Some of Khomeini's supporters, such as Mohammed Beheshti, his future chief justice, successfully managed the difficult juggling act of reaching an accommodation with the Shah's regime while at the same time remaining loyal to Khomeini. Others, like Hashemi Rafsanjani, were constantly rubbing up against the state's security apparatus in their attempts to maintain contact with militant anti-Shah groups. Die-hard Khomeini supporters continued to keep his name alive within the confines of Iran's clerical institutions, and in Qom annual demonstrations were held calling for the ayatollah to be allowed to return home.[4] It was during this time that Khomeini and his followers made the first tentative steps towards establishing links with Iranian student groups in Europe and the United States that later made a significant contribution to the success of the 1979 Revolution.

In Najaf Khomeini had only a small group of followers who had joined him in exile; the rest were either in Qom or scattered around the rest of the country. Mostafa, his eldest son, who had accompanied him on the journey from Turkey to Iraq, acted as his *chef de cabinet*, arranging his diary and making sure that the administrative wheels of his father's organization ran smoothly. He was soon joined by his wife, Batoul, and the rest of the family, including his younger son Ahmad. Mostafa, who did not inherit his father's intellectual gifts and achieved only a basic level of Islamic study, had developed an abiding hatred of the Pahlavi dynasty, upon whom he blamed 'the wrongness of everything in this wrong world' and lost no opportunity to call for revenge on the Pahlavis. He was charged with taking down his father's statements for distribution to the outside world, which were often littered with grammatical and spelling errors. As there were no copying machines available in Najaf, Mostafa and his younger brother Ahmad had to make hundreds of copies of their father's utterances by hand.

With his sons' help, Khomeini managed to correspond with a number of mullahs inside Iran, writing as many as half a dozen letters a day. The letters were sent to prearranged addresses specially chosen to avoid detection by the small army of SAVAK agents deployed by General Nematollah Nassiri, the chief of the intelligence service, to interdict the seditious correspondence. Early in his exile Khomeini attempted to strike up a correspondence with Amir-Abbas Hoveyda, the cultured politician who had replaced Mansur as the Shah's prime minister after the latter's assassination. Hoveyda, a lawyer by training who was himself related to a grand ayatollah, had initially considered writing detailed replies to Khomeini, but was persuaded against the idea by General Nassiri. Khomeini ultimately had his revenge on both men, who were executed by his Revolutionary Guard firing squads in 1979.

For the most part Khomeini lived a modest life in Najaf. When he was not teaching at Najaf's prestigious theological school, he spent much of the day secluded in his tiny room where he read and prayed. He rarely visited the nearby golden shrine to Imam Ali because he wanted to avoid members of the local Shia hierarchy, who had effectively ostracized him from Najaf's ruling elite. In the evenings he would sit in his room listening to Radio Iran's main news bulletin, and the BBC's Persian service. Sometimes Mostafa would join him and they would sit together discussing the implications of various news items.

Students who followed Khomeini from Qom to study with him at Najaf noticed several changes in his demeanour. 'The Khomeini who taught us in Najaf was very different to the one who had taught us in Qom,' one of his former students recalled. 'In Qom he had wanted to be a religious leader; in Najaf he wanted to be a political leader.' In public his former students found him less forthcoming than he had been in Iran, a change they ascribed to the fact he had little backing from the other ayatollahs in Iraq. 'When he arrived in Najaf he thought he would be one of the leading ayatollahs, but he encountered stiff opposition from the existing Shia hierarchy which did not approve of what he was doing.' As in Qom, Khomeini continued to live a simple life. 'It was extremely hot in the summer, but he never bought an air-conditioning system, like the other ayatollahs in Najaf. He just had a simple fan in his room.' The more senior Iraqi clerics had their own cars and drivers, but Khomeini either walked or took a taxi. Khomeini undoubtedly missed his homeland, but he never showed it so far as his students were concerned, 'He never gave us any indication that he was homesick.'[5]

Khomeini turned to Iraqi mullahs of a more radical persuasion, and one of the more important relationships he developed was with Mohammed Bakr al-Sadr, the head of Iraq's recently formed Dawa (the Call) Islamic party. The Sadr family was among the most distinguished of the Iraqi Shia. Gertrude Bell, the remarkable orientalist who worked for the British High Commission during the creation of Iraq in the 1920s, described the Sadr clan as 'possibly more distinguished for religious learning than any other family in the whole Shia world'.[6] Sadr's family had played a prominent role in the Shia revolt against British rule in the 1920s, and have remained in the vanguard of militant Islamic activity in Iraq to this day.

Khomeini's friend Mohammed al-Sadr had been prompted to enter the political arena by Israel's shock victory over the Arabs in the 1967 Six Day War. Sadr shared Khomeini's enthusiasm for creating a universal Islamic state, but had a more modern outlook than the conservative-minded Khomeini. Sadr took a close interest in modern science, and had written a definitive book on the practical application of Islamic economics. He argued that it was crucial for the Shia clergy to become well acquainted with modern disciplines such as politics and economics to prepare themselves for government. Like Khomeini, Sadr had no qualms about supporting militant action to achieve his goals, and some of the founder members of the

Dawa were drawn from the Iraqi remnants of Navab Savafi's Fedayeen, which Khomeini had supported in the 1950s.[7] The friendship between Khomeini and Sadr survived for several years until Sadr's execution by Saddam Hussein in 1980 for supporting a Shia revolt against the Baathist regime. But the connection between modern-day Iran and the Sadr family continues to this day. His grandson, the radical Shia cleric Muqtada al-Sadr, is the leader of the Iranian-backed militia that played a lead role in the insurgency to drive United States-led coalition forces out of Iraq following the overthrow of Saddam's regime in 2003.

It was partly as a result of his friendship with Sadr that Khomeini came to define his vision for an Islamic state, which in turn became the manifesto for Islamic fundamentalist regimes throughout the world. Following the death of Grand Ayatollah Hakim in 1968, a similar doctrinal vacuum developed in Najaf to the one that had existed in Qom following Borujerdi's death in 1963, and which Khomeini had successfully exploited to press his own claim for leadership of Iran's Shia. As a foreigner he had little chance of asserting his authority over Iraq's fiercely nationalistic Shia as their *marja*, but that did not prevent him, with Sadr's encouragement, from participating in the vigorous theological debate that inevitably followed Hakim's death. The most senior Iraqi Shia leader, the *marja*, was now Grand Ayatollah Khoei who, like his predecessor, believed the faithful should refrain from involvement in politics.

But these were turbulent times in Iraq. In 1968 the Baath party had staged the coup that would eventually bring Saddam Hussein to power, and many of the younger Shia clergy were agitating to become more involved in the exciting political events unfolding in Baghdad. At first Khoei distanced himself from the debate, but to silence some of the more excitable Iraqi clergy he delivered a series of lectures in which he reaffirmed the Shia clergy's traditional view that the mullahs needed to remain above secular society so that they could serve as its watchdogs. Khomeini's son Mostafa attended the lectures and took copious notes, which he passed on to his father. The views expressed by Khoei in his lectures were diametrically opposed to Khomeini's and, at Sadr's prompting, he resolved to deliver a series of lectures of his own that clearly articulated his own position. The lectures were subsequently printed in a slim volume entitled *Velayat-e Faqih*, the 'regency of the theologian', which was Khomeini's blueprint for an Islamic government. In fact Khomeini's lectures were more than a template for the establishment of Islamic government: they set out Khomeini's radical religious philosophy for the application of government based on the strict interpretation of Sharia law that would become more popularly known as Islamic fundamentalism.

The lectures were the culmination of Khomeini's rigorous theological studies stretching back over four decades, but incorporated the new line of clerical populism that he developed after going into exile in Najaf. At the time of publication in 1970 his lectures had little circulation beyond the narrow group of theology students who attended his lectures at Najaf, and only became more widely known after the 1979 Revolution, by which time Khomeini had achieved the fait accompli of establishing an Islamic government in Iran under the guise of a popular revolution. But had any of the enthusiastic young students who supported Khomeini's revolution studied his lectures on Islamic government beforehand, they may have been less inclined to lend him their unqualified support.

According to Khomeini's radical new interpretation of Shia Islam, senior clerics who specialized in Islamic law (*feqh*) – of which Khomeini was one – had the ultimate authority to rule the state, rather than giving their blessing to the appointment of a secular ruler such as the Shah, which was the present custom. This unique conclusion – which had no precedent either in the Koran or Sharia – was arrived at through conventional Shia premises. God had sent the Prophets and Imams to guide the faithful; these Prophets and Imams had left behind the Sharia to guide the faithful on the path to righteousness, and in the absence of the Twelfth Imam, or Mahdi, it was the duty of senior Shia clerics, or *mojtaheds*, to uphold the principles of Sharia law.

Khomeini argued that the reason his ideas might sound strange to modern Muslims was that for centuries monarchists, imperialists and others had worked hard to falsify Islam. For Khomeini, the monarchy, whether in Iran or anywhere else, was a pagan institution that was a relic from the era of polytheism, and therefore incompatible with true Islam. According to Khomeini, Islam was the supreme religion, and lesser faiths, such as Christianity and Judaism, were to be physically suppressed so as not to pollute the purity of the true faith. He preached that Muslims had a sacred duty to oppose all monarchies and imperialist institutions, such as the liberal democracies of the West, and to rise up against them. Most kings, to Khomeini's mind, had been criminals, oppressors and mass murderers, and in calling for the root-and-branch destruction of the monarchy in Iran, he was overturning twelve centuries of Shia tradition where the clergy had accepted monarchical rule as a necessary safeguard against the perils of anarchy.[8] In short, this was fanaticism dressed up as Islam.

But Khomeini was careful to keep these inflammatory and highly contentious teachings to the confines of the seminary. In his public pronouncements at Najaf, he continued his assault on the Shah on the basis of his political, social and economic shortcomings. He denounced the Shah for supporting Israel against the Muslim world, allying with the West in the Cold War, wasting resources on the ever-expanding military, neglecting agriculture so the country could be flooded with cheap American goods and allowing society to degenerate to a level where crime, alcoholism, prostitution and drug addiction were rife. He gradually adopted the use of populist slogans that stressed the importance of Islam as a force in liberating the country from the Shah's incompetent government. Many of these pithy catchphrases became popular chants during the 1979 Revolution, such as, 'Islam belongs to the oppressed, not the oppressors', 'The poor die for the revolution, the rich plot against the revolution', and 'Neither East nor West, but Islam'.[9]

Not everyone was impressed with the radical new persona Khomeini adopted in Najaf. 'More and more we came to see him as a fake,' said one of his former students who later joined an opposition group to Khomeini's government. 'The more he talked about his version of Islamic government, the more we realized that this was not just constructive criticism of the Shah's regime; this was Khomeini setting out his doctrine for taking over not just Iran, but the rest of the Islamic world. Khomeini sought total domination over all Muslims, and this was his way of achieving it.'[10]

*

'To all intents and purposes, the Shah was the regime: monarchy and state had become virtually synonymous.'[11] That was how the distinguished British diplomat Sir Anthony Parsons viewed the political situation in Tehran when he arrived to take up his post as Britain's ambassador in the mid-1970s. The excitement generated by the White Revolution, where the Shah had proposed a more equitable distribution of political and economic power, had subsided with President Kennedy's assassination in 1963. Having toyed with the notion of presiding over a more democratic form of government, the Shah had reverted to his old autocratic ways, where he relied on the strength of the military and the brutality of his security apparatus to govern the country.

The Shah's short-lived experiment with open government began to unravel after he was the target of an assassination attempt in the spring of 1965. The would-be assassin was a serving member of the Shah's elite imperial guard, and under interrogation revealed he belonged to a left-wing group of European-educated intellectuals who opposed the regime. Coming just months after the murder of his prime minister, the Shah used the attacks as an excuse to impose a nation-wide clampdown on political dissent. From the mid-1960s until the 1979 Revolution the Shah displayed no further interest in indulging in a dialogue with his opponents, not even the moderate secularists who were broadly supportive of his regime. Although elections to the Majlis were held every four years, the ballots were rigged, and the Iranian parliament was reduced to the status of rubber-stamping the Shah's decrees.

SAVAK, the Shah's all-pervasive intelligence service, became the most powerful state institution, and it was given a free rein to infiltrate every aspect of Iranian society. By the 1970s SAVAK was said to employ 500,000 full-time and part-time workers and informers, and its network infiltrated every aspect of Iranian life to the extent that people were advised not to trust anyone, including members of their own family. The Shah appointed Nematollah Nassiri as SAVAK's new chief in 1965 after criticizing the previous leadership for not being more effective in suppressing the religious opposition led by Khomeini. Nassiri, a sycophant who became a national hate figure because of the brutal methods he used, was provided with a vast budget and all the resources he needed to keep the Shah in power. Secular opposition groups were systematically moni-tored and intimidated, and in the bazaars and theological col-leges there was hardly a Khomeini supporter who was not on the receiving end of SAVAK's strong-arm tactics. Torture was commonplace in the SAVAK-run prisons, and many of the prominent political dissidents who were spared execution later died in prison from the maltreatment they received at the hands of their captors. The methods of torture described by Amnesty International in the 1970s included electric shocks, beating the soles of the feet with electric cables, burning on a heated metal grille and the insertion of bottles and hot eggs into the anus.

An Iranian poet who was detained by SAVAK in 1973 told of seeing a SAVAK torture room with 'all sizes of whips' and instruments designed to pluck out the fingernails of victims. 'They hang you upside down,' he said, 'and then someone beats you with a mace on your legs or on your genitals, or they lower you down, pull your pants up and then one of them tries to rape you while you are still hanging upside down.'[12] By the 1970s the Shah's regime had become every bit as repressive and brutal as the one his father had administered in the 1930s.

The dislocation of the Shah from his people became even more pronounced as the country experienced an unprecedented economic boom fuelled by the rapid growth of the oil industry. The dramatic increase in demand for oil from the industrialized economies in the 1960s saw Iran's oil revenues increase threefold in the space of just five years, and the Shah spent much of his new-found wealth on strengthening the country's armed forces. With the Johnson administration in Washington obsessed with the Vietnam War, a subtle, but significant, change occurred in the Shah's relationship with the United States. Before the petrodollars began to flow into the imperial coffers the Shah had relied heavily on Washington for economic support. But American aid to Iran began to dwindle as Iran's oil wealth grew, and by the 1960s the relationship between Washington and Tehran became more equal as America became ever more dependent on Iranian oil. In 1966 Iran ceased to be a recipient of American aid, and American arms companies became the beneficiaries of the Shah's drive to turn Iran into a regional military superpower. Orders were placed for F-4 Phantom fighter jets and tanks, and the Shah was constantly hectoring American officials to approve orders of the most sophisticated military equipment.

The oil price boom of the 1970s that followed the 1973 Yom Kippur War between Israel and the Arabs made matters even worse in terms of the disconnection between the Shah and his people. The undreamt-of wealth inspired the Shah to dream of elevating Iran into a major force in world affairs, and he talked constantly about making Iran one of the five great powers of the world, with the third most powerful military. These delusions of grandeur coincided with the Nixon administration's decision to appoint the Shah as its regional sheriff in the Gulf. Henry Kissinger, Nixon's foreign policy guru, was deeply impressed by the Shah's unequivocal support for Washington and described him as 'that rarest of leaders, an unconditional ally'.[13] In return the Americans allowed the Shah unconditional access to its non-nuclear military inventory so that by the mid-1970s Iran had become the most important purchaser of American arms. In 1972 the Shah took advantage of Nixon's open-ended commitment to purchase the brand-new F-14 fighter, the most expensive and advanced fighter aircraft in the world which no other country – not even Israel – had been allowed to purchase. The Shah read military magazines such as *Jane's Defence Weekly* as if they were shopping catalogues, and his profligate spending on military equipment saw the defence budget leap from $1.4 billion in 1972 to $9.4 billion in 1977. The vast military expenditure led to the influx of American officials and military advisers, which deepened the sense of resentment throughout Iran that the country was once again being taken over by foreign interlopers.

The Shah's pro-American foreign policy generated much ill will. The emergence of Israel as the dominant regional military power following its stunning success in the Israeli–Arab wars of 1967 and 1973 had caused much resentment throughout the Muslim world, particularly in the Arab states, where anti-Israeli sentiment led to the creation of pro-Palestinian terror groups. But the Shah confounded the regional trend by establishing close relations with Israel, which led to Israel's Mossad intelligence service working closely with SAVAK. There were so many Israeli diplomats and advisers working in Tehran by the mid-1970s that Israel had effectively established a 'virtual embassy' in Tehran. At the same time the Shah opposed the

1: Sheikh Fazlollah Nuri

2: Khomeini as a young man

3: Khomeini with fellow students at Qom

4: US President Richard M. Nixon, right, clasps the hands of Mohammad Reza Pahlavi, the Shah of Iran, as he and first lady Pat Nixon, centre, prepare to leave Iran after a visit in May 1972. The Shah's wife, Farah Diba, is seen at left.

5: 1 February 1979. After fourteen years in exile in France, Khomeini leaves Neauphle-le-Chateau for Iran.

6: Khomeini sits inside the chartered Air France Boeing 747 which was to fly him back to Tehran. He is shown a few minutes before the plane took off from Paris.

7: Although Iran's US-backed Shah had already fled the country, the 747's landing on 1 February is seen as the true start of the Islamic revolution.

8: Khomeini is ringed by turbaned and robed Moslem marshals of the special 'security service' organized to protect the religious leader upon his arrival.

9: 12 February 1979. A woman, in black chador and carrying a G-3 machine gun, holds up her hand in a gesture of defiance to the camera. She is amongst the forces occupying Tehran University a day after the victory of the Islamic Revolution.

10: Khomeini on the roof of the Refah School in Tehran where he orchestrated the revolution following his return from Paris.

11: The Shah of Iran, with his wife Empress Farah, and sons Prince Ali Reza, Crown Prince, right, and daughter Leila, front centre, during their stay in the Bahamas, April 1979.

12: Chapour Bakhtiar, the last Prime Minister appointed by the Shah of Iran, speaks out against the Ayatollah Khomeini and his regime at a press conference in Paris on 3 August 1979.

13: On 4 November 1979 the Revolutionary Guard stormed the US Embassy in Tehran and took more than sixty people hostage. Demonstrating outside the Embassy two days later, a girl clutching a picture of Khomeini screams 'Death to the Great Satan, Carter. Death to the USA'.

14: One of the hostages, blindfolded and with his hands bound, being displayed to the crowd outside the Embassy. At least two former hostages say they believe the bearded man, third from right, is future president Mahmoud Ahmadinejad. He has dismissed allegations of his involvement as 'baseless'.

15: Demonstrators burn an American flag atop the wall of the Embassy.

16: The first released group of US Embassy staffers hold a press conference 18 November 1979, the day after Khomeini ordered the release of all women and black US hostages.

17 & 18: During an aborted commando raid on 26 April 1980 to rescue the US embassy hostages, eight members of the raiding party died in a crash between a cargo plane and a helicopter in the eastern desert region of Iran. A propeller from the burned-out American C-130 lies amidst the plane's wreckage (*above*) and the remains of the burned-out US helicopter lies in front of an abandoned chopper (*below*).

radical Egyptian President Gamal Abdel Nasser and other Arab radicals, such as Yasser Arafat, the chairman of the Palestine Liberation Organisation, and he also took a dim view of Communism and the Soviet Union.

But the Shah seemed oblivious to his growing isolation from the Iranian people, and the event that best encapsulated his growing departure from political reality concerned the celebrations staged in October 1971 to celebrate the 2,500th year of the Iranian monarchy. In what was essentially an exercise to justify the legitimacy of the Pahlavi dynasty established by his father in 1925, the Shah spent an estimated $100 million commemorating the capture of Babylon by Cyrus the Great on 12 October in 539 BC. Two weeks of lavish celebrations were held near the ruins of Persepolis, the ancient capital of Persia. Cynthia Helms, the wife of the American ambassador, wrote that 'one hundred and sixty desert acres were covered with some seventy tents, sumptuously decorated by Jansen's of Paris with French crystal, china and linens, and hung with red silk and velvet and glittering chandeliers . . . the royal court had new uniforms designed by Lanvin, and stitched with nearly one mile of gold thread.'[14] The event was more directed at impressing the outside world than the Iranian people, and the Shah referred to the Persepolis celebration as 'the greatest gathering of Heads of State in history.'[15] Mrs Helms recorded that 'five hundred guests from sixty-nine countries, including nine kings, five queens, sixteen presidents, and three premiers' attended the festivities.[16] The occasion was greeted with sullen resentment by the Iranian people, who took particular exception to all the foreign workmen and companies drafted in to provide the furnishings and catering, which they took as a grave insult to their own ability and expertise.

For a man who had been thrust onto the throne at the age of twenty-two following his father's forced abdication, had been forced to flee (albeit briefly) into exile, and had survived numerous assassination attempts, it was perhaps not surprising that the Shah always seemed to be seeking to justify himself. Western diplomats who dealt with him on a regular basis identified a schizophrenic personality who desperately sought to hide his deep feelings of insecurity. Anthony Parsons, the British ambassador, found his public manner 'harsh, arrogant, patronizing and didactic', while in private he was 'quiet, reflective, remarkably well-informed on foreign affairs and military matters ... Socially he was shy, withdrawn and devoid of small talk.'[17] William H. Sullivan, the American ambassador, reached a similar conclusion, writing that while in public he liked to portray himself as 'a forceful personality', this was not his natural character. In private he was 'relaxed, and talked in his usual easy, gracious way about a number of things'. But the moment he had to appear in public 'he transformed himself suddenly to a steely, ramrod straight autocrat. This involved not only adjusting his uniform and donning dark glasses but also throwing out his chest, raising his chin and fixing his lips in a grim line.'[18] The satirical British magazine *Private Eye* had an altogether different take on the Shah's autocratic demeanour. It took to referring to him in print as 'the Shit of Persia'.

The other issue that increasingly affected the Shah's public persona was the knowledge that he was suffering from lymphatic leukaemia, which was diagnosed in the spring of 1974. Although the French doctors treating him said the illness was not necessarily fatal and could be controlled with medication, the condition affected the Shah's general disposition. When he gave an interview to *Time* magazine that spring, the interviewer noted that 'the highly active 54-year-old monarch sighed frequently as he talked, his voice sometimes dropping to a whisper, as though betraying the burden he feels as the absolute ruler of Iran's 34 million people.'[19]

The final confirmation that tensions between the state and society were reaching an irretrievable breach came with the Shah's decision in 1975 to turn the country into a one-party state. The few remaining Iranian political parties were dissolved, to be replaced by the new Resurgence Party (*Hezb-e Rastakhiz*). From now on all facets of political life would come under the supervision of the movement; all citizens were required to join the party and vote in national elections, and those who refused were denounced as 'traitors' or 'secret Communists' and given the choice of either going to prison or leaving the country for the Soviet Union. Hoveyda, the Shah's urbane prime minister, became the secretary-general of a 200-strong politburo which announced it would observe the principles of 'democratic centralism', a synthesis of the best facets of capitalism and socialism. The new government was committed to helping the Great Leader, the Shah, in completing his White Revolution – now named the Shah–People Revolution – in leading the people towards the new Great Civilization.

The Shah himself assumed the status of a deity, and became known as the 'Aryan Sun' (*Arya Mehr*), who was 'not just the political leader of Iran. He is in the first instance the teacher and spiritual guide. He is the helmsman who not only builds for his nation roads, bridges, dams and underground canals, but also the spirit, thought and hearts of his people.[20] The Shah seemed genuinely to believe that he was on a divinely appointed mission to lead his country to a new era of greatness. He told Oriana Fallaci, the Italian journalist, that throughout his life he had received 'messages' and 'visions' from the prophets, from Imam Ali and from God himself. 'I am accompanied by a force others can't see – my mythical force. I get messages. Religious messages . . . if God didn't exist it would be necessary to invent him.'[21] When other European journalists pointed out the Shah's new political doctrine completely contradicted the democratic aspirations of the White Revolution he responded, 'Freedom of Thought? Freedom of Thought? Democracy? Democracy? What do these words mean? I don't want any part of them.'[22] Unfortunately for the Shah, he had committed to print his enthusiasm for multi-party systems of government and economic and social reform in his memoirs *Mission for My Country*, and SAVAK acted quickly to remove all copies of the book from the nation's libraries and bookshops.

Khomeini followed the gradual erosion of the Shah's popularity with growing interest, and missed no opportunity to denounce him from exile in Najaf. The move to one-party rule proved to be particularly unpopular, especially after the Resurgence Party declared war on the bazaars – where support for Khomeini still remained strong – to deal with the inflation that hit the country in 1975. The government appointed 10,000 officials to wage 'a merciless crusade against profiteers, cheaters, hoarders and unscrupulous capitalists'. A Guilds Court set up by SAVAK imposed 250,000 fines, banned 23,000 from their home towns, handed out 8,000 prison sentences ranging from two months to three years and brought charges against another 180,000.[23] Virtually every *bazaari* family was affected by the clampdown, and the bitterness they felt was intense.

Resurgence Party activists were sufficiently foolhardy to launch a simultaneous assault on the clergy. The Shah was promoted as the country's spiritual leader, as well as its political one, and the traditional clergy were denounced as 'black medieval reactionaries'. The government reopened the sensitive issue of women's rights by promulgating new laws that gave greater freedom for women, whose interests were protected by a new ministry for women's affairs. The marriageable age was raised to eighteen, birth control clinics were expanded and abortion permitted during the first twelve weeks of pregnancy. By far the most bizarre change undertaken to put Iran on the road to becoming a Great Civilization was to supplement the Muslim calendar with a new imperial calendar, which allocated 2,500 years for the presumed length of the Iranian monarchy and another thirty-five years for the reign of Mohammed Reza Shah. Overnight Iran jumped from the Muslim year 1355 to the imperial year 2535.

Khomeini issued a fatwa banning the faithful from joining

the Resurgence Party on the grounds that it was designed to destroy not just the bazaars and the farmers but the whole of Iran and Islam. Many leading clerics in Iran followed suit, issuing a flurry of fatwas declaring the party to be unconstitutional, against the interests of Iran and contrary to the teachings of Islam. In Qom the Feizeyeh seminary where Khomeini had taught closed down in protest. SAVAK responded with the uncompromising tactics that had become its hallmark. Some 250 students from the Qom seminary were drafted into the army, and one died soon after in prison. A few days after Khomeini's fatwa was published SAVAK rounded up all of his known associates, including many who would play leading roles in the revolution to come. Never before in Iranian history had so many clerics found themselves in prison at the same time.

The speed with which Khomeini and his supporters were able to respond to the Shah's latest assault on the status of the clergy illustrated the strength and depth of his support base. The unhappy combination of the Shah's centralization of power and a booming economy that neglected the material needs of ordinary Iranians led, from the early 1970s, to the emergence of a number of political groups that employed terror tactics to attack the regime. The Persepolis celebrations in 1971 had taken place against a background of a massive security operation launched in response to the outbreak of urban terrorist activity. In February that year a leftist, Cuban-style group called Fedayeen-e Khalq (Warriors of the People), took over a provincial police post. They were quickly overpowered by local villagers and, together with other members of the group discovered by SAVAK, were executed a month later. In August, just before the celebrations were about to begin, SAVAK detained sixty-nine members of another, hitherto unknown, underground group called Mujahideen-e Khalq-e-Iran (The Holy Warriors of the Iranian People), which had planned to blow up Tehran's main power station and disrupt the celebrations. Eleven of the organization's founders and members of its central committee were executed, and the others condemned to long prison sentences. Both these groups had been formed in great secrecy during the 1960s, and were comprised of young Iranians who had previously been associated with the religious wing of the National Front. Their founders, impressed by the logic of Marxism, attempted to show that true Islam was as revolutionary as Marxism without abandoning the spiritual dimension of life.

Khomeini greatly admired the tenacity of the Mujahideen, especially their courage in continuing to attack the Shah's regime when they knew that they faced torture and certain death if they were caught. In the early 1970s Khomeini authorized his lieutenants to fund the Mujahideen-e Khalq and its armed operations against the Shah. Hashami Rafsanjani, who was rapidly emerging as one of Khomeini's most effective organizers, was given responsibility for maintaining links with clandestine opposition groups, even those, like the Mujahideen, whose political philosophy did not conform to Khomeini's worldview. As Rafsanjani later explained, opposition forces at the time were so few, 'we considered any form of struggle against SAVAK a blessing'.[24] Rafsanjani was constantly being detained by SAVAK for his anti-Shah activities, but they could never muster sufficient evidence to prosecute him. He was imprisoned briefly after Mansur's murder in 1965, and again on the eve of the Shah's coronation in 1967. In 1971 he was arrested again, but SAVAK was unable to prove he was the author of a letter to Khomeini urging him to support the Mujahideen.

Khomeini worked hard to broaden his contacts with other radical Islamic groups, particularly in southern Lebanon where he struck up a close friendship with the radical Shia cleric Musa al-Sadr. Khomeini got to know Sadr, a scion of the distinguished Sadr clan in Iraq whom Khomeini had befriended in Najaf, after the Lebanese cleric's niece married Ahmad

Khomeini, the ayatollah's youngest son. (Musa al-Sadr was himself the brother-in-law of Mohammed Bakr al-Sadr, the leader of Dawa in Iraq.) Musa al-Sadr was an Iranian by birth who had studied at Qom and moved to Lebanon in 1959 to further his career. By the early 1970s Sadr had become the leader of the Shia Muslims who were the dominant religious group in southern Lebanon. He formed Amal (Hope), a religious party that looked after the Shia's interests, and later set up a militia, which was the forerunner of the radical Hizbollah militia created by Khomeini in southern Lebanon in the early 1980s. One of Sadr's key aides in southern Lebanon was Mostafa Chamran, a fellow Iranian who had trained as a physicist in America before joining Sadr in southern Lebanon. While in Lebanon Chamran befriended Khomeini, and later became one of the founders of the Revolutionary Guards, and he was responsible for appointing the firing squads that carried out the first executions following the 1979 Revolution.

For centuries the Shia of southern Lebanon had looked to Najaf for leadership, and Sadr had voted for Grand Ayatollah Khoei over Khomeini when the Iraqi Shia were electing a new *marja* in 1970 on the grounds that Khomeini was a relative newcomer to the Najaf scene.[25] Even so, Sadr provided staunch support for Khomeini's cause, and became a powerful and vociferous critic of the Shah, so much so that his mysterious disappearance while visiting Libya in 1978 was blamed 'on events in Iran', suggesting that he was another victim of SAVAK's assassination squads.[26] One of Musa al-Sadr's last acts before departing for Libya was to give an interview in which he praised 'Imam Khomeini' whom he believed expressed the 'national, cultural, libertarian dimensions' of the Iranian Revolution.[27]

The development of Khomeini's links with southern Lebanon in the early 1970s was an important part of his effort to develop a wider network of support throughout the entire Shia Muslim community. His friendship with Mohammed al-Sadr in

Najaf allowed him to build up an important alliance with the militant Dawa Islamic party in southern Iraq. And his relationship with Musa al-Sadr helped to expand his support base among the Shia of southern Lebanon, which would eventually lead to the creation of Hizbollah, the Revolutionary Guards' most powerful ally outside Iran. Indeed, the support base that Khomeini established in southern Iraq and southern Lebanon in the 1970s survives to this day. The Mahdi Army of Muqtada al-Sadr, Mohammed al-Sadr's grandson and one of the most militant supporters of the insurgency against the American-led coalition, is one of Tehran's most important allies in modern-day Iraq, while Hizbollah remains at the forefront of Iran's attempts to intimidate Israel from its base in southern Lebanon.

The links with Lebanon proved particularly useful for Khomeini's efforts to develop a more militant dimension to his anti-Shah campaign. Both his sons, Mostafa and Ahmad, were frequent visitors to Lebanon where they received political and military training at Amal camps in southern Lebanon, and later from the PLO in Beirut.[28] Although relations were strained between Yasser Arafat, the PLO chairman, and Musa al-Sadr, this did not prevent Arafat from maintaining links with Khomeini, and the PLO leader visited the ayatollah on two occasions in Najaf. The meetings led to an arrangement whereby a number of Khomeini's supporters were trained by the PLO. Among those who underwent guerrilla training in Lebanon was Mohammed Montazeri, the son of a leading ayatollah, who won notoriety after the 1979 Revolution as 'Ayatollah Ringo' for his gun-toting antics, and was one of Khomeini's closest allies during the 1979 Revolution. Many of the young Iranians who underwent training in Lebanon were recruited by the underground network run in Iran by Morteza Motahhari, another of Khomeini's key allies who remained active in Iran in spite of SAVAK's efforts to suppress the clerical opposition.

By 1977 it was estimated that about 700 of Khomeini's

supporters had been trained at guerrilla camps in Lebanon. In 1975 Rafsanjani secretly travelled to Lebanon to meet with members of the Islamic opposition working abroad and to oversee the training of Khomeini's supporters at the PLO camps. While he was abroad SAVAK detained a leading member of the Mujahideen, who under interrogation revealed details of Rafsanjani's involvement. Rafsanjani was arrested for the umpteenth time on his return, and on this occasion he was badly treated. He later recalled how he was lashed on the soles of his feet with an electric cable. 'The flesh was torn apart, and the bones jutted out. There were multiple fractures.' The agents, he said, also held a knife to his throat for hours, making small nicks and asking him to guess 'when the blade might go all the way down and sever my head.'[29]

Rafsanjani claimed he was seeking 'to correct the ideological thinking' of the Mujahideen at the time of his arrest, for the group's attempts to fuse Marxism with militant Islam were always going to clash with Khomeini's exclusively Islamic doctrine; Khomeini finally cut his ties with the Mujahideen soon after the revolution, but not before they had helped him to gain power. Rafsanjani was one of several of Khomeini's key organizers to be detained by SAVAK as the Shah instituted yet another anti-clerical crackdown. They included Montazeri, who was jailed for ten years, while Rafsanjani received a six-year sentence. Another key Khomeini ally, Ali Khamenei, who replaced Khomeini as Iran's supreme leader in 1989, was arrested on numerous occasions but still managed to ensure that charitable donations made in Khomeini's name found their way to Najaf. Mohsen Rafiqdost, a wealthy *bazaari* merchant who had trained in Lebanon and was one of the founder members of the Revolutionary Guards, was arrested in 1976 for supporting the Mujahideen, and was severely tortured by SAVAK. Rafiqdost was related to Rafsanjani, and the two men became close friends during their time at Evin.[30]

By the mid-1970s many of Khomeini's activists in his

underground network in Iran were languishing in SAVAK prisons. Two of them, Reza Saidi and Hossein Ghaffari, died in prison as a result of the injuries they received under torture. The Shah clearly believed that his terror tactics had succeeded in removing Khomeini from the political scene. Asked about the ayatollah in the course of a lengthy interview, the Shah replied, 'Khomeini? No one mentions him any more in Iran, except, perhaps, the terrorists. The so-called Islamic Marxists pronounce his name every now and then. That's all.'[31]

But no matter how hard SAVAK tried to undermine Khomeini, it was unable to halt his growing popularity among the wider Shia community, which resulted in a significant increase in his personal wealth, as he was now receiving donations from Iran, Iraq and Lebanon. In 1972 he was able to buy a new and larger house in Najaf to accommodate his expanding family – both his sons had three children. A significant proportion of the donations were used to finance the training of young militants in Lebanon. Khomeini had made the most of his enforced exile in Najaf, and he was about to reap the rewards of all his hard work. Khomeini had written his manifesto for the Islamic revolution, and he had the underground network of militant activists in place that was necessary to support his bid for power. All he needed to do was judge the right moment to make his move.

*

The first indication the political prisoners being held at Tehran's Evin prison had that change was in the air came when the guards started being nice to them. Evin was the place where SAVAK's sadistic guards were allowed to perpetrate their barbaric torture techniques, and many of the prisoners held there had suffered horribly, and some had died of their injuries. The majority of political prisoners were either supporters of Khomeini or groups such as the Mujahideen. Many of Khomeini's key lieutenants, such as Rafsanjani, Montazeri and Khamenei, were among those being held as the government persisted with its attempts to suppress clerical opposition. One estimate suggested that the regime killed, tortured or exiled at least 600 Iranian clerics during the 1970s alone.

But then in 1977 the atmosphere at the prison suddenly changed, and the attitude of the guards became more sympathetic. 'It happened quite abruptly,' recalled one former Mujahideen prisoner who was held at Evin with some of Khomeini's followers. 'All of a sudden the sadist who had been torturing me on and off for two years disappeared and a new police chief appeared to take charge of us. He was very nice to us and asked us if we'd like some tea, or if we'd like a cigarette. We just couldn't believe it.'[32]

Unknown to the prisoners, the Shah, responding to the arrival of President Jimmy Carter at the White House in early 1977, had ordered his security chiefs to ease the crackdown on political dissent. The Shah fully expected to come under pressure from Washington to improve his human rights record, as he had after President Kennedy's election in the 1960s. He was determined to maintain good relations with America, which was the cornerstone of his foreign policy, and he wanted to remove any pretext Washington might have for criticizing his regime. Amnesty International had recently described him as 'one of the worst violators of human rights in the world', a label he was keen to cast aside. But the genie of popular unrest in Iran was already well and truly out of the bottle. The high-handed manner in which the Shah had introduced one-party rule, while elevating his own status, had managed to alienate virtually every segment of society. The army remained loyal to its king, as did the small circle of trusted advisers who helped him to run the country. But the rest of the country – including the great landowners – had lost faith in him and his increasingly erratic conduct, and seethed at the various injustices perpetrated against them, their families, their friends and their interests.

The Carter administration's clumsy interventions hardly helped the Shah's cause. When Cyrus Vance, Carter's Secretary of State, visited Tehran in May 1977 he declared his satisfaction with the progress the government was making on improving its human rights record. Then in virtually his next breath he announced the administration's approval for the sale of 160 F-16 fighter jets and 7 AWACS, which contained the latest state-of-the-art technology and had not been sold outside NATO. Washington's fundamental misunderstanding of the deep currents of anti-Shah dissatisfaction coursing through the country were epitomized by President Carter when he attended a state banquet in Tehran the following January. In his toast to the Shah, Carter declared that 'Iran, because of the great leadership of the Shah, is an island of stability in one of the most troubled areas of the world.'

If anything it was the opposite, and the widely held perception that the Shah was under pressure from Washington to reform his autocratic style of government saw an explosion of anti-Shah criticism, with newspapers pressing the boundaries of press freedom with inflammatory articles, such as the front page editorial in the leading daily *Kayhan*, asking, 'What is wrong with Iran?', which received 40,000 letters of complaint in return about different aspects of government policy. Previously suppressed political parties reappeared, such as the National Front and Mehdi Barzagan's Liberation Movement of Iran. Iranian lawyers got together and demanded a strict adherence to the law and an end to the regime's special courts, and by October 1977 students were protesting on the campuses on a regular basis.

The Shah was caught between a rock and a hard place. If he sent in the security forces to crack down on the dissent, he risked alienating his backers in Washington. If he allowed the criticism to continue, he risked losing his throne. Intimations of his own mortality also played an important part in his calculations. By 1977 the Shah had come to appreciate that he was seriously ill, and might soon need to give up the throne in favour of his son. During one of his regular meetings with the British and American ambassadors, he informed them he had rejected the military option because he did not believe he could suppress political dissent through military force alone. 'Then, in the first allusion to his ill health, he said he would probably be turning over authority to his son, the crown prince, in the course of the next few years, and after his departure from the scene the young man would not be able to continue to rule by military force.'[33] The Shah therefore determined to establish a democratic political system that would sustain the dynasty after his own departure. But he also nurtured doubts about whether the Carter administration really wanted him to remain in power. He later lamented the fact that the lack of guidance he received from Washington as the political crisis unfolded 'explains everything about the American attitude . . . they wanted me out.'[34]

The Shah's predicament was made worse by the collapse of the economic boom that had been fuelled by spiralling oil prices. As the industrialized economies went into recession, Tehran suffered a dramatic decline in its oil revenues. The country's emerging middle classes, who depended heavily on high levels of government spending for their livelihoods, were left high and dry and became yet another disaffected group calling for political reform. One indication that the country had become a political tinderbox came in August 1977 when the mayor of Tehran sent bulldozers to demolish part of the city's slums to make way for a new highway without bothering to inform the slum-dwellers in advance. On this occasion the residents cast aside their fear of SAVAK and rose up against the authorities, and a number of people were killed in fierce fighting.

Another incident that reflected the mounting political tension was the death of Khomeini's eldest son Mostafa in mysterious circumstances in Iraq on 23 October 1977. In all likelihood

Mostafa died of a heart attack, but such was the febrile atmosphere in Iran that Khomeini's supporters readily believed that he had been killed by SAVAK agents. Rumours circulated that on a trip to Syria and Lebanon a few weeks previously Mostafa had been contacted by two visitors from Iran. They discussed recent events with him and arranged to meet him in Najaf after he had returned. On the night of his death two guests had arrived at his house, but had left without anyone seeing them. Mostafa was found dead the following morning. But neither Khomeini nor Ahmad ever gave any credence to the conspiracy theories. When Khomeini was told of his son's death he simply repeated the Koranic verse, 'We belong to God and to him we shall return.'[35] Mostafa's death nevertheless had the effect of placing Khomeini's name back in the public domain in Iran, and in Qom people flocked to offer their condolences to his elder brother Morteza. Memorial services were held in Tehran where praise for Khomeini was freely voiced. Khomeini wrote a message of thanks to the Iranian people in which he said, 'We are facing a great calamity and should not mention personal tragedies.' Demonstrations started to take place in Qom on a regular basis calling for Khomeini to be allowed to return from exile.

Khomeini had been waiting patiently to make his move, and the growing atmosphere of political tension throughout the course of 1977 led him to conclude the time had come to act. Not only was political dissent on the increase, but Khomeini learnt from his followers who were detained in prison that the fight appeared to have gone out of the regime. 'All the guards wanted to know from us was how they could stop the students from demonstrating,' recalled one former prisoner at Evin. The authorities began the gradual release of political prisoners from the second half of 1977. Initially they attempted to set conditions, such as obtaining an undertaking that the released prisoner would refrain from political activity. 'It was a futile exercise, and the guards knew it,' the prisoner continued. 'As soon as they got out of prison they helped to set up Khomeini's revolutionary committees.' Hashemi Rafsanjani was particularly active during this period, and spent most of his time negotiating with the SAVAK guards over who should be released. 'Rafsanjani was not badly treated in prison towards the end of his imprisonment,' said one of his fellow prisoners. 'He had a good relationship with the guards. He often used to give SAVAK intelligence on what was going on inside Khomeini's movement, and they were grateful for that. In return Rafsanjani was able to call the shots in the prison.'[36]

In December 1977 Khomeini decided to intervene. Morteza Motahhari, one of the few Khomeini activists in Iran who had managed to escape SAVAK's clutches, was instructed to set up an organizational framework that could better coordinate the various clergy-related anti-Shah opposition groups within Iran. The Society of Militant Clergy, which Motahhari founded, became the forerunner of the revolutionary committees that would eventually implement the 1979 Revolution. The Society was just the latest manifestation of the Coalition of Islamic Societies Khomeini had set up in the 1960s before his exile, and had much the same support base. In Tehran, with the help of the *bazaaris*, the Society quickly formed eight branches which set up bases to organize debates, distribute leaflets, recruit local youth, organize strikes and distribute Khomeini's statements and cassette tapes. Khomeini wrote to Motahhari, a white-turbaned scholar whom SAVAK believed was solely engaged with his academic pursuits, urging him to prepare for jihad and committing the movement to the 'dethronement' of the Shah and a total boycott of 'the government of Satan'.

The Shah then chose the worst possible moment to play into Khomeini's hands. On 6 January 1978, still believing that Khomeini was a busted flush, the government-controlled newspaper *Ettela'at* published a scurrilous attack on Khomeini and the clergy. Under the title, 'Iran and Black and Red Imperialism', the article accused the clergy of being 'black reactionaries who were in cahoots with feudalism, imperialism and communism'. But the comments about Khomeini were nothing less than defamation. He was denounced as a foreigner (because his family originally came from India), an agent of the British, a drunkard, and a closet homosexual. Immediately after publication of the article, riots erupted in Qom as students took to the streets, burning *Ettela'at* news-stands and persuading the local bazaars to close down. The students then attacked the local police station, where the police responded with violence, killing several people (including mullahs) and wounding many more.

The controversy over the *Ettela'at* article succeeded in making Khomeini the symbol of the Iranian revolution. During the days that followed Khomeini was able to demonstrate that he had the organizational infrastructure to sustain a serious challenge to the Shah's authority. Also, the fact that Khomeini was the only opposition leader of stature who demanded unequivocally that the Shah had to go meant that he had the support of millions of Iranians who, for one reason or another, had become thoroughly disenchanted with the Shah's regime.

The clashes at Qom quickly escalated into a nationwide anti-Shah campaign, which Khomeini was able to orchestrate from his base in Najaf. In mid-February a demonstration in Tabriz to mark the fortieth day of mourning for the Qom killings resulted in the Shah sending in tanks and helicopter gunships to restore order, which resulted in yet further deaths. The cycle of violence was repeated forty days later in Yazd and Isfahan, where there were violent clashes between Khomeini's supporters and the Shah's security forces. Yet another round of clashes erupted in twenty-four cities the following month in which scores more of Khomeini's supporters were killed and injured. But while the regime fought to contain the demonstrations, the Shah refrained from going on the offensive and launching a nationwide crackdown against the protesters, which only served to give them greater confidence. He also demoralized his own government by instigating a purge of senior government and security officials, including General Nassiri, the head of SAVAK, accusing them of corruption and violence. A fire at a cinema in Abadan in August that killed 477 people further eroded public confidence in the Shah's regime, and the Shah responded by appointing Sharif Emami as the new prime minister.

The more the Shah tried to control the situation, the more Khomeini seized the moment, flooding the country with pamphlets, speeches and cassettes calling unequivocally for the Shah's overthrow. Even when Sharif Emami began to overturn some of the Shah's policies, such as abolishing the 'imperial' calendar and committing the government to multi-party democracy, he was unable to halt the revolutionary momentum that was building inexorably in Khomeini's favour. Yet further blood-letting occurred on 8 September – immediately after the Shah had declared martial law – when hundreds of pro-Khomeini demonstrators were gunned down by the Imperial Guards during a demonstration in Jaleh Square, in south-east Tehran, to mark the end of the Ramadan fast. It was later claimed that the organizers were not aware that martial law had been declared when they arranged the demonstration, and would have cancelled it if they had known. But the ensuing bloodshed meant the day became known as 'Black Friday', and finally closed off any possibility of a compromise between government and opposition.

Anthony Parsons, the British ambassador, met with the Shah soon after Black Friday, and 'was horrified by the change in his appearance and manner. He looked shrunken, his face was yellow and he moved slowly. He seemed exhausted and drained of spirit.'[37] At the meeting the Shah asked plaintively why it was the masses had turned against him after all that he had done for them. The ambassador's reply amounted to a devastating indictment of the Shah's misrule. 'The massive influx into the cities had produced a rootless and discontented proletariat. Many of them were engaged in construction work. They spent their days building houses for the rich and returned at night to shanties or even holes in the ground lined with plastic. Crass materialism at all levels had led to insecurity when the good life had not arrived. It was no wonder in such circumstances that the people had turned to their traditional leaders, the mullahs who had always opposed the Shah . . . Iran had become a land of unfulfilled promises.'[38] Iran was a country ripe for a revolution.

Not only was the Shah incapable of running the country, his medical condition was rapidly deteriorating through cancer, which was affecting his judgement. The following month he made yet another catastrophic error, when he allowed his regime to pressure the Iraqi government to end Khomeini's comfortable exile in Najaf. At first the Iraqis tried to persuade Khomeini to withdraw from politics in return for being allowed to stay in Najaf. But when Khomeini refused, he was asked to leave. His first thought was to move to the neighbouring state of Kuwait which, located at the head of the Gulf, is within easy reach of Iran. But the Kuwaitis refused him permission to enter. Finally, helped by the international network of Iranian exiles whose support he had acquired, Khomeini settled for Paris, a move that proved to be disastrous for the Shah. Suddenly Khomeini had easy access to telephones and transport, which made it easier for him to communicate with his support network in Iran. It now seemed simply a question of time before Khomeini returned to Iran in triumph.

PART TWO

LEGACY

6

The Revolution Unveiled

From the moment Khomeini assumed control of Iran in February 1979 his ambition lay far beyond controlling the destiny of the 60 million Iranians whose uncertain fate now lay in his hands. Khomeini could never allow his spiritual and political aspirations to be restricted by the mere physical limitations of Iran's geographical borders. The radical Islamic philosophy he had developed during decades of study at Iran's leading theological colleges, and later in exile among the Shia diaspora, was aimed at the entire Muslim world, not just Iran. His uncompromising doctrine of Islamic fundamentalism, where all governments were obliged to observe the will of God and base their rule on the strict interpretation of Sharia law, was to be either adapted or imposed throughout the entire Muslim world and beyond. From the Maghreb states of North Africa to Indonesia in South East Asia, from Afghanistan's wild frontiers to the Muslim-dominated suburbs of European cities, Khomeini's vision encompassed the world's 1.25 billion Muslims conducting their lives according to his strict interpretation of God's will and law.

Khomeini was more than aware that he could never achieve these goals merely through the appeal of his reasoning and rhetoric. The vested interests of the West, and the resistance of the autocratic Sunni Muslim regimes that dominated the Middle East, meant that Khomeini would on occasion need to resort to force to achieve his ends. The formation of the Revolutionary Guards in the early days of the Islamic revolution was designed to ensure its radical agenda would in time be exported throughout the Muslim world, as well as protecting Iran's new government from counter-revolutionary attack. Khomeini was prepared to consider the use of any military force at Iran's disposal – including nuclear weapons – to safeguard the sanctity of his Islamic revolution from corruption by the insidious forces of Western secularism, whether in Iran or the wider Islamic world. But before he could devote his energies to exporting his Islamic agenda, Khomeini's first priority was to secure the triumph of his own revolution in Iran.

The summary executions that Khomeini authorized the founder members of the Revolutionary Guards to conduct on the roof of Refah School in mid-February was just the beginning of a nationwide purge that would see thousands of those deemed to be 'enemies of the Islamic revolution' sent to their deaths. Khomeini had moved quickly to consolidate his own political position with the appointment of Mehdi Bazargan as his first prime minister just five days after his return from Paris. He was mindful of the Shah's successful 1953 tactic of abandoning the country while the provisional government struggled to restore order, and then returning once the danger had passed. But this time there was to be no repetition. The failure of the Shah's armed forces to reassert their authority following the uprising of junior ranks in Khomeini's favour in early February, which was followed by the inevitable resignation on 11 February of Shapour Bakhtiar, the Shah's last prime minister, meant that Khomeini's claim to leadership of the country was uncontested. Bazargan, who at seventy-five was nearly Khomeini's direct contemporary, was a veteran of the National Front's ill-fated pro-democracy campaign in the 1950s under Mosaddeq, whose anti-Shah credentials made him the ideal candidate to oversee a transitional government. 'There was a lengthy discussion in the Revolutionary Council about the appointment of prime minister,' the mild-mannered Barzargan later recalled. 'Since no other name came to mind,

the gentlemen proposed me as the most suitable candidate.'
Khomeini accepted the proposal, remarking, 'You put my mind
at rest. It was a good choice, which the two sides should be
content with.'[1] By which Khomeini meant the nationalists and
the clergy, the two most important political constituencies
whose different political agendas needed to be reconciled if the
revolution were to succeed.

The Revolutionary Council, which was comprised of a
mixture of clerical and secular Khomeini supporters, drew up
a decree of appointment, which was signed by Khomeini and
read out by Rafsanjani. It stated that Bazargan's duties as the
country's provisional prime minister were, namely: to get the
government administration and the economy functioning again
after more than a year of strikes and disruption, and to prepare
the ground for the Islamic Republic that would follow.[2] Bazargan was an experienced politician who had spent his entire
political career campaigning for democracy and constitutional
rule. He was prepared to accept the challenge of steering the
country as it made the difficult journey from monarchical
dictatorship to the uncharted territory of an Islamic Republic.
A devout Muslim, he believed that Iran's future political
development lay in reconciling religious faith to political activism, and Islam to nationalism.

Bazargan was keen to establish the rule of law and respect
for human rights, but his quasi-liberal credentials soon put him
at odds with Khomeini and his followers, who were more
concerned with consolidating the gains of their exclusively
Islamic revolution. Bazargan himself acknowledged the difference in style between himself and the ayatollah when he
addressed an audience at Tehran University shortly after his
appointment. 'Don't expect me to act in the manner of Khomeini who, head down, moves ahead like a bulldozer, crushing
rocks, roots and stones in his path. I am a delicate passenger
car and must ride on a smooth asphalted road.'[3] Bazargan duly
formed a cabinet to take on the daunting task of restoring

order to the country having informed Khomeini and the
Revolutionary Council that he was a 'stickler' for order and
regulations. 'I avoid haste and extremes. I am given to careful
study and gradualism. I was this way in the past and will not
change my approach in the future.'[4] Bazargan's cabinet consisted of men from Iran's new middle class and did not include
any clerics, and his government took control of the administration, the police and the remnants of the army. But from the
outset the role of Bazargan's government was secondary to that
of Khomeini's Revolutionary Council, the identity of whose
members was not disclosed, and the precedent – which continues to this day – was set whereby Iran's political rulers were
subservient to the wishes of the religious elite.

Bazargan was powerless to change this arrangement because
Khomeini's widespread popularity during the first few weeks
after his return from Paris made him virtually untouchable in
the eyes of Iran's adoring public. He was hailed as a messianic
figure who had accomplished the astonishing feat of routing
the omnipotent Shah and his powerful backers in the United
States. The constant stream of propaganda that the Iranian
masses had been fed by Khomeini and his supporters was filled
with powerful religious imagery, and it did not take a great
leap of imagination on the part of the throngs of uneducated
Iranian peasants who flocked to the capital to see Khomeini as
a new Moses throwing out the corrupt Pharaoh. Khomeini had
made especially good use of his four-month sojourn at Neuphle-
le-Château, where his access to modern communications had
enabled him to raise his international profile to a level that
had not been possible when he was in Najaf. He gave over 120
interviews to a wide range of international media during his
four months in Paris, sometimes at the rate of five or six a day,
which helped to increase his stature in Iran as a credible
opposition leader and gained the Iranian opposition movement
the world's sympathy and acceptance.[5]

The excellent air and telecommunications links between

Tehran and Paris enabled him to maintain much closer links with the underground network of Islamic sympathizers that had developed in Iran under such figures as Motahhari, Beheshti and Rafsanjani. Every day Khomeini's latest declarations were telephoned through to Tehran, where they were taped, transcribed and circulated throughout the country, and a constant stream of visitors made their way from Tehran to Paris to discuss the political drama unfolding in Iran. It was in Paris that Khomeini was able to assume leadership of the opposition movement, but it was in Tehran that he made it count.

With the government in his pocket Khomeini's biggest challenge was to control the hundreds of revolutionary *komitehs*, or committees, that had sprung up throughout the country during the early weeks of the new regime. For the most part the *komiteh*s consisted of young, idealistic radicals who, empowered by their overthrow of the Shah and their possession of weapons, took it upon themselves to fill the vacuum created by the absence of an effective state-controlled security apparatus. Whether Marxist, Islamic Marxist or Islamic, many of these *komiteh*s were a law unto themselves which were willing to initiate their own edicts, irrespective of the wishes of their political masters.[6] The superior organization and discipline of Khomeini's network gave him a distinct advantage over the other groups, which were mainly linked to the Marxist Fedayeen groups that had waged a guerrilla war against the Shah's regime. In Tehran alone, it was estimated there were 1,500 revolutionary *komitehs* and, as Bazargan ruefully remarked on taking office, 'the committees are everywhere, and no one knows how many exist, not even the Imam himself.'[7] The fact that the committees were constantly bickering among themselves over issues of jurisdiction, legitimacy and the application of revolutionary justice seriously jeopardized the success of Khomeini's revolution, particularly as there was a deepening gulf in the various interpretations of Islamic law and Marxist doctrine.

Khomeini needed to exert his authority if he was to prevent the revolution from running out of control. In his message to the nation on 13 February he urged people to hand in their weapons. 'You should take note that the sale of arms is prohibited by our religion,' declared Khomeini. 'Uproar should be avoided. The people must not think that now they have won victory they should disturb public peace, they should do this or that. You should act with order, discipline, with humanity, in the Islamic spirit.'[8] But not even Khomeini's stature could stem the tide of tit-for-tat killings, as people took revenge on former regime members, and rival groups engaged in running street battles. A few days later the government berated 'unnecessary shooting by individuals who are using their weapons as toys' and implored individuals to refrain from making threatening phone calls to former regime members who had 'made certain errors'. Yet another indication of the country's rapid descent into lawlessness came on 14 February when groups of demonstrators briefly occupied the American embassy, holding hostage the ambassador, seventy diplomatic staff and twenty US Marines. An international crisis was averted only by the intervention of Bazargan's government with Khomeini's full backing.

The executions at Refah School were Khomeini's way of demonstrating who was in charge and bringing the fractious revolutionary groups to their senses. The execution of the four generals – including General Nassiri, the Shah's hardline security chief – on the evening of 15 February was the start of a succession of executions that continued non-stop for several weeks of former members of the Shah's regime. The bloodletting caused fierce division within the provisional government, with Khomeini arguing that a degree of bloodletting was necessary to satiate the public's desire for revenge after decades of Pahlavi repression. But Bazargan and the rest of the cabinet, who had publicly committed themselves to restoring the rule of law, were horrified, and tried to rein in the Islamic com-

mittees' penchant for summary justice. The protests did succeed in causing the executions to be halted for a three-week
spell from mid-March, but they resumed again with the
execution of the Shah's longest-serving prime minister, the
urbane and cultured Amir-Abbas Hoveyda.

Hoveyda's death in particular caused an international outcry, not least because, when in office, he had tried to curb the
Shah's autocratic streak, and had on occasion intervened to
spare the lives of Islamic militants sentenced to death by the
Shah's regime. Bazargan tried to intervene and secure Hoveyda
a proper judicial trial, but was outmanoeuvred by Sadeq
Khalkhali, the Robespierre of Khomeini's revolution, who personally took charge of Hoveyda's case.

In an interview with the BBC some years later, Khalkhali
proudly related how he had gone to the prison where Hoveyda
was being held (he had originally been arrested – together with
General Nassiri – by the Shah in one of his last attempts to
placate the mounting popular unrest). After arranging for
Hoveyda to have a simple lunch of rice and beans, 'I ordered
the prison doors to be closed, then I put all the phones inside
the fridge and locked them so that no news would leak out.'
Hoveyda was brought before Khalkhali's kangaroo court and
spent the next two and a half hours pleading for his life.
According to Khalkhali, Hoveyda's basic argument was that
'I was prime minister in a system and I was powerless. The
system should be blamed for mistakes and shortcomings, not
the individual.' But Khalkhali dismissed Hoveyda's arguments,
and replied that in the thirteen years he had served as prime
minister 'many things occurred against the interest of Iran and
in favour of imperialism'. He claimed Hoveyda had been
responsible for giving the United States 'free oil' during the
Vietnam War, and had supplied Israel with oil products and
food during the 1973 Yom Kippur War. Hoveyda was found
guilty of 'corruption on Earth', and sentenced to death.[9] Khalkhali then told Hoveyda to write his will, and when that was

completed, the former prime minister was led outside and immediately executed by firing squad. That evening pictures of Hoveyda's corpse lying in the Tehran mortuary, surrounded by smiling, gun-toting Islamic revolutionaries, was broadcast on state television.

The execution of Hoveyda, together with the other ad hoc killings taking place in towns and cities throughout the country, graphically illustrated the reality of Khomeini's Islamic revolution. Khalkhali, who appeared to take a pathological delight in his role as Khomeini's judicial enforcer, took his orders directly from the Imam and made sure his wishes were fully implemented. So far as Khomeini was concerned, Hoveyda's execution was the settling of an old score that went back to 1967, when Khomeini had sent the prime minister an open letter from exile in Iraq threatening him with 'the people's rage' for supporting Israel during the Six Day War, the Shah's subservience to the United States and undermining Islam and the clergy. For all the talk of democracy and the rule of law, Khomeini and his followers had no qualms about waging a bloody vendetta against the former regime and anyone associated with it.

Even so the provisional government felt obliged to justify its actions, and a statement broadcast on Tehran Radio the day after Hoveyda's death claimed the executions were necessary 'to destroy and kill evil . . . to execute evildoers is the great mission of Muslims in order to realize the perfection of nature and society.'[10] Driven by Khalkhali's determination to liquidate 'the enemies of the revolution', hundreds more former regime members – civil servants, police chiefs, military officers and politicians – were paraded before Khomeini's firing squads. Inspired by the fanaticism of 'judge blood', revolutionary komitehs cooperated with newly formed units of the Revolutionary Guards to take the law into their own hands. Throughout the country the merest suggestion that an individual might have worked for SAVAK was sufficient to have them paraded before a 'court' and sentenced to death. Nor was the slaughter solely the work of committees affiliated with Khomeini's cause. Groups of all political persuasions indulged in retribution, settling old scores which had little or nothing to do with revolutionary or counter-revolutionary activity.

With the country on the brink of total anarchy, Khomeini struggled to maintain control. While millions of Iranians celebrated what became known as the 'Spring of Freedom', Khomeini and the Revolutionary Council intensified their efforts to make sure they did not lose control of the streets to rival Marxist and left-wing guerrilla groups, such as the Muhajideen-e Khalq and the Fedayeen. To start with, Khomeini and his followers relied heavily on organized gangs of strong-arm thugs known as Hizbollah, the descendants of the militant Islamic group of the same name that had assassinated Iranian Prime Minister Mansur in 1965. Khomeini had managed to maintain links with Hizbollah's supporters and sympathizers and other radical Islamic groups, such as the Society of Militant Clergy, despite the close attention of SAVAK's agents and informers. During the revolution Hizbollah supporters attacked rival demonstrators who challenged Khomeini's position, the offices of newspapers critical of the direction in which the post-revolutionary government was moving, and the premises of opposition groups. Hizbollah's activities were directly controlled by Khomeini and his inner circle and were designed to frustrate attempts by the better-organized left-wing groups to seize control of the revolution.[11]

The organization in which Khomeini took the closest interest, though, was the Revolutionary Guards, or Pasdaran, whose formation Khomeini had authorized at the Refah School meeting shortly after his return. Khomeini had identified the need for some form of Islamic paramilitary organization while he was still in Paris. In his speeches he often made reference to the fact that Iran needed 'an Islamic Army', without going into much detail. He entrusted Ibrahim Yazdi, one of his key advisers at Neauphle-le-Château, with responsibility for liaising with the underground movement in Iran headed by Ayatollah Mohammed Beheshti, another staunch Khomeini loyalist. Once back in Tehran Khomeini wasted no time putting his plan into action, and the newly formed Guards' primary mission was 'to protect the revolution from destructive forces and counter-revolutionaries'. From their inception the Guards were responsible directly to the Revolutionary Council, and were given a wide degree of independence – including their own budget – and soon acquired supreme administrative and legislative authority.

The importance of the Revolutionary Guards to the success of the Islamic revolution was immediately recognized by Khomeini's inner circle, and there was intense competition among the leading mullahs to head the new organization, including Mohammed Yazdi, Khomeini's chief adviser in Paris who had become the deputy prime minister for revolutionary affairs. Overall control of the Guards was initially entrusted by Khomeini to a moderate religious leader, Ayatollah Hasan Lahuti. But other leading revolutionary figures sought to influence the Guards' development, including Rafsanjani, who had proved himself to be one of Khomeini's most effective behind-the-scenes organizers in the build-up to the revolution. Rafsanjani was the main driving force behind the Guards' original foundation, and was initially put in charge of military training. From the outset the organization charged with protecting the revolution had an international dimension, and drew heavily on the hundreds of young Islamic militants who had passed through guerrilla training camps in Lebanon.

The experience of combat-trained Islamic militants such as Mostafa Chamran – the organizer of the Refah School firing squads – proved invaluable in turning the Guards into an effective paramilitary organization. Chamran was an iconic figure in the Guards' early development and his background was typical of many of the organization's early recruits. Born in Tehran in 1932, Chamran undertook his higher education at the University of California where he studied Electrical Engineering and Computer Sciences in the 1960s. A convert to Khomeini's radical Islamic philosophy in the 1970s, he went to southern Lebanon at the start of the Lebanese civil war to help defend the country's Shia community, and helped to set up the Shia Muslim Amal militia in southern Lebanon, the forerunner of Hizbollah. The creation of Amal in the mid-1970s, which was set up to enable the Shia of southern Lebanon to defend themselves against Israel, was the brainchild of Musa al-Sadr, the militant Iranian-born Shia cleric whom Khomeini had befriended while in exile in Najaf. Chamran, who was killed in action during the Iran–Iraq War in 1981, remained a close confidant of Khomeini, and his contribution to the Guards was later rewarded with his appointment as defence minister.

Another pivotal figure in the formation of the Revolutionary Guards was Mohsen Rafiqdost, the wealthy Tehran *bazaari* who had driven Khomeini on his triumphant parade through the capital. Like Chamran, Rafiqdost, who came from an influential Tehran *bazaari* family, was an early convert to Khomeini's radical Islamic creed. He was a key figure in the resistance movement against the Shah during the mid-1970s and spent a year training in southern Lebanon. Like Rafsanjani, he was eventually captured and imprisoned by SAVAK, and was severely tortured. Related to Rafsanjani by marriage, Rafiqdost became a prominent figure in the development of the Guards, and was later rewarded for his efforts with several senior positions in the post-revolution government. He was also heavily implicated in the 1983 suicide truck bombing of the American marine base in Beirut that killed 241 people. Other founder members of the Revolutionary Guards who would later occupy key positions in the regime were Javed Mansuri, who in 2008 became Iran's ambassador to China, and Mohsen Rezai, who became the Revolutionary Guards' longest-serving commander.

Khomeini did not control the Guards' day-to-day activities, but merely made statements setting out policy and left it to the Guards' commanders to interpret how his intentions might best be implemented. In the early stages he also took little interest in the Guards' recruitment, so long as there were sufficient numbers to make it an effective group. Many of the Guards' early commanders were drawn from an eclectic group of militant Islamic organizations who were broadly supportive of Khomeini's aims. But only scant attention was paid at this time to the level of their support and dedication to Khomeini's cause, as the pressing need was to get the Guards up and running and capable of presenting effective resistance to the competing revolutionary groups. While some of the recruits were trained by Amal in Lebanon, others had benefited from the training provided by Yasser Arafat's Palestine Liberation Organisation in Lebanon, part of the arrangement Khomeini negotiated with Arafat in Najaf. Some of the more fanatical Guards leaders, such as Chamran and Rafiqdost, who opposed the secularism of Arafat's PLO, wanted only to recruit those trained by Shia Muslim militias, and sought to place strict entry conditions. 'Chamran and his associates believed that anyone who was not totally devoted to Khomeini and his radical philosophy should be excluded from membership of the Revolutionary Guards,' said a former member of the Guards. 'If the Guards were to be the guardians of the revolution, they argued, then only those who fully supported its objectives should be allowed membership.'[12]

The formation of the Guards was officially confirmed by a decree Khomeini passed on 5 May, and by the spring of 1979 their total strength was estimated at 4,000 to 6,000. When they staged their first parade in Tehran in the summer of 1979 they looked a distinctly unimpressive outfit. But the constant demands of policing the revolution, and their involvement in suppressing provincial rebellions later in the year, provided them with invaluable experience, and it was not long before they were firmly established as the pre-eminent guardians of Khomeini's Islamic revolution, both at home and abroad. By late 1979 they had grown in number to about 30,000. Khomeini paid a personal tribute to the seminal role the Guards had played in securing the revolution when he declared in a speech in August, 'If the Revolutionary Guards did not exist, the country would not exist. The Revolutionary Guards are very dear to me. I look to you. You have no background apart from an Islamic one. I am very thankful to all of you.'[13]

*

Khomeini had put in place an effective security structure to protect the revolution, and had taken control of the government. His next move was to hold a referendum where the people would have the opportunity to decide what kind of government they would like to govern them in future. In essence the referendum, which was held in March, offered the electorate a choice between a monarchy and a republic. The enduring hostility most Iranians felt towards the monarchy meant that the result was a foregone conclusion, even if the details of what kind of republic might replace the Pahlavi dynasty had yet to be fleshed out. There was much debate in the Iranian press as to whether or not Iran should become a democratic or Islamic republic. While Khomeini and his supporters maintained a discreet silence as to their true intentions regarding an Islamic republic, the ayatollah ended any discussion of Iran becoming a democratic republic when he declared, 'What the nation wants is an Islamic republic: not just a republic, not a democratic republic, not a democratic Islamic republic. Do not use this term "democratic". That is western style.'[14] When the referendum was held at the end of the March it was boycotted by many of the pro-democracy parties. Consequently the result declared on 31 March showed that 98 per cent of the country had voted in favour of the abolition of the monarchy and the establishment of an Islamic republic.

A few weeks before the referendum was held Khomeini left Tehran to return to Qom, the first time he had seen his family home for fifteen years. His arrival in Qom was taken by many of his supporters to be the signal that Khomeini, having achieved his goal of overthrowing the Shah, would withdraw from public life and seek to return to his former life of study and teaching. However much the 76-year-old Khomeini might have yearned for a return to private life, though, the forces unleashed by the Shah's overthrow and the collapse of the government meant this was entirely unrealistic. In the few weeks since his return to Iran he had become not just the leader of the revolution: he was the revolution. He had achieved almost mythical status amongst the people, and even experienced politicians such as Bazargan thought of him as a 'saint', an image that Khomeini did not exactly seek to dispel. So far as the masses were concerned, he was the man who had single-handedly triumphed over the forces of darkness and freed the country so that a new generation could take over the reins of government.

Just how much Khomeini intended to withdraw from public life is a matter of dispute. He had certainly handed control of the day-to-day administration of the country to Bazargan and the other members of the provisional government. But all of them owed their positions to the Ayatollah, without whom they were isolated individuals with no organized support base. And having devoted the latter years of his life to campaigning for the creation of an Islamic state, it is unlikely he was prepared to give the provisional government a free hand in moulding the country's future government. As Ibrahim Yazdi, Khomeini's close ally who had become the provisional government's foreign minister, remarked when Khomeini left for Qom, 'the revolution consisted of one man, the Imam, and the

millions of his followers, with nothing in between.'[15] Consequently, when Khomeini relocated to Qom, Tehran simply
followed after him. For the nine months that Khomeini
remained in the shrine city it became the country's unofficial
capital, with politicians and officials making their way across
the dusty desert to consult with him on all the important
decisions.

Much of Khomeini's time at Qom was taken up with discussions over the proposed new constitution – the next stage
towards securing the revolution following the abolition of the
monarchy. A rough draft of a new constitution had been drawn
up while Khomeini was still living in Paris by a group of liberal
Islamists, which was kept under wraps until he had returned
to Iran. The draft was handed over to the newly established
Revolutionary Council after Khomeini's return, and then passed
on to a committee set up by Bazargan's Freedom Movement.
The final document made no mention of Khomeini's highly contentious concept of *velayat-e faqih*, where supreme authority
for running the country would be invested in the country's
most revered religious figure. An early draft of the proposed
constitution was finally unveiled in mid-June, and the ensuing
debate very quickly developed into a struggle between Khomeini and his disciples, who were determined to implement his
concept of *velayat-e faqih*, and the secularists around Bazargan
who sought to draw up a more secular constitution.

Although Khomeini wanted to transform Iranian society
and establish an Islamic state based on Sharia rule, he still had
only a vague notion of the kind of government he would need
to create for this purpose, and as to how he himself would fit
into the new arrangement. He did not want to be a ruler per
se, nor could he simply become a private citizen. One solution
was that he should become a kind of arbiter, whose judgement
and guidance was sought on important decisions and matters
and policy, but who would not be involved in their day-to-day
administration and application. Many of Khomeini's ideas on

Islamic government derived from the seventh-century Islamic community the Prophet had established in Saudi Arabia, and were therefore simplistic, and not suited to the administration of a modern, twentieth-century state. Khomeini's view was that the government should undertake the traditional duties of protecting Islam, defending the country's borders, administering justice and collecting taxes, but otherwise he had little understanding or knowledge of the complex bureaucratic structures needed for a country to function efficiently.

Barzagan, on the other hand, talked about creating a Democratic Islamic Republic, and still clung to the hope that the new government could be modelled on Charles de Gaulle's Fifth Republic. But Bazargan's provisional government struggled to compete with the stranglehold Khomeini's shadow clerical government had over the country. The Revolutionary Council and the Islamic Republican Party, which had been set up by Ayatollah Mohammed Beheshti to contest any future elections, meant that Bazargan's options were limited. 'In theory, the government is in charge; but, in reality, it is Khomeini who is in charge,' lamented Bazargan. 'He with his Revolutionary Council, his revolutionary *komitehs*, and his relationship with the masses . . . They put a knife in my hands, but it's a knife with only a handle. Others are holding the blade.'[16]

When elections were held in August to appoint the Assembly of Experts, the seventy-three-man body responsible for drafting the new constitution, Khomeini's Republican Party won an overwhelming majority of seats. More than fifty of those elected were directly sponsored by Khomeini's party, giving him the final say on the drafting process for the Islamic constitution. When the Assembly convened on 18 August to begin work, Khomeini personally set the parameters for debate, declaring the final document must be 'one hundred per cent Islamic', and stating that 'discussion of proposals contrary to Islam lies outside the scope of its mandate'. Even so, Bazargan managed to inject some vestige of democratic government into the document, such as granting the general electorate – defined as all adults including women – the authority to elect the president, the Majlis, the provincial and local councils as well as the Assembly of Experts. But these were token gestures, as the final document stipulated that the president, who was to be elected every four years and was restricted to serving two terms, would be 'the highest official authority after the Supreme Leader'. The Supreme Leader, of course, would be Khomeini, a role specially created to enable him to lead the country without having day-to-day responsibility for governing it.

The powers entrusted to the Supreme Leader in the constitution's final draft compare favourably to those claimed by Europe's fascist dictators, with the exception that Khomeini had the added bonus of claiming divine inspiration. All the principles for Islamic government set out in Khomeini's *velayat-e faqih* blueprint for fundamentalist rule, contained in the book 'Islamic Government' he had published in Najaf, found their way into the new constitution. Not only was Khomeini declared Supreme Leader for life, but his unique position as the spiritual guardian of the revolution was confirmed through the constitution's recognition of his status as the 'Imam of the Muslim Umma', the prophet of the entire Muslim world. Never before in the history of Shia Islam – or any other form of Islam, for that matter – had this sacred title, with its connotations of infallibility, been bestowed upon a living person. The document stipulated that the new constitution was to remain in force until the return of the Mahdi, whose manifestation upon earth the faithful believe will herald the end of the world. On Khomeini's death the Assembly of Experts could either replace him with one paramount religious figure or, if no such person emerged, then with a Council of Leadership formed of three or five senior ayatollahs.

The authority devolved on the Supreme Leader was as much temporal as it was spiritual. Some of the responsibilities he acquired in the 175-clause document were vague: he could 'determine the interests of Islam, set guidelines for the Islamic Republic, supervise policy implementation and mediate between the executive, legislative and judiciary'. Others were more specific. He could dismiss presidents, as well as vet candidates for high office. He was to be the nation's commander-in-chief, with the power to declare war and peace, mobilize the armed forces, appoint their commanders and convene a national security council. He had the right to appoint senior officials across a broad range of national institutions, including the director of the national television network and the editors of the country's two leading newspapers, *Ettela'at* and *Kayhan*. The appointment of the country's chief justice, as well as lower court judges, were in his gift, as were appointments to the newly formed Guardian Council, which had the power to veto bills deemed to be contrary to either the spirit of the constitution or Sharia. The Council also had the power to vet candidates running for public office – including the Majlis.

This new, all-powerful position was entirely Khomeini's creation, and one that he had cleverly sought to conceal from the wider Iranian public during his rise to power. Most Iranians were unclear how the new constitutional arrangement would work in practice, and only a few fully understood and approved of the all-encompassing authority that would be invested in one man. 'Khomeini was determined to create this all-powerful position for himself because, if it was approved, it meant the ayatollahs were free to do anything they wanted,' a former revolutionary activist explained. 'It meant there could be a complete break with the past, and the new regime would not be impeded by any obligations previous governments had undertaken.'[17]

Another key function of the Supreme Leader was the task of appointing the commander of the Revolutionary Guards, whose role as the guardians of the revolution – both at home and abroad – was set out in the constitution's preamble. Under the heading 'An Ideological Army' the constitution stated that the 'Islamic Revolutionary Guards Corp are to be organized in conformity' with the principles of the Islamic revolution. 'They will be responsible not only for guarding and preserving the frontiers of the country, but also for fulfilling the ideological mission of jihad in God's way; that is, extending the sovereignty of God's law throughout the world (this in accordance with the Koranic verse 8.6: 'Prepare against them whatever force you are able to muster, and strings of horses, striking fear into the enemy of God and your enemy, and others besides them'.

The Guards' constitutional role in protecting and exporting Iran's Islamic revolution was included at Khomeini's personal insistence, and he took seriously his obligation to appoint the organization's commander, which was reflected in the calibre of people selected for a position that acquired increasing importance in the new governmental structure. Ayatollah Hasan Lahuti, the Guards' first commander, was followed first by Hashemi Rafsanjani and then by Ali Khamenei, both of whom later served as presidents of Iran. Another crucial role assigned to the Guards by the constitution was the requirement – also contained in the preamble under the heading 'The Form of Government in Islam' – to provide 'the necessary basis for ensuring the continuation of the Revolution at home and abroad. In particular . . . the Constitution will strive with other Islamic and popular movements to prepare the way for the formation of a single world community and to assure the continuation of the struggle for the liberation of all deprived and oppressed peoples in the world.'

The new constitution left no one in any doubt that Khomeini's ambition for his Islamic fundamentalist agenda lay far beyond the borders of Iran. 'Exporting the revolution throughout the Islamic world helped to justify the regime's existence, because it meant Iran was committed to a permanent state of revolution,' said one former Khomeini supporter. 'The fact that the Revolutionary Guards had a constitutional responsibility to export the revolution meant they had a mandate to interfere in the affairs of other nations, such as Lebanon, Iraq and Afghanistan, to name but a few. The Islamic republic assumed responsibility for the reunification of the Islamic world – so far as the revolution is concerned, Islam has no boundaries. The Revolutionary Guards were central to Khomeini's dream of claiming leadership of the entire Islamic world. Without the Revolutionary Guards Khomeini would have found it very hard to survive in power.'[18]

Khomeini was unapologetic about this unprecedented power grab, which gave him authority and jurisdiction far beyond any of the shahs' wildest ambitions. Even at the height of their megalomania the shahs had never succeeded in claiming ownership of the nation's souls. But Khomeini's vision for the perfect Islamic nation did not distinguish between government and religion, politics and faith, and he argued that the new constitution did not contradict the people's desire for democracy because 'the people love the clergy, have faith in the clergy and want to be guided by the clergy . . . It is right that the supreme religious authority should oversee the work of the president and other state officials to make sure that they don't make mistakes or go against the law and the Koran.'[19] These comments were made in an interview Khomeini gave to the redoubtable Italian journalist Orianna Fallaci in October 1979 at his home in Qom while negotiations over the constitution's final draft were still underway. It was only the second interview Khomeini had granted to the Western media since returning from exile, and he chose Fallaci because he remembered the torrid time she had given the Shah when she interviewed him in 1973 over his appalling human rights record. Fallaci said she was impressed by Khomeini's 'great dignity and splendid bearing – it was the first time that I have ever felt charisma,' she said afterwards – but that did not prevent the ayatollah from finding himself on the receiving end of her acerbic tongue.

To show Khomeini respect, Fallaci dressed in a chador, the traditional floor-length black veil the regime required all women to wear, on the grounds that 'I don't wear blue jeans to interview the Pope.' But the chador soon became the subject of a heated exchange with Khomeini when Fallaci suggested that the chador was symbolic of the segregation into which women had been cast by the revolution. 'They had to take a dip apart [from men] in their chadors,' she complained. 'By the way, how do you swim in a chador?' 'Our customs are none of your business,' Khomeini replied testily. 'If you do not like Islamic dress, you're not obliged to wear it because Islamic dress is for good and proper young women.' To which the spirited Fallaci replied, 'That's very kind of you. And since you said so, I'm going to take off this stupid, medieval rag now.' As she did so, Khomeini, according to Fallaci's account, got up 'like a young cat' and left the room without saying a word.[20]

Khomeini's efforts to mould the constitution to his liking as the details became known were not without their critics. Two of the most prominent anti-Shah political movements that predated the revolution, the National Front and Bazargan's Freedom Movement, both sought a more Western-style parliamentary system with strict limitations imposed on the power of president. The left-wing parties, such as the Communist Tudeh party and the Mujahideen-e Khalq, were more inclined to support the restrictions on individual liberty so long as the government took firm action to curb foreign influence and undertook a radical redistribution of the nation's wealth. The most challenging opposition to Khomeini's campaign to implement his extreme form of Islamic government, however, came from Grand Ayatollah Kazem Shariatmadari, his chief religious rival at Qom. A Shia cleric steeped in traditional Shia learning, Shariatmadari was deeply sceptical of the claims made by Khomeini's concept of *velayat-e faqih*. He took issue with Khomeini's declaration that a true Islamic state could only be created if it were administered by a supreme religious figure, and his supporters argued strongly at the Assembly of Experts that the notion of appointing an all-powerful Islamic jurist to oversee the country conflicted with the principle of popular sovereignty. Others argued that making religious authority vulnerable to the criticism normally directed at politicians would spell 'the beginning of the decline of Islam'.[21] The traditional Shia clergy saw no place for Islam in the affairs of the state. All they required was that the government recognize Islam as the national religion, and observe the customs and culture of Islamic tradition.

Not all the opposition to Khomeini's agenda was peaceful. In the spring an anti-clerical Islamist group called Forqan launched a campaign of assassination against Khomeini's close supporters. Among those gunned down was Morteza Motahhari, Khomeini's long-standing confidant who had been appointed chairman of the Revolutionary Council and was the ayatollah's closest adviser among the clergy. Khomeini was broken-hearted by the loss of the man he called 'my dearest son' and 'the fruit of my life', and at the memorial service he held for Motahhari at the Feizeyeh school at Qom he sat clutching his handkerchief, sobbing and sometimes crying out loudly for his friend.[22]

The bitterness of the opposition to his constitutional proposals only served to stiffen Khomeini's resolve. 'We thought we were dealing with human beings. It is evident we are not,' he declared in a speech in August. 'We are dealing with wild animals. We will not tolerate them anymore.'[23] He rejected the suggestion that defendants should have open trials and have proper legal representation as a reflection of 'the Western sickness among us', and declared that those on trial were criminals, and 'criminals should not be tried, they should be killed'.[24] The significant majority he enjoyed at the Assembly of Experts meant that his supporters were able to defeat comfortably most opposition amendments, particularly those concerning the all important article 5, which implemented Khomeini's *velayat-e faqih* by conferring 'the vice-regency and the leadership of the nation' on a just, pious, courageous and capable jurist – such as Khomeini. Even suggestions that this provision should only last for Khomeini's lifetime were dismissed by Mohammed Beheshti, who chaired the key meetings and was charged by Khomeini with ensuring the final draft reflected his wishes.

On the streets, meanwhile, Khomeini continued to rely on the muscle of Iran's Hizbollahis, the partisans of the Party of God headed by Hadi Ghaffari. Their rallying cry: 'Only one party – of Allah: only one leader – Ruhollah' resonated throughout the country as they targeted any group deemed to oppose Khomeini's wishes. The Hizbollah gangs became known more colloquially as *chomaqdars*, the club wielders, because of their proficiency with the clubs they used to break up rival political gatherings.[25] In August a number of popular newspapers which reflected the views of the various political and ethnic groups that felt disenfranchised were closed down by the Hizbollahis. When demonstrations were organized to protest at the closure of the newspapers, they were violently attacked by the Hizbollahis. Ghaffari, the Hizbollah leader and a founder member of the Revolutionary Guards, orchestrated attacks against the headquarters of left-wing groups, who were forced into hiding.

The only person who seemed to stand a realistic chance of blocking the creation of the most uncompromising and dictatorial Islamic regime in world history was the provisional prime minister, Mehdi Bazargan. Despite being assailed from all sides over the course and conduct of the revolution, Bazargan still managed to put up a creditable rearguard action to thwart Khomeini's designs. Bazargan had established a working relationship with Khomeini, and once a week travelled to Qom with his cabinet to discuss key issues. In May he managed to get Khomeini to impose restrictions on the number of summary executions being carried out by the revolutionary courts, and in July he secured a general amnesty for all former members of the regime, although this did little to interrupt the bloodletting of Khalkhali, who applied the catch-all charge of 'sowing corruption on earth' against the regime's opponents to keep the revolutionary firing squads fully occupied.

By October Bazargan felt sufficiently emboldened to put his name to a memorandum addressed to Khomeini asking for the Assembly of Experts to be dissolved on the grounds that the original draft constitution – based on Bazargan's ideal of France's Fifth Republic – had been revised beyond recognition. Supported by Grand Ayatollah Shariatmadari, Bazargan went so far as to describe the Assembly's revamped constitution as 'a revolution against the revolution' and threatened to publish his original draft which, had it been made public, may well have proved the more popular version. Shariatmadari's support was particularly troubling for Khomeini, as he was the only cleric of comparable religious stature, and he was not afraid to speak out against the excesses of Khomeini's revolution. He earned a harsh reprimand from Khomeini when he received a delegation of university professors at Qom and sympathized with their complaints about public whippings and executions, 'possibly even of pregnant women, 12-year-old children and 90-year-old men'. One of Khomeini's closest disciples later claimed that Bazargan and Shariatmadari had been 'plotting' to eliminate the Assembly of Experts and undo the entire Islamic revolution.[26]

Whatever hopes Bazargan and Shariatmadari had of heading off Khomeini's Islamic autocracy were dashed in late October when President Carter, against the advice of his senior officials, granted the Shah permission to receive urgent medical treatment for his cancer in the United States. Since fleeing the country in January, the Shah had become a sad and somewhat dejected figure as he moved from one country to another seeking refuge. Having first settled in Egypt, he subsequently lived in Morocco, the Bahamas and Mexico before his cancer became so bad that he required top quality medical care. The timing of the Carter administration's decision could not have come at a worse time for Bazargan, who had embarked on the highly risky strategy of seeking to normalize relations between revolutionary Iran and the United States.

Bazargan had maintained relations with American diplomats since before the revolution, and had many reasons for wanting to develop a constructive relationship. Iran's military relied heavily on the United States for spare parts, which were in desperately short supply after the convulsions of the revolution. He was also concerned about the Soviet Union's intentions towards Tehran, and suspected that Moscow was working with Saddam Hussein, Iraq's newly installed dictator, to assist rebel Kurds in Iran. Bazargan believed he had the support of Khomeini and the Revolutionary Council in seeking to open a diplomatic dialogue, and Khomeini was certainly in favour of acquiring military spare parts from the United States. But Bazargan still had to contend with the visceral anti-American feeling that ran deep within all sections of Iranian society, which saw Washington as the Shah's ally and blamed American imperialism as the cause of many of Iran's difficulties.

On 1 November Bazargan, accompanied by Ibrahim Yazdi, the foreign minister, and Mostafa Chamran, the Revolutionary Guard commander who held the defence portfolio, travelled to Algiers to meet with Zbigniew Brzezinski, Carter's National Security adviser. Just as the two sides sat down to discuss security issues of mutual concern, the Shah arrived in the United States to begin his cancer treatment. Bazargan's opponents in Tehran seized their moment. The American embassy in Tehran had been occupied on several occasions since the February revolution, and on 4 November a group of 400 revolutionary students calling themselves 'students following the Imam's line' decided to stage a sit-in at the diplomatic complex. The protest was as much a demonstration against Bazargan's meeting with Brzezinski as it was the Shah's admission to America, and the huge demonstrations that subsequently took place in Tehran denounced both the United States and Bazargan. Two days later Bazargan made his own protest at this blatant attempt to undermine his authority and resigned.

Khomeini does not appear to have had forewarning of the students' plans, although it is inconceivable that senior revolutionary officials were not consulted. Ibrahim Asgharzadeh, the students' leader, had only intended the protest to last a few days, and said that the main aim of the sit-in was to make a highly public protest against the Shah's admission to America, and ingratiate themselves with Khomeini.[27] Asgharzadeh was a member of a radical student group called 'Strengthen the Unity', which also included Mahmoud Ahmadinejad, who became Iran's president in 2005 and was a young Revolutionary Guard commander at the time of the occupation. Although Ahmadinejad has strongly denied claims made by five former American captives that he was involved in the embassy takeover, he was undoubtedly one of the central players in the group of student activists responsible for taking over the embassy.[28] Western journalists who covered the embassy siege have also identified Ahmadinejad as having been present in the embassy compound in the early days of the occupation.[29] The furthest senior Iranian government officials from the time will go towards confirming Ahmadinejad's involvement is to say that he worked as a liaison officer between the occupiers and Khomeini's office.[30]

At first Khomeini was not sure how to react to the occupation of the embassy. In the past when overenthusiastic students had occupied the building, he had ordered their removal, and they had complied. The British embassy had also been occupied that same day, but the occupation had ended peacefully, and there seemed no reason why the protest at the American embassy should not end the same way. American security officials at the embassy initially took a relaxed view of the protest, believing that it would end peacefully, as when left-wing activists had occupied the embassy the previous February. But other, more radical elements associated with the Revolutionary Guards, soon took over, and it was not long before the captives were being paraded blindfolded before the world's media.

When Ibrahim Yazdi, the foreign minister, visited Khomeini at Qom the day after the students started their sit-in, the ayatollah demanded, 'Who are they? Why have they done this?' and told Yazdi 'Go and kick them out.'[31] But by the time Yazdi got back to Tehran he was surprised to discover Khomeini had changed his mind and had issued a public statement backing the students' takeover. For Yazdi, this was just another example of Khomeini's vacillating nature, and he realized that the ayatollah's approach had been swayed by the jubilant scenes taking place outside the embassy that were shown on national television. Khomeini had been reassured by Mohammed Khoeniha, a popular Tehran cleric who was students' 'spiritual leader', that the hostage-takers were devout Muslims, unlike the left-wing militants who had occupied the embassy the previous February. Khomeini nevertheless sent his son Ahmad, who was friends with Khoeniha, to Tehran to check on what was going on, and when Ahmad arrived he was literally carried away by the rapture of the crowds, and physically lifted over the embassy walls, where his presence was taken by the students as confirmation of Khomeini's approval of their action.

Khomeini was undoubtedly swayed by the popular euphoria that the occupation had created, particularly in the press, and he could not resist riding the crest of the populist wave. Khomeini's first public comment, in which he denounced the embassy as a 'nest of spies', effectively gave his blessing to the occupation. The result was that fifty-two American diplomats and embassy staff would be held hostage for a total of 444 days and cause what would prove to be an irrevocable split in relations between Washington and Tehran. Khomeini's support for the occupation was a classic exercise in political opportunism, for it quickly became the central focus of the revolutionary movement. Fratricidal infighting was set aside in the interests of taking a united stand against 'the Great Satan'. Those political parties, such as the National Front, which did not support the occupation, were isolated from mainstream politics. And, crucially for Khomeini, he no longer had to contend with opposition to his constitutional proposals for an Islamic republic, which, prior to the occupation, had been in danger of becoming a formidable obstacle towards the end of Bazargan's administration. Bazargan's resignation merely confirmed the fact that he had lost his long-running struggle to impose his authority on the competing demands of the revolution.

Khomeini had no hesitation in accepting Bazargan's resignation, and seized the opportunity to press ahead with his radical constitutional agenda. The fall of Bazargan meant that the Revolutionary Council took responsibility for running the country, and the day after Bazargan's resignation Khomeini issued the Council with instructions to prepare for a referendum on the new Islamic constitution, and for presidential and parliamentary elections. Khomeini still entertained reservations about the constitution's final draft, which he still felt was contaminated by Western notions of democracy. He was aggrieved, for example, that he only had the power to confirm the appointment of the president, rather than make the appointment himself.[32] But he consoled himself with the thought that the combination of his stature as a religious figure, together with his powers of veto, would enable him to overcome any potential resistance to his will.

During the run-up to the referendum, which was scheduled for 3 December, Khomeini skilfully manipulated the siege of the American embassy to isolate the various opposition groups that were still holding out for democratic representation. Having backed the occupation, and realizing the West had no clear-cut strategy for ending the crisis, Khomeini approved the appointment of Mohammed Khoeniha, on his son Ahmad's recommendation, to supervise the students. Khoeniha gave the protest legitimacy as it was now seen to have Khomeini's personal representative guiding events. From now on, when the students made demands, they could genuinely do so in Khomeini's name. Their basic demand was that they would release the hostages only if the American government handed over the Shah, who by this time was receiving cancer treatment at a New York clinic. This demand, which became the central issue of the hostage crisis, was made in the knowledge that the students had Khomeini's full support, although, as one of them remarked to their American captives, most Iranians were in two minds as to whether or not they really wanted the Shah back. 'They wouldn't know whether to torture him, shoot him or hang him.'[33] The more the hostage crisis developed, the more Khomeini grew in confidence, at one point boasting, 'The Americans can't do a damned thing . . . How can America militarily intervene in this country? It is not possible. The whole world is watching. Can America stand up to the world and intervene here? America would not dare.'[34]

The American embassy siege proved to be a defining moment both for Khomeini and the Islamic revolution. Whereas previously he had sought to control the wilder excesses of the revolution, such as limiting the number of executions, now he fully embraced the concept of revolutionary action, and gave the student revolutionaries free rein to confront the negative influences of imperialism, liberalism and democracy. For decades Khomeini had denounced Washington's pernicious influence in Iranian affairs: now he had the opportunity to humiliate the United States and make an unequivocal statement of where true power now resided in Tehran. Khomeini was so moved by the powerful nationalistic forces unleashed by the occupation of the American embassy that he called it 'the second Islamic Revolution'.

The referendum result on 3 December returned an overwhelming endorsement for the new constitution. The only significant opposition had come from Grand Ayatollah Shariatmadari, who publicly announced his refusal to participate unless the article relating to the *velayat-e faqih* was modified. But Shariatmadari was no match for Khomeini, and soon after the result of the referendum was announced Khomeini used the same strong-arm tactics that had silenced the secular opposition against the grand ayatollah. A large crowd of Hizbollahis gathered outside his house in Qom and chanted slogans in favour of the constitution, and a propaganda campaign was launched against Shariatmadari's party, claiming it was penetrated by 'anti-Islamic foreign agents'. The grand ayatollah's supporters tried to defend their leader, staging pro-Shariatmadari demonstrations in Tabriz, capital of the Iranian province of East Azerbaijan and Shariatmadari's stronghold, that attracted more than one million followers. Tabriz had been the centre of the provincial unrest that had led to the Shah's overthrow, and the mullahs were concerned that, if Shariatmadari was able to garner enough support, he could have a similar effect on the Iranian revolution. But unlike Khomeini, the more benign Shariatmadari was disinclined to lend his name to violence, and the potential unrest was suppressed by the Revolutionary Guards. Many of Shariatmadari's aides were arrested and the grand ayatollah placed under permanent house arrest.

Many other opposition groups – including the National Front and the Mujahideen – and professional associations had abstained from voting on the constitution because of their concerns over the erosion of civil rights, which meant that the turn-out was much lower than the previous referendum on the abolition of the monarchy (20 million voted in March, 16 million in December[35]). Realizing that he still needed to tread carefully if he was to achieve his goal of creating an Islamic state, Khomeini banned clerics from putting their names forward to contest the forthcoming presidential election that was scheduled for January 1980. But he still held the trump card as the new constitution stipulated that any candidate had to be approved by the *velayat-e faqih*, and Khomeini used his new powers to veto candidates, such as Masud Rajavi, the leader of the Marxist Mujahideen-e Khalq, on the grounds that he had boycotted the constitutional referendum. His preferred candidate was Jalaleddin Farsi, a member of the Islamic Republican Party, who had close links with the Fedayeen militant Islamic group, but he was disqualified because his father was an Afghan, and the constitution insisted all candidates must be of Iranian nationality and origin.

That left the field wide open for Abol Hassan Bani-Sadr, who had been a close confidant of Khomeini since the two men became allies in Paris. Bani-Sadr's election helped to assuage the doubts of the secularists about the direction the country was taking. Although he was regarded as one of Khomeini's 'favourite sons', Bani-Sadr was an Islamic moderate who had formerly been a member of the National Front, and had spoken out against the imposition of the more uncompromising Islamic aspects of the new constitution, such as the *velayat-e faqih*, during the deliberations of the Assembly of Experts. Thus when Bani-Sadr received Khomeini's endorsement as the country's first democratically elected president on 4 February 1980, the ayatollah's comments hardly amounted to a ringing endorsement of his one-time protégé. 'I will say one word to Mr Bani-Sadr,' said Khomeini. 'Whatever office man achieves, it will be taken away from him one day, on an unspecified day. One must take care not to become too proud with high office. I ask Mr Bani-Sadr not to change because of the office. I ask everyone to support him as long as he acts according to the principles of Islam.' Khomeini may have had his reservations about Bani-Sadr, but he had nevertheless achieved his primary objective. In the space of just one year he had accomplished his life-long ambition of creating an Islamic state based on the strict interpretation of Sharia law.

7

Taking on the World

Trouble had been brewing between Iran and its near neighbour Iraq from the moment Baathist dictator Saddam Hussein seized power in Baghdad in July 1979, just five months after Khomeini launched his Islamic revolution in Tehran. The 42-year-old Saddam was a proud secular nationalist who, like Khomeini, sought to dominate the Arab world, although the Iraqi leader hoped to achieve his goal by uniting all the Arab nations under the banner of revolutionary Baathist ideology, rather than Khomeini's brand of Islamic fundamentalism. Saddam's decision to stage a bloodless coup against President Ahmad Hassan al-Bakr, the military dictator who had been Saddam's mentor in the Baath Party for more than a decade, was partly motivated by Saddam's deepening concern over the effect Khomeini's revolution was having on Iraq's majority Shia population, many of whom openly supported the establishment of a radical Islamic government in Baghdad as well as Tehran.

Relations between Saddam and Khomeini had first become strained towards the end of the ayatollah's period of exile in Najaf. Although still only the country's vice-president, by the late 1970s Saddam was generally recognized to be the power behind the throne of President al-Bakr. As part of his ruthless drive to force Iraq's disparate ethnic and religious groups to submit to Baathist rule Saddam had launched a persecution campaign against the country's Shia population, particularly the Dawa (the Call) Islamic party, which had been founded by Khomeini's friend and Iraqi Shia ally Mohammed al-Sadr. In

1977, following an anti-Saddam demonstration near Najaf
by Dawa sympathizers, the Iraqi strongman had retaliated by
sending attack helicopters and armoured units to break up the
protest, which resulted in the deaths of sixteen demonstrators
and 2,000 arrests. Even though Sadr was not directly involved
in organizing the demonstration, his activities were closely
monitored by Saddam's all pervasive security police, who
reported that Sadr was encouraging his supporters to attend
Khomeini's lectures at Najaf. Thus when the Shah asked the
authorities in Baghdad to expel Khomeini from Najaf, Saddam
had made it his personal business to see to it that the radical
ayatollah was escorted to the airport and flown to Paris.[1]
Khomeini held Saddam personally responsible for his deportation and when asked, during an interview shortly after his
arrival in Paris, to list his enemies, he replied, 'First, the Shah;
then the American Satan; then Saddam Hussein and his infidel
Baath Party.'[2]

Saddam's persecution of Sadr and Iraq's radical Shia intensified after Khomeini seized power in February 1979. Sadr, who
had tried to distance himself from political activism prior to the
Iranian revolution, threw caution to the winds and declared a
three-day holiday at Najaf to celebrate Khomeini's triumphant
return to Tehran. Sadr sent a personal emissary to Tehran to
congratulate Khomeini, and demonstrators in Najaf carried
pictures of Khomeini. Sadr himself declared that he accepted
Khomeini as the undisputed leader of Iraq's Shia, and that he
would act as the ayatollah's official deputy. Saddam feared
Iraq's Shia militants were attempting to replicate the same
tactics that Khomeini's supporters had used to overthrow the
Shah, and in June the Iraqi government responded by arresting Sadr and taking him to Baghdad for interrogation. Sadr's
detention provoked an international outcry, which forced the
Iraqi government to back down and release him from prison.
This prompted a furious debate within the Baath Party's ruling
Revolutionary Command Council over the degree of violence to

be used in combating Islamic extremism in Iraq, the upshot of which was Saddam's decision to depose President Bakr and seize power for himself.

Having conducted a bloody purge of the Baath party, in which Saddam's opponents were publicly denounced and executed, the new Iraqi dictator launched another persecution campaign against the Shia. Sadr was placed under house arrest, and between 4,000 and 5,000 members of his Dawa party were arrested, of whom 200 were executed. Sadr responded by trying to recruit anti-Baathist soldiers, and forming underground commando cells whose primary goal was to assassinate Saddam. In April 1980 a radical Iraqi Shia group, trained by the Amal militia that Sadr's cousin Musa al-Sadr had set up in southern Lebanon, attempted to assassinate Tariq Aziz, Saddam's newly appointed foreign minister. Aziz survived, but the following day Saddam's security forces arrested Mohammed al-Sadr and his sister, Bint al-Huda, who were taken to Baghdad for interrogation. There seems little doubt that the cleric and sister were tortured by Saddam's half-brother, Barzan al-Tikriti, the head of Iraqi intelligence, before being hanged in secret after a summary trial. Their bodies were returned to the family home the following day, and when relatives open the coffins marks on the faces of both showed they had been tortured.[3] It is more than likely that Khomeini himself would have suffered a similar fate had he still been living in Najaf, such was the closeness of his relationship with Sadr. As news of the hangings reached the Shia heartlands of southern Iraq, widespread riots erupted, which were brutally suppressed by Saddam's security forces. Hundreds of Shia demonstrators were killed, and thousands arrested. A few weeks later Saddam instituted one of his favourite mass punishment routines, rounding up an estimated 35,000 Iraqi Shia and forcibly deporting them to Iran.

The execution of Sadr and Saddam's persecution of Iraq's Shia prompted a furious response from Khomeini. 'The war that the Iraqi Baath wants to ignite is a war against Islam . . . The people and army of Iraq must turn their backs on the Baath regime and overthrow it . . . because the regime is attacking Iran, attacking Islam and the Koran.'[4] Khomeini's rallying cry would later be taken up by Sadr's grandson, the radical Islamic cleric Muqtada al-Sadr, who would be one of the leaders of the violent insurgency against Coalition forces following the overthrow of Saddam's regime in 2003. So far as Khomeini was concerned, though, Sadr's execution was just the excuse he needed to call for Saddam's overthrow.

From the earliest days of the Iranian revolution Khomeini and his followers had identified Saddam as one the main obstacles preventing the Iraqi Shia from becoming the beneficiaries of radical Islamic government. Soon after the ayatollahs seized power, Sadeq Khalkhali, Iran's infamous 'judge blood', publicly declared the regime's determination to overthrow Saddam. 'We have taken the path of true Islam and our aim in defeating Saddam Hussein lies in the fact that we consider him the main obstacle to the advance of Islam in the region.'[5] By the time of Sadr's execution, exporting the Islamic revolution to neighbouring Muslim countries had become an article of faith enshrined in the new Iranian constitution, a point that was not lost on Iran's new ambassador to Baghdad, a firebrand mullah, who took his revolutionary duties so seriously that he made numerous vitriolic denunciations of the host government while calling on the Iraqi people to launch their own Islamic revolution.

Saddam's decision to invade Iran on 22 September 1980 – the start of a conflict that would last for eight years and cost an estimated 1 million lives – was more a calculated act of opportunism than a response to Iranian provocation. Saddam had never got over the humiliation he had felt in 1975 when, as vice president, he had been forced to sign the Algiers Agreement with the Shah, which gave Tehran control of the Shatt al-Arab waterway, Iraq's only outlet to the Gulf. Saddam had been looking for an opportunity to exact revenge on Iran, and the constant in-fighting in Tehran led him eto believe that an attack would meet with minimal resistance, particularly as the effectiveness of Iran's armed forces was known to have been severely diminished by the revolution. Saddam was encouraged in this view by a number of former Iranian politicians and senior officers from the Shah's era who had sought sanctuary in Iraq.

Saddam believed that, apart from negotiating more favourable terms over the Shatt al-Arab in any future peace deal with Tehran, he would also be able to occupy portions of the oil-rich region of Khuzestan in south-western Iran, which possessed a sizeable Arab population and, until the rule of Reza Shah, had been known as 'Arabistan'. To highlight Iraq's claim to the region, Saddam's intelligence officials persuaded a group of Iranian Arabs from the region to stage a high-profile terrorist attack to draw attention to their plight. On 30 April 1980 six armed Iranians laid siege to the Iranian embassy in London, holding twenty-six Iranian diplomats and other embassy workers hostage, to draw world attention to the plight of oppressed Arabs in Iran. But the siege was brought to an abrupt end after the British prime minister ordered the SAS to storm the building and free the captives. The Carter administration's hopes of staging its own rescue operation to free the hostages held at the American embassy in Tehran a few days earlier ended in failure after one of the rescue helicopters crashed into a C130 transport aircraft, killing eight American service personnel. Khomeini gloated over the American 'defeat' and chastised President Carter for his foolish manoeuvre, and warned that any further action by the United States would result in the immediate execution of all the American hostages. By the time Saddam invaded Iran, Carter was concentrating all his efforts on getting re-elected and fighting off Ronald Reagan's bid to succeed him at the White House. Washington did little to restrain Iraqi war plans, but also did little to encourage them.

Just as the American embassy siege had helped Khomeini to

rally popular support behind the Islamic government, the sudden bombing of Tehran airport – the opening salvo in Saddam's military offensive – and the subsequent capture of large areas of western Iran, including the country's largest port and the centre of its oil industry, gave the leadership another opportunity to exploit a national crisis to its advantage. Khomeini's immediate response was to reassure the nation, 'A thief has come, thrown a pebble and fled back to his home and, God willing, will not be able to repeat his action.'[6] But at heart he was deeply concerned that Saddam's surprise attack might actually succeed in achieving its goals. No one knew better than Khomeini just how unprepared Iran's armed forces were to defend the country. The entire armed forces – army, navy and air force – were equipped with American weaponry, and it was unlikely that much-needed spare parts would be forthcoming so long as there was no resolution to the hostage crisis at the American embassy. Khomeini genuinely believed the regime might be on the point of collapse, and desperately sought to rally support to the cause of the Islamic revolution.

One of Khomeini's first tasks was to try to mend relations with President Bani-Sadr, against whom he had been waging a systematic campaign to undermine his authority since his election the previous January. Though sympathetic to the ideals of the Islamic revolution, Bani-Sadr, who had won an overwhelming victory in the presidential election, believed he had a mandate to redress the balance of the revolution and rescue it from its more fanatical exponents whom he described as 'a fistful of fascist clerics'.[7] Like Bazargan before him, what Bani-Sadr wanted most of all was to return the country to something approaching normality. He wanted to revive the national police force and army, and make the judicial system function according to Iranian, rather than Sharia, law. He made no secret of his determination to dismantle the various revolutionary organizations which he described as 'multiple centres of authority'. The clerics were to be subjected to the law of the state, and the Revolutionary Guards absorbed into the regular army, while the revolutionary courts and the committees that ran them would be dismantled. To begin with it appeared that he had Khomeini's backing after the ayatollah issued a statement describing support for Bani-Sadr as being incumbent on the people. Following Khomeini's lead, other clerics made statements in Bani-Sadr's favour, including Ali Khamenei, one of Khomeini's inner circle who had the prestigious position of leading Friday prayers in Tehran, who urged the faithful 'respect him, follow him, support him in the field, cooperate with him, do not undermine him'.[8]

But from the outset of his presidency Bani-Sadr had to contend with the confusion that surrounded the president's role in the new constitution, a situation that was not helped when Khomeini used his own constitutional prerogative to appoint Ayatollah Mohammed Beheshti, one of his key allies, as the country's new chief justice, a powerful position that meant Khomeini effectively controlled key government appointments. Beheshti had been Khomeini's main representative at the Assembly of Experts during the discussions on the new constitution, which made him well placed to exploit legal loopholes in Khomeini's favour. As chief justice Beheshti was also able to control the machinery of revolutionary terror, and prevent secularists from exercising any influence over judicial reform.

Despite Bani-Sadr's assertion that he wanted to enforce the rule of law, the pace of quasi-judicial trials and executions increased dramatically, especially after Bani-Sadr gave Sadeq Khalkhali, the notorious 'judge blood', responsibility for spearheading an anti-narcotics campaign. Khalkhali marked his appointment on 20 May by ordering the execution of twenty drug traffickers. On 8 July Khalkhali had seven alleged drug offenders shot by firing squad in full public view in Tehran. Later that month Khalkhali had a makeshift gallows built on a Tehran street, and eight drug traffickers were made to stand on discarded Coke and Pepsi-Cola cartons, with nooses round their necks. But when the cartons were kicked away, the gallows collapsed. Undeterred Khalkhali had the eight women and men shot. And when in the same month the revolutionary courts carried out the first public stonings of two men and two women accused of sexual impropriety, Khalkhali defended this barbaric method of execution on the grounds that, 'We approve of anything in the Koran.'[9] Khalkhali's excesses were too much even for Ayatollah Beheshti, who sent a circular to the revolutionary courts ordering that no further executions be carried out without written consent. He also forced Khalkhali's resignation after it was discovered that $14 million of confiscated drug funds were unaccounted for.

Bani-Sadr's hopes of asserting his authority over the chaos created by the Islamic revolution rested on the outcome of the elections for the Majlis which took place soon after the presidential contest. But unlike the contest for president, where the mullahs had been excluded from participation, the parliamentary elections were open to all parties. The Islamic Revolutionary Party, which had been set up by Beheshti and Hashemi Rafsanjani, mobilized its highly effective networks among the clergy, the komitehs and the Revolutionary Guards to ensure the party was well represented. The IRP also enlisted the street muscle of the Hizbollahis who enthusiastically attacked opposition rallies and offices, mainly belonging to the Mojahideen-e Khalq. The IRP's tactics paid off and it won 85 of the 270 seats in the new parliament, while the majority of the other seats went to members of the clergy. Rafsanjani was appointed the speaker of Iran's first post-revolution Majlis, and it was not long before the newly elected parliament had embarked on a bitter confrontation over the choice of Iran's new prime minister. The dispute was only resolved in August when Khomeini intervened and forced Bani-Sadr to accept his preferred choice, Ali Rajai. Like Beheshti and Rafsanjani, Rajai had been deeply involved in the underground Islamic militant groups that plotted the Shah's overthrow, and was a founder member of the Revolutionary Guards.

Bani-Sadr refused to accept Rajai's appointment on the grounds that he lacked experience, and the wrangle over the appointment of a new government continued long after Saddam had launched his invasion. Khomeini tried to strengthen Bani-Sadr's position after the Iraqi invasion by appointing him chairman of the Supreme Defence Council in addition to commander-in-chief of the armed forces, but the infighting between Bani-Sadr and the clergy showed no let-up, even when it came to the conduct of the war. One of Bani-Sadr's first moves was to free air force pilots and military commanders who were suspected of plotting to overthrow the Islamic revolution. But this only confirmed the clerics' view that Bani-Sadr was secretly plotting with the military establishment to neutralize the influence of the clergy. Bani-Sadr continued to insist that the time had arrived for the mullahs to withdraw to their mosques and leave the running of the country to professional politicians and technocrats. But this suggestion was bitterly resisted by the clergy, which turned increasingly to the Revolutionary Guards to fight their corner.

*

The war with Iraq was the making of Khomeini's Revolutionary Guards, and helped the ayatollah to consolidate his stranglehold over the country even further. An organization that had started as a motley collection of like-minded Islamic militants, drawn from a wide variety of revolutionary backgrounds, had gradually formed itself into an organized and effective paramilitary force. The Guards' development had been greatly helped by the experience they acquired from their military intervention against Kurdish rebels in August 1979, when Saddam Hussein had encouraged Iraqi Kurds to launch cross-border raids. The Guards also played a prominent role in suppressing the unrest created by followers of Grand Ayatollah Shariatmadari in

Tabriz during the December referendum. When Shariatmadari's loyalists seized control of the radio and television centre in Tabriz and started broadcasting anti-Khomeini messages, the Revolutionary Guards stormed the building and detained the principle agitators.

From the summer of 1979 onwards the Guards instituted a number of measures to improve their operational effectiveness. Senior commanders, such as Mostafa Chamran, began a purge to expel those who were not considered to be totally loyal to Khomeini's Islamic agenda. In July Mohsen Rezai, who would later command the Guards for sixteen years, was placed in charge of the new intelligence wing, which reported directly to Khomeini.[10] Rezai recruited scores of former SAVAK agents who had succeeded in persuading the Guards' commanders that the skills they had learned spying for the Shah could be employed just as usefully for the mullahs. Arrangements were put in place for recruits to the intelligence unit to receive secret training from experienced Syrian officers who set up a temporary headquarters at a large house in central Tehran. The main purpose of the intelligence wing was to spy on the various counter-revolutionary groups that were still active in Iran, from the communist Tudeh Party to left-wing guerrilla groups. In early 1980 another section was established under the control of another Revolutionary Guard commander, Mehdi Hashemi, to support overseas liberation movements, particularly those, like the Shia Muslim Amal movement in southern Lebanon, that were sympathetic to the Iranian revolution. Hashemi was a protégé of Ayatollah Hossein Ali Montazeri, a leading figure within the IRP and an ally of Khomeini, who strongly advocated that Iran's Islamic government based its foreign policy on the promotion of revolutionary Islam throughout the world. Another key figure in the Guards' development during this period was Mohsen Rafiqdost, who established the Foundation of the Dispossessed. The Foundation was a charitable organization that sought to redistribute the nation's wealth from large landowners to impoverished families, and proved to be a highly successful public relations vehicle for generating popular support for the Guards.

By the summer of 1980 the Revolutionary Guards had firmly established themselves as the revolution's storm troops, and took a direct interest in administering Islamic justice as well as defending the regime from possible attack. When a group of senior army officers was detained on suspicion of mounting a plot to kill Khomeini and overthrow the government, the Revolutionary Guards burst into the prison where they were being held and killed ten of the ringleaders. They played a prominent role in the national demonstrations that took place in the summer of 1980 in support of Khomeini's call for a purge of the country's bureaucracy. The Guards were active in conducting a nationwide purge of the civil service and the armed forces, which led to 4,000 civil servants losing their jobs and between 2,000 and 4,000 high-ranking officers being dismissed from the armed forces. The removal of so many skilled civilian and military personnel from senior positions was one of the reasons Saddam Hussein believed his invasion of Iran would achieve a swift victory.

The Revolutionary Guards were among eleven different paramilitary groups that rushed to south-west Iran to defend the country against the Iraqi attack, the other principal militias being the Mujahideen and the Fedayeen. The main thrust of Iraq's initial offensive was directed at the key port of Khorramshahr and at the heart of the Iranian oil industry, centred on Abadan and Ahwaz. Saddam calculated that, cut off from its oil resources and revenues, the Iranian economy would collapse and the regime forced to make peace. Khorramshahr fell at the end of October. But although the Iraqis laid siege to Abadan and other major cities, the Iranians managed to arrest the Iraqi advance. Khomeini was not alone in Iran in thinking the Iraqi invasion was supported and encouraged by Washington, and his stubborn determination to resist what he saw as an American plot against the Islamic revolution inspired many Iranians to believe that it was their duty to fight and die in defence of the revolution. The Iraqis had certainly not bargained for the ferocity of the Iranian resistance, with the Revolutionary Guards organizing a staunch defence of the major towns. Iraqi commanders were unwilling to be drawn into urban street fighting, for which the Guards, with their extensive experience of urban fighting during the revolution, were well suited. Far from parading in triumph through Tehran, the Iraqis quickly found themselves bogged down in a bitter and protracted war of attrition.

Bani-Sadr, who had relocated from Tehran to Iran's main military base in Khuzestan, received much of the credit for organizing Iran's spirited resistance to the Iraqi invasion. The revival of Iranian nationalism, and the nation's determination to defend the revolution and support Khomeini, were a potent mix which Bani-Sadr carefully manipulated to keep the flame of resistance alive when it appeared that an Iranian collapse was imminent. His insistence on releasing from prison Iranian air force pilots and senior officers proved to be a masterstroke. The pilots inflicted severe damage on key Iraqi installations and crippled Iraq's oil-exporting facilities, while the army officers rallied their forces sufficiently to arrest the Iraqis in their tracks. Bani-Sadr wanted to exploit the military success to establish a national spirit of unity, and he tried hard to reconcile the armed forces and the Revolutionary Guards, who still entertained suspicions that the officer corps – for all the purges – remained loyal to the *ancien régime*.

But the reverse happened, and instead Bani-Sadr became the victim of the mullahs' jealousy who feared the president might use the military's new-found prowess for his own political ends. Their concern was that, once the war was over, Bani-Sadr might use the military as his personal support base to seize power for himself. As Khomeini's grandson Hussein later remarked, 'I have heard them say that it is preferable to lose half of Iran than for Bani-Sadr to become the ruler.'[11]

The deep divisions between Bani-Sadr and the IRP-dominated Majlis surfaced virtually every week when he travelled to Tehran to discuss the progress of the war with Khomeini, with whom the president still maintained a close relationship. Khomeini had also relocated at the outbreak of hostilities, moving from Qom to take up residence in the village of Jamaran in the northern part of Tehran, where he would live for the rest of his life. Khomeini ordered the president and his clerical opponents to set aside their political differences for the duration of the conflict, but to no avail. When Bani-Sadr reported back on the war's progress to the Majlis, he tried to give the regular armed forces the credit for halting the Iraqi advance, but the clerics tried to claim the glory for the Revolutionary Guards. They claimed the army was deliberately staying in the background so that the Revolutionary Guards bore the brunt of the fighting, and the IRP introduced a Bill to parliament requiring the Guards to be equipped with heavy weapons and to be given first choice of army recruits. Khomeini tried to act as a peacemaker between Bani-Sadr and the IRP, and in March 1981 he summoned the two sides to his residence to settle their differences. But Bani-Sadr refused to acknowledge the IRP's right to interfere in key areas of government, and Khomeini was reduced to issuing a decree banning the two sides from making speeches or publishing articles that might inflame tensions until the end of the war.

By this stage the rivalry between Bani-Sadr and the IRP had reached the stage where reconciliation proved impossible, and neither side was prepared to abide by Khomeini's decree. Ayatollah Beheshti and others in the IRP had alienated Bani-Sadr by circulating a proposal at the Majlis that the president should be relieved of his responsibility as commander-in-chief. Bani-Sadr's followers responded by organizing demonstrations at which his loyalists chanted slogans condemning the corrupt three, 'Khamenei, Rafsanjani and Beheshti'. Even staunch supporters of the revolution, such as Ibrahim Yazdi, the former foreign minister and a close Khomeini ally, publicly denounced the IRP for its 'Stalinist and un-Islamic methods', while other religious leaders wrote an open letter to Khomeini comparing the activities of the Revolutionary Guards to the Shah's secret police, and describing it as 'a new SAVAK'. The Revolutionary Guards, who worked closely with Rafsanjani and Beheshti, were certainly active in supporting the IRP's efforts to out-manoeuvre Bani-Sadr. The offices of newspapers critical of the Majlis were attacked and rallies organized by radical clerics, including Ayatollah Lahuti, the Revolutionary Guards' first commander, were brutally disrupted.

Apart from having to wage war against Iraq, the country was rapidly descending into civil war, particularly after Bani-Sadr linked up with the left-wing Mujahideen-e Khalq to help him counter the Revolutionary Guards. The Mujahideen had experienced a complicated relationship with the leaders of the Islamic revolution. Under the leadership of the charismatic Masud Rajavi, the Mujahideen had been one of the more effective underground resistance movements against the Shah. Many of the organization's leaders, including Rajavi, were imprisoned, where they established good relations with underground Islamic leaders, such as Hashemi Rafsanjani.[12] Although they broadly supported the Islamic revolution, Khomeini felt uncomfortable with the Mujahideen's left-wing agenda, and was wary of the support Rajavi attracted when he organized one of his regular rallies at one of Tehran's universities, which attracted thousands of supporters. Rajavi's ideology was based upon an eclectic mix of Islam, Darwinism, Marxism and critiques of capitalism, and his message was one of social revolution, where Iran moved towards a classless society, rather than an Islamic one based on religious equality. 'The struggle is over two kinds of Islam,' he said at one of his rallies. 'One, an Islam of class, which ultimately protects the exploiter; and a pure, authentic and popular Islam, which is against classes and exploitation.'[13] Khomeini denounced the Mujahideen's ideology as 'the training of our youth in the interests of the West',[14] which was taken by the Guards as an open invitation to attack any rally organized by the Mujahideen, and Tehran University became the scene of constant running battles between the Guards and the Mujahideen.

Khomeini's decree in March 1981 urging restraint between the two sides made little impact, and clashes continued between the Mujahideen and the Guards at Tehran University and in provincial towns throughout the spring. But even with the backing of the Mujahideen, Bani-Sadr was no match for the better organized and more fanatical supporters of the IRP. In April and May more than a dozen Bani-Sadr supporters were killed in street battles with the Guards and other militant Islamic groups, such as the Hizbollahis. And any hopes Bani-Sadr still entertained of getting the IRP to acknowledge his authority evaporated in May when Khomeini publicly sealed his split with his former protégé, declaring, 'The nation is hostile to the cult of personality.'

Although Khomeini had sought to resolve the differences between Bani-Sadr and the IRP, his patience had been wearing thin with his president since the start of the year when a successful resolution of the American embassy siege was concluded in January. The death of the Shah in July 1980 had removed the primary justification for holding fifty-two American embassy personnel hostage, and the Iraqi invasion added to the urgency of Tehran ending the siege. As one of Khomeini's negotiators remarked, 'The hostages are like a fruit from which all the juice has been squeezed out.' The government negotiated a hasty conclusion to the crisis where, just as President Carter prepared to leave office, all the hostages were released, in return for which Washington agreed to release some $11–12 billion of assets that had been frozen in retaliation for the initial occupation of the embassy. But the settlement negotiated by the IRP-dominated government meant that nearly $6 billion of these assets were handed over to American and foreign banks to pay outstanding debts, and to cover the cost of any compensation claims by the hostages. Bani-Sadr publicly condemned the government's incompetence in negotiating such a disadvantageous deal. His open denunciation of the IRP, together with his continued refusal to countenance the IRP's claim to control key government departments, such as the judiciary, led Khomeini to conclude that the time had come to dispense with the country's first post-revolutionary president.

Khomeini used his constitutional position as the country's supreme leader to criticize Bani-Sadr's refusal to cooperate with the IRP-dominated Majlis. 'The dictator is the one who does not bow to the Majlis, the laws of the Majlis, the judicial authority,' Khomeini warned in a speech in early June. 'The day I feel danger to the Islamic Republic I will cut everybody's hand off.'[15] Even after this warning Bani-Sadr failed to recognize that his presidency was in mortal danger, and he compounded the split with Khomeini by writing to him warning that he was 'committing suicide' by handing power over to the 'power hungry' Majlis, and demanded the immediate dissolution of the Majlis and the government which he claimed had only gained power by rigging the elections. Khomeini responded by dismissing Bani-Sadr as commander-in-chief and was so angered by Bani-Sadr's reply that he would no longer read his letters. Bani-Sadr, sensing that his falling-out with Khomeini was irrevocable, went into hiding, from whence he issued statements defending his record in office, claiming, with some justice, that just as he was on the point of defeating Iraq's aggression, 'I was stabbed in the back.'[16]

With Bani-Sadr in hiding, the Mujahideen made one last effort to muster support for the beleaguered president, and staged a massive rally on 10 June at Revolution Square, close to Tehran University, which was attended by tens of thousands of supporters who, for the first time, publicly blamed Khomeini for the repression and reign of terror that the country was suffering. But before the organizers could arrange another rally for 15 June, Khomeini effectively sealed Bani-Sadr's fate – and the rest of the anti-clerical opposition – by addressing the nation in a radio broadcast in which he denounced the organizers of the protest rallies as 'apostates', and the rallies themselves as 'an invitation to uprising, an invitation to insurrection'. He accused Bani-Sadr of fuelling dissent throughout the country, and demanded that he make a full public apology. 'I want him to go on television and announce his repentance and say he has been wrong in inviting the people to revolt.'[17]

There was no way back now for Bani-Sadr, and the Revolutionary Guards and their associates lost no time in mobilizing their forces to ensure there were no more anti-government rallies. Most of those attending were middle-class professionals who were still clinging to the hope that the post-revolution political settlement could be altered to dilute the all-encompassing power of the clergy, but confronted by the brute force of the Revolutionary Guards and the Hizbollahis, they realized they were no match for Khomeini's superior forces, and the proposed rally was quietly cancelled. The Mujahideen were alone in continuing their campaign to force the government to change course, committing themselves to 'revolutionary resistance in all its forms'. The Revolutionary Guards responded by attacking Mujahideen supporters, and dozens were killed in running street battles that took place in most of the major cities. Rafsanjani, the speaker of the Majlis, and other prominent members of the clerical faction, interpreted the Mujahideen's statement as a declaration of war, and linked their campaign to Bani-Sadr. 'These people have made war against God. They are oppressors. They have revolted against the Islamic Republic. They have shed blood.'[18] The following morning fifteen people who had been involved in street clashes with the Guards were executed at Evin prison, and a large crowd gathered in front of the Majlis building in Imam Khomeini Avenue in central Tehran demanding Bani-Sadr's execution.

Under the constitution Khomeini could not dismiss Bani-Sadr unless the Majlis declared him 'incompetent', and Rafsanjani moved quickly to arrange a debate on Bani-Sadr's competence on 20 June. All the prominent clerical figures in the campaign to unseat the president would later hold senior positions in the Islamic government. Rafsanjani would one day become president, as would Ali Khamenei, while Ali-Akbar Velayati would serve as foreign minister. From the moment the debate was arranged the outcome was a foregone conclusion, such was the IRP's stranglehold over the Majlis. The atmosphere of menace and intimidation which accompanied the proceedings was so intense that many of the deputies that had been signed up to speak in Bani-Sadr's defence withdrew their names.

The charge list against the president was all-encompassing: he was accused of making common cause with the opposition, criticizing the Imam, lacking faith in the principle of *velayat-e-faqih*, discrediting revolutionary organizations such as the Guards and sowing dissent within the Islamic Republic. Even his conduct of the war came in for criticism, and he was accused, in his former capacity as commander-in-chief, of leaving the country exposed to foreign aggression. As the deputies debated the president's future, the crowd outside the Majlis demanded Bani-Sadr's death. When the motion was finally taken, 177 deputies voted in favour of declaring the president incompetent, and only one voted against. When Rafsanjani and other senior clerics appeared on the Majlis balcony to announce the result of the vote, the crowd burst into chants of 'Death to Bani-Sadr'. Rafsanjani made a brief speech, declaring 'With your help, one of the greatest barriers to the continuation of the revolution has been eliminated. From this moment Bani-Sadr is removed from the Islamic Republic. Switch your slogans to America.' To which the crowd responded by chanting, 'Death to America.'[19]

Khomeini formally dismissed Bani-Sadr the following day, but that was by no means the end of the dispute. From his secret hideout Bani-Sadr made calls for a mass uprising to overthrow the clerical dictatorship, and the Mujahideen continued to hold impromptu demonstrations. The authorities responded to the continued challenge to Khomeini's authority with unprecedented violence, with the Guards conducting public summary executions of opponents of the religious leadership. The Mujahideen was no match for the Guards' use of indiscriminate violence, but the opposition managed to exact their revenge on the IRP on 28 June 1981 when a massive bomb destroyed the party's headquarters in central Tehran. The blast happened as party leaders were holding emergency talks on the future government of the country, and among the seventy people killed in the explosion were Ayatollah Mohammed Beheshti, one of Khomeini's closest aides and one of the architects of the Islamic Republic.

Khomeini was devastated both by the loss of a man who had been a close personal friend and a leading figure in the Islamic revolution, but he quickly gathered his composure and authorized the authorities to institute a nationwide purge of the Mujahideen, whom he held responsible for the bombing, even though the organization never officially claimed responsibility for it. The bloody reprisals began almost immediately, with opposition politicians dragged from their prison cells and shot. Thousands of Mujahideen supporters were imprisoned and hundreds executed. Amnesty International later estimated that by the end of 1981 more than 2,500 Mujahideen supporters had been executed as the Revolutionary Guards embarked upon a systematic campaign to destroy the last remnants of resistance to the Islamic regime.[20] Bani-Sadr and Rajavi realized the game was up, and escaped into exile in an air force plane to Paris, where they continued their attempts to rally opposition to the mullahs' rule, a campaign that continues to this day.[21]

Despite the regime's brutal repression of the Mujahideen, the organization maintained its attacks on the government, and on 30 August managed to assassinate Mohammed Ali Rajai, the IRP's former prime minister who had succeeded Bani-Sadr to the presidency, and Mohammed Bahonar, the new prime minister. But while the Mujahideen continued to mount sporadic attacks against the regime, assassinating leading officials and supporters of the Islamic government, the organization never regained its ability to pose a serious threat to Khomeini's Islamic revolution, and its effectiveness waned. The appointment of Ali Khamenei, one of Khomeini's closest supporters, as the Islamic republic's third president in October 1981 set the seal on Khomeini's triumph in eradicating the last vestiges of domestic opposition to his radical Islamic programme. Khamenei's appointment was important in that it signified the end of Khomeini's conceit that the clergy should not be directly involved in the running of the country, even though the IRP, through its dominance of the Majlis, was already firmly established as the dominant force in Iranian politics. By appointing Khamenei, who had been a loyal ally for more than twenty years, Khomeini was declaring that he wanted the clergy to be more, not less, involved in politics. From now on mullahs would be actively encouraged to take over key positions in the government and civil service, and the clergy would take responsibility for running the country. After nearly two years of unremitting bloodshed, and against considerable odds, Khomeini had unequivocally achieved his goal of turning Iran into one of the most uncompromising Islamic states the world has ever seen.

*

The consolidation of Khomeini's power base in Tehran gave the Islamic regime the confidence to turn its attention further afield. Freed from the pressures of trying to contain an incipient civil war, the new government of President Khamenei, with Khomeini acting as its spiritual guardian, was able to concentrate its full attention on prosecuting the war with Iraq. The clerics had repeatedly criticized Bani-Sadr for not being adventurous enough in taking the offensive against Iraq. The Iraqi advance had been halted in no small part due to the heroism of the Revolutionary Guards, whose devotion to Islam and the Imam meant they thought nothing of sacrificing their lives in defence of the Islamic republic. With Bani-Sadr out of the way, the government was able to reconcile the rivalry between the traditional armed forces, which insisted on conducting well-planned and well-organized operations according to established military practice, and the Guards, whose cavalier approach was based on the belief that religious zeal and determination would prevail. No one in the Guards was in any doubt that they had God on their side, and that if they were killed in action they would receive their just reward in heaven.

Khomeini's new government was able to pull off the remarkable feat of moulding the respective strengths of the military and the Guards into a cohesive and effective fighting unit. The armed forces provided the logistical backup, air power and overall coordination while the Guards provided the divinely inspired manpower. The Guards now became a fully fledged military force called Sepah-e Pasdaran-e Enqelabi (Army of the Revolutionary Guards). With their own ministry the Revolutionary Guards numbered as many as 120,000 men and controlled their own small naval and air units.[22]

One of the more dramatic tactics employed during the renewed offensives Iran launched in late 1981 and early 1982 was the use of human wave attacks, in which thousands of volunteers cleared minefields by walking over them and drawing the enemy's fire, thereby opening the way for more conventional armed units to attack Iraqi positions. The Iranians were forced to adopt these desperate tactics because the military, which relied heavily on the United States and Britain for supplies, lacked the equipment and resources to confront the better-equipped Iraqis, who from the start of the war benefited from the West's willingness to provide a constant stream of military hardware.

Iranian commanders realized their best resource was the deep, untapped reservoir of highly motivated, religiously inspired volunteers who, despite their lack of training and equipment, lacked nothing in courage. The Basij, Iran's army of mass volunteers, was largely made up from age groups not normally associated with combat, primarily young boys aged between ten and sixteen, but at the other end of the age spectrum also including unemployed old men in their eighties. The boys were inspired to respond to the mullahs' appeal for a mass mobilization by the excitement generated by the war effort, much as teenage British boys responded to Lord Kitchener's appeal for recruits during the First World War. Many of them received only the most basic training before being dispatched to the front. Basij volunteers wore a red headband, which signified their readiness for martyrdom, and were given a gun and a couple of hand grenades before being sent in their thousands to run through minefields in what amounted to mass suicide, as those who managed to get through this first ordeal were promptly mown down by the well-entrenched Iraqi machine-gun positions.

'We all assembled in a field where there must have been thousands of us, young boys, some younger than me, and old men as well,' recalled one thirteen-year-old Basij who survived a human wave attack and was captured by the Iraqis. 'The commander told us we were going to attack an Iraqi position north-east of Basra . . . The sun was coming up as we started to walk towards the Iraqi lines, and boy, was I scared! . . .

When we got to the top of the hill we started running down the other side towards the enemy position. I wasn't afraid anymore. We all shouted "Allahu Akbar", as we ran, and I could see the line of soldiers in front of us – a line of helmets – then they started firing. People dropped all around me, but I kept on running and shouting, kept going while many were being killed. By the time I'd reached the trenches, I'd thrown my grenades and somehow lost my gun, but I don't remember how. Then I was hit in the leg and fell over and lay for a long time right in front of the lines.'[23] The constant use of human wave attacks, which continued for the duration of the war, was the primary reason Iran suffered such a high fatality rate during the course of the war, with some estimates putting the total number of Iranian war dead as high as 500,000, although the Iranian government's official figure is much lower at around 200,000.

The Iranian tactics might have been rudimentary, but they were highly effective, and in May 1982 the combined efforts of the armed forces and the Guards succeeded in breaking the year-long siege of Khorramshahr, the country's most important port. Khomeini was jubilant, and immediately delivered an up-beat message to the Iranian people in which he seemed to imply that he was ready to negotiate an end to the conflict with Baghdad. 'I should advise . . . our neighbours that we have your good at heart providing you do not follow the United States and treat us according to the holy Koran,' he declared in a radio broadcast. The liberation of Khorramshahr was undoubtedly a defining moment in the development of the Islamic revolution, and showed what could be achieved when the country was united and determined to succeed.

Khomeini certainly gave the impression that he was keen to stop the war, and exploit the government's success in driving the Iraqis out of Iran to consolidate the domestic revolution. But other leading revolutionary figures such as Hashemi Raf-sanjani, and most of the commanders of the Revolutionary

Guards, argued that the military offensive should press on into Iraq, and that by maintaining the military momentum Iran would be in a strong position to force the Iraqis to pay war reparations. Khomeini's son Ahmad said that his father cautioned against continuing the war, warning, 'if you continue the war and do not succeed, this war will never end. Now is the best time to end the war.'[24]

But Khomeini seems to have been genuinely in two minds as to whether to persist with the campaign, and was eventually persuaded that the Iranian offensive should continue at least until the crucial Shatt al-Arab waterway, Iraq's only access to the sea and vital for its oil exports, was captured. Some of the Revolutionary Guard commanders who had been responsible for masterminding the successful campaign to recapture Khorramshahr had an almost Messianic belief in continuing the war. Colonel Sayyid Shirazi, a young Guards officer who had been acclaimed for revitalizing the military campaign against Iraq, argued that Iran should 'continue the war until Saddam falls and we can pray in Karbala', one of the holiest shrines in Shia Islam located in southern Iraq. Khomeini effectively ended the debate on 21 June when he issued a statement calling for Saddam's overthrow. Part of Khomeini's calculation was that if Saddam fell there might be the possibility of establishing an Islamic regime in Baghdad similar to the one he had built in Tehran, forming the nucleus of a string of Islamic states throughout the Gulf region. In his speech announcing his intention to seek Saddam's overthrow, Khomeini predicted that the Iraqi people would establish an Islamic government, and 'if Iran and Iraq unite and link up with one another, the other, smaller nations of the region will join them as well.'[25]

Ali Khamenei, the Iranian president who replaced Khomeini as the country's Supreme Leader after his death, went even further, claiming that Khomeini's elevated religious status meant that he was entitled to claim leadership over the world's entire Muslim community. 'The future government of Iraq should Iraq should be an Islamic and a popular one,' Khamenei declared. 'The policy of *velayat-e faqih* will be Iraq's future policy, and the leader of the Islamic nation is Imam Khomeini. There is no difference between the two nations of Iran and Iraq in accepting the Imam as the leader, and following the Imam and his line. Government and state officials are limited to international borders, but the Imam is not limited by geographical frontiers.' Even though Khomeini would not live to see Saddam's overthrow in 2003 by an American-led military coalition, Iran, with Khamenei aspiring to fulfil Khomeini's role as a global Islamic leader, entertained similar ambitions for post-Saddam Iraq.[26]

In the middle of July the Iranians launched the first in a series of offensives to take the war into Iraq and quickly discovered, as the Iraqis had done before them when they first invaded Iran, that an army puts up far more determined resistance when it is fighting on home, rather than foreign, soil. In a succession of campaigns over the next five years Iran's motley coalition of armed forces, Guards and Basij displayed great ingenuity and resourcefulness, but made little headway against a better organized and well-equipped Iraqi army, which enjoyed the added bonus of receiving the support of regional and international allies. The conflict soon degenerated into a bitter and protracted war of attrition, not dissimilar to that fought in the trenches of the First World War, where each side attempted mass set-piece attacks, achieving modest gains at the expense of colossal casualties.

Khomeini had passed up a golden opportunity to end the war with Iraq in triumph, and the fateful decision to carry on with the conflict gradually dissipated the great surge of patriotism and devotion to the revolution that had accompanied the Iraqis' defeat at Khorramshahr. The fact that he had personally called for Saddam's overthrow also painted the Iranians into a corner, as their war effort – like that of the Bush administration in 2003 – was now dedicated to achieving regime change in

Baghdad, rather than gaining a sufficient military advantage to force Iraq into accepting a peace settlement advantageous to Tehran. For Khomeini, the war was personal. In August 1983, when a possible peace agreement was considered, Khomeini rejected the deal so long as Saddam remained in power. 'The Islamic government of Iran cannot sit at a peace table with a government that has no faith in Islam and in humanity,' he said. 'Islam does not allow peace between us and Saddam, between a Muslim and an infidel.'[27] To achieve his aim of establishing an Iranian-style government in Baghdad, Khomeini authorized the formation of the Supreme Council of the Islamic Revolution of Iraq (SCIRI) under the leadership of Mohammed Bakr al-Hakim, a leading Iraqi Shia scholar who was living in exile in Iran. Iranian officials openly referred to Hakim as the leader of Iraq's future Islamic state, and SCIRI played a central role in Iran's attempts to establish an Islamic theocracy in Baghdad following Saddam's overthrow in 2003.

Having decided to prolong hostilities, Khomeini came round to the view that the war was 'God's hidden gift'. He was persuaded by Rafsanjani and other leading revolutionaries that continuation of the war would actually help to prolong support for the Islamic revolution, which might otherwise subside if his Islamic agenda was confined to Iran. The war provided Khomeini with the opportunity to promote himself as an international leader of Islamic revolution, and in public he began to assume the mantle of the leader of the world's oppressed Muslims, and to declare his interest in exporting the virtues of Iran's Islamic revolution throughout the entire Islamic community. 'We do not want to occupy Iraq,' Khomeini declared soon after the decision had been taken to continue the offensive against Iraq. 'Our aim is to rid Iraq of its tyrannical rulers and to liberate Jerusalem.'[28] Khomeini's son Ahmad, who was one of his closest confidants, later wrote of his father's motives, 'The war gave us an opportunity to tell the world about the power of the revolution, the power of the Imam and our cultural and ideological values in relation to Western values . . . Every missile we sent to Iraq carried with it the Imam's thoughts to the world. It was the Imam's line of communication to every single Muslim. It led to the creation of resistance cells among the Muslims.'[29]

Iran was now fully committed to exporting its Islamic revolution, fulfilling its constitutional obligation to 'extend the sovereignty of God's law throughout the world'. Apart from establishing an Islamic government in Iraq, Khomeini sought to expand his militant brand of politicized Islam throughout the Muslim world. The regime became active in a number of Islamic countries, from the West coast of Africa to the Philippines and Malaysia, although the main focus of its activities were those countries, such as Iraq, Lebanon and the Gulf states, where Tehran believed the Shia communities were susceptible to Iranian influence. Senior figures in the government, such as Ayatollah Hossein Ali Montazeri, who was married to one of Khomeini's sisters and had helped to draft the Islamic constitution, led the parliamentary faction that stated the government's foreign policy should be based on the promotion of revolutionary Islam.

Khomeini decreed that the annual *hajj* pilgrimage to Mecca, which devout Muslims are obliged to undertake at least once in their lifetime as part of the Five Pillars of Islam, was a useful opportunity for promoting the advantages of the Iranian revolution. The ayatollahs had a low regard for the Saudi royal family, the Sunni Muslim guardians of the holy Muslim shrines of Mecca and Medina, whom Montazeri publicly condemned as 'a bunch of pleasure-seekers and mercenaries'. In late 1982 an estimated 100,000 Iranian pilgrims clashed with Saudi police when they staged protests, displayed Khomeini's portrait and shouted slogans against Israel and America. The following year, Khomeini went even further, urging Iranian pilgrims to use the *hajj* as an opportunity to launch an 'Islamic uprising' and to make it 'a vibrant *hajj*, a crushing *hajj*, a *hajj* that condemns

the criminal Soviet Union and the criminal America.'[30] Montazeri openly challenged the Saudis' suitability to remain the
custodians of the holy places, and called for an international
committee of Islamic nations to take charge.

Saudi Arabia was not the only Gulf state to find itself on
the receiving end of Iran's unwelcome interference. Iranian
agents were active in many of the Gulf sheikhdoms, such as
the United Arab Emirates, Kuwait and Bahrain, where they
had long-standing and unresolved territorial disputes. The
Kingdom of Bahrain, the majority of whose population are Shia
Muslims, was particularly targeted by pro-Iranian activists,
and in December 1981 the government uncovered an Iranian-
organized plot to overthrow the government. All of the seventy-three suspects, who came from Bahrain, Saudi Arabia,
Oman and Kuwait, were Shia and had been trained and indoctrinated by Iran. On a smaller scale the Iranians supported
Islamic liberation movements in the Philippines and Malaysia.
Revolutionary Guards units also made exploratory visits to
Africa's Ivory Coast, where there is a large community of
Lebanese Shia Muslim traders. But by far the most significant
investment in exporting the Iranian revolution was made in
Lebanon, which would become the front line in Iran's relentless
campaign to destroy the state of Israel.

8

The Legacy Defined

The Israeli invasion of Lebanon in the summer of 1982 provided Khomeini with a golden opportunity to sow the seeds of Islamic revolution in another foreign land, and the Revolutionary Guards were quick to seize the opportunity. The links Khomeini and his supporters had built up with Lebanon's 1.5 million Shia Muslims put him in a strong position to exploit Lebanon's political divisions. At the same time it provided the leaders of the Islamic revolution with their first chance to confront their sworn foe, the state of Israel.

The primary objective of Israeli Prime Minister Menachem Begin in launching Operation Peace for Galilee in June 1982 was to destroy the military infrastructure of Yasser Arafat's Palestine Liberation Organisation in Lebanon, which was held responsible for launching attacks on Israeli towns and villages in the Galilee region of northern Israel. The Israeli offensive was aimed at PLO targets in Beirut and southern Lebanon, and at first the local Shia population in southern Lebanon welcomed the advancing Israelis with rose petals, the traditional Lebanese greeting, such was their contempt for the PLO. But the mood soon turned sour as the invasion inflicted widespread devastation on Lebanon's civilian population, particularly among the main Shia population centres in southern Lebanon and Beirut's southern suburbs. The Christian Phalange militias, which had been involved for seven years in a bitter civil war with the PLO and its Lebanese Muslim allies, supported the Israeli offensive, while the Lebanese Muslims, both

Sunni and Shia, belatedly rallied to defend the country from Israel's incursion.

The main point of contact for Iran with radical Shia leaders in southern Lebanon was Amal, the Lebanese Shia militia, which had been formed under the leadership of Nabih Berri in the 1970s to protect the interests of the country's Shia population during the civil war. Musa al-Sadr, the Iranian-born cleric who had befriended Khomeini in the 1970s, had been the spiritual driving force behind the creation of Amal before he disappeared in mysterious circumstances on a visit to Libya in 1978. Khomeini's ties to the radical Shia of southern Lebanon were strengthened after one of his daughters married a close relative of Sadr's, and the relationship between the two families led to Sadr arranging for scores of Khomeini's Islamic supporters to undergo military training, both with Amal and Yasser Arafat's PLO in Beirut.

Most of the key figures in Khomeini's government, including Khamenei, the president, and Rafsanjani, the speaker of the Majlis, had received military training in Lebanon. Mostafa Chamran, the founder member of the Revolutionary Guards who organized Khomeini's firing squads and became the revolution's first defence minister, had also trained in Lebanon but was killed in action in 1981 during the war against Iraq. (Chamran today is regarded as one of the principal martyrs of the revolution, and his death is commemorated each year with a ceremony attended by senior Iranian government officials.) The relationship between Sadr and Khomeini had become so close that when the cleric disappeared during his trip to Libya,[1] supporters pinned up pictures of Khomeini alongside those of the missing Imam in Shia villages throughout southern Lebanon. After Sadr's disappearance, Khomeini referred to him as a son and disciple. 'I can say that I nearly raised him,' he declared.[2]

The strength of the bond between the leaders of Iran's Islamic revolution and the Shia of southern Lebanon meant that the Revolutionary Guards had no difficulty in exploiting the security vacuum created by the Israeli invasion. In return for providing military training for Khomeini's supporters in Lebanon, many radicalized young Lebanese Shia were sent to important Iranian religious centres such as Qom to study the principles of the Iranian revolution. One militant group based in Lebanon with ties to the Revolutionary Guards was the Dawa, the remnants of the Iraqi Shia party created by Khomeini's ally and Musa al-Sadr's cousin, Mohammed al-Sadr, which had been brutally repressed by Saddam Hussein. Prior to the Israeli invasion the Lebanese Dawa had been held responsible for a series of terrorist attacks against French targets in retaliation for France's decision to offer political asylum to former members of the Shah's regime, and providing military support to Iraq. In July 1980 a Christian Lebanese, who had converted to Islam and pledged allegiance to Khomeini, was arrested following a failed attempt to assassinate the former Iranian prime minister Shapour Bakhtiar. The Dawa was blamed for bombing the Iraqi embassy in Beirut in December 1981, and the following year the group was implicated in the murder of the French ambassador to Lebanon, Louis Delamare, in September 1981. The following March it bombed the French embassy in Beirut, in which nine people were killed and twenty-seven wounded.[3]

Within days of Israel launching its invasion Khomeini approved the dispatch of a contingent of between 500 and 1,000 Revolutionary Guards to Lebanon to help organize the Shia resistance. Soon afterwards Ayatollah Montazeri, one of Khomeini's closest ideological supporters, told a visiting delegation of Lebanese Shia clerics who had come to Tehran to lobby for support against the Israeli occupation of southern Lebanon, that: 'It is disgraceful for Muslims to keep silent and let Zionists ruthlessly transgress their territory causing so much damage, ruin and loss of life . . . it is the duty of all Muslims to react and deal a blow upon the enemy.'[4]

The Guards based themselves in the ancient Roman city of Baalbeck in the Bekaa Valley, and quickly established a network of training camps for young Lebanese Shia recruits. The Guards' deployment to Lebanon was greatly facilitated by the assistance of Syria, which had seized military control of eastern Lebanon soon after the start of the civil war in 1976. The enmity between President Asad, the Baathist Syrian dictator, and his Baathist counterpart in Iraq, Saddam Hussein, was so deep-seated that Asad had immediately allied himself with Iran following the Iraqi invasion. Although Asad's secularist Arab regime shared little common ground with the Iranian Shia and Khomeini's outlook, he was prepared to consider any alliance that put his deadly rival Saddam Hussein at a disadvantage – a classic example of the old Arab saying, the enemy of my enemy is my friend. Asad was initially reluctant to allow the Iranians to meddle in a region that Damascus jealously regarded as its own sphere of influence, but with the might of Israel's armed forces threatening Damascus, Asad was soon persuaded that any contribution from Iran that could help to disrupt the Israeli offensive was welcome.

Ali Akbar Mohtashemi, the Iranian ambassador to Damascus and another staunch Khomeini loyalist, was a key figure in helping to establish the Revolutionary Guards in Lebanon, and the newly built four-storey Iranian embassy complex in Damascus – located next to the British embassy – became the main conduit for passing directions from Tehran to the Revolutionary Guard contingent in Baalbeck. Mohtashemi added a whole new dimension to the traditional use of the diplomatic pouch, which is supposed to be immune from inspection by the host country. Intelligence officers based in Damascus at the time concluded that the Iranians were using the 'pouch' to ship crates of arms, funds and supplies to their new revolutionary outpost in Lebanon, a conduit that exists to this day.[5] When David Dodge, the acting president of the American University in Beirut, became the first American to be taken hostage in

Lebanon two weeks after the Israeli invasion, the Revolutionary Guards drugged him, put him in a crate and shipped him
to Tehran's notorious Evin prison, via the Iranian embassy in
Damascus, which exploited its diplomatic immunity to facilitate
the shipment. Dodge's transfer from Lebanon to Tehran was
personally supervised by Mohsen Rafiqdost, one of Khomeini's
closest security advisers and a founding member of the Revolutionary Guards.[6]

The Iranian media made much of the Guards' role in
confronting the Israelis, but in fact they had little contact with
the Israelis, who were based thirty-five miles south of Baalbeck.
At this stage in the Guards' development, a modest contingent
of Islamic militants equipped with only basic military equipment was in no position to tackle Israel's intimidating military
machine, and the Iranian commanders were smart enough to
know their limits. Instead they concentrated their energies on
the main purpose of their mission – to export the Iranian
revolution to the Lebanese Shia. As one of the Guards told a
British reporter, 'Our only goal is to Islamicize this place and,
as the Imam Khomeini says, we have to export the Islamic
revolution to the world. So, like any other Muslims, we have
come here with the aim of saving the deprived.'[7]

With the Lebanese government preoccupied with the chaos
of the Lebanese civil war and the devastation caused by the
Israeli invasion, the Guards managed to tighten their grip
around Baalbeck. They entrenched themselves in three major
offices, taking over the Lebanese Army's regional headquarters
at the Sheikh Abdullah barracks, as well as a local clinic, which
was renamed 'Hospital Khomeini', and the Hotel Khayyam.
They became active in local schools, where they propagated
Islamic doctrine, and within the space of a few months the
ancient city had assumed the appearance of a miniature Tehran.
Shia women took to wearing the chador, the traditional black
Islamic dress, which covers all but the face, and the walls of
the city were festooned with vivid posters and murals that

depicted Khomeini leading bloodstained Islamic warriors fighting for the liberation of Jerusalem. Alcohol disappeared from shop shelves, and the Guards roamed the streets making sure Islamic customs were strictly observed.

The Guards consolidated their ties with militant Lebanese Shia leaders, such as Hussein Musawi. Musawi was a protégé of Mostafa Chamran, who had arranged for the young Lebanese to study in Tehran. Musawi had been a leading figure in Nabih Berri's mainstream Amal movement, but had set up his own splinter group – Islamic Amal – following the arrival in August of an American-led multinational force to monitor the ceasefire between the Israelis and Palestinians negotiated by Washington. Musawi had taken exception to Berri's moderate stance towards American involvement in ending the fighting; Musawi and other radical Shias argued that Washington was to blame for the Israeli invasion in the first place. He was also disillusioned with the secular-minded Berri's lack of the enthusiasm for the Iranian revolution, and responded by relocating his followers to the Guards' new base in Baalbeck, where the Iranians provided him with support to establish his own militia which was more akin to the Guards' own goals. Musawi compared the relationship between the Guards and Islamic Amal to that of 'a mother to her son. We are her children. We are seeking to formulate an Islamic society which in the final analysis will produce an Islamic state.'[8]

The deployment of the Revolutionary Guards to Lebanon acted as a catalyst for the formation of another militant Islamic movement that would become one of the Iranian revolution's most important allies. The emergence of Hizbollah, the radical Lebanese Shia militia, can be traced back to the early months of the Guards' deployment to Baalbeck. The group was modelled on the organization of the same name that had been in the vanguard of Khomeini's attempts to suppress political opposition to the Islamic revolution in Iran. It was formed from the young and poor Lebanese Shia peasants who were indoctrinated through films and 'ideological seminars'. They were so inspired by the call of revolutionary Islam that the local mosque carried a banner proclaiming it to be 'Martyrdom's Headquarters', while posters on the streets carried slogans such as 'Death to America' and 'Martyrdom is the aim and hope of God's worshippers'. For eight hours a day a local radio station transmitted 'The Voice of the Iranian Revolution', which included songs, sermons and interviews with Khomeini's supporters. Some of the radical young Shia who made their way to Baalbeck were members of the Lebanese Dawa who had already demonstrated their proficiency in conducting terrorist attacks against the French and Iraqis. Subhi Tufeili, a founder member of Hizbollah, acknowledged that the group was 'in essence the Dawa party', and its early formation drew heavily on the Dawa's terrorist expertise.

It was not long before the radicalization of Lebanon's Shia by Khomeini's agents had a dramatic impact on the course of the conflict in Lebanon. At 1.05 p.m. on the afternoon of 18 April 1983, a dark delivery van drove into the parking area of the American embassy in Beirut and detonated a massive bomb. The attack took place minutes after Robert Ames, a senior CIA officer, had convened a meeting of eight intelligence officials on the top floor of the embassy's north wing. The force of the blast caused the front of the building to collapse, and sixty-three people were killed and more than one hundred injured in what was then the bloodiest terrorist attack ever undertaken against an American diplomatic mission. Six months later, at shortly after 6 a.m. on 23 October, the Americans suffered an even more devastating attack when a suicide truck bomb destroyed the compound used to house US Marines serving with the multinational force. At the same time another truck bomb destroyed the command post used by the French contingent. The carefully coordinated attacks claimed the lives of more than 300 American and French soldiers, with scores more sustaining horrific injuries. For the United States it amounted to the worst disaster suffered by the American military since the Vietnam War.

The introduction of the modern curse of the Islamic suicide bomber to the lexicon of international terrorism – which reached its catastrophic apogee with the September 11 attacks – can be traced back directly to Khomeini's decision to deploy the Revolutionary Guards to Lebanon in 1982. A tactic that has now become widespread throughout the Middle East and beyond was relatively unknown at the time of the 1983 attacks, and consequently caught the French and Americans completely off guard. But while the Iranians officially denied any involvement, the subsequent American investigation demonstrated that the Revolutionary Guards had played an important role in planning and supporting the attacks, which were aimed at forcing the American and French governments to withdrawn their troops from Lebanon, an objective that was achieved when the multinational force withdrew the following year.

The terrorist mastermind responsible for the three suicide bomb attacks was eventually identified by American investigators as Imad Mughniyeh, a radical Lebanese Shia who had been trained and recruited by the Revolutionary Guards. Born in Tyre in 1962, Mughniyeh, who would become one of the world's most sought-after terrorists with a $25-million bounty offered by the FBI for his capture, came from a religious Lebanese Shia family and spent a year studying at the American University in Beirut. During the Lebanese civil war he fought with the elite Force 17 unit of Yasser Arafat's PLO, where he became an expert in the use of explosives. After the PLO was forced to evacuate its forces from Lebanon as part of the ceasefire deal negotiated by Washington, Mughniyeh joined Musawi's Islamic Amal, and was soon introduced to commanders of the Revolutionary Guards in Baalbeck. Abu Wafa, a former Guards' commander, recalled that during Mughniyeh's first trip to Iran in the 1980s, the young Lebanese militant proved his military ability and excelled in training. Together with a group of Lebanese Shia trainees, Mughniyeh volunteered to fight in the war against Iraq, and took part in several daring operations behind Iraqi lines.[9]

On his return to Beirut the local Revolutionary Guard commander appointed Mughniyeh the head of security for the newly established Hizbollah militia, and it was in this capacity that he was given responsibility for planning the deadly attacks against the American and French missions. Mughniyeh, who linked up with a former leader of the Dawa, Mustapha Badredeen, to plan the attack, began by conducting an exhaustive reconnaissance of the American and French compounds, and also recruited volunteers to conduct the suicide missions. For the attack on the US Marine compound Mughniyeh is reputed to have watched through his binoculars from the rooftop of a building located a safe distance away as the grinning truck driver drove his deadly cargo through the gates.

The success of the suicide bomb attacks against the Americans and the French confirmed Mughniyeh's position as a vital asset for the Revolutionary Guards and, with their backing, he went on to mastermind a number of high-profile terrorist operations. Similar suicide bomb attacks were carried out against Israeli positions in southern Lebanon, and Mughniyeh was the architect of the Lebanese hostage crisis, in which dozens of foreign nationals were abducted, including, in March 1984, William Buckley, who had taken over the CIA's Lebanon operation after the embassy bombing and was subsequently tortured to death by his kidnappers. Videos of him being tortured by Mughniyeh were sent to the CIA headquarters in the United States. Mughniyeh also helped to organize the bombing of the American embassy in Kuwait. He finally achieved international notoriety in 1985 after he led the team of hijackers who seized TWA flight 847 at Beirut airport in 1985, where he was filmed dumping the body of US Navy diver Robert Stethem on the airport tarmac having shot him in the head.

As a result of Mughniyeh's various terrorist exploits, President Ronald Reagan officially held Iran responsible for the attacks, and Tehran was placed on the State Department's list of countries responsible for 'state-sponsored terrorism'. A reward was also offered for Mughniyeh's capture – dead or alive. Tehran responded by granting Mughniyeh Iranian citizenship and allowing him to move with his family to Tehran to prevent him from being captured by the West. Long before Osama bin Laden emerged on the international terrorist scene, Imad Mughniyeh, Tehran's very own terror mastermind, pioneered the use of the modern suicide bomb, and inflicted a reign of terror against America and its allies that would not be surpassed until the September 11 attacks. For the next two decades Mughniyeh remained a key asset for the Revolutionary Guards, assisting them with their attempts to export the Islamic revolution throughout the world, while at the same time playing a key role in the development of Hizbollah as the Islamic revolution's most successful overseas export. As a former Hizbollah official later recalled, 'When Mughniyeh joined the Guards he did so on the basis of first conforming with the declared agenda of establishing a resistance movement . . . while this resistance movement would be of Lebanese nationality, it would also be of Iranian affiliation.'[10]

*

Iran's deepening involvement in the Lebanon conflict and the regime's support for Islamic terrorism reflected the growing self-confidence and assertiveness of Khomeini's government in Tehran. Having approved the initial strategy for deploying the Revolutionary Guards to Lebanon, Khomeini did not involve himself in the day-to-day planning and execution of policy, and only became involved when it was feared that the Revolutionary Guards' enthusiasm for exporting the revolution and launching terrorist attacks might work against Iran's wider interests. One occasion where Khomeini was obliged to intervene was when Mughniyeh hijacked TWA flight 847 in Beirut. Hashemi Rafsanjani, who had skilfully exploited his position as speaker of the Majlis to become Khomeini's most trusted adviser on foreign policy issues, managed to persuade Khomeini that it was not in Iran's interests to provoke another hostage crisis with America in the middle of the war with Iraq, particularly as scores of Westerners were already being held captive in Lebanon – the majority of them at the Revolutionary Guards' headquarters at Baalbeck. Khomeini agreed, and with his support Rafsanjani was able to pressure Mughniyeh and the other hijackers to release their hostages.[11]

Khomeini's intervention in the TWA hijack confirmed Washington's suspicions that most of the terrorist attacks against American interests in the region were being orchestrated from Tehran. For although the Revolutionary Guards had established an elaborate network of contacts within Lebanon's Shia community, Western officials were still uncertain whether to blame indigenous Shia radicals or Tehran for the constant terrorist threat they faced in Lebanon, particularly when it came to trying to negotiate the release of the scores of Western hostages who had been abducted by Islamic militants. The TWA hijacking seemed to confirm western beliefs that, while local militia groups might be responsible for waging the terrorist campaign, it was Tehran that was pulling the strings, a pattern that would later be repeated following the American-led invasion of Iraq in 2003. As a consequence the United States, Britain and France focused more of their attention on Tehran when it came to resolving the hostage crisis. Nor did the positive intervention of Hashemi Rafsanjani in resolving the TWA hijack pass unnoticed, for it raised the tantalizing prospect – certainly in Washington – that there might be moderate or pragmatic political figures in Iran such as Rafsanjani with whom the United States might be able to do business.

From Khomeini's point of view, though, Iran's involvement in Lebanon gave him great personal satisfaction on a number of levels. The deployment of the Revolutionary Guards to the Bekaa Valley meant that the regime had taken an important first step towards fulfilling its constitutional commitment to export the Iranian revolution. And the activities of Mughniyeh and Tehran's other terrorist proxies in the region meant that Tehran was able to wage war against its bitterest enemies – America and Israel – without having to resort to a direct confrontation that it could ill afford.

The success of the Revolutionary Guards' mission to Lebanon was just one of many factors that helped Khomeini to consolidate his position as Iran's spiritual leader and to ensure the survival of the Islamic revolution for future generations. For all the tumult the revolution had caused, Iran's oil revenues produced a healthy income of $15 billion a year, which was more than sufficient to sustain the needs of the revolution, and helped to finance a massive increase in the revolutionary bureaucracy, which grew from 304,000 civil servants at the end of the Shah's reign to a massive 850,000 by 1982. New ministries for intelligence, the Revolutionary Guards, Islamic Guidance and reconstruction were formed, mainly prompted by the continuing war effort, which from 1982 onwards seemed to be moving in Iran's favour. Having undertaken a radical restructuring of the military and the Revolutionary Guards to combine them into an effective force, the regime instituted the religious variant of the Communist commissar system, using 270 clerics to keep watch on key divisions and report back on their performance to the ayatollahs in Tehran.[12]

The continuation of the war acted as a highly potent rallying cry to unite Iranians of every religious and political hue behind the cause of defeating Saddam Hussein, and Khomeini exploited the popular support to strengthen the state's stranglehold over everyday administration of the state. Various practical measures were introduced, such as ration cards for all basic goods, which also served to increase government control over ordinary Iranians. Other measures were little more than a blatant power grab, such as nationalizing all the country's major companies and banks. Many of these were taken over by the state at the expense of wealthy entrepreneurs – many of whom had fled abroad with the Shah – who had dominated Iran's pre-revolutionary economic landscape. The justice ministry assumed control of every aspect of the legal system, from the Supreme Court to the revolutionary courts, with Khomeini's clerical supporters occupying nearly all of the key judicial positions.

Newspapers, books, films and the broadcast media were subjected to censorship, and the state-controlled television stations were ordered to broadcast features showing the clergy in a favourable light. Heroic footage of leading figures in the Revolutionary Guards, such as Mostafa Chamran commanding units on the Iraqi front line, were regularly broadcast to show there was much more to the clergy than simply preaching at the local mosque. The newly created Ministry of Islamic Guidance instigated a 'cultural revolution' to eradicate any traces of Western culture, from the use of Western names to changing the names of any public institution related to the Shahs. An Islamic code of public appearance, which required women to wear headscarves and long coats and discouraged men from wearing ties, was strictly enforced, with transgressors receiving fines or even public beatings.

A network of semi-public religious foundations was established ostensibly to help the poor, but in practice they were used to reward those who fully embraced and supported the tenets of the Islamic revolution. Funding for the main charity, the Foundation for the Oppressed and Disabled, which was run by the Revolutionary Guards commander Mohsen Rafiqdost, initially came from the confiscated property of fifty millionaires, and was distributed to families who contributed to the war effort. Rafiqdost turned the Foundation, or *bonayad*, into one of Iran's largest commercial conglomerates, and by the late 1980s its assets totalled more than $20 billion, including 140 factories, 470 commercial farms, 100 construction firms, 64 mines and 250 commercial companies. It owned the Iranian Coca-Cola franchise – nicknamed Zam Zam Cola, the former Hyatt and Hilton hotels as well as the two leading national newspapers *Ettela'at* and *Kayhan*. Rafiqdost maintained his close links with the Revolutionary Guards, and many former Guards who had good war records were rewarded with highly sought-after jobs in Rafiqdost's burgeoning commercial empire. By the end of the decade it was estimated that in excess of 400,000 people were employed by the Foundation and its charitable affiliates, and their combined budgets were half that of the central government.[13] The Revolutionary Guards and their associates were effectively building a state within a state that would give them enormous political leverage in deciding government policy.

This hectic bout of activity was initiated immediately following the destruction of President Bani-Sadr's political career in June 1981, and persisted for the rest of the decade as the clerics made a sustained effort to bring all the institutions of the state under their direct control. The process of consolidation was greatly assisted by the nationwide purge that followed the fall of Bani-Sadr, which removed the last traces of opposition to clerical rule. The Mujahideen were the primary target of a ruthless reign of terror that would have done the Jacobins proud. Having backed Bani-Sadr's attempt to dismantle the Islamic government, they took the foolhardy course of launching a campaign of assassination against prominent regime members. Scores of senior Islamic leaders were killed, and many others injured, including Khomeini's key aides, Hashemi Rafsanjani and Ali Khamenei.

Khomeini responded by empowering the revolutionary courts to take effective action, and they responded with unrestrained vigour. Between February 1979 and June 1981, when the sadistic Sadeq Khalkhali was at the height of his powers, the revolutionary courts sanctioned the execution of 497 political opponents as 'counter-revolutionaries' and 'sowers of corruption on earth'. Between June 1981 and June 1985 the revolutionary courts executed 8,000 opponents as the revolution turned on its own. The Mujahideen, who had lent Khomeini their full support during the difficult early days of the revolution, bore the brunt of the purge, but supporters of other political factions were not immune. Communists, National Front supporters and followers of Shariatmadari were all paraded before the firing squads, with many of them forced to recant their views on television before they met their deaths.

As a leading ayatollah in his own right, Shariatmadari, who continued to uphold the Shia tradition of quietism, where the clergy did not involve itself in politics, was too senior a figure to suffer the indignity of being tried by the revolutionary courts. Instead he was implicated in a plot to assassinate Khomeini which involved the former foreign minister Sadeq Qotbzadeh, who had served as one of the ayatollah's closest advisers while he was in Paris. Qotbzadeh and seventy accomplices were executed, but not before they had confessed, under interrogation, that Shariatmadari had known of the plan to murder Khomeini. Echoing the worst of the Stalinist show trials, Shariatmadari, whose son was threatened with execution if he did not cooperate, was forced to make a public confession on television and beg Khomeini's forgiveness. Shariatmadari was the last remaining cleric of stature who opposed Khomeini's fundamentalist interpretation of Islam, and Khomeini determined to destroy his reputation as a spiritual leader. Shariatmadari was defrocked – a move without precedent in Shia Islam – and placed under permanent house arrest, where he no longer had any contact with his supporters.

Khomeini had become Iran's supreme leader in every sense of the word, and though he remained one step removed from the day-to-day business of government, his aura permeated every level of the country's administration. No action was initiated if the official involved felt that it might in any way be contrary to Khomeini's wishes. Khomeini kept in close touch with all aspects of daily government by maintaining his habit, which he had begun at the start of the revolution, of holding regular audiences with groups representing various organizations and interests at the local mosque next to his house in the Jamaran district of Tehran. The meetings took place five times or more a week, and would commence with a speech or a petition from the visiting group, and visitors were encouraged to give vent to their frustrations. Thus Khomeini would get to hear of the difficulties caused by food rationing and other economic problems that were being created by the war effort.

Responding to these complaints, Khomeini reminded his audience that the Islamic revolution was not about improving the material well-being of the people, and chided them that they had not 'served Islam simply for the purpose of filling your stomachs'. But Khomeini, who was in his eighties and suffered periodic bouts of bad health, was particularly sensitive to the accusation that he was out of touch with what was going on in his own country. 'You said that I am not informed,' he responded during one such session. 'But this is said by those who want to imply that I am an ill-informed man and therefore what I say cannot be correct. I am not an ill-informed man. You came and sat and told me all you wanted.'[14] Even so, those responsible for running the country, such as Khamenei and Rafsanjani, were expected to interpret Khomeini's speeches on any given subject, and then act accordingly.

*

The origins of the ayatollahs' interest in developing nuclear weapons can be traced back to the early 1980s when Khomeini's regime was looking at various options to protect the Islamic revolution from future attack. From the moment Iran took the decision to take the war to Iraq, the Iraqis had resorted to using chemical weapons, which proved to be a highly effective tactic in repelling the 'human wave' attacks launched by the Revolutionary Guards. The introduction of weapons of mass destruction (WMD) into the Iran–Iraq war by Saddam Hussein, and the failure of the West to take seriously Iran's claims that Iraq was using chemical weapons, prompted Khomeini to revive his own interest in the possibility of Iran developing a WMD programme. The Iranians had been alarmed to discover that their deadly Iraqi rival had been secretly developing his own nuclear weapons arsenal, which was severely disrupted after Israeli warplanes destroyed the Osirak reactor in 1981, where the clandestine weapons programme was based.

When he came to power in 1979, Khomeini inherited a well-advanced nuclear programme that had been initiated by the Shah as part of his drive to modernize Iran, and work had already begun on building two nuclear plants at Bushehr and Ahwaz. But Khomeini regarded the Shah's nuclear programme as yet another symbol of the former regime's attempts to Westernize the country, and cancelled the contracts to build the power stations. It was only after Saddam Hussein introduced WMD to the battlefield that Khomeini had second thoughts about his cavalier dismissal of the benefits of nuclear technology, and urged his senior officials to revive Iran's nuclear programme with a view to developing atomic weapons. Before his death in the 1981 terrorist attack on the IRP's headquaters, Ayatollah Mohammed Beheshti, arguably the most influential Islamic leader in Iran after Khomeini, had been a keen advocate of Iran resuming its nuclear programme, and his arguments no doubt helped to persuade Khomeini to change his mind. An Iranian nuclear scientist, Dr Fereidoun Feshakaki, recalled how he had been called to Beheshti's office in Tehran in 1979, who told him he must build an atom bomb. 'It is your duty to build this bomb for the Islamic Republic,' Feshakaki, who later defected to the West, recalled Beheshti telling him.[15] Ali Larijani, who became Iran's chief negotiator with the West over Iran's nuclear programme, told officials at the

International Atomic Energy Agency (IAEA) that the origins of Khomeini's project could be traced back to the early 1980s.[16]

Iran's nuclear programme had originally been conceived in the 1960s. The Shah's $30-billion plan envisaged the construction of twenty nuclear power plants by the year 2000. During the 1970s, when most of the nuclear development work was undertaken, the entire nuclear programme was supervised by the Atomic Energy Agency of Iran (AEOI) and subject to regular inspections by the Vienna-based IAEA under an agreement the Shah had signed in 1974. As part of the international cooperation on Iran's nuclear programme, thousands of Iranians were invited to study nuclear technology in Germany, France, Britain, America and India. Iran was also a signatory to the Treaty on the Non-Proliferation of Nuclear Weapons (NPT), the international agreement that limited the development of nuclear weapons. Iranian nuclear scientists undertook preliminary research to explore the possibility of adapting the nuclear programme for military use, and in 1975 work was commissioned on building a set of lasers that could separate weapons-grade uranium from natural uranium. The same technology could be used to produce plutonium.[17] The export of the lasers to the Shah was approved by the US government, and by the time Khomeini came to power in 1979 Iran's nuclear programme was regarded as 'by far the most ambitious in the Middle East'.[18]

After Khomeini had given the green light for Iran to explore the possibility of acquiring nuclear weapons, the Revolutionary Guards, acting in conjunction with the Ministry of Defence, moved quickly to assume responsibility for the military programme which they determined to keep secret from the outside world. In 1983 a special unit devoted to nuclear research and technology was set up by the Guards and located in a suburb of north Tehran. Nuclear scientists who had gone through the official training programme organized by the research division of the AEOI were seconded to work in the new unit.[19] At the same time the Ministry of Defence, which had responsibility for developing the missile systems capable of carrying nuclear warheads, set up its own special research unit which was placed under the control of a senior Revolutionary Guards officer. The AEOI was to remain the official face of Iran's nuclear programme, and continue its dialogue with international monitoring agencies, such as the IAEA, while the Revolutionary Guards would oversee work on the clandestine weapons programme. According to an Iranian nuclear physicist who defected to the West in 1992, Mohsen Rezai, who had assumed overall command of the Revolutionary Guards in 1981, revealed that the regime had allocated a budget of $800 million for the atom bomb programme. The defector recalled that Rezai had told him, 'Iran needs to arm itself with anything needed for victory, and we need to have all the technical requirements in our possession to even build a nuclear bomb, if and when needed.'[20]

From the mid-1980s onwards the regime expended an enormous amount of effort on developing its nuclear capability. In 1984 a new nuclear research laboratory was built at Isfahan at the site of an existing complex dating back to the Shah, which had originally been designed to train staff to work at the new Bushehr nuclear power station. Hashemi Rafsanjani, in his capacity at Khomeini's main foreign policy adviser, negotiated a deal with China to provide training, expertise and materials for the nuclear programme, and the Chinese installed the first of four 'training' reactors at Isfahan in 1985. Rafsanjani negotiated another deal with North Korea to assist with uranium exploration and development. Other nuclear cooperation deals were negotiated with the Soviet Union and Pakistan, where the Pakistani nuclear scientist Dr Abdul Qadeer Khan was making good progress on developing Pakistan's atom bomb, which was successfully test-fired in 1998.

Much of Iran's early research work on its nuclear military programme took place at Isfahan, where it conducted experiments in uranium conversion and fuel production, which constituted a clear breach of its NPT obligations. Iranian officials scoured the international black market for nuclear material, and by 1985 Iran was in a position to undertake experiments on uranium enrichment – the first step towards producing fissile material for a nuclear warhead. They also succeeded in acquiring the blueprint for a centrifuge design – centrifuges are used to enrich uranium to weapons grade – from an unnamed 'foreign intermediary', most likely Pakistan.[21] All of this activity, which the regime would later claim was part of its research into the development of nuclear power, was deliberately concealed from the IAEA's nuclear inspectors on their regular visits to monitor progress of Iran's nuclear energy programme. In 2003 the IAEA published a report which concluded that 'practically all of the materials important to uranium conversion had been produced in laboratory and bench scale experiments between 1981 and 1993 without having been reported to the Agency'.[22] The fact that these experiments, and the rest of Iran's clandestine nuclear programme, were controlled by the Revolutionary Guards, as opposed to the AEOI, appeared to confirm the fears of Western nuclear experts that Iran was developing its own nuclear weapons capability.[23]

Khomeini's determination to persist with the war against Iraq until Saddam Hussein's regime was overthrown led the government to explore some unlikely avenues in pursuit of arms procurement, and revealed potentially damaging splits in the regime's ruling echelons. For all the effort invested in the nuclear project, Iran's most pressing need was to get hold of military equipment to support the war effort. Most of the military infrastructure inherited from the Shah – the warplanes, the naval vessels, the field munitions etc. – originated from America, but Tehran had been denied access to spare parts and equipment needed by the embargo Washington had imposed in retaliation for the occupation of the American embassy. After American President Ronald Reagan privately sent Hashemi Rafsanjani a message of thanks for his helpful intervention in resolving the TWA hijack, the wily Rafsanjani sensed an opportunity to do a deal with Washington.

Although Ali Khamenei, the president, and Mir Hossein Musavi, the prime minister, held more senior positions, it was the hard-working and skilful speaker of the Iranian parliament who had replaced Beheshti as Khomeini's most trusted political adviser. Rafsanjani's long-standing friendship with Khomeini's son Ahmad gave him the advantage over his political rivals in terms of his access to the country's spiritual leader. Rafsanjani had become so adept at interpreting Khomeini's wishes that Khomeini arranged for him and his family to move into a neighbouring mansion in the north Tehran suburb of Jamaran.

Rafsanjani was confident enough to believe he did not need Khomeini's blessing to explore the possibility of a deal with the Americans: his main priority was to support the war effort. A complex negotiating process, which, was brokered by a number of Israeli middle men, began in which the Iranians sought to buy American arms in return for using their influence over the radical Lebanese groups they had helped establish to free the Western hostages held in Lebanon. Washington's involvement was partly motivated by the desire to discover whether there was a moderate faction in Tehran it could do business with. Within a few months an arrangement was entered into whereby Israel, acting on Washington's behalf, delivered 2,000 anti-tank missiles and 18 HAWK surface-to-air missiles to Tehran, in return for which the Iranians were supposed to persuade their Lebanese proxy groups to release the American hostages held in Beirut. But while the Americans kept their end of the bargain, only three American hostages were released. And no sooner had they returned home than another three Americans were kidnapped, suggesting that the Iranians intended to keep their arms for hostages trade going for as long as it was beneficial to Tehran.

Some senior officials within the Reagan administration were

so encouraged by their new negotiating channel with Tehran that in May 1986 Robert McFarlane, the former US National Security Adviser and a trusted confidant of Reagan, paid a personal visit to Tehran in a vain attempt to open a dialogue with Khomeini. Travelling on a false Irish passport, McFarlane and his party arrived in an Israeli Boeing 707 filled with vital spare parts for Iran's war effort. McFarlane himself was carrying an iced cake and a Bible – the cake, which was decorated with a brass key, was supposed to symbolize unlocking the door to better relations between America and Iran, while the Bible, which bore President Reagan's personal inscription, was meant to highlight the historical relationship between Christianity and Islam. But the overture came to nothing when Khomeini learned of the American party's presence in Tehran, and personally forbade any of his ministers to meet the American delegation. McFarlane's entourage was kept waiting unceremoniously at Tehran airport for several hours while a group of young Revolutionary Guards ate the cake, and were then ordered to leave without having been given the opportunity to deliver any of their offerings.[24]

Apart from the obvious embarrassment Iran's diplomatic rebuff caused the Americans, the revelation that Rafsanjani had opened a dialogue with Washington revealed deep divisions among the country's leading revolutionary establishment. Rafsanjani's position as Khomeini's favourite inevitably aroused jealousy among the regime's other leading clerics, particularly the supporters of Ayatollah Montazeri, whom Khomeini had officially nominated as his successor in November 1985. Under the terms of the constitution, Khomeini, who was now well into his eighties, could either select an individual equal in religious stature to himself, or appoint a council of three to five jurists. Montazeri, who had been a devoted follower of Khomeini since attending his classes at Qom, was a man of outstanding learning and a militant jurist. As president of the Assembly of Experts, he had managed the heated debates over the constitution, and as a senior member of the IRP he had championed the export of the Islamic revolution, and by designating Montazeri as his official successor Khomeini was picking the obvious candidate.

The main Revolutionary Guards' unit responsible for exporting the revolution, the Office for World Islamic Liberation Movements, was run by Mehdi Hashemi, who was related to Montazeri by marriage. Hashemi was one of the more extreme of the radical mullahs vying for influence in Tehran, and had close links to both Hizbollah in Lebanon and the Iranian-funded Mujahideen in Afghanistan. Like Montazeri, Hashemi was deeply suspicious of Rafsanjani's attempts to impose a measure of legitimacy on the Iranian government, which the Montazeri camp feared would destroy the purity of the revolution. Through his Lebanese contacts Hashemi got to hear of Rafsanjani's extraordinary dealings with the Americans, and it was not long before Tehran was abuzz with accounts of the arrival of the strange American delegation at the airport. The revelation that Rafsanjani had not only been in secret talks with the hated Americans, but had also allowed Israel to supply arms for Iran's war effort, could have proved fatal. Rafsanjani moved quickly, and on 12 October Hashemi and a large number of his followers were arrested on trumped-up treason charges. By having Hashemi arrested Rafsanjani had hoped to prevent the details of his dealings with the Americans being made public, but Hashemi had taken the precaution of providing his friends in Beirut with chapter and verse on the McFarlane visit, which was duly published in the left-wing Lebanese news magazine *Ash-Shiraa* on 3 November 1986.

When details of Iran's unlikely arms deals with the United States and Israel became public, Khomeini was quick to distance himself from the whole affair, and allowed Rafsanjani and the other pragmatists responsible for setting up the negotiations to take the blame. While he did not name Rafsanjani, Khomeini accused unidentified officials of falling prey to 'foreign propaganda' from the White House, which he called 'the Black House'. More ominously, Khomeini declared, 'I never expected such things from these people. At this time they should have been screaming at America.'[25]

This could well have been the end for Rafsanjani, but ultimately he was saved by Khomeini's intervention. Khomeini had no wish to engage in a dialogue with the Americans, but at the same time he had no desire to see the career of his political protégé destroyed. With Khomeini's backing, Rafsanjani went on the offensive, and Hashemi was put on trial at the Special Court for the Clergy, which Khomeini had set up especially for the occasion. Hashemi was found guilty of treason and sentenced to death, and his execution by firing squad on 27 September 1987 represented a major victory for Rafsanjani, and silenced the radicals around Montazeri who had tried to undermine his attempts to steer the revolution along a more pragmatic course. Rafsanjani emerged from this unseemly episode as the real power behind Khomeini's throne, and his decisive move against Hashemi was a salutary lesson to those radicals, particularly within the Revolutionary Guards, who felt the Majlis speaker was curbing the enthusiasm of Islamic revolutionaries. But as Khomeini's representative on the Supreme Defence Council, which was responsible for the war effort, Rafsanjani's position appeared to be inviolable.

The ongoing war with Iraq, which had been the underlying motivation for Tehran's overture to Washington, remained the most pressing concern for both the government and the country at large. The successful capture of the Fao peninsula by Iranian forces in February 1986, which put the Iranians in a commanding position over the crucial Shatt al-Arab waterway, also raised the alarming prospect, from the West's point of view, that Basra, Iraq's second city and the centre of Iraq's oil industry, might fall under Iranian control. So long as the two sides were bogged down in a grim war of attrition, with neither side capable of making a significant breakthrough, the attitude of most Western governments was best summed up by former US Secretary of State Dr Henry Kissinger's remark, 'It's a shame they both can't lose.' But the idea that the Islamic revolution might establish a toehold in the Shia heartlands of southern Iraq, with the future possibility of Khomeini controlling a crescent of radicalized Shia from Tehran to Baghdad, was sufficient to prompt the West to undertake a wide-ranging review of its policy towards the conflict.

In Britain the Thatcher government secretly relaxed the strict guidelines on the export of arms to either of the combatants, and millions of pounds of military supplies were shipped to Iraq. Washington was even more proactive, and was so determined to assist the Iraqis to arrest the Iranian advance that the Americans took the unprecedented decision to provide the Iraqis with real-time satellite information so that Iran's troop movements could be closely monitored. During the course of the next year the Americans, prompted by their desire to even the score for their humiliation over the arms-for-hostages affair, openly sided with the Iraqi war effort. The US Navy, supported by Britain and other European allies, was dispatched to the Gulf to protect the vital oil artery from attack by Iranian warplanes and patrol boats. The patent anti-Iranian bias of the American operation was demonstrated in May 1987 when twenty-eight American sailors were killed when an Iraqi warplane fired an Exocet missile at the USS *Stark* in the Gulf, and the Reagan administration blamed Tehran for being the cause of the attack by continuing its policy of trying to destabilize the Gulf.

The West's support for Iraq, and Iran's own failure to press home its advantage after achieving the initial breakthrough in the Fao peninsula, saw a gradual erosion of support for the war among ordinary Iranians. The Revolutionary Guards and the army had made good use of the weaponry provided by Washington to make important strategic gains in Fao, but transportation shortages seriously impeded their efforts to exploit their advantage. Even so Rafsanjani, who had his own reasons for demonstrating his revolutionary credentials after the embarrassment of the Hashemi affair, backed the commanders who wanted to continue the advance into Iraq and capture Basra. The army's ground forces commander, Brigadier General Ali Shirazi, who was concerned about the enormous casualties the Iranian forces had already suffered, urged caution, and actually came to blows with Mohsen Rezai, the Revolutionary Guards commander, during an argument over whether or not the advance should continue. Khomeini himself was forced to intervene and relieve Shirazi of his command. When a fresh offensive was launched the following January, the Iraqis were better prepared, and the Iranians suffered an estimated 70,000 to 80,000 casualties out of a force of 200,000.[26]

Popular support for the war effort in Iran continued to decline, and even Revolutionary Guards units began to hold demonstrations in favour of 'forgiving' Saddam Hussein. The pool of volunteers for the Basij began to dry up as the national appetite waned for conducting mass suicide attacks against the Iraqis for no tangible gains, forcing the government to extend compulsory conscription from twenty-four to twenty-eight months. In private many Iranians complained about the war and tried to dodge the draft, and the shortage of troops at the front constrained attempts to launch new offensives. The presence of a large contingent of Western warships in the Gulf, and the active support Iraq was receiving from the West, severely limited Iran's other military options. Some Iranian politicians still clung to the hope that they might be able to incite an Islamic revolution in Baghdad, but Saddam's fearsome security forces had the country's radical Shia firmly in their grip. When it was clear that Iran would not be able to improve on its short-lived success in capturing the Fao peninsula, a number of senior Iranian clerics – including Rafsanjani – tried to persuade Khomeini that the time had come to end the war, but Khomeini would not contemplate such a move so long as Saddam was still in power.[27]

In the event Khomeini's hand was forced after Iraq launched a successful offensive in the spring of 1988 which succeeded in recapturing the Fao peninsula. Iraq's elite Republican Guard, with American help, had been completely retrained and re-equipped, and the inferior Iranian forces were totally overwhelmed by the offensive. Iraq was also able to strike a massive psychological blow against Iran's civilian population by launching a barrage of Scud missiles whose range had been extended to enable them to strike Iran's main cities, with Tehran and Qom bearing the brunt of the hits. More than 200 missiles were fired, the heaviest bombardment the civilian population had suffered in seven years of conflict and, as rumours spread that the warheads might contain chemical weapons, there was mass exodus from the cities, with more than 1 million people deserting Tehran alone. When the Iranians tried to plant mines in the Gulf to disrupt the West's main oil shipping artery, the Americans launched Operation Praying Mantis, which started with American warships destroying three oil platforms used by the Revolutionary Guards to attack Gulf shipping.

When the Iranians tried to respond by dispatching their fleet and air force to confront the Americans, the US Navy effortlessly destroyed three Iranian naval vessels and shot down an F-4. For the next three months the Iraqis maintained their well-organized offensive, virtually destroying Iran's defensive capability so that by the end of June they were in a position to march on Tehran if they so desired. The final straw for the Iranians, though, came on 3 July, when the American warship USS *Vincennes* accidentally shot down an Iran Air Airbus after it had left Bandar Abbas airport, which was used by military, as well as civilian, aircraft. The Americans were involved in a skirmish with Iranian naval vessels at the time, and mistook the Airbus for an F-14. Two hundred and ninety passengers and crew were killed in the catastrophe, the sixth worst disaster in aviation history.

In a last, desperate attempt to revive the Iranian war effort, Khomeini appointed Rafsanjani acting commander-in-chief of all Iran's armed forces in early June. Despite all the setbacks and growing internal criticism of the war effort, Khomeini continued to insist that the fate of the war should be 'decided on the battlefields and not at the negotiating table'. Khomeini's health was now so frail that he relied on his son Ahmad to read his statement at the inauguration of the third session of the Majlis on 28 May, in which he called for the government to remove the 'bottlenecks, limitations and problems' that he believed were hampering the war effort. But as soon as Rafsanjani assumed control of the war effort, he immediately recognized the hopelessness of Iran's predicament. The situation was so desperate that the only proposal the Revolutionary Guards could put forward was to use its own chemical weapons, but Rafsanjani persuaded Khomeini to reject the idea, arguing that it would further increase Tehran's international isolation, and provoke the Iraqis into launching more missile attacks, possibly with chemical warheads, against Iran's already demoralized citizens. Although the Americans insisted the destruction of the Iran Airbus was a tragic mistake, Rafsanjani and the rest of the clerical establishment were convinced that America was intent on destroying the Islamic revolution, and Khamenei, the Majlis, the commanders of the Revolutionary Guards and the military unanimously concluded that Khomeini must be persuaded to change his mind and accept a peace deal.

Rafsanjani was deputed to talk Khomeini round, and he spent several days trying to persuade the ayatollah that pursuing the war any longer could lead to the destruction of the Islamic Republic. Finally, and with great reluctance, Khomeini agreed to end the war. Previously Khomeini had rejected a number of United Nations Security Council resolutions designed to impose a ceasefire in the long-running conflict on the grounds that they did not allocate blame to Iraq for starting the war in the first place. Khomeini now gave his authorization to the government to accept unconditionally Resolution 598, which the UN had adopted the previous year, and on 18 July Iran formally announced the war was over. Khomeini was distraught at the thought of having to concede defeat to Iraq, which is how he regarded Iran's acceptance of the ceasefire. In a written statement issued two days later, Khomeini made no attempt to conceal his disappointment. 'Had it not been in the interests of Islam and Muslims, I would never have accepted this, and would have preferred death and martyrdom instead. But we have no choice and we should give in to what God wants us to do. I reiterate that the acceptance of this issue is more bitter than poison for me, but I drink this chalice of poison for the Almighty and for His satisfaction.'[28]

The humiliating end to the Iran–Iraq War took a heavy toll on Khomeini. Had it not been for his stubbornness, Iran could have ended the war in 1982, after the liberation of Khorramshahr, and saved the nation the terrible suffering it had to endure for another six years. The country would have ended the war on a high note and been the beneficiary of $70 billion that the Gulf Arabs had offered Tehran as a reward for terminating the conflict. Instead by 1988 the country was economically almost on its knees: inflation was running at between 40 and 50 per cent, unemployment stood at 30 per cent despite the nationwide draft, and expenditure on the war was outstripping state revenues. Khomeini had forced the Iranians to persist with a policy that caused them tremendous harm and achieved nothing. But the fact that Iran's spiritual leader, through sheer force of will, had been able to force Iran to pursue the conflict long after most people thought it was winnable demonstrated the strength of his all-pervading influence over the country.

Khomeini seemed to appreciate the implications of his grave

miscalculation over prolonging the war, and the setback took a heavy toll on his general well-being. He was nearly eighty-six and was suffering from cancer, as well as heart problems that had affected him intermittently since the early 1980s. His eyesight was failing, and he relied on his grandchildren to read newspapers, books and official reports for him. His public appearances had become increasingly rare, and after the cease-fire he became a virtual recluse. Ahmad Khomeini recalled the moment his father knew he had to accept the ceasefire. 'The television was showing our soldiers and he kept hitting himself with his fists, saying "Ah". No one dared to see him. After accepting the ceasefire he could no longer walk. He kept saying, "My Lord, I submit to your will." He never again spoke in public. He never again went to speak at the mosque, and he fell ill and was taken to hospital.'[29]

Khomeini knew he did not have much longer to live, but before he met his maker he was determined to ensure that his legacy was in order so that future generations of Iranians and their supporters would forever be committed to upholding the principles of his Islamic revolution.

9

The Global Brand

The finishing touches to Khomeini's legacy of radical Islam were applied in the final months of the ailing ayatollah's life. In poor health and rarely seen in public, Khomeini was still mentally alert. In life, Khomeini enjoyed total dominance of the country's political and religious affairs in the ten years he had ruled as Iran's spiritual guardian. As he neared the end of his long and eventful involvement in making Iran one of the most radical Islamic states in world history, his main preoccupation was that the achievements of the Islamic republic should continue long after his death.

Uppermost in his thoughts was the problematic issue of the succession. Ayatollah Mohammed Montazeri, one of Khomeini's lifelong followers and a dedicated supporter of the Islamic revolution, had already been designated Khomeini's official successor. But even though Khomeini retained a high regard for Montazeri's religious learning and stature, he had started to entertain doubts about Montazeri's suitability for the position as the nation's guardian. In the aftermath of the war with Iraq there was growing public pressure for a relaxation of the all-encompassing powers invested in Khomeini's position, not least because it was widely held that the ayatollah's conduct during the military campaign had demonstrated a lack of clear economic, social and political strategy. In a series of lectures delivered at Qom in late 1988 and early 1989, Montazeri appeared to address these concerns when he spelled out a more open type of Islamic government, one that provided more scope

for popular participation than had been tolerated under Khomeini. Montazeri made no attempt to disguise his view that the
country had become a religious dictatorship.

Montazeri's mounting disillusion with the regime intensified after the war when Khomeini personally authorized the
mass execution of thousands of political prisoners. The order
was issued following an ill-advised invasion of the country by
the Mujahideen, the former supporters of the Islamic revolution
who had fled into exile in the 1980s and built up a substantial
base in Iraq during the war. The invasion took place two days
after Khomeini officially ended the war, and was easily suppressed, but Khomeini feared the Mujahideen were planning a
national uprising. He issued an order to intelligence officials
that any prisoners who still declared their support for the
Mujahideen should be executed immediately. International
human rights bodies estimate that several thousand prisoners
were either hanged or shot during the next two months.[1] Many
of those killed had nothing to do with the Mujahideen, and
had been held in prison for many years for their involvement
with other political parties. In some cases former prisoners who
had been released after serving their sentences were re-arrested
and executed even though they had not taken part in political
activities since their release. Leftists were executed for 'apostasy' on the grounds they had turned their back on God, the
Prophet, the Koran, and the Resurrection. One plausible
explanation for this appalling bloodbath was that Khomeini
was seeking to bond together his followers in the common
experience of mass executions, with the killings testing their
mettle, weeding out the half-hearted from the true believers,
the weak-willed from the fully committed.[2]

Whatever Khomeini's motive, Montazeri, who as deputy
leader had responsibility for assessing prisoners' sentences, was
appalled, and wrote to Khomeini arguing that the mass executions were against the interests of the Islamic state. Apart from

the fact that people who were totally innocent were being executed, Montazeri believed the bloodletting would further turn world opinion against Iran and damage the Islamic Republic's reputation for future generations. In one of his letters to Khomeini, which was made public, Montazeri complained that Iran had become known in the world only for its executions. Khomeini's response was to force Montazeri to resign his position as designated successor to the supreme leader.

In March 1989 Khomeini wrote a letter to Montazeri running to several pages in which he accused the grand ayatollah of seeking to hand over 'the Muslim people of Iran to the liberals'. Montazeri responded by writing a short, five-line reply in which he announced he was resigning from the succession, a position he said he had never wanted in the first place. Montazeri's resignation nevertheless caused the regime severe difficulties, as there were no other obvious candidates. Khomeini's preferred choice was Ali Khamenei, the then president, but Khamenei was too junior in the country's religous hierarchy, and his scholarly qualifications not good enough for such an important religious position. With Khomeini's health rapidly fading, he convened a special meeting of the Assembly for Revising the Constitution, which duly amended the constitution to allow Khamenei to become the designated successor.

Khomeini dismissed Montazeri to ensure that the purity of the Islamic revolution was maintained. In January 1988 Khomeini had written a letter addressed to Khamenei and the Council of Guardians, the body responsible for making sure the principles of the revolution were upheld, stating unequivocally that the authority of the *faqih*, the supreme religious leader, was absolute and his duty to preserve the Islamic Republic took precedence over all others. The *faqih*, moreover, was empowered by God to take whatever action was necessary to protect the Islamic revolution, even if it meant going against well-established religious law or the objections of senior clerics.

Khomeini's edict meant that his successors as supreme leader would enjoy the same powers he had exercised since the foundation of the Islamic Republic.

Khomeini also made sure that after his death Iran would continue work on its nuclear weapons programme. He was under no illusions that Iran had effectively conceded defeat to Iraq, and he was determined that, in any future conflict, Iran would have all the necessary weapons to achieve victory. On 16 July 1988, just four days before Khomeini announced that he had agreed to accept UN Security Resolution 598, which called for an immediate ceasefire to end the war with Iraq, he wrote a letter to Iran's military and political leaders. The letter was in response to a 'shocking report' he had received from Mohsen Rezai, the commander of the Revolutionary Guards, in which Rezai expressed utter despair at the course the war was taking. Khomeini's letter argued that Iran should do everything to acquire the military capability to ensure that it did not find itself in the same humiliating position the next time the country went to war. 'If we have at hand the instruments which we will obtain over five years, it is possible for us to have the power to carry out destructive or reciprocal operations,' Khomeini wrote. 'If we have 350 infantry brigades, 2,500 tanks, 3,000 artillery units, 300 fighter jets, 300 helicopters and the ability to create noticeable quantities of laser and atomic weapons which are the requirements of war in this day and age, I can say that by God's will we could carry out an offensive operation.' This letter, whose existence was kept secret for many years, is the only known occasion when Khomeini personally referred to the necessity of Iraq acquiring nuclear weapons.[3]

Khomeini's letter had a profound and lasting effect on the development of Iran's nuclear programme. Until this point there had been a degree of ambiguity within the ruling echelons as to whether Khomeini really supported the development of nuclear weapons or not. After Khomeini had initially

opposed resuming work on the Shah's nuclear power programme, many of his supporters had come to believe that he
also regarded nuclear weapons as unIslamic. But this letter, in
which he unequivocally declared his support for an Iranian
atom bomb, made it clear to his successors that a nuclear-armed
Iran should be one of the revolution's key objectives after his
death. However much Iran's nuclear programme might bring
the country into conflict with the West, there was little the
ayatollahs could do to change course, irrespective of the damage the pursuit of a nuclear weapons arsenal might cause the
country. The quest for the atom bomb was a central part of
Khomeini's legacy, and so long as the Islamic Republic survived, the Islamic revolutionaries who governed the country
would never give up on their nuclear ambitions.

Another of Khomeini's deathbed interventions was aimed at
making sure Iran maintained its confrontational policy with the
West. At the end of the war with Iraq a lively debate developed
between the pragmatists, led by Rafsanjani and Khamenei, who
argued it was in Iran's interests to attempt a rapprochement
with the West to help rebuild the country, and the radicals
within the Revolutionary Guards who insisted Iran was perfectly capable of coping on its own. By early 1989 it appeared
the pragmatists had the upper hand, and several editorials
appeared in the government-controlled press arguing that Iran
had nothing to lose by establishing proper relations with the
West.

The arrival of President George Bush at the White House in
January saw Washington attempt to take a more conciliatory
tone with Tehran, and in his inaugural address the president
openly asked for Iran's help in freeing the Western hostages
still held in Lebanon, assuring the Iranians that 'Goodwill
begets goodwill.' Rafsanjani in particular was greatly encouraged by this veiled overture from the United States, and he
responded by suggesting Iran adopt a less confrontational
attitude towards the West. He also suggested that the Iranian

constitution was in need of reform, and that continuing the war with Iraq had been a mistake. Khomeini was incensed by this overt challenge both to his legacy and to his authority. But rather than become involved in a public dispute with Rafsanjani and the pragmatists over future policy, Khomeini hit upon a simple expedient that put paid to any possibility of a rapprochement with the West. He issued his infamous fatwa denouncing Salman Rushdie's book *The Satanic Verses*.

For five months Iran had studiously refrained from getting involved in the controversy surrounding the book written by Rushdie, an Indian-born Muslim, which had provoked world-wide protests from Muslims over what they regarded as the blasphemous depiction of the Prophet Mohammed. Then on Valentine's Day 1989 Khomeini published his ruling declaring that 'The author of *The Satanic Verses* book, which is against Islam, the Prophet and the Koran, and all of those involved in its publication who were aware of its content, are sentenced to death. I call on zealous Muslims to promptly execute them on the spot they find them.' One of Iran's religious charities, or *bonyads*, offered a reward of $2.6 million for Rushdie's death.

At a stroke Khomeini's religious ruling destroyed any hopes the pragmatists still entertained of improving relations with the West. As Muslim supporters of the fatwa attacked bookstores selling *The Satanic Verses* in Britain, Italy and the United States, European governments that had just restored relations with Tehran quickly withdrew their ambassadors in protest. A Muslim cleric in Belgium who criticized the fatwa was killed by a team of Revolutionary Guards assassins, while in Japan the book's translator was assassinated by a Guards hit team. By issuing the fatwa Khomeini had guaranteed that Iran would maintain its hostile attitude towards the West and Western culture long after his own death. Rather than reaching an accommodation with the West, Khomeini wanted the Islamic revolution to confront the West.

It was within the context of Iran's institutional hostility to

Western interests that suspicions arose about Iran's involvement in the terrorist attack against Pan Am flight 103, which was destroyed by a bomb as it flew over the Scottish village of Lockerbie in December 1988 with the loss of 270 lives. Almost immediately Western intelligence officials saw the attack as Iran's revenge for the destruction of the Iran Air Airbus by the USS *Vincennes* the previous July. A number of leading clerics close to Khomeini made public statements vowing revenge for the disaster, including Ali Akbar Mohtashemi, who had become Iran's Interior Minister, who declared there would be a 'rain of blood' over the West in retaliation for the disaster.

Previously Mohtashemi had served as Iran's ambassador to Damascus where he had played a central role in the development of the militant Lebanese Shia militia Hizbollah, which had been linked to the suicide truck-bomb attacks against the Americans and French in 1983 and the hostage crisis. During his time in Damascus Mohtashemi had dealings with Ahmed Jibril, the leader of the radical Popular Front for the Liberation of Palestine — General Command (PLFP-GC), which was labelled a terrorist group by the US State Department. For months after the Lockerbie disaster British and American officials were convinced that the Iranian government was behind the atrocity, and evidence emerged that Mohtashemi had paid $10 million to Jibril's organization. Mohtashemi was also known to have had close links with the notorious Palestinian terrorist Abu Nidal, another key suspect in the Lockerbie investigation, members of whose group were frequent visitors to the Iranian embassy in Damascus when Mohtashemi was ambassador.[4] The investigation focused on the arrest two months before the bombing of fifteen terrorists linked to the PLFP-GC in Germany who were found to have a number of home-made bombs, consisting of Toshiba cassette recorders filled with Semtex explosive, similar to the one used in the Lockerbie attack. Investigators eventually discounted the PLFP-GC plot and instead turned their attentions to Colonel Gaddafi's Libya, and two Libyan intelligence agents were later charged and put on trial for the attack.

But many campaigners and officials close to the investigation believed Iran had got off lightly because there was insufficient evidence to mount a successful prosecution. 'We had clear indications that Iran was somehow involved in the Lockerbie bombing, but not enough to make the charges stick,' said a senior Western intelligence official who was directly involved in the investigation. 'The Iranians are far too smart to be caught red-handed on something as big as this.'[5] As with the suicide truck-bomb attacks in Beirut and the Lebanon hostage crisis, Tehran took great care not to be implicated directly in the terror strategy even though most Western governments privately acknowledged that Iran was active behind the scenes directing operations. This would become a familiar problem for Western officials investigating Islamist-inspired terror plots in the years to come, from the hostage crisis in Lebanon to the Revolutionary Guards' links to Osama bin Laden's terrorist organization. While there were often suspicions that the attacks had been masterminded by Tehran, finding the evidence to prove it was a different matter. This was the case with Lockerbie where the investigation was further undermined by suspicions that the newly elected Bush administration was prepared to turn a blind eye to Iran's possible involvement as part of its attempts to improve relations with Tehran and negotiate the release of its hostages held in Beirut.[6]

The real story about who was ultimately responsible for the Lockerbie disaster may never be known, but fresh evidence continued to emerge that linked Khomeini's regime directly to the attack long after one of the Libyan agents was convicted and jailed for life for his role in the atrocity. In 1997 a former Iranian intelligence officer was reported to have told German investigators that Khomeini had personally ordered the attack to avenge the Iran Air disaster, and that Libyan and Palestinian terrorists had been 'hired' to carry out the bombing.[7] Other Iranian defectors claiming to be intelligence officers and former members of the Revolutionary Guards made similar claims, and various intelligence reports entered the public domain that appeared to suggest a direct link between Khomeini and the PLFP-GC. But no conclusive evidence was produced to prove Iranian complicity and the Iranian authorities studiously denied that the regime had anything to do with the Lockerbie bombing.

The truth about Pan Am flight 103 was one of many secrets Khomeini took with him to the grave when his health finally gave out shortly before midnight on Saturday, 3 June 1989. His physical condition had been in steady decline since he had suffered a near fatal heart attack in the summer of 1986, which had been kept a strict secret from the outside world. But from late 1988 onwards even Khomeini knew that his body was giving up on him. By early June Khomeini had been admitted to a clinic close to his residence in north Tehran, and on Friday 2 June Khomeini called his close family to his bedside to inform them that he was dying. He bade them farewell with the words of a man who knew he was soon to meet his maker. In his last recorded words he told his family, 'This is a very difficult path . . . watch all your words and deeds . . . I have nothing more to add. Those who want to stay, may do so; those who don't may go. Put the light out. I want to sleep.'[8] Attended by his son Ahmad and his daughter Zahra, he fell into a deep slumber.

Khomeini was the first Iranian ruler in over eighty years not to be exiled or assassinated, but to die peacefully in his bed. His death was officially announced on Tehran Radio the following morning by a presenter who sobbed uncontrollably as he read: 'The lofty Spirit of Allah has joined the celestial heaven.' Rafsanjani, Khamenei and other leading regime members issued a joint statement in which they set the tone for the dead leader's eulogies, describing him as 'the most divine personality in the history of Islam after the Prophet and the Imams.' Rafsanjani, who had effectively been running the country as Khomeini's health declined, declared a state of emergency, and all the telephone lines were cut. Rafsanjani and his clerical colleagues feared that the removal of Khomeini's towering presence from the country's political life might provoke instability. Airports, borders and key installations were all closed down and Revolutionary Guards units deployed to tackle any disturbances.

Khomeini's family wanted the funeral to take place the following day, according to Islamic custom, but the government felt obliged to postpone the event for a week to allow the proper arrangements to be made to accommodate all the foreign guests that were expected to attend, not to mention the millions of distraught Iranian mourners who were already making their way to Khomeini's house to pay their last respects. The government was also keen to use the intervening period to confirm the succession so that Khomeini's legacy was fully implemented. Not everyone rejoiced at the prospect of Khomeini's extreme brand of Islamic fundamentalism being prolonged long after his death, with one long-standing critic remarking, 'The long night of tyranny is over. We are at the threshold of a new dawn.'

But the clerical cabal that Khomeini had gathered around him in the final years of his life had their own ideas, and while the funeral arrangements were being made Rafsanjani convened a special meeting of the Assembly of Experts to implement Khomeini's plan for the succession. Khamenei, who had been raised to the position of ayatollah by Khomeini shortly before his death, was appointed the country's new supreme spiritual leader, or *faqih*, with Rafsanjani seamlessly replacing Khamenei as president, in line with Khomeini's wishes. There were concerns that Khamenei lacked the religious qualifications to hold such a prestigious position, and the Shia religious establishment at Qom steadfastly refused to acknowledge Khamenei's arbitrary election to the status of ayatollah, which is typically

won through the acclamation of peers and followers.[9] Sensitive
to any suggestion that the post-Khomeini settlement lacked
legitimacy, Rafsanjani moved quickly to redress the constitutional balance by abolishing the post of prime minister and
transferring all the prerogatives previously held by that office
to the presidency. Rafsanjani's status as the main power broker
in the land was confirmed when the Revolutionary Guards and
the army issued a joint statement pledging their allegiance to
him as their new commander-in-chief.

While the Assembly of Experts put the finishing touches to
the succession, Khomeini's body was moved to a hilltop area of
north Tehran to lie in state. Covered in a white shroud with
his feet facing towards Mecca, Khomeini's presence attracted
tens of thousands of mourners desperate to pay their last
respects. The authorities were overwhelmed by the sheer volume of people trying to see the Imam's body laid out in an air-
conditioned glass case, and the Tehran fire brigade had to spray
water over the excited crowd to prevent them from fainting.
When the time came for the funeral itself the crowd was so
immense and uncontrollable that it proved impossible for the
funeral cortège to pass from Khomeini's home in north Tehran
to his final resting place at the Behesht-e Zahra cemetery.

An estimated 2 million Iranians converged on Tehran for
the funeral, and the authorities eventually had to resort to
using a helicopter to transport the body to the cemetery. But
the moment the helicopter landed the crowd surged forward
and seized the body, tearing at the white shroud so that the
pieces might be kept as holy relics. The Revolutionary Guards
had to fire their guns in the air to retrieve the body, which
was flown back to north Tehran so that it could be redressed
for burial. The Guards eventually succeeded in transporting
the body in a sealed metal container to the cemetery, where it
was interred facing Mecca. But that did not stop the frenzy.
The Iranian media reported that more than 10,000 people were
treated for injuries they received during the funeral ceremony,

and dozens lost their lives. Khomeini's death had proved to be as tumultuous as his life.

*

The heirs to Khomeini's legacy lost no time in consolidating their eagerly awaited inheritance. The Reform Council set up by Khomeini weeks before his death, ostensibly to legitimize Khamenei's claim to the succession, made an important number of other changes to the constitution which diluted the requirements necessary for the appointment of a *faqih*. One member of the council even argued that a *faqih* was not essential for Khomeini's *velayat-e faqih*, and that henceforward the Supreme Leader, far from being the country's most acclaimed religious scholar, merely needed to be a seminary-trained cleric to qualify for the position, so long as he had the right qualities of piety, courage and was 'versed in the political issues of the age'.[10] The dilution of a position that had been conceived by Khomeini for Khomeini meant that henceforward Khamenei would simply be called the Supreme Leader, while the term *faqih* fell into abeyance.

The Reform Council initiated a series of other measures designed to make the government less bureaucratic and more effective, the most significant of which was the establishment of the Expediency Council as a permanent body to adjudicate over disputes between the legislative, the Majlis, and the executive, in the form of President Hashemi Rafsanjani and Supreme Leader Ali Khamenei. Representatives of the government, the armed forces, the intelligence services and the Guardian Council, which remained responsible for upholding the tenets of the Islamic revolution, were all represented on the forty-four-member Expediency Council, which effectively became Iran's upper house.

Seven weeks after Khomeini's death, in July 1989, all these constitutional amendments were subjected to a national referendum, as were the appointments of Khamenei and Rafsanjani.

Rafsanjani went through the motions of contesting the election against a rival candidate who was completely unknown to the rest of the country, which meant that the result was a forgone conclusion. The amendments to the constitution received 97 per cent of the vote, while Rafsanjani polled 94 per cent. The turnout, though, was less than 55 per cent – a 20 per cent drop since the last referendum had been held nearly a decade previously to ratify the principles of Khomeini's revolution.

Given the reputation Khamenei and Rafsanjani had enjoyed as pragmatists during Khomeini's final years, most Iranians might have been forgiven for expecting a relaxation in the more unpalatable aspects of Khomeini's Islamic ideology, such as the public stonings and floggings. But the persistent doubts over Khamenei's suitability to occupy the office of Supreme Leader, particularly concerning his religious credentials, made him compensate for his shortcomings by aligning himself with the hardliners. As one Iranian political commentator at the time remarked of Khamenei, 'From a tepid liberal he turned overnight into an irredeemable hardliner.' Khamenei's main legitimacy derived from the fact that Khomeini had personally chosen him as his successor, and so far as most Iranians were concerned his authority derived solely from his ability to execute the will of the Imam. Khomeini had carefully arranged his legacy so that he remained the source of all legitimacy in Iran long after his death, and Khamenei had no alternative other than to adhere strictly to Khomeini's posthumous wishes.

That had no doubt been Khomeini's reason for choosing Khamenei over Montazeri in the first place. Montazeri was a senior Islamic jurist in his own right and, from Khomeini's point of view, had shown a worrying independence of mind when it came to interpreting the principles of the Islamic revolution. With Khamenei, Khomeini knew he need not worry. Born in 1939 in Mashhad, Khamenei, who had been imprisoned under the Shah, had proved himself to be a devoted supporter of the revolution who had worked his way through the ranks of the Islamic Republican Party to become its secretary general. Khamenei had been one of Khomeini's students at Qom and later became a close ally of Khomeini's for more than twenty years, but always took care to show due deference to his master.

An eloquent and well-educated orator, Khamenei's instincts were probably more liberal than those of Khomeini. After Khomeini had issued his fatwa against Salman Rushdie, Khamenei suggested that the whole affair would blow over if Rushdie 'apologizes and disowns the book'. But when Rushdie issued a carefully worded statement regretting the 'distress' he had caused to the Muslim world, Khomeini ignored the gesture and insisted that even an apology could not overrule the death sentence. On another occasion Khomeini publicly humiliated Khamenei when, as president, he made a speech in 1987 indicating reform might be possible on various social issues. Khomeini angrily wrote to Khamenei saying he did not understand the principles of *velayat-e faqih*. Ordinary people, he insisted, did not have a say in the running of the country; their duty was to respect Islam and the will of God. 'Khomeini laid down the law that if you want an Islamic country then you have to have the absolute rule of the clergy,' said one of Khomeini's former aides. 'Even though Khamenei was the President, Khomeini often treated him as a rather dim student.'[11] So far as securing his legacy was concerned, Khomeini knew that in Khamenei's hands the Islamic revolution was safe.

Rafsanjani, the new president, was an altogether different proposition. Another devotee of the Islamic revolution who had been imprisoned on several occasions because of his opposition to the Shah, Rafsanjani was a wily political operator and a successful businessman in his own right who had made a personal fortune during the commercial boom of the 1970s. Born in 1934 to a pistachio farmer in the remote town of Rafsanjan, the future president was educated in Qom, and soon became involved in politics, becoming a member of the

'Devotees of Islam' which campaigned for the nationalization of Iran's oil industry in the 1950s. When Khomeini went into exile Rafsanjani had become a key figure in the underground resistance. After the revolution he quickly earned a reputation as Iran's 'smiling power broker', but although he may well have been a true moderate, his motivation was always predicated by what was best for his own career.

Extremely ambitious, Rafsanjani acquired a reputation as a thoroughly unprincipled political animal, who would deploy every means at his disposal, from rigging elections in his favour to publicly disowning politicians who had formerly been his close allies. His political mastery nevertheless impressed Khomeini, and he became the ayatollah's closest and most trusted political adviser, a bond that was strong enough to enable Rafsanjani to emerge unscathed from the humiliation of the arms-for-hostages scandal in the 1980s. Rafsanjani repaid Khomeini's faith in his political ability by skilfully confirming Khamenei's position as Supreme Leader and his own as the new president. Most Iranians believe that Rafsanjani's ultimate ambition is to succeed Khamenei as Supreme Leader, assuming he manages to live that long.

One of Khamenei's most pressing priorities after becoming president was to strengthen the Revolutionary Guards to make them a more effective force in terms of defending the Islamic revolution at home and exporting it abroad. A strong Guards Corps was also essential to shoring up Khamenei's presidency. Not everyone in Iran was convinced about the legitimacy of Iran's post-Khomeini political settlement, and the unconditional support of the Guards, who were totally committed to the Islamic revolution, helped to provide Khamenei with another source of legitimacy.

During the Iran–Iraq War the Guards had evolved into a formidable, self-contained military establishment. By 1986 it consisted of 350,000 personnel – three times the size of the British Army – who were organized in battalion-size units that either operated independently or with units of the regular armed forces. In 1986 the Guards also acquired small naval and air units. The main responsibility of the naval force, which was formed following an order Khomeini issued in 1985, was to protect Iran's interests in the Gulf. Although it was only equipped with small patrol launches, the Guards' navy proved highly effective at causing disruption to Gulf shipping towards the end of the war. During the 1980s the main activity of the air force was to develop effective missile systems for the war with Iraq and for Iran's nascent nuclear programme.

Under Khamenei the three Revolutionary Guards divisions – army, navy and air force – were expanded to five. The two new sections created by Khamenei were the Basij and the Quds force. The Basij, the army of volunteers who had performed so heroically during the war, was given responsibility for providing domestic security, while the Quds (Jerusalem) force was dedicated to supporting the regime's overseas operations, such as intelligence gathering and helping to export of the Iranian revolution by supporting radical Islamic liberation groups. After Mecca and Medina, Jerusalem is one of the holiest sites in Islam where the Prophet Mohammed is said to have ascended to heaven. Jerusalem had been an emotive rallying cry during the war against Iraq, and Khomeini had frequently made speeches to the effect that the path to the liberation of Jerusalem from Israeli control lay through the conquest of Baghdad. The distance between Tehran and Jerusalem meant that it was unlikely that Iran's armed forces would ever find themselves in a direct confrontation with Israel, but the presence of Hizbollah, Iran's heavily armed Lebanese Shia militia, on Israel's northern border, was the ayatollahs' way of making sure they had a significant stake in the long-running Arab–Israeli dispute.

The Quds force soon developed into the spearhead of the regime's attempts to export the revolution. Its main function was to develop and support radical Islamic groups, many of which Washington accused of involvement in acts of terrorism.[12] Ahmad Vahidi, the first Quds force commander who was appointed in 1990, was a close ally of Mohsen Rezai, the head of the Revolutionary Guards, and had formerly headed the Guards intelligence unit during the 1980s, as well as helping to establish the unit responsible for helping overseas Islamic liberation movements. In 1983 Vahidi was given responsibility for helping to establish the 1,000-strong Guards detachment that was deployed to Lebanon in 1982 and helped to set up Hizbollah. Vahidi was one of several Iranians who were implicated by Washington in the 1983 suicide truck-bomb attacks in Beirut. From the outset Vahidi reported directly to Khamenei, rather than the commander of the Revolutionary Guards, which was indicative of Khamenei's personal commitment to exporting the Iranian revolution.

Under Vahidi's command, the Quds force, which comprised 800 Revolutionary Guards who had proved their revolutionary credentials, moved quickly to establish an international network of Islamic revolutionaries. Apart from continuing to build Hizbollah's operational infrastructure in south Lebanon, one of the Quds force's most notable early successes was to establish an alliance with the Sudanese regime of Hassan al-Turabi. A Sunni Muslim, al-Turabi was keen to develop links to any radical Islamic government, even a Shia regime like Iran. The Iranians responded by posting Ali Akbar Mohtashemi, the former ambassador to Damascus who had helped found Hizbollah, as Iran's new ambassador to Khartoum. Over the next two years Sudan allowed the Revolutionary Guards to set up two training camps south of Khartoum, where hundreds of Islamic militants from a variety of Middle Eastern countries underwent basic military training. A year after the Revolutionary Guards established bases in Sudan, Osama bin Laden, the founder of the al-Qaeda Islamic terror network, also moved to Sudan, where he established the foundations of his international terror network.[13] The presence of the Revolutionary

Guards and Osama bin Laden in Sudan at the same time in 1991 led to concerns within the Western intelligence community that, despite their different Shia and Sunni backgrounds, Iran and al-Qaeda were prepared to pool their resources cooperating in terrorist operations.

The development of Iran's international terrorism network coincided with the intensification of its quest for nuclear weapons. Both Khamenei and Rafsanjani were united in their desire to press ahead with the development of atomic weapons, not least because they would deter Saddam Hussein or any country hostile to Iran invading or attacking the country in the future. At the end of the Iran–Iraq War Rafsanjani told a meeting of Revolutionary Guards commanders, 'We should fully equip ourselves both in the offensive and defensive use of chemical, bacteriological and radiological weapons. From now on you should make use of the opportunity and perform this task.'[14] Khomeini himself had committed Iran to develop nuclear weapons in the letter he wrote in the last year of his life, and the ayatollah's legacy meant Khamenei and Rafsanjani would adhere to his wishes.

The discovery by the IAEA's nuclear inspectors at the end of the first Gulf War in 1991 that Saddam Hussein's regime had been within a few months of building an atom bomb also concentrated the minds of the ayatollahs in Tehran. The Iraqis had managed to develop their atom bomb despite regular inspections by the IAEA. If Saddam could trick the world into believing his nuclear ambitions were entirely peaceful, there was no reason why Iran could not follow suit. Thus, despite making impressive progress on the clandestine nuclear weapons programme, in public Tehran always denied any desire to acquire nuclear weapons. For example, in an address to foreign diplomats in 1995, Rafsanjani insisted that Iran's strict adherence to the tenets of Islam did not allow it to develop 'destructive and anti-human weapons'.[15]

After Khomeini's death Rafsanjani and Khamenei presided

19: During the Iran–Iraq War, a young woman makes Molotov cocktails for the Pasdarans (Revolutionary Guards) in the mosque at Abadan. A large poster of the Ayatollah Ruhollah Khomeini is plastered on the mosaics.

20: Khomeini lies in a Tehran hospital surrounded by his son Ahmed and three of his grandchildren, February 1980. Khomeini died on 4 June 1989, aged 87.

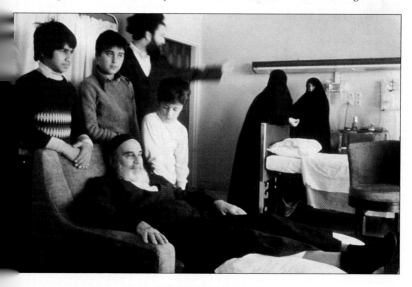

21: A young Iranian soldier shouts 'Allahu Akhbar' (God is Great), the battle cry from the trenches during the Iran–Iraq War, in Ein Khosh, Iran, November 1982. Tens of thousands of teenage Iranians volunteered for service at the front.

22 & 23: US Marines, armed with automatic rifles, stand guard in front of the American Embassy in West Beirut, Lebanon, after a huge car-bomb blast collapsed the entire front of the seven-story structure, 18 April 1983.

24 (*above*): Former designated successor to the late Ayatollah Khomeini, Hossein Ali Montazeri.

25 (*above, right*): The author touring Iranian front line positions with the Revolutionary Guards in 1987.

26 (*right*): 20 April 1988. Iraqi soldiers pose in front of a huge bullet-pocked mural of Khomeini in the strategic Faw peninsula of southeast Iraq that was partly occupied by Iranian forces during the Iran–Iraq war.

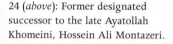

27: Demonstrators in Tehran call for the death of Indian–British writer Salman Rushdie after a fatwa was issued by Khomeini condemning him to death for blasphemy after the publication of his novel *The Satanic Verses* in 1989.

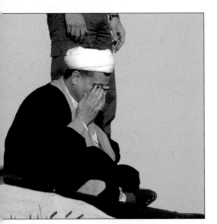

28, 29 & 30 (*opposite*): Iranian politician Hashemi Rafsanjani cries as the Ayatollah Ruhollah Khomeini lies in state in Tehran on 5 June 1989, the day before his funeral. About one million Iranians surround the glass show box at the Mossala prayer ground.

31 (*right*): In Shia Islam tradition, men self-flagellate near the burial ground.

32: 9 August 1991. British journalist John McCarthy touches down on home soil, after being held hostage for five years in Lebanon.

33: Associated Press chief Middle East correspondent Terry Anderson is surrounded by journalists and well-wishers as he leaves the Syrian Foreign Ministry in Damascus on 4 December 1991. Anderson was freed after more than six years of captivity in Lebanon.

34: An Iranian officer briefs his troops during military manoeuvres in the Zabol area on the Iran-Afghan border, 1 November 1998. Iran dispatched 200,000 troops for its unprecedented Zolfaqar-2 manoeuvres.

35: UN weapons inspectors have applied their knowledge acquired searching WMDs in Iraq to make sure Iran is conforming with UN regulations.

36: A Hizbollah fighter uses binoculars to watch over Israeli army positions on the outskirts of the southern village of Aitaroun, close to the town of Bint Jbeil, August 2006.

37: Israeli soldiers carry a wounded comrade off an armoured personnel carrier. Eleven Israeli soldiers were killed in heavy fighting with Hizbollah guerrillas near the border.

38: Former Iranian president Ali Akbar Hashemi Rafsanjani, speaks during a Friday prayer ceremony in Tehran in September 2006. Despite losing the 2005 election, he remains a powerful force behind the scenes.

39: The radical Shiite cleric Muqtada al-Sadr delivers a Friday sermon in a Mosque in Kufa, Iraq, 2006. American commanders believed al-Sadr had orders from Tehran to precipitate a civil war in Iraq.

40: British navy personnel, seized by Iran, left and centre foreground, meet with Iranian President Mahmoud Ahmadinejad, right, in Tehran, 4 April 2007. Ahmadinejad announced that his government would release fifteen detained British sailors and marines as an Easter season gift to the British people.

41: Lebanese Hizbollah women, hold mock Katyusha and RPG rocket launchers, during a rally in Saksakkiyeh village, southern Lebanon in 2007. Hizbollah leader Sheik Hassan Nasrallah claimed his group possesses an arsenal of rockets that can reach 'any corner' of the state of Israel.

42: Exterior view of the reactor building at the Bushehr nuclear power plant at the Iranian port town of Bushehr, 1200 km south of Tehran.

43: Iranian President Mahmoud Ahmadinejad meeting former UN Secretary General Kofi Annan in Tehran in October 2008. Annan was participating in a 'Conference on Religion in the Modern World' organized by Iran's Dialogue Between Civilizations Organization headed by former reformist Iranian president Mohammad Khatami.

over a rapid expansion of Iran's nuclear project. By 1989 Iran had made impressive progress in the acquisition of nuclear technology and expertise. Nuclear cooperation deals Tehran had signed with the Soviet Union and China were highly productive, and in addition to providing Iran with four research reactors the Chinese delivered a calutron, a crude device that can be used to enrich uranium. Tehran had also succeeded in negotiating a secret deal in 1987 with the Pakistani nuclear scientist Dr Abdul Qadeer Khan. Khan later provided Tehran with the blueprints for the design of P2 centrifuges, which can be used to enrich uranium to weapons grade. In addition Khan arranged for a group of Iranian scientists to be trained in Pakistan, arranging for some of them to work at his own facility. The negotiations with Khan were made by a team of Revolutionary Guards, which reported directly to Khamenei. By the early 1990s the Guards had set up their own nuclear research centre and worked separately from the AEOI, Iran's official nuclear body, prompting Western intelligence to suspect that the Guards were working on their own clandestine nuclear weapons programme.[16]

Iran's development of an international terrorist infrastructure and the intensification of its efforts to acquire nuclear weapons were undertaken while the regime's official line was that it wanted to normalize relations with the West following Khomeini's death. The parlous state of the Iranian economy was one pressing reason why Rafsanjani hoped to use his presidency to have a more constructive dialogue with the West. By the summer of 1990 nearly half the nation's workforce was unemployed, one-third of the country lived below the poverty line and inflation was running at 200 per cent. Rafsanjani was keen to exploit Washington's more conciliatory mood towards Tehran following the election of the first Bush administration, which made the first move by easing some of the sanctions applied during the Iran–Iraq War. Rafsanjani and some of the other pragmatists may have been genuine in their attempts to improve relations, and negotiations were entered into via a third party to try to resolve the hostage crisis in Lebanon which, now that Western forces had withdrawn from Beirut, served no real purpose other than to tarnish Iran's international reputation. But the ghost of Khomeini's legacy continued to haunt the deliberations of Tehran's ruling elite, and there was a limit to how far Rafsanjani could pursue his efforts to improve relations with the 'Great Satan'. Washington soon detected this ambivalent attitude in Tehran and reluctantly concluded that there was no point talking to a faction in Tehran that could not deliver on its commitments.

Saddam Hussein's invasion of Kuwait in August 1990 distracted Washington's attention away from Iran, and its only interest in Tehran was to persuade the Iranians to remain neutral while the United States assembled a multinational coalition to evict Iraq's armed forces from the sheikhdom. Having suffered terribly during their own war with Iraq, the Iranians were more than happy to let the coalition destroy Saddam's military capability. It was only when the war was over, and Saddam's bedraggled forces had been forced to retreat from Kuwait, that the Iranians suddenly took an opportunistic interest in the post-war possibilities in Iraq. With Saddam's repressive security apparatus in disarray, militant Shia groups in southern Iraq – encouraged by the West – launched an uprising to overthrow the Baathist dictatorship in the spring of 1991.

Khomeini had long harboured the desire to establish an Islamic government in Baghdad. His heirs sensed an opportunity to exploit the Shia revolt for their own interests. Prior to the revolt the Revolutionary Guards' Quds force had helped to train the Badr Corps, a militia made up of radical Iraqi Shias who had fled to Iran to escape Saddam's brutality. Another unit of the Quds force had established close links with Kurdish militias in northern Iraq that were seeking to establish an independent state. But the prospect of Iran exploiting Iraq's weakness to replace Saddam's regime with an Islamic state was too much for Washington, which withdrew its support for the Shia uprising in southern Iraq. Eventually Saddam was able to rally his forces and launch a brutal repression of the Shia. But long after Saddam had crushed the Shia revolt the Quds force continued to train and support the Badr Corps, which twelve years later would become an important factor in Shia politics when another US-led coalition went to war with Saddam Hussein.

The end of the Gulf War provided Rafsanjani and the pragmatists with a new opportunity to move towards repairing relations with Washington, even if the hawks in Washington remained concerned about Iran's deepening involvement with radical Islamist groups. But any prospect of a thaw in relations was severely diminished in August when an Iranian hit team murdered Shapour Bakhtiar, the Shah's last prime minister, in Paris. After fleeing into exile in 1979 Bakhtiar had formed the National Resistance Movement to campaign for the restoration of democracy in Iran, and had already escaped several assassination attempts. But the Iranians finally succeeded in silencing him when a three-man assassination squad broke into Bakhtiar's villa in a suburb of Paris and killed him and his secretary before fleeing back to Tehran on an Iran Air flight. Bakhtiar was found by French security officials the following morning sitting in his chair with his throat and wrists slit.

Bakhtiar's murder was part of Tehran's attempts to eradicate the last vestiges of Iranian opposition to the revolution, which had started when Khomeini had authorized the mass execution of political prisoners held in Iran's jails before he died. But the brutality of Bakhtiar's murder, and the incontrovertible evidence acquired by French investigators that proved the involvement of the Revolutionary Guards, persuaded the Americans that nothing much had changed in post-Khomeini Iran. Even though the pragmatists eventually managed to secure the release of the Western hostages held in Lebanon at the end of

1991, Washington was by then in no mood to engage in a constructive dialogue. Rafsanjani had hoped at the very least for some expression of gratitude from Washington for using his influence to secure the hostages' release, but none was forthcoming, as most American officials were disinclined to thank the Iranians when they had been instrumental in directing the hostage crisis from the outset.

Another factor that contributed to a shift in Iran's attitude towards Washington was the announcement that Bush was convening a peace conference in Madrid to attempt to resolve the Israeli–Palestinian dispute. From the mullahs' perspective, if the Americans succeeded in achieving their stated objective of concluding a lasting peace agreement, it would legitimize Israel's right to exist, whereas the mullahs were committed to Israel's ultimate destruction. Khomeini had been consistent in his denunciation of the Zionist state since the 1950s, and in 1979 had declared that the last day of Ramadan should be marked as al-Quds, or Jerusalem, day, when devout Muslims prayed for the liberation of Jerusalem from Israeli control. Khamenei continued Khomeini's line of anti-Israeli rhetoric by always referring in public to the state of Israel as 'the cancerous tumour'. A Middle East deal would also seriously constrain Iran's prospects of exporting Khomeini's revolution. The longer the stand-off between the Arabs and Israel continued, the more likely it was that impressionable young Muslims might be seduced by the appeal of radical Islam. And if a peace deal were successful, it would need to include Syria, which would have serious repercussions for Iran's future support for Hizbollah as Tehran depended heavily on Syrian goodwill to maintain the communication and supply lines between Tehran and the Bekaa Valley.

However much Rafsanjani might originally have hoped to reach a better understanding with the West, by the end of 1991 the Iranian regime found itself adopting a far more confrontational attitude, and instead of looking for opportunities to improve relations with Western governments it sought allies that would support its hard-line, rejectionist approach to Western policy. When the Middle East peace conference finally convened in Madrid at the end of October, Tehran issued an uncompromising statement condemning the conference and threatening to murder any Arab delegates who agreed to participate.[17] At the same time the West's attitude began to harden towards Iran when the first clear evidence emerged that the ayatollahs were trying to develop nuclear weapons. While the Madrid conference was taking place Washington produced its first national intelligence estimate on Iran's nuclear programme, which concluded that the Iranian regime appeared intent on developing nuclear weapons. The brief, cautiously worded assessment conceded – correctly – that Iran's nuclear programme was disorganized and only at the initial stage of development. But the extent of Iran's nuclear cooperation with China, and its relentless search for nuclear-related technology from countries like China, India, Argentina, Pakistan and Germany, prompted a lively debate within the first Bush administration about Iran's true intentions, with many senior officials arguing that Iran's nuclear threat was more serious than that portrayed in the intelligence estimate.[18] The controversy over Iran's real nuclear ambitions was set to continue for many years to come.

*

The rest of the 1990s was characterized by Iran's deepening involvement in Islamic-motivated terrorist groups and the West's confused response to the mounting security threat posed by Iran's Islamic revolution. One moment some European governments were calling for a constructive dialogue with those Iranian leaders deemed to be moderates, and the next they found themselves unilaterally cutting diplomatic ties following Iran's involvement in some new outrage. The West's indecision was in part a reaction to the deepening

rivalry over policy that developed between Rafsanjani and
Khamenei, with Rafsanjani trying to position himself as the
reformer who wanted to establish the rule of law over all
aspects of Iranian society, while Khamenei grew closer to the
conservative hardliners who had won a majority of the seats at
the Majlis elections in 1992 and wanted to maintain Khomeini's
status quo.

Rafsanjani's priority after becoming president was to
rebuild Iran after the devastation of the war years and introduce a measure of order to the chaotic administration of the
country, which he called 'the era of reconstruction'. The
various law enforcement agencies were combined into one
formal structure and he stated publicly that those covert units
used to assassinate opponents during the war would now be
terminated, having served their purpose. But despite Rafsanjani's efforts, many of the ad hoc revolutionary organizations
remained in place and beyond the state's control, including
most of the Revolutionary Guards' structure. These also
included the *bonyads*, the large religious charities that had
multiplied during the war. The largest *bonyad*, the Foundation
of the Oppressed, was controlled by Mohsen Rafiqdost, who
diverted much of its funding to financing radical Islamic groups
overseas, such as Hizbollah in Lebanon.

Khamenei and his conservative supporters became increasingly suspicious about Rafsanjani's attempts to reform the
government, particularly his efforts to bring the revolution's
religious bodies under state control. Khamenei and the hardliners still controlled the Revolutionary Guards and the newly
created Quds force which they used to carry on Khomeini's
legacy of anti-Americanism and exporting the revolution. The
next few years registered an explosion of activity by the
Revolutionary Guards overseas which saw them seeking to
establish a foothold throughout the Middle East, North Africa,
Central Asia, Europe, the Balkans and even Latin America.

Their primary focus was the Middle East, where their main

objective was to disrupt Washington's attempts to broker a peace deal between Israel and the Palestinians, and to subvert America's regional hegemony. All the resources that had previously been tied up fighting the war against Iraq and suppressing domestic opposition were unleashed on an unsuspecting world as Iran unfurled the banner of radical Islam. The strategic alliance with Hizbollah in southern Lebanon and with the Sudanese government proved to be invaluable in training and equipping Islamic militants for the campaign of political destabilization and terrorism.

Following the end of the Lebanese civil war in 1991, Tehran donated millions of dollars through the Foundation of the Oppressed in humanitarian assistance to help the Shia of southern Lebanon rebuild their lives. Iran literally bought the support of Lebanon's Shia population by building schools and hospitals and generally taking care of the welfare of the population. The flag of the Iranian revolution was proudly displayed from the roofs of the new buildings, while inside portraits of Ayatollah Khomeini were hung on the walls next to those of local Lebanese Shia leaders. By the early 1990s southern Lebanon was developing into a mini Iranian republic where every aspect of life, from hospital care to education, from building new homes to refurbishing government buildings, was paid for and administered by Hizbollah. At the same time the militia, boosted by its success in forcing the Israeli army to withdraw from southern Lebanon, strengthened its military capability to the extent that Lebanon's southern border in effect became Iran's front line in its undeclared war against Israel.

The development of Iran's welfare and security infrastructure in southern Lebanon was greatly facilitated by the support of Syria which, having allied itself to the United States for Operation Desert Storm, adopted a more ambiguous policy towards the West after Washington announced it would be attempting to mediate a peace deal between Israel and the

Palestinians. Of all the Arab states Syria was the most recalcitrant when it came to dealing with Israel, and the new axis between Damascus and Tehran was crucial to Iran's strategy of confronting the United States and Israel.

In December 1992, Iran's determination to undermine the Israeli–Palestinian negotiating process received an unexpected boost when the Israeli government made the calamitous decision to deport more than 400 Palestinian militants to southern Lebanon. The Palestinians were nearly all members of Hamas, the radical Islamic Palestinian group that had emerged to challenge Yasser Arafat's PLO for overall leadership of the Palestinian cause. Arafat's initial good relations with Iran's Islamic revolutionaries had waned after the PLO leader sided with Saddam Hussein during the Iran–Iraq War. Hamas, which wanted to create an Islamic Palestinian state and was committed to the destruction of Israel, was, like many Sunni Muslim militant movements, wary of linking up with the Shia of Iran. But the forcible relocation of Hamas' top leadership to Hizbollah-controlled southern Lebanon inevitably brought the two sides together.

When the expelled Hamas activists arrived in southern Lebanon Hizbollah officials helped them to set up a camp in Marj-el-Zhour, the Valley of the Flowers, and provided food and other essential supplies. During the course of the next year several Hamas leaders were invited to meet with prominent Shia leaders in Beirut, ultimately laying the foundations for a mutually beneficial cooperation pact between Hamas and Tehran. The burgeoning alliance was further strengthened when a Hamas delegation visited Tehran and was received personally by Khamenei. Following the meeting Iran agreed to pay Hamas an annual contribution of $34 million to fund its operations, with the first payment being made in early 1993.[19]

The new strategic relationship Iran developed with Sudan was another feature of the Islamic revolution's expansionist policy. The importance to Tehran of the alliance with Sudan was demonstrated when Rafsanjani made a six-day state visit to Khartoum in December 1991. He was accompanied by the foreign minister, defence minister, the head of intelligence and the commander of the Revolutionary Guards. Sudan under al-Turabi was attempting to position itself at the head of a radical, pan-Islamic movement. In the spring of 1991 he set up the Popular Islamic Conference in which delegates from fifty-five Islamic states committed themselves to the struggle of radical Islam against the West. Rafsanjani's flirtation with improving relations with the West was easily forgotten as he grasped the opportunity to acquire an important ally for the broader struggle of confronting Western influence in the Muslim world.

Tehran's alliance with Sudan was the first tangible evidence that the traditional distrust between the rival traditions of Sunni and Shia Islam could be set aside in the mutual interest of waging jihad, or holy war, against Western interests. Rafsanjani's visit resulted in a series of economic and military agreements, with Iran promising to provide $20-million worth of weapons and training, ostensibly to help Khartoum with its war against the Christian uprising in the south.[20] A number of Iranian officials and Revolutionary Guards remained in Khartoum to help the Sudanese establish the National Islamic Front militia, which was modelled on, and trained by, Iran's Revolutionary Guards. Sudan's new militia took preference over the traditional armed forces when it came to the allocation of manpower, resources and weapons, and by 1992 it had recruited 90,000 fighters and volunteers.

In addition to setting up Sudanese militias the Revolutionary Guards were allowed to establish two training camps at al-Shambat and al-Mazrah, south of the capital, Khartoum, where Islamic militants from North Africa and the Horn of Africa were trained in a variety of terrorist techniques. A number of Islamic radicals who had fought in Afghanistan against the Soviet Union in the 1980s made their way to Sudan, including Osama bin Laden, who had flown to the country with his family on his private jet in 1991.[21] Bin Laden and al-Turabi came to an understanding whereby, in return for bin Laden investing millions of dollars in the Sudanese economy (bin Laden came from one of Saudi Arabia's wealthiest families) al-Turabi allowed the terrorist mastermind complete freedom in Sudan. While there bin Laden struck up a close working relationship with the NIF, the militia that had been set up by the Revolutionary Guards, which he provided with communications equipment and weapons, in return for which Sudan provided al-Qaeda with 200 passports, which enabled al-Qaeda operatives to move from one country to another with new and fictitious identities.[22]

The deployment of American forces to the neighbouring war-torn state of Somalia in December 1992, part of President Bush's ill-fated attempt to assert a 'new world order' after America's victory in the first Gulf War, provided Tehran and Khartoum with the perfect opportunity to test the strength and effectiveness of their new alliance. The success of the Western military coalition in defeating a Muslim nation – even if it was the secularist Iraqi regime of Saddam Hussein – had caused great consternation throughout the Muslim world, and the event was described in radical Islamic circles as *Atzma*, the crisis. The American mission to Somalia, which was part of a United Nations peacekeeping operation, was perceived by both Iran and Sudan not only as a direct threat to their interests, but as a golden opportunity to avenge the success of Operation Desert Storm. From the moment US Marines landed in Somalia, Iran and Sudan decided to wage a terror campaign to force the Americans to withdraw.[23] Just a few months before the American deployment Rahim Safavi, the deputy commander of the Revolutionary Guards, led a joint Iranian–Sudanese delegation to Somalia to advise the militias set up by radical Somalis. With bin Laden's financial backing, a number of Somali training camps were set up in Ethiopia and Ogaden, while the Revolutionary Guards helped with the provision of weapons and other equipment.

Backed by Iran and Sudan, General Aidid, the Somali warlord, initiated a highly effective terror campaign against the UN mission and American forces. By the summer of 1993, the Revolutionary Guards had established a base at the Somali port of Bossaso to support the Somali insurgency campaign. American officials accused the Revolutionary Guards of teaching hundreds of General Aidid's militiamen how to use anti-aircraft weaponry and rocket-propelled grenades, how to develop intelligence systems that evaded US detection, and how to plant and conceal remote-controlled mines.[24] On 3 June Aidid's militia demonstrated its newfound proficiency when it killed twenty-six Pakistani peacekeepers in an ambush. When, the following October, US forces tried to arrest two of Aidid's senior lieutenants as they drove through Mogadishu, American marines became involved in a ferocious firefight with the Somali insurgents, which resulted in eighteen American soldiers being killed after the Somalis succeeded in shooting down two Sikorsky Black Hawk helicopters.

The number of American casualties was small compared with the number of Americans killed in the suicide truck-bomb attacks in Beirut ten years previously, but the effect was the same. Within months American President Bill Clinton, who had taken office the previous January, ordered the withdrawal of America's military forces from Somalia, a move that only served to confirm Tehran's suspicions that Washington had no stomach for a fight. Iran had suffered hundreds of thousands of casualties during the war with Iraq. Yet the deaths of a few hundred Americans and French in Lebanon had been sufficient to persuade President Reagan to withdraw American forces out of harm's way, while a decade later the loss of just eighteen American lives had been too much for President Clinton, who reacted the same way. So far as Iran's Revolutionary Guards were concerned, it seemed that a few, well-organized terrorist attacks were all that were needed to have the world's last remaining superpower running for cover.

Sudan proved to be a useful training ground for providing support to Egyptian Islamic fundamentalists attempting to overthrow the regime of President Hosni Mubarak. The Egyptians, like the Syrians, had fought alongside coalition troops to liberate Kuwait, and had subsequently incurred the wrath of radical Islamic groups. Egypt was another key player in the Middle East peace process, and to undermine Mubarak the Iranians provided support to Egypt's Gama'a Islami, which waged a highly effective terrorist campaign and came close to assassinating Mubarak in June 1995. The Iranian interests section in Cairo was closed down after the police found evidence of direct Iranian involvement in plots to overthrow the Egyptian government. Tehran launched a similar campaign of destabilization in Jordan, another important contributor to the peace negotiations, and Iranian diplomats in Amman were accused of funding and advising fundamentalist candidates in the Jordanian parliamentary elections in 1992, which resulted in the election of twenty fundamentalist MPs.[25]

Iran was particularly interested in targeting Saudi Arabia. Despite the long-standing hostility that existed between Saudi Arabia's Sunni fundamentalist Wahhabi sect and Iran's Shia revolutionaries, the Guards nevertheless succeeded in establishing Hizbollah bases among the Shia communities in the east of the country. The small, oil-rich sheikhdoms of the Gulf were another favoured target and a special training camp was set up to train dissidents, prepare alternative governments and put saboteurs in place. They stepped up their funding for dissident groups, especially in Bahrain, which had a majority Shia population. To intimidate the other Gulf states in 1992 the Revolutionary Guards seized Abu Musa Island in the Strait of Hormuz from Dubai, and when the United States failed to intervene they staged large-scale naval and air manoeuvres in the Gulf.

Nor were efforts confined to the Middle East. Iran became the main arms supplier for Bosnian Muslims during the civil war in the Balkans, setting up an effective smuggling network run from the Iranian embassy in Zagreb. Elsewhere in Europe, a four-man Iranian hit team gunned down four Kurdish dissidents at the Mykonos Restaurant in Berlin in September 1992. The murders were part of a broader assassination campaign ordered by Tehran to liquidate all remaining political dissent to the regime. The judge at the trial of the assassins blamed the leaders of the Iranian regime for the killings, and issued an arrest warrant for Iran's then intelligence minister, Ali Fallahian. The Revolutionary Guards became involved in Pakistan's campaign to assume control of the Indian state of Kashmir. Mohsen Rezai, the commander, declared that Iran was prepared to go into battle in Kashmir 'alongside their brothers', while Khamenei threatened India by warning Delhi that it was mistaken if it thought it could subjugate Kashmir's Muslims forever.

Even further afield Hizbollah was active in Brazil and Uruguay, but its most controversial activity was in Argentina where in March 1992 Hizbollah, working closely with the Iranian embassy, detonated a bomb at the Israeli embassy in Buenos Aires, killing twenty-nine diplomats and embassy workers. Hizbollah boasted of its exploits by releasing a videotape it had filmed of the embassy prior to the bombing. In 1994 Hizbollah struck again, this time working with local neo-Nazi groups, and bombed a Jewish community centre in Buenos Aires, killing eighty-five people and wounding two hundred. The Argentine authorities later issued an international warrant for the arrest of five Iranians for the bombings, including Ahmad Vahidi, the commander of the Quds Force, and Mohsen Rezai, commander-in-chief of the Revolutionary Guards.

*

The global terror network that Iran established in the four years after Khomeini's death led the US State Department to conclude in early 1993 that Tehran had become the world's 'most dangerous state sponsor of terrorism'.[26] From the moment the Clinton national security team entered the White House in 1993 it was made fully aware of the threat posed to American interests in the Middle East, particularly President Clinton's attempts to negotiate an Israeli–Palestinian peace deal. Although the Israeli–Palestinian peace talks had been initiated by Clinton's Republican predecessor, many of the president's senior Democrat advisers believed the root of most of the region's problems lay in the long-running dispute, and whole-heartedly endorsed the Bush administration's initiative. The previous big Middle East breakthrough, the Camp David peace deal between Israel and Egypt, had been negotiated by Jimmy Carter, the last Democratic president to occupy the White House, and Clinton was keen to emulate his success by conclud-ing a settlement of the Palestinian issue.

Iran was implacably opposed to any deal that legitimized Israel's existence, and the Clinton administration believed the only way to negate Iran's insidious influence was to initiate a policy of containment against Tehran, similar to the one that had been imposed against Iraq at the end of the Gulf War. The attitude to Iran was best summed up by Warren Christopher, the US Secretary of State, who said in a speech at Georgetown University in late 1993, 'Iran is the world's most significant state sponsor of terrorism and the most ardent opponent of the Middle East peace process . . . Iran is intent on projecting terror and extremism across the Middle East and beyond.'[27]

Rafsanjani and the pragmatists understood that so long as the conservatives around Khamenei held the upper hand in terms of exporting the revolution and supporting radical Islamic groups, there was little prospect of an improvement in relations between the United States and Tehran. The Iranians responded to their growing isolation from the West by intensi-fying their military build-up. Russia and the former Soviet Republics provided the bulk of the weapons and equipment, including submarines, fighter aircraft and conventional weapons. A $1.3-billion deal was struck with China to provide a whole range of anti-ship and anti-aircraft missiles, and help with Iran's attempts with its own missile development programme. The main supplier of ballistic missile technology, though, was North Korea, which provided modified versions of the old Soviet Scud missile system, the prototype for Iran's short-range and medium-range Shahab (Meteor) ballistic systems. In January 1995 international concern deepened about the direction Iran's military build-up was taking in January 1995 when Tehran concluded a deal with Moscow for the Russians to complete work on building the Bushehr nuclear power station in the Gulf, which had been badly damaged during the war. The agreement inevitably raised fears that Iran would use the development of the Bushehr plant as cover to expand its military nuclear capability, even though the Russians insisted that the light water reactor they were supplying could not be used to provide weapons-grade nuclear material.

Relations between Washington and Tehran took another serious turn for the worse after the Republicans swept to power in Congress in early 1995. Iran's new aggressive policy, particularly its attempts to torpedo the Israeli–Palestinian peace negotiations, provided the Republicans with ample opportunity to demonize Iran in the eyes of the American public. Despite the diplomatic tensions between the two countries, American businesses were still doing a roaring trade with Iran; in 1995 the United States was Iran's third largest trading partner and the largest purchaser of its oil.[28] The Republicans were determined to put an end to this lucrative business, which they believed was helping to finance the international terror network. In January 1995 Republican Senator Alfonse D'Amato introduced legislation to ban all American trade with Iran. Despite opposition from American business leaders, the ban was authorized by President Clinton in May 1995. Not content with that, Republican leader Newt Gingrich persuaded Clinton to give the

CIA $18 million to fund a programme of covert action to destabilize the Iranian regime.

Khamenei and the hardline conservative faction in Tehran saw the American action, with some justification, as tantamount to a declaration of war, and their reaction came close to provoking all-out conflict between the two countries. When Khomeini was still alive he had never forgotten Washington's success in overthrowing the Mosaddeq government in the 1950s, and had always feared that Washington was plotting a similar move against the Islamic revolution. His successors felt the same way and, rather than be intimidated by Congress's hostile actions, Khamenei and the hardliners decided to renew their attacks on America and its allies in the Middle East.

The most obvious target was Israel, where the country was still trying to come to terms with the assassination of Prime Minister Yitzhak Rabin, who was killed by a right-wing Jewish extremist in Tel Aviv in November 1995. Before his death Rabin had signed the Oslo Accords with PLO leader Yasser Arafat, committing the two sides to a lasting peace settlement. When Shimon Peres, Rabin's successor, decided to call a general election in the spring of 1996, the Iranians saw an opportunity to wreck the Oslo Accords. Peres was arguably more committed to the peace process than Rabin, but Benjamin Netanyahu, his right-wing opponent in the elections, wanted to end the negotiations with Arafat, whom he regarded as a terrorist. Peres had a reputation as a dove in Israeli politics, and Tehran calculated that by launching attacks against Israel the Israeli public would be persuaded to vote for the more hawkish Netanyahu.

By this stage the Revolutionary Guards had established close links with the radical group Palestinian Islamic Jihad, whose policies were even more extreme than those of Hamas. In February 1996, with Iran's help, Islamic Jihad carried out four suicide bomb attacks in Israel within four days, the first time Israelis had experienced the destructive force of Islamist suicide bombers on home soil. The suicide bombings were followed by an escalation in cross-border attacks by Hizbollah militants based in southern Lebanon, which targeted Israeli civilian targets in the north of the country. Desperate to prove his hawkish credentials, in April Peres launched Operation Grapes of Wrath, Israel's first coordinated military assault on Hizbollah's infrastructure in southern Lebanon. The high level of Lebanese civilian deaths caused by the Israeli incursion provoked an international outcry, and Peres was forced to call a halt to the operation. As Iran had calculated, Israel's abortive intervention in southern Lebanon cost Shimon Peres the premiership when the election was held in May, and the Israeli electorate voted the hawkish Netanyahu into office, thereby ending any prospect of progress being made in the Oslo Accords. The Iranians acknowledged their thanks to Hizbollah by increasing their annual contribution to the militia to $100 million.[29]

By the summer of 1996 Western intelligence agencies had identified eleven camps that the Guards' Quds force had organized in Iran to train Islamic terrorists for operations around the world. Every year an estimated 5,000 extremists passed through the camps, which were set up on the orders of Rafsanjani in his capacity as head of Iran's Supreme Security Council. Each of the camps was assigned for a different purpose. The Abyek camp at Qasvim was used to train potential assassins while the Nahavand camp at Hamadan was used exclusively by Hizbollah activists from Lebanon.[30]

After Israel the other main area of Revolutionary Guards activity was the Gulf, where the Guards launched a campaign to destabilize regimes that were closely allied to Washington. In Bahrain, where the ruling Sunni Muslim Khalifa family presided over a predominantly Shia population, the government provided Washington in June 1996 with documentary proof of a plot hatched by the Revolutionary Guards to overthrow the regime and install a pro-Iranian government. The

Guards had set up a cell called Hizbollah-Bahrain in Qom in 1993 which was dedicated to establishing a Shia government in Bahrain. Most of the cell members had undergone training in Lebanon and Iran. Of the forty-four members of the group, twenty-nine were detained by the Bahrainis while the rest fled to Iran.[31]

Two weeks after the Bahrain coup plot was exposed Tehran came close to provoking an all-out war with the United States when a truck bomb destroyed the Khobar Towers housing complex in eastern Saudi Arabia, which was used to house American military personnel. Nineteen Americans were killed in the blast, and another 372 wounded. The force of the blast, which was similar to the suicide truck-bomb attacks against Americans and French in Beirut in 1983, was so powerful that it tore the front off the eight-storey apartment block and was felt twenty miles away in Bahrain. It was carried out by a group called Saudi Hizbollah, whose members were drawn from the Saudi Arabian Shia community in the east of the country. The Saudi terrorists had undergone training in Lebanon and at one of the training facilities set up by the Quds force in Iran, the Imam Ali camp in east Tehran.[32]

American investigators eventually discovered the Quds force had ordered the Saudi terrorists to begin planning for an attack against American targets at least two years previously. The Iranians were interested in carrying out a terrorist attack in Saudi Arabia for a number of reasons. From an early stage in the Islamic revolution Khomeini had been at loggerheads with the Saudi royal family, which he regarded as corrupt and unworthy to be the guardians of Mecca and Medina, the two holiest sites in Islam. In 1983 Khomeini had ordered Iranian pilgrims making the annual *hajj* – which Khomeini had undertaken himself as a young man – to treat the occasion as an 'Islamic uprising'. Iranian pilgrims often provoked riots at the holy sites, and Khomeini posthumously denounced the Saudis in his will in the most uncompromising terms. Muslims, he wrote, 'should curse tyrants, including the Saudi royal family, these traitors to God's great shrine, may God's curse and that of his prophets and angels be upon them.'[33] Attacking the Saudis was part of Khomeini's legacy, and the choice of an American target was aimed at forcing Washington to remove its infidel forces from the sacred land of the Prophet. The Americans had continued to maintain a strong military presence in Saudi Arabia after Operation Desert Storm to protect the oil-rich Gulf states. If well-timed terrorist attacks had forced the Americans to retreat from Beirut in 1983 and Somalia in 1993, why not Saudi Arabia in 1996?

The Saudi terror cell had set up its own camp in Lebanon's Bekaa Valley which was run by a Saudi Shia named Mugassal, who had been recruited by the Quds force.[34] During their stay in Lebanon the Saudi militants received expert advice from Imad Mughniyeh, the mastermind of the Beirut suicide bomb attacks in the 1980s. By the 1990s Mughniyeh had moved to Qom in Iran with his wife and three children. After Washington put a reward on his head for his part in the 1985 TWA hijacking, the Iranians gave him citizenship and made him an officer in the Revolutionary Guards for the role he had played in helping to establish Hizbollah. Using forged passports and a variety of aliases, Mughniyeh travelled frequently between Tehran and the Bekaa Valley, as well as other Quds force training camps, such as those in Sudan. The Israelis believed he was the mastermind behind the devastating bomb attacks against the Israeli embassy and cultural centre in Buenos Aires, and the Khobar Towers bombing had all the hallmarks of a Mughniyeh attack. Several attempts were made to catch him — most notably at Paris's Charles de Gaulle airport in 1988 and in Saudi Arabia in 1995, but on both occasions he managed to escape.

While Iran was eventually identified as the main culprit, to start with the Americans believed Osama bin Laden's al-Qaeda network was responsible for the Khobar Towers attack. After linking up with the Revolutionary Guards in Sudan, by 1995 al-Qaeda militants were travelling regularly to Lebanon to receive training. Al-Qaeda purchased its own guest house in the Bekaa Valley, and the group received instruction from Mughniyeh on how to make truck bombs.[35] According to a former al-Qaeda terrorist captured by the Americans, during this period Mughniyeh travelled to Sudan where he had a face-to-face meeting with bin Laden.[36] In November 1995, al-Qaeda was blamed for a truck bomb that exploded outside a Saudi–US joint facility in the Saudi capital Riyadh. Saudi authorities detained four suspects, who confessed to having been inspired by bin Laden. But they were sentenced to death and beheaded before American investigators had a chance to interview them, raising question marks about the level of al-Qaeda's involvement. Bin Laden himself denied any direct connection in an interview broadcast on CNN in 1997. 'I have great respect for the people who did this action,' he said. 'What they did is a big honour that I missed participating in.'[37] His organization was nevertheless active in the region, and he issued a fatwa urging the Saudi people to wage a jihad against the Saudi royal family for tolerating the presence of American troops. Although Washington ultimately concluded that the Iranian-trained Saudi Hizbollah terrorist cell was responsible for the Khobar Towers attacks, the 9/11 Commission Report found that 'there are also signs that al-Qaeda played some kind of role, as yet unknown'.[38] If al-Qaeda was involved in the Khobar Towers attack, it meant that the heirs to Khomeini's revolution had succeeded in uniting rival Sunni and Shia radicals in the common cause of waging holy war against the West.

While part of the American investigation continued to explore the possibility of an al-Qaeda connection, the primary focus remained Iran, and the likely involvement of the Quds force and Saudi Hizbollah. Several of Clinton's security advisers were convinced that Iran was responsible, but the CIA urged caution, arguing that the possibility of Iranian involvement was only one of several theories that needed to be examined.[39] It was several weeks before the Clinton administration had a strong case that Iran was behind the attack, but not one that would stand up in a court of law. America's attempts to identify the culprits were hampered by the Saudis, who were reluctant to hand over valuable information (conclusive evidence of Iranian involvement in the attacks was not finally handed over to Washington until 1999).

Even so Clinton wanted to teach the Iranians a lesson. They had caused serious disruption to the Middle East peace process, and they had, in all likelihood, killed nineteen American soldiers. Clinton ordered his national security officials to draw up plans for retaliatory strikes against Iran with the instruction, 'I don't want any pissant half-measures.'[40] But while the planners at the Pentagon looked at various military options – including a full-scale ground invasion of Iran of the type used during Operation Desert Storm – Clinton eventually backed away from launching military action against Iran, not least because the Saudi authorities wanted to negotiate their own resolution of the crisis with Iran. The Saudis eventually did a deal with Tehran whereby Iran agreed not to carry out any further terrorist attacks on Saudi territory, in return for which the Saudis would persuade Washington not to launch retaliatory military action. In the end Clinton had to console himself with passing the Iran–Libya Sanctions Act, which, while strengthening the economic blockade against the Islamic revolution, once again suggested that Washington had no stomach for a fight with the forces of radical Islam. The lesson of the Khobar Towers bombing, and all the other terrorist attacks carried out in the name of revolutionary Islam, was that the Revolutionary Guards had succeeded in wreaking havoc against the West and its allies and had got away with it.

10

Rogue Regime

The leaders of Iran's Islamic revolution responded to the September 11 attacks against the United States in 2001 by sending President George W. Bush and the American people a message of condolence. A statement issued by the Iranian government expressed its 'deep regret and sympathy with the victims' and declared 'it is an international duty to try to undermine terrorism'. A country that had spent most of the 1990s being denounced as an international pariah for its role in Islamic terrorism suddenly found itself offering its sincere condolences to an enemy it regularly demonized as 'the Great Satan'. Far from rejoicing that the United States had suffered the worst terrorist attack in history, the Islamic Republic of Iran joined the rest of the civilized world in offering its help and support in America's hour of need. In Tehran crowds of sympathizers held spontaneous candlelight vigils for those who perished in the attacks, the only country in the Middle East to do so.

This remarkable turnaround in Iran's attitude to the United States had been made possible by the election four years previously of Mohammed Khatami as Iran's fifth post-revolution president. Khatami's success in the 1997 presidential election was as much a surprise for the Iranian people as it was to the outside world. A mild-mannered academic who had twice served as minister of guidance and Islamic culture, Khatami's only claim to public prominence had come in 1992 when the hardliners had forced him to resign for allowing Iran's media

and entertainment industry too much licence. At the time of
the election Khatami was head of Iran's National Library,
hardly a position of great influence. He was, though, an Hojjat-
al-Islam, the clerical rank below that of an ayatollah, and
Khatami had been a steadfast supporter of the Islamic revolution from its inception. The Council of Guardians, which vetted
candidates for the election, therefore allowed him to stand
because they needed a few names to put forward against
Khamenei's preferred candidate, Ali Akbar Nuri, whose success, given the rigged nature of Iran's elections, was supposed
to be a forgone conclusion.

In an ideal world President Rafsanjani would have been
allowed to stand for a third term, but his supporters failed in
their bid to amend the constitution, which stipulated that the
president could only serve for two four-year terms. With
Rafsanjani out of the running, Nuri, a hardliner who had
ensured the principles of the Islamic revolution were upheld at
the Majlis, was considered the most suitable replacement by
the clerical establishment. Khamenei officially endorsed him as
the Supreme Leader's candidate and Mohsen Rezai, the Revolutionary Guards commander, issued written orders to all his
troops to vote for him.

But by 1997 the Iranian people had grown disillusioned
with their revolutionary government, which they blamed for
the parlous state of the Iranian economy and the country's
isolation from the rest of the world. Inflation was running at
close to 40 per cent, the value of the currency had halved and
unemployment stood at 30 per cent, which was partly the
result of Rafsanjani's economic mismanagement, but also due
to the economic sanctions applied by the American Congress.
Even though Khatami was largely unknown to the wider
Iranian public, during the election his name nevertheless
became synonymous with their desire for change – much like
Barack Obama in the 2008 US presidential election contest.
Despite the regime's brazen attempts to rig the result, Khatami

won nearly 70 per cent of the vote, which would have been even higher had it not been for the hardliners' inept attempts to fix the result.

The size of Khatami's majority enabled him to make sweeping changes of the government's senior ranks. In particular he sidelined many of the hardliners who had presided over Iran's aggressive policy of confrontation with the West. Ali Akbar Velayati, the combative foreign minister, was replaced, as was Mohsen Rezai, whose personal intervention with the Revolutionary Guards had failed to swing the election result in favour of Khatami's main rival, and Ali Fallahian, the intelligence chief, who was the subject of several international arrest warrants for his involvement in various terrorist operations around the world. But the old guard were not completely silenced by Khatami's election victory. Having stepped down as president Rafsanjani became head of the highly influential Expediency Council, the body Khomeini set up at the end of his life to mediate inter-governmental disputes, while Mohsen Rezai became the Council's administrative secretary.

When Khatami was elected president Tehran had already taken steps to tone down its aggressive foreign policy and support for terrorism. With the Khobar Towers attack and its involvement in other terrorist operations Iran had come close to provoking Washington into launching military action, and Tehran's subsequent isolation by America and Europe had given the hardliners a sharp reality check. It was one thing to fulfil Khomeini's legacy of exporting the revolution; another to provoke the world's most powerful military powers into launching a campaign that could result in the overthrow of the Islamic republic. Khatami accelerated the pace of Iran's more accommodating attitude towards the West, and actively sought to put relations with Washington on a more normal diplomatic footing. In his inaugural speech to the Majlis Khatami called for a 'dialogue among civilizations' and said he was prepared to have diplomatic relations with 'any state which respects our independence'.[1] In early January 1998, he went further, giving an interview to CNN in which he suggested America and Iran should take the first steps towards establishing contacts between the two countries through the exchange of academics, artists and athletes.[2] The United States responded by sending a team of wrestlers to compete in Tehran.

Khatami made many other attempts to change the world's perception of Iran. At home he promised to ban 'superstition and fanaticism' from the government, and generally allowed a relaxation of the more irksome governmental restrictions. The press was encouraged to write critical articles and university students were urged to take a more active role in politics. Diplomatic efforts were made to restore relations with Saudi Arabia and the other Gulf states, and Tehran reduced its support for Islamic opposition groups. Perhaps the most significant act that suggested the atmosphere in Tehran was undergoing a radical change came in September 1998 when Khatami announced he was lifting the fatwa against British author Salman Rushie. But while Khatami pursued his reform agenda with vigour, he still had to contend with the opposition of the hardliners who continued to control most of the judiciary and the legislature.

In his all-powerful position as Supreme Leader, Khamenei made it clear he did not approve of Khatami's reform programme, and Khamenei's conservative supporters did their best to frustrate Khatami's attempts to change and improve the way the country was run. Iranian officials and academics who were encouraged by Khatami to visit the United States as a first step towards normalizing relations told their American interlocutors that Khatami's greatest strength was the broad support he enjoyed from the Iranian people, and his biggest hurdle was the entrenched position of the old guard around Khamenei who were not prepared to surrender control of Iranian policy.[3] By liberalizing social controls and attempting to improve relations with America, Khatami was challenging two of the central

pillars of Khomeini's legacy, and the hardliners were determined to destroy Khatami's presidency, which they regarded
as a dangerous aberration from the principles of Khomeini's
revolution.

Other more sinister forces were at work trying to undermine
Khatami's administration. From late September to early January
1999 five prominent liberals were brutally murdered in mysterious circumstances that became widely known as the 'serial
killings'. Khamenei showed little sympathy for the victims of
the serial killings, describing those who died as 'apostates'. But
Khatami took a different view and set up a special commission
of inquiry which produced compelling evidence that the murders had been carried out by members of Iran's security forces,
who believed they had been acting in the interests of protecting
the revolution. The investigators eventually made the alarming
discovery that a secret committee comprising intelligence officials, Revolutionary Guards and members of Khamenei's office
had been conducting a programme of assassination against
prominent dissidents for ten years, both at home and abroad.
At least fifty dissidents had been murdered, although the
investigators suspected the figure was far higher. Khatami
responded by sacking the intelligence chief and conducting a
widespread purge of Iran's intelligence forces, which resulted
in an estimated 80 per cent of them losing their jobs.

Khatami's cleansing of the intelligence services was halted
by Khamenei, and the hardliners, who still enjoyed a majority
in the Majlis, continued their campaign to undermine Khatami's
campaign of social reform. In early July they passed a bill to
curb press freedoms, prompting demonstrations by students at
Tehran University. The Hizbollahis, the street thugs who had
been so effective in suppressing opposition to the Islamic
revolution in the early 1980s, made an unwelcome return to
Iran's political scene. They broke into the university dormitories and beat up a number of the students, causing some of them
to fall to their deaths from the windows. The following day

more students took to the streets, and within days Tehran was suffering its worst street demonstrations since the 1979 Revolution, with the students fighting running battles with the Hizbollahis, whose ranks were boosted by Lebanese volunteers who had flown to Tehran to support the hardliners.[4] The students chanted 'either Islam and the law, or another revolution', a reference to the fact that Khamenei and the clerics still enjoyed total dominance of the judiciary, as well as the legislature. The students even burned Khamenei's portrait, a graphic illustration of their disenchantment with the Islamic revolution.

Under pressure from Khamenei and the Revolutionary Guards, which had deployed several divisions around the capital and threatened to crush the protests by force, Khatami declined to accept the protesters' appeals to him to lead a new revolution. After the Guards' commanders wrote to Khatami warning him not to take 'any revolutionary decisions' but to 'act in accordance with your Islamic and national mission', Khatami publicly denounced the protesters and accused them of undermining his attempts to implement his reform programme. The security forces took this as a signal to move in, and within days the protests had been crushed. Dozens of students were injured and 1,400 arrested.

The suppression of the student protests in Tehran in the summer of 1999 effectively brought the campaign for a more liberal regime to an end. Faced with the Guards' brute force, the custodians of Khomeini's revolution, Khatami's courage failed him, and he conceded defeat to the hardliners. The reformers made one, last valiant effort to curb the excesses of the Islamic revolution the following year when they contested the Majlis elections and won 73 per cent of the votes. But the reform-minded majority of the Iranian public were thwarted by the hardliners who by now had the upper hand, and they stepped up intimidation of those liberal politicians and journalists who continued to campaign for reform. Abdullah Nuri, the popular mayor of Tehran and a key ally of President Khatami, was jailed for five years on charges of endorsing better relations with the United States and Israel. Rafsanjani, in his position as head of the Expediency Council, and Mohammed Yazdi, the hardline justice minister, took various measures to protect the Islamic revolution. Many of the newly elected reformist members of the Majlis were simply deposed, while the security forces continued their campaign of assassination against prominent liberals.

By the time of the September 11 attacks Khatami, who had succeeded in getting himself re-elected in the summer of 2001, was still nominally in charge of the country, but his authority was much diminished. Washington had belatedly woken up to Khatami's attempts to change Tehran's political climate the previous year when Madeleine Albright, Clinton's Secretary of State, sought to improve relations by easing Washington's economic sanctions, and even attempted to make a public apology for America's past intervention in Iranian affairs. Her appeal for a 'new beginning' was received in the spirit it was meant by Khatami, but the conservatives in Tehran made sure he had limited room for manoeuvre.

The Clinton administration also entertained strong reservations about the wisdom of establishing a dialogue with Tehran as Washington continued to receive intelligence reports pointing to Iran's continued involvement in Islamic terrorism. In August 1998 al-Qaeda exploded two devastating truck bombs at the American embassies in Kenya and Tanzania, killing 224 people and wounding an estimated 5,000 others. The attacks were the first carried out by bin Laden's terror group against the United States, and followed the famous fatwa he issued the previous February calling on Muslims to wage holy war against the Americans and their allies. The bomb-making technology used for the attacks was the same as used for the attacks in Beirut in 1983 and in Dhahran in 1996, and the al-Qaeda cells responsible for the bombings had been trained by Hizbollah in south Lebanon.[5] Even if Iran was not directly responsible for the bombings, it had provided Osama bin Laden's group with the necessary terrorist training. Washington responded to the attacks by bombing the training camps the Revolutionary Guards had helped to set up in Sudan in the early 1990s, as well as al-Qaeda's training facilities in Afghanistan, where bin Laden had been forced to relocate in 1996.

Similar suspicions surfaced in October 2000 when al-Qaeda suicide bombers attacked the US Navy destroyer USS *Cole*, killing seventeen members of the ship's crew and wounding at least forty. Whether or not Iran had provided technical support for the attack on the USS *Cole*, the CIA regarded the potential threat posed by Iran's terror network to be equal to that of bin Laden's al-Qaeda organization. In late December 2000 George Tenet, the CIA director, wrote to President Clinton warning him of 'an increased risk of attacks on our country's interests'. While bin Laden posed the greatest threat, Tenet warned the president that 'Iran and Hizbollah also maintain a woldwide terrorism presence and have an extensive array of off-the-shelf contingency plans for terrorist attacks, beyond their recent focus in Israel and the Palestinian areas.'[6]

There was a change of mood in Washington with the arrival of President George W. Bush at the White House in January 2001. Many senior members of the new administration, such as Vice President Dick Cheney and Defense Secretary Donald Rumsfeld, had painful memories of Washington's dealings with Iran going back to the Reagan administration. The Beirut suicide bombings and the arms-for-hostages scandal, to name but a few of the atrocities committed against American and Western interests, had neither been forgotten nor forgiven, and the new administration was wary of taking Khatami's reform agenda seriously. The hard-headed Republican realists who were now running American policy worked on the basis of deliverable results, not vague promises, and, for all the talk of a Prague Spring taking hold in Tehran, the new policy-making team was immediately confronted with compelling evidence of

Iran's direct involvement in one of the more recent high-profile terrorist attacks against American interests.

In 1999 the Saudis had finally handed over conclusive proof that Iran was behind the 1996 Khobar Towers bombing in eastern Saudi Arabia that killed nineteen American service-men. It had taken the FBI nearly two years to put together a watertight case, so that it fell to the Bush administration to issue the forty-six-count indictment in June 2001 which accused the Iranian-trained Saudi Hizbollah of being respon-sible for the attacks. Thirteen Saudis and one Lebanese – assumed to be Imad Mughniyeh – were accused of the bomb-ings, and the indictment alleged that the suspects had been directed by Iranian government officials. The Clinton adminis-tration had come close to launching retaliatory military action against Iran in the immediate aftermath of the Dhahran bomb-ing, but the time for such measures had now passed. President Bush issued a statement to the families of those killed and injured in the attacks that 'your government will not forget your loss and will continue working, based on the evidence, to make sure that justice is done'. But the main focus of their effort would now be to bring the culprits to justice rather than launch military action.

The Bush administration was quickly made aware that, while Tehran was supposed to have scaled down its overseas terrorist commitments following the Khobar Towers attacks, it continued to support radical Islamist groups, particularly the more radical members of the Palestinian Islamic group Hamas, who were viscerally opposed to the Israeli–Palestinian peace process. In 1999 the Quds force set up a special training camp on the outskirts of Tehran to train Hamas militants,[7] and the ties between Hamas and Iran were further strengthened in August 2000, shortly after the collapse of the Camp David peace talks hosted by President Clinton, when a high-level delegation of Iranian officials visited Damascus to strengthen ties with Hamas leaders based in the Syrian capital. The Iranian delegation was led by Ali Akbar Velayati, who, after his dismissal as Iran's foreign minister by Khatami, worked as a special adviser to Khamenei.[8] Yasser Arafat, the PLO leader, was reported to have met with Khamenei's representatives, as was Khaled Meshaal, the hardline Hamas leader based in Damascus.

Shortly afterwards the second Palestinian intifada erupted in the West Bank and Gaza, prompting Khamenei to declare, 'there is only one remedy and there is only one cure . . . and that is to destroy the root cause of the crisis – the Zionist enemy.'[9] The Revolutionary Guards responded to the outbreak of the intifada by calling for the removal of 'the cancerous tumour Israel off the region's map' and offering to go to the 'divine battlefields' of the occupied Palestinian territories to defend the honour of Islam and liberate Jerusalem.[10] The Guards had also extended their activities further afield, with the ubiquitous Imad Mughniyeh reported to be working with Chechen rebels in their war of independence against Moscow.[11] Not surprisingly the US State Department, in its annual assessment of global terrorism in 2001, described Iran as 'the most active state supporter of terrorism'.[12]

More alarming still was the CIA's mounting concern over the direction Iran's nuclear programme was taking. In a briefing to the new Bush team, George Tenet, the CIA director, provided details of the latest intelligence estimate which concluded that Iran remained one of the most active countries seeking to acquire nuclear technology from abroad – primarily from Russia, China and North Korea – that can be used to develop weapons of mass destruction.[13] Just how much Khatami knew about these activities was a moot point as both the activities of the Revolutionary Guards and the development of a nuclear weapons programme were directly controlled by Khamenei. But however much Khatami might have sought better relations with the West, the charitable view within the Bush administration was that important areas of Iranian policy remained beyond the president's control, and that Iran itself remained a serious threat to global security.

In the immediate aftermath of the September 11 attacks, Iran was not the Bush administration's primary concern. The top priority was to destroy Osama bin Laden's al-Qaeda terrorist network which had been set up in southern Afghanistan following his expulsion from Sudan in 1996. Bin Laden had been invited to base himself in Afghanistan by the Taliban, a radical Islamic group which had established a stranglehold over large tracts of a country rendered ungovernable by decades of incessant conflict. Once it became clear that the Taliban was not prepared to hand over bin Laden and the other architects of the September 11 attacks, Washington resolved to take military action against Afghanistan to overthrow the Taliban and bring bin Laden and his accomplices to justice.

There was no love lost between the Taliban and Tehran and, apart from offering his condolences, Khatami found himself in the curious position of offering Washington Iran's practical support for the forthcoming military campaign. Relations between the Taliban and the Islamic revolution had been strained since the 1990s when the Afghani fundamentalists seized control of the country. The Shia revolutionaries in Iran had a long-standing rivalry with their Sunni Muslim counterparts in Afghanistan dating back to the Mujahideen campaign against the Soviet occupation in the 1980s. These tensions worsened considerably when the Taliban, backed by Pakistan and Saudi Arabia, took control of most of the country in 1996 and launched a bloody persecution of the country's Shia Muslims, many of whom are members of the Hazari minority. The Quds force immediately swung into action, setting up training camps to help the Afghan minorities defend themselves against the Taliban's medieval barbarity. Relations deteriorated even further in 1999 when the Taliban overran the northern town of Mazar-I Sharif and killed eleven Revolutionary Guards who had been acting as advisers to the Afghan opposition.

Tehran was incensed by the killings, and 200,000 troops were immediately dispatched to the border as the government deliberated over whether or not to invade. The Revolutionary Guards were desperate to avenge the murders of their comrades, but Khamenei was persuaded, in view of Afghanistan's brutal history of repelling foreign invaders, of the prudence of not becoming embroiled in a protracted and bloody conflict that in all probability Iran could never win.

The Islamic Republic's residual hostility to the Taliban did mean, though, that Khatami, having publicly condemned the September 11 attacks, was prepared to offer Washington assistance in overthrowing the Afghan government. The Bush administration also reacted positively to Tehran's message of condolence, and sent a message back, via the Swiss, requesting that Iran joined the campaign against al-Qaeda and the Taliban.

From the start of what became known as the 'war on terror' there was ambiguity in both Washington and Tehran about how the two countries should proceed in the post-9/11 world. The Bush administration might have sought Iran's assistance in defeating the Taliban and al-Qaeda, but at the same time President Bush was sending out strong signals that Washington regarded Iran, in its capacity as one of the world's leading sponsors of terrorism, as a potential future target in the global campaign against terrorism. In his address to Congress shortly after the September 11 attacks Bush warned that any government found to be providing aid or safe haven to terrorists would be regarded as an enemy, irrespective of whether or not they had been involved in the attacks on America. The State Department's view that Iran was the world's leading exporter of terrorism certainly suggested that in the post-9/11 climate Iran could soon find itself on the receiving end of American action if it did not radically change policy.

Tehran was in a quandary over how best to respond to Washington's request for assistance. Iran was no friend of the Taliban, and Khatami was inclined to provide limited support for the American-led military campaign, by allowing coalition forces to transit through Iranian air space and offering other logistical support, such as allowing American transport aircraft the use of staging facilities in eastern Iran. But the glowering presence of Khamenei, who remained deeply suspicious of American intentions, inhibited Khatami's room for manoeuvre.

The deep divisions within the Iranian regime over how best to respond to the Afghan issue were revealed when Jack Straw, the British foreign secretary, visited Tehran in late September to seek Iran's cooperation. The British government under Prime Minister Tony Blair had immediately allied itself to Washington following the 9/11 attacks, and Britain embarked on a frenzied bout of diplomatic activity on Washington's behalf to build an international coalition against the Taliban and al-Qaeda. Straw's visit to Tehran – the first by a British foreign secretary since the 1979 revolution – was undertaken as much on Washington's behalf as it was Britain's, and he had a constructive meeting with Khatami at which he discussed the need for Iran to confront the problem of international terrorism. But no sooner had Khatami offered to cooperate with the forthcoming campaign against Afghanistan than Khamenei issued a statement that totally contradicted what Khatami had been saying. 'Iran will not extend any assistance to the US and its allies in attacking the already suffering Muslim neighbours in Afghanistan,' Khamenei declared. 'America has its hands deep in blood for the crimes committed by the Zionist regime.'[14]

Some senior advisers to the Bush administration expressed their reservations about the value of Straw's mission. While the White House had given Straw its backing, Richard Perle, the chairman of the Pentagon's Defense Advisory Board and a key Bush adviser, publicly denounced Straw's visit, calling it 'absurd'. 'We are not going to fight terrorism effectively by inviting into the (coalition) the very states that are sponsoring terrorists.'[15] This was an opinion that would be heard many times in Washington over the forthcoming months as the Bush administration gradually formulated its post-9/11 policy.

For all their internal divisions the Iranians did provide the coalition with tangible support for the military campaign to overthrow the Taliban government in Afghanistan, Operation Enduring Freedom, which began in October 2001. Iran agreed to perform search-and-rescue missions for downed American air crew who bailed out over Iran, and allowed the Americans to ship humanitarian aid through their ports to landlocked Afghanistan. On the diplomatic front the Iranians were active in persuading the Northern Alliance, the main Afghan opposition group to the Taliban, to support the American-led offensive. At one point the Iranians became so committed to the success of the American campaign that they expressed their frustration at the slow progress of the military offensive.[16]

But Iran's schizophrenic attitude to the war in Afghanistan was revealed in the aftermath of the Taliban's overthrow in November. Khamenei had adopted a realpolitik view of the American offensive: there was nothing to be gained from opposing the military campaign, which was going to happen anyway and probably succeed in doing Iran a favour in getting rid of the detested Taliban. But that did not mean he wanted to abandon Iran's traditional hostility to the 'Great Satan', which, after all, was one of the principal pillars of Khomeini's legacy. The Supreme Leader's ambivalence certainly affected Iran's postwar response to Afghanistan. On the one hand Iran's diplomatic corps, which had developed good relations with their American counterparts during negotiations at the United Nations in the build-up to the conflict, were ready to cooperate fully with the daunting task of rebuilding Afghanistan after almost thirty years of uninterrupted civil war. According to American officials, the Iranians made a significant contribution to the success of the United Nations conference at the end of the war, and persuaded the former king, Zahir Shah, to participate in the process.

At the same time the Iranians played a crucial role in helping the remnants of bin Laden's al-Qaeda terror organization to escape from Afghanistan into Iran. Once again the rival Shia and Sunni Islamic traditions set aside their differences to make common cause in confronting the United States. Ahmad Vahidi, the founder of the Revolutionary Guards Quds force who had become Iran's deputy defence minister, was the main organizer of the rescue mission, which resulted in an estimated 500 al-Qaeda fighters seeking refuge in Iran.[17] To get to Iran the al-Qaeda fighters took a three-day drive across the Baluchistan desert along a route frequented by heroin smugglers. Among those who were provided with a safe haven in Iran after the fall of the Taliban were Saif Adel, al-Qaeda's chief of staff who was wanted for his role in the 1998 bombings of the American embassies in Kenya and Tanzania, and Osama bin Laden's son Saad. The presence of such prominent al-Qaeda militants in Iran, which would last for many years, together with Tehran's continued support for radical Islamic groups around the world, was yet another issue that would undermine Khatami's attempts to improve relations with the West.

*

Any confusion about where the Bush administration stood in relation to the Islamic Republic of Iran was finally resolved in Bush's State of the Union speech on 29 January 2002. Iran, together with North Korea and Iraq, were identified by the president as constituting an 'axis of evil' which threatened global security. 'By seeking weapons of mass destruction, these regimes pose a grave and growing danger. They could provide these arms to terrorists, giving them the means to match their hatred,' Bush declared. And he vowed to work with America's coalition partners 'to deny terrorists and their state sponsors the materials, technology, and expertise to make and deliver weapons of mass destruction. We will develop and deploy effective missile defences to protect America and our allies from sudden attack.'

Iran's new status as one of the world's three leading rogue nations came about more by accident than design. After the success of the military campaign in Afghanistan, Washington was turning its sights towards Saddam Hussein's Iraq, which had a long history of involvement with terrorist groups going back to the 1970s, and was still refusing to comply with the ceasefire terms it had accepted at the end of the Gulf War in 1991. The president's speech was primarily meant as a warning to Saddam to comply with his international obligations, or face the consequences. Michael Gerson, Bush's speechwriter, had come up with the phrase 'axis of evil' to describe the link between rogue states like Iraq and their support for terror groups. But White House officials were concerned that if only Iraq were mentioned in the speech, it would be tantamount to a declaration of war against Baghdad. Condoleezza Rice, Bush's National Security Advisor, suggested that other countries should be added to the list, and North Korea and Iran were selected because they both supported terrorism and pursued weapons of mass destruction.[18]

Iran's support for terrorism was particularly topical in Washington at this time for, just a few weeks before Bush made his speech, Israeli security officials had intercepted a ship, the *Karine A*, in the Red Sea which was found to be carrying a substantial cargo of Iranian-made weapons being shipped to Palestinian militants in the Gaza Strip. The cargo contained Katyusha rockets, mortars, sniper rifles, rocket-propelled grenades and explosives. It had been loaded on the ship at Kish Island in Iran, and many of the weapons were still in their factory wrappings. The weapons were packaged in eighty-three watertight crates attached to buoys so that they could be dumped overboard and retrieved by smaller vessels to save the ship from docking at port.[19]

American intelligence continued to receive reports about the assistance Iran was providing in helping al-Qaeda to escape from Afghanistan to Iran. By now the links between al-Qaeda and Iran's Revolutionary Guards went back nearly a decade, and there was evidence that suggested Iran might have had some involvement in the September 11 attacks. Intelligence reports prepared by the CIA in October 2001 claimed that, at the very least, Iran had allowed between eight and ten of the 9/11 hijackers to travel through Iran on their way to and from their training bases in Afghanistan and Saudi Arabia. Iranian border officials were told not to place stamps in the passports of al-Qaeda travellers. A top Hizbollah official – believed to be Imad Mughniyeh – was said to have accompanied the hijackers on their flights between Iran, Lebanon and Saudi Arabia and had meetings with Saudi Hizbollah, which had links with the hijackers, the majority of whom were Saudi citizens.

The authors of the 9/11 Commission report later concluded that 'there was strong evidence that Iran facilitated the transit of al-Qaeda members into and out of Afghanistan before 9/11, and that some of these were future 9/11 hijackers', although it concluded that 'we have no evidence that Iran or Hizbollah was aware of the planning for what later became the 9/11 attack'.[20] But the commissioners did recommend that US officials conduct further enquiries into the extent of the assistance Iran provided to the 9/11 hijackers.

The effect of Iran's inclusion in Bush's State of the Union address in 2002 was to end any chance of a constructive dialogue being established between Tehran and Washington. The low-level cooperation between American and Iranian officials during the invasion of Afghanistan continued after the main combat operations were concluded, and strayed beyond the main agenda issue of the post-Taliban reconstruction of Afghanistan. But after Bush's speech the Iranians suspended their involvement in the talks, and Khamenei issued an angry response, calling the American president 'a man thirsty for human blood' and declaring that 'Iran is proud to be at the receiving end of the anger of the most-hated Satanic power in the world.'[21]

For all the inflammatory rhetoric, though, the Iranians understood that Iraq was the main target of Washington's military objectives, and by March the dialogue between American and Iranian officials had resumed because Tehran was desperate to learn what the Americans were planning for Iraq, which would have a direct bearing on Iran. As with the Taliban in Afghanistan, there was nothing Tehran wanted more than to see the overthrow of Saddam Hussein's dictatorship in Baghdad. But the removal of the Baathist dictatorship would have profound implications for Iran too. The ayatollahs in Tehran had maintained close relations with the dominant Shia population of southern Iraq that Khomeini had established during his years in exile in Najaf. They wanted to make sure they were well prepared for any future opportunities the Americans might create for them to exploit these links.

But Washington was not taken in by Iran's willingness to maintain a dialogue, mainly because it continued to receive intelligence reports about Iran's support for global terrorism and its involvement with nuclear proliferation. For example, while the United States and its allies were busy trying to deny radical Islamic groups bases in the Middle East, further details emerged of the network of training camps the Quds force had established in Iran to train a broad range of Islamist radicals, including al-Qaeda. The main focus for terrorist training was the Imam Ali camp in Tehran where fifty recruits, in groups of ten, received instruction in conducting ambushes, bomb-making, counter-surveillance and hand-to-hand combat. A second training camp was operated at the Bahonar garrison in north Tehran where groups of militants underwent courses in urban guerrilla warfare and Islamic fundamentalism.[22]

By far the most damaging revelations, which appeared to

justify the Bush administration's decision to include Iran in its 'axis of evil' list of rogue states, came in August 2002, with the discovery that Iran had secretly built two nuclear facilities that could make a vital contribution to the ayatollahs' quest for nuclear weapons. The National Council of Resistance of Iran (NCRI), the political wing of the Mujahideen militia that had been violently suppressed by Khomeini in the early 1980s, made the startling disclosure that Iran had constructed a gas centrifuge plant at Natanz, 200 miles south of Tehran. This could be used to enrich uranium to weapons grade. There was also a heavy-water production facility at Arak, 150 miles south of Tehran, that could be used to extract plutonium, which can also be used to construct an atom bomb. A few months later American intelligence officials confirmed they had verified the existence of the two sites and their intended use. Both sites have been built despite the constant monitoring of Iran's nuclear programme by the IAEA's inspection teams. The Natanz plant caused particular concern as the main enrichment chambers had been constructed deep underground and covered with a thick concrete coating to protect them from attack. The Iranians had clearly learned from the Iraqis' experience in 1981 when Israeli warplanes easily destroyed the Osirak reactor which was being used to develop atomic weapons.

The secrecy surrounding the construction of Natanz was so tight that the governor of the province of Isfahan, where the plant is located, had not even been informed, and he was refused entry when he tried to visit it after its existence was revealed. The clandestine facilities were eventually inspected by the UN's nuclear experts when a team headed by Dr Mohamed ElBaradei, the head of the IAEA, visited Iran in February 2003. The inspectors were taken aback by the sheer scale of the progress the Iranians had made with their secret nuclear programme. At Natanz they found that 160 centrifuges, the sophisticated equipment used for enriching uranium, had been assembled as part of a pilot programme. In the main building they entered a vast, bomb-proof underground hall which had been designed to house up to 50,000 centrifuges, sufficient to enrich uranium on an industrial scale. When fully operational the plant would be able to provide enough fissile material for roughly twenty-five to fifty nuclear warheads each year. In addition the inspectors found the Iranians had developed the more sophisticated P2 centrifuge that had been used by the Pakistani nuclear scientist Dr Abdul Qadeer Khan to develop Pakistan's nuclear bomb. When Khan's international nuclear smuggling ring was finally exposed in 2004 it was revealed the Iranians had bought the complete blueprint for Pakistan's atom bomb. Small traces of enriched uranium were found on the pilot centrifuges which suggested they had already been used to enrich uranium, a clear breach of Iran's obligations under the Nuclear Non-Proliferation Treaty (NPT).

The more the inspectors probed, the more they found evidence of Iran's elaborate and wide-ranging deception of the IAEA. Iran had acquired two tons of refined uranium, known as 'yellowcake' from China, and other quantities of uranium from two other countries, including Pakistan. Just before the inspectors arrived, Khatami made a public announcement that Iran had started work on mining its own uranium, with most of the mining work concentrated on the Savand area, 125 miles from the city of Yazd. Iran had already announced in 1995 that it was building a uranium conversion plant at the Isfahan Nuclear Research Centre, which turns stocks of uranium ore into uranium hexafluoride (UF_6) which, when fed into the gas centrifuges, produces enriched uranium.

The material collected by the IAEA provided a clear indication that Iran was well on the way to becoming entirely self-sufficient in the production of enriched uranium, which meant that there would be no impediment to Tehran developing nuclear weapons if it so desired. More than that, Iran had an ambitious programme to have total control over the entire nuclear fuel cycle. The raw uranium ore extracted from the mines at Yazd would be taken to Isfahan where it would be converted into UF_6. From Isfahan the UF_6 gas would be transported to Natanz where it would be fed into the centrifuges and turned into enriched uranium. And depending on the level of enrichment, the Iranians would have the capability to produce their own weapons grade fissile material. And just in case there was a breakdown in this system IAEA inspectors found that the Iranians had also developed a laser isotope separation programme, which can also be used to enrich uranium. Iran's admission that it had been mining uranium in particular raised concerns that Tehran was trying to build an atom bomb. Under the terms of the agreement Tehran had signed with Moscow to rebuild the Bushehr nuclear reactor in the Gulf, the Russians had agreed to provide all the power station's uranium fuel. There was no need for Iran to construct its own uranium enrichment process if Tehran's nuclear intentions were peaceful.[23] Similar concerns were raised about the Arak heavy water facility, and also about the Iranians' failure to disclose other important aspects of the nuclear programme.

While in public the Iranians continued to insist that all the research was being undertaken for Iran's nuclear power programme, Rafsanjani gave his clearest hint yet that it was in Iran's interests to have nuclear weapons. Addressing the congregation of Friday prayers in Tehran in December 2001, Rafsanjani, who still controlled Iran's national defence council, sought to reconcile the tenets of Islam with the need for nuclear weapons. 'We do not want to fall victim to insecurity,' he said. 'If a day comes when the world of Islam is duly equipped with the arms Israel has in its possession, the strategy of colonialism would face a stalemate because the exchange of atomic bombs would leave nothing of Israel, while only damaging the Muslim world.' Israel by this time was known to have a substantial arsenal of nuclear warheads, and Rafsanjani's speech suggested Iran was seeking to introduce the old Cold War doctrine of mutually assured destruction to the Middle East.

The discoveries made by the IAEA teams led them to conclude that there was a strong possibility that Iran had other secret nuclear facilities it was trying to hide from the outside world. One of the more bizarre episodes concerned a nuclear research centre at Lavizan in north-east Tehran whose existence did not become known to the IAEA until May 2003. But when the IAEA asked to inspect the site, which they believed was conducting research on nuclear weapons, Iran's National Security Council ordered that the entire site be demolished. Before the bulldozers moved in all the equipment was moved to a new 60-acre facility, including two whole body counters that are used to detect radiation contamination to the human body. The site was then completely razed to the ground and six inches of topsoil was removed to ensure that no incriminating traces of enriched uranium were found. When the IAEA's inspectors were finally allowed to inspect the site in June 2004 there was nothing to see but empty wasteland. Even the trees from the surrounding park land had been cut down in case their leaves contained traces of incriminating material, such as traces of uranium.[24]

When the full extent of Iran's deception became public it set Iran on a collision course with the West that quickly escalated into a major international crisis. The more hawkish members of the Bush administration and Israel called for military action to be launched against Iran to prevent it from developing nuclear weapons. Israel was particularly concerned about the rapid progress being made in the development of Iran's nuclear capability as they regarded the Jewish state as the most likely target of Iranian nuclear weapons. The Islamic revolutionaries, after all, had made no secret of their visceral opposition to the existence of the Jewish state, a policy that had been bequeathed to them by Khomeini. In June the Israeli foreign minister, Silvan Shalom, was so concerned about the Iranian programme that he predicted that 'Iran will possess weapons of mass destruction by the end of 2005 or early in

2006.' While his forecast proved to be erroneous, Israel was not alone in concluding that the IAEA's startling revelations indicated that Iran had a clandestine nuclear weapons programme. Why, otherwise, would the regime have gone to such extraordinary lengths to conceal the existence of key nuclear facilities if their purpose, as the Iranian government kept insisting, was entirely peaceful?

What was most disturbing for the West about the discovery of Iran's clandestine nuclear programme was that much of the development work had been undertaken during the presidency of the reform-minded, supposedly pro-Western Khatami. Construction at Natanz had only started in 2000 after the Clinton administration had successfully persuaded the Russians not to provide Tehran with uranium enrichment technology. After that rebuff the Iranians had clearly decided that, if they could not rely on the help of the outside world to develop their nuclear capability, they would have to do it themselves. It was on Khatami's watch that Iran decided to commence its own uranium mining activities, and he took a personal interest in overseeing the programme's development. When Khatami became president the programme was being run by scientists who had been chosen for their revolutionary credentials rather than their technical expertise. Khatami changed that by appointing Gholamreza Aghazadeh as the new head of Iran's Atomic Energy Organisation (AEOI), who in turn made dramatic improvements to the technical capabilities of the nuclear development teams. Under Khatami the nuclear programme was controlled by the office of the president, the commander of the Revolutionary Guards, the head of the Defence Industries Organisation and Aghazadeh. Khamenei, the Supreme Leader, was also kept fully informed of developments by the Guards. Iran's entire political, military and religious establishment was in some way or another committed to the success of the nuclear programme, not least because, in the final year of his life, Khomeini had written about the importance of Iran acquiring nuclear weapons. So far as the standard-bearers of Iran's Islamic revolution were concerned, they were fulfilling Khomeini's dying wish.

Fortunately for Iran the controversy over the exposure of its nuclear programme was overshadowed by the Bush administration's obsession with Iraq and overthrowing Saddam Hussein's regime. By the time ElBaradei confirmed in February 2003 the extent of Iran's nuclear deception, informing American officials that the Natanz facility was 'comprehensive and sophisticated',[25] Washington's plans for the invasion of Iraq were already too well advanced to turn back. Otherwise the Bush administration might well have concluded, under the terms of the war on terror doctrine the president had articulated in his State of the Union address, that there was a more convincing case for launching military action against Tehran, rather than Baghdad. By early 2003 Iran's involvement in global terrorism was well documented in Washington, evidence was emerging that, at the very least, Iran had facilitated al-Qaeda during the planning stages of the 9/11 attacks, and the revelation that Iran was working on a clandestine nuclear weapons programme certainly qualified it as a potential target for an administration that was obsessed with the possibility of rogue states acquiring nuclear weapons. The Bush administration was not in any doubt about how the new details concerning Iran's nuclear programme should be interpreted. Before the UN inspectors had even had a chance to inspect the facilities, Richard Boucher, the US State Department spokesman, announced that the United States had 'reached the conclusion that Iran is actively working to develop a nuclear weapons capability'.[26]

The overthrow of Saddam Hussein's regime in April 2003, and Iraq's rapid descent into anarchy following the removal of the country's Baathist security infrastructure, meant the issue of Iran's nuclear ambitions was put on hold. The reason the first Bush administration had pulled back from launching a full-scale invasion of Iraq in 1991 was the fear that the Shia of southern Iraq would link up with their Iranian co-religionists to create a 'Shia Crescent' stretching from the Levant to Central Asia. Washington wanted Iran to be on its best behaviour while it undertook the delicate task of removing Saddam from power, a policy that Tehran, which was glad to see the back of Saddam Hussein's regime, was only too happy to see implemented. But Iran's ability to destabilize post-Saddam Iraq could not be taken for granted by Tehran. It was still only fifteen years since the Shia of Iraq and the Shia of Iran had been involved in a bloody, eight-year war which had caused massive loss of life and untold suffering. While the Quds force had maintained close ties with the more radical Shia elements in Iraq, the ayatollahs in Tehran understood that they needed to proceed with caution if they were to establish good relations with Iraq's Shia.

Following Saddam's overthrow Iran moved cautiously, and the Quds force was deployed into the country to make sure Tehran was fully informed about ongoing political developments. In the early days of the American occupation the Iranians took great care not to be accused of causing trouble for the occupying power, not least because, with upwards of 100,000 American troops stationed across their border, there was always the risk of provoking American military retaliation against Iran. Tehran had funded and supported many of the Shia militias that now made their way back to Iraq, such as the Supreme Council for the Islamic Revolution in Iraq (SCIRI) and the Dawa. Many Dawa supporters had fled into exile in Iran after Saddam executed the group's spiritual leader, Mohammed al-Sadr, Khomeini's friend from the time of his exile in Najaf. Moqtada al-Sadr, the grandson of the cleric executed by Saddam, was intent on setting up his own militia, the Mahdi Army, to oppose the American occupation of Iraq after Saddam's overthrow. In Tehran Rahim Safavi, the Revolutionary Guards commander, and other radical figures in Iran argued strongly in favour of moving into Iraq in force, and challenging the new American hegemony. But they were held back by Khamenei, who took a more cautious approach and wanted to see how the post-Saddam political landscape took shape in Iraq before making any firm commitments.

For all Iran's insistence that it wanted to cooperate with the Americans in Iraq local Iraqis and American officials had little doubt that Tehran was behind the murder in April 2003 of Ayatollah Majid al-Khoei, the 41-year-old spiritual head of SCIRI, who was hacked to death by a Shia mob after being dragged, his hands bound, from the Imam Ali shrine in Najaf. Khoei, who had been forced to flee into exile in London following the failed Shia revolt against Saddam Hussein at the end of the 1991 Gulf War, had been a staunch opponent of Saddam's rule, and had just returned to Iraq following the dictator's overthrow. Although his party was funded and supported by Iran, Khoei had fully supported the US-led invasion and had committed SCIRI to work with the Americans to set up an interim government in Iraq. But this was too much for Muqtada al-Sadr, who his own close links with Tehran. Muqtada al-Sadr responded to Washington's plans to set up a US-controlled provisional government to replace Saddam's regime by remarking, 'The smaller devil has gone but the bigger devil has come,'[27] a sentiment that was no doubt shared by many of the more radical mullahs in Tehran. Although al-Sadr denied responsibility for Khoei's murder, survivors of the attack said the radical cleric's supporters wielded the knives that hacked Khoei to death. Certainly most Iraqis held Muqtada al-Sadr responsible, and in November an Iraqi judge issued an arrest warrant for him for Khoei's murder.

Before Saddam's overthrow Muqtada al-Sadr was relatively unknown outside Iraq. But by the late spring of 2003 he had turned the Sadr city Shia slums in Baghdad into his personal fiefdom and posed a serious threat to the US-led coalition's chances of establishing order. Soon after he had been implicated in the murder of Ayatollah al-Khoei, Muqtada al-Sadr was invited to Tehran to meet with Khamenei. During his stay in Tehran he also met Qassem Suleimani, the newly appointed head of the Quds force. During his visit to Tehran he discussed the details of his idea for forming the Mahdi Army, which would later play a lead role in opposing the coalition in Iraq.

Even at this early stage in Washington's troubled involvement in Iraq Paul Bremer, the American head of Iraq's provisional government, believed Muqtada al-Sadr to be so powerful that he predicted, 'Muqtada al-Sadr has the potential of ripping this country apart.'[28] The American pro-consul was also concerned about Tehran's growing influence in southern Iraq, even though Iran's presence was not universally welcomed by the Iraqi Shia. Early on in his mission Bremer informed Bush that 'the Iranians may be playing around a bit' in Iraq. Bush asked Bremer what the Iraqis made of Iran meddling in Iraqi affairs, to which Bremer replied that, based on his talks with Iraqi Shia leaders in southern Iraq, 'they don't want those guys from Iran mucking around in Iraq'.[29] Certainly the Iraqis were as confused as the Americans about Iran's true intentions in Iraq. By the following year Iran was supporting so many different Shia groups – the Mahdi Army, SCIRI, Dawa, the Badr Corps to name but a few – that one local Iraqi Shia commented, 'It is impossible to oppose Iran because they are paying all the pro-Iran parties – and they are paying all the anti-Iranian parties as well.'[30]

Iran was playing a deeply duplicitous game, and a dangerous one too. With most of the resources of the coalition absorbed in Iraq fighting what was at this point still a predominantly Sunni-inspired insurgency, Washington was in no position to confront Iran. But wherever US intelligence officials looked they saw Iran maintaining its involvement with the most unlikely terrorist allies. Arguably the most remarkable alliance was the assistance the Quds force was said to have provided Abu Musab al-Zarqawi, the fanatical Sunni terrorist responsible for establishing al-Qaeda in Iraq after the fall of Saddam. The Jordanian-born al-Zarqawi, who waged a sustained campaign of suicide bombings and kidnappings in Iraq against the coalition, was held responsible for the suicide car-bomb attack that killed Ayatollah Bakr al-Hakim in late August 2003. Hakim's father had been another one of Khomeini's mentors, and his son subscribed to Khomeini's view that Islam had a central role to play in the government of the country. Hakim was one of Tehran's closest allies in Iraq, and his militia, the Badr Corps, was armed and equipped by Iran. His death was a significant blow to Tehran's attempts to influence the political development of post-Saddam Iraq.

But that did not prevent the Revolutionary Guards from providing support to al-Zarqawi the following year when he was forced to flee following the US military's assault on his base in the Iraqi town of Fallujah. According to a BBC report, in August 2004 Qassem Suleimani, the commander of the Quds force, admitted that Iran had allowed free passage across the Iranian border to al-Zarqawi and his fighters to escape the American offensive. Although al-Zarqawi was known for his hatred for Shia Muslims, whom he regarded as heretics, Suleimani said Iran was prepared to help him because the leaders of the Islamic revolution were becoming increasingly concerned that the United States might succeed in its goal of establishing a secular, pro-Western regime in Baghdad.[31] While in Iran al-Zarqawi was even reported to have met with Imad Mughniyeh, the Revolutionary Guards' master terrorist, who was himself fully engaged at the time in finding and training fighters for Muqtada al-Sadr's fledgling Mahdi Army. Mughniyeh's terrorist handiwork was evident in the carefully coordinated suicide car-bomb attacks that became a feature of daily life in southern Iraq in 2004. In one particularly gruesome attack in April 2004, seventy-three people were killed – including eighteen children – when five suicide car bombs exploded at the same time outside Iraqi police stations in the British-controlled sector. As one Western intelligence official commented, 'This is all part of a strategy devised by the hardliners in Iran to repeat their success in Lebanon and drive coalition troops out of Iraq.'[32]

Nor was al-Zarqawi the only al-Qaeda-related terrorist receiving support from the Revolutionary Guards during this turbulent period. On 12 May 2003, just as the Americans announced the end of their military campaign to overthrow Saddam's regime, three truck bombs were detonated almost simultaneously in the Saudi capital Riyadh at the housing complexes where foreign workers lived, killing twenty people, including seven Americans. Within months American investigators had solid proof that the attack had been carried out by Saudi terrorists working for an al-Qaeda terrorist cell run by Saif Adel, bin Laden's former chief of staff, who had based himself in Iran following the overthrow of the Taliban. The Iranians claimed they had no control over Adel and the other al-Qaeda members, whom they claimed were living in the lawless eastern area of the country. But for the Americans and their allies, this seemed like just another lame excuse by the Iranians for their increasingly threatening behaviour. So far as Washington was concerned, Iran was rapidly running out of excuses to justify its behaviour.

11

In Search of the Apocalypse

The election in July 2005 of the former Revolutionary Guards commander Mahmoud Ahmadinejad as the Islamic republic's sixth president had an immediate and dramatic impact on Iran's relations with the outside world. Born in the desert town of Aradan in 1956, Ahmadinejad had risen from obscurity to become the mayor of Tehran. A devoted supporter of Khomeini, he had been involved with the student movement responsible for laying siege to the American embassy in 1979, and had subsequently acquired a reputation as one of the revolution's hard-line conservatives. During this heady period in the development of Iran's revolution Ahmadinejad met Khomeini several times; he made a deep and lasting impression on the young activist. Like many young revolutionaries, Ahmadinejad regarded Khomeini as his political mentor as well as his religious leader. Ahmadinejad's involvement in student politics also meant that he met many of the other key figures in the Islamic revolution, notably Khamenei and Rafsanjani, whom Khomeini had nominated as his interlocutors with the students.

Ahmadinejad joined the Revolutionary Guards at its inception in 1979 while still a student at Tehran's University of Science and Technology, where he studied development engineering. He was active in championing the virtues of the revolution, explaining that it was vital for Islamists 'to defend the totality of the new regime and respond to its needs'.[1] During the Iran–Iraq War he served with the engineers on the Kurdish border, although he saw little front-line action. But he made many important contacts within the Guards and the Basij, both of which later made significant contributions to his rise to power. After a spell teaching traffic management at his old university in Tehran, he gradually involved himself in politics, first joining the conservative faction on Tehran's city council before becoming mayor in 2003.

A bitter opponent of Khatami's reform agenda, during the 2005 presidential election Ahmadinejad drew heavily on his contacts in the Revolutionary Guards to steer the result in his favour. Ever since Khatami's surprise victory in 1997 the reactionaries had intensified their efforts to rig elections in favour of the hardliners. Khatami's re-election in June 2001, when the reformists were still able to muster a majority of the vote, only served to encourage the hardliners in their efforts to destroy the reform movement. By the time of the 2004 Majlis election, Khamenei and his supporters succeeded in rigging the ballot so that the majority of Khatami's reformist supporters were ejected. Khamenei, the judiciary, the Revolutionary Guards, and the entire revolutionary establishment were united in the determination to re-establish the credentials of Khomeini's revolution.

The conservative hardliners allied to Khamenei had already started to reassert their authority the previous year when, encouraged by the presence of pro-democracy coalition forces in neighbouring Iraq, thousands of students took to the streets in a series of anti-government protests. The demonstrations were in many respects a rerun of the pro-democracy protests that had broken out in the summer of 1999 and had been crushed by the intervention of the Hizbollahis and the Guards, who always seemed at hand to crush any hint of dissent to the regime. As in 1999 some of the protesters were sufficiently emboldened to chant, 'Death to Khamenei'. And just like 1999 they were savagely attacked by the self-appointed guardians of the revolution, who stormed the students' dormitories at Tehran university and subjected the protesters to savage beatings.

After three days of pitched street battles, the protests were eventually crushed by the Guards and their supporters who arrested more than 4,000 students. Iran's pro-democracy genie had been well and truly put back in its bottle.

The student protests of 2003 had once again demonstrated the general disquiet throughout the country at the uncompromising policies of the ruling elite, but this, for the most part, silent majority had no means of expression through the institutions of the state. President Bush attempted to lend encouragement to the protesters by suggesting they overthrow the theocratic dictatorship. But his words had the opposite effect, with Khamenei appealing to Iran's anti-Western instincts by claiming that Washington was behind the demonstrations. The Bush administration's support for the pro-democracy protests led to the hardliners tightening their grip over the country's institutions to prevent the reformists from having a platform from which to express their views. But the unheard voices of Iran's oppressed population continued to rise to the surface. In 2003 the Iranian writer Shirin Ebadi, a former judge who had been sacked because of her gender, won the Nobel Peace Prize for her book *Iran Awakening*, in which she wrote an emotional account of the repression educated Iranian women suffered at the hands of the mullahs' regime.

Prior to the Majlis elections in February 2004 the Council of Guardians systematically vetted all the candidates, and disqualified virtually any politician associated with the country's reform movements. Many senior members of Khatami's government resigned in protest, but that merely played into the hands of the hardliners, who won a comfortable majority, prompting Khamenei to declare, 'The losers in this election are the United States, Zionism and the enemies of the Iranian nation.'[2] The same tactics were deployed by the hardliners for the 2005 presidential contest where Ahmadinejad's main rival was the septuagenarian Rafsanjani, who bizarrely positioned himself as the champion of Iranian youth. But once Khamenei, who had

always been wary of Rafsanjani's political cunning, had indicated that Ahmadinejad was his preferred choice, the Guards
moved into action and implemented what one Guards commander described as a 'multi-layered plan' to ensure his victory, which resulted in Ahmadinejad somehow acquiring an
unexpected 6 million extra votes. The ballot was littered with
irregularities, and on at least one occasion the total votes for a
district surpassed the number of registered voters. The vote-
rigging was so transparent that the vanquished Rafsanjani
claimed that some of the extra votes Ahmadinejad had received
were actually the unexpired birth certificates of dead people.[3]

When he became president Ahmadinejad was almost
unknown outside Iran. But his hard-line adherence to the
principles of Khomeini's revolution, and his uncompromising
views about the West and Israel, were soon exposed for the
entire world to see. At a conference held in Tehran in October
titled 'The World Without Zionism', Ahmadinejad declared
that Israel was a 'disgraceful blot' that should be 'wiped off
the face of the earth'. The comments immediately provoked an
international uproar, but Ahmadinejad defended himself by
insisting he had merely been quoting the words of Khomeini,
the founder of Iran's Islamic revolution. 'As the Imam said,
Israel must be wiped off the map.'

Ahmadinejad's controversial outburst was just one example
of the new Iranian leader's extremist views. At one of his first
cabinet meetings the new president revealed his deep devotion
to the Twelfth Imam, whom devout Shia regard as a direct
descendant of the Prophet Mohammed who went into 'occlu-
sion' at the age of five. According to tradition, the Hidden
Imam, as he is also known, will only return after a period of
cosmic chaos, war and bloodshed – what Christians call the
Apocalypse – and then lead the world to an era of universal
peace. Ahmadinejad told his newly appointed ministers, 'We
have to turn Iran into a modern and divine country to be the

model for all nations, and which will serve as the basis for the return of the Twelfth Imam.' One minister helpfully suggested the government should undertake a programme of hotel expansion to accommodate all the visitors that would flock to Iran when the Mahdi finally returned. Several months later, while on a tour of the provinces, Ahmadinejad made the outlandish suggestion that the Western powers were so concerned about the Mahdi's possible return that they were scouring the world trying to find him, to prevent him returning to Iran and establishing justice on earth.[4]

In the early days of his presidency Ahmadinejad worked hard to adopt the revolutionary persona that had served Khomeini so well during the early days of the revolution. Ahmadinejad's power base, both in the cities and the countryside, lay with the poor and the dispossessed, the *sans-culottes* of the revolution, and he spent much of his time touring the provinces seeking to rekindle the flames of the early revolution and return to the values of Khomeini's early years. He often used Khomeini's language to denounce the United States and Iran's other perceived enemies, and was highly critical of their opposition to Iran's pursuit of nuclear technology, which he regarded as Iran's 'legitimate right'.

The election of an Iranian president who entertained a truly apocalyptic vision of the world further aroused concern about the direction in which the Iranian revolution was heading. This was particularly true in Israel, the target of so much of Ahmadinejad's inflammatory rhetoric, where in December the Israeli prime minister, Ariel Sharon, quietly ordered his military chiefs to make preparations for possible air strikes against Iran's nuclear facilities. Nor was it just Israel that expressed concern at the prospect of the new, hardline regime in Tehran acquiring nuclear weapons. Following the revelations about Iran's clandestine nuclear facilities in 2002, the European powers, led by Britain, Germany and France – the so-called

EU3 – embarked on an intensive round of diplomatic activity aimed at persuading the Iranians to halt their uranium enrichment activities at Natanz.

Washington was, initially, prepared to let the EU3 make all the running in the negotiations with Iran, not least because it had its hands full trying to deal with the rapidly deteriorating security situation in Iraq. The decision to invade Iraq had caused a deep rift in relations between continental Europe and Washington, and there was a feeling among some senior members of the Bush administration that it would be good for the Europeans to experience for themselves what it was like trying to deal with rogue regimes like Saddam Hussein's Iraq and revolutionary Iran. The European negotiations eventually succeeded in late 2003 in persuading Iran to suspend its enrichment activities, although the deal fell well short of Washington's demand that the Natanz programme be halted for good. Despite this gesture from Iran, UN inspectors continued to find compelling evidence that the regime still had undeclared nuclear facilities that could be part of a secret military programme.

In 2004 the inspectors found traces of uranium that had been enriched to weapons grade, which blew a hole in the Iranians' insistence that all their activity was concentrated on becoming self-sufficient in nuclear power. Nuclear power stations do not require uranium to be enriched to weapons grade. And the inspectors finally confirmed that Iran had acquired the more sophisticated P2 centrifuge from Pakistan, another important element of the nuclear programme that Tehran had failed to disclose to the IAEA. But far from being embarrassed by these discoveries, Iran's response when confronted with this incriminating evidence was to demand the right to resume work on its nuclear programme. This prompted John Bolton, the Bush administration's hawkish Undersecretary of State, to issue a stark warning to the European negotiators that Iran would soon be able to develop nuclear weapons. 'If we permit Iran's deception to go on much longer, it will be too late. Iran will have nuclear weapons.'[5]

Work on Iran's nuclear programme was still technically suspended when Ahmadinejad became president, although the IAEA suspected Iranian technicians had continued conducting research on the all-important centrifuges at Natanz.[6] But as soon as Ahmadinejad became president Iran officially asked the IAEA to remove its seals at the Isfahan Uranium Conversion Facility so that work could begin immediately on converting uranium ore, or yellowcake, into UF_6, the feeder material needed for the uranium enrichment process. Ahmadinejad then sacked the team of negotiators who had been working closely with the IAEA and EU3 on a resolution of the nuclear crisis, and their replacements were ordered to adopt a more aggressive approach in their dealings with the West.

Almost immediately this resulted in Tehran rejecting a wide-ranging package put together by the EU3 which offered Iran economic incentives in return for suspending all its nuclear activities. In an address to the Majlis, Ahmadinejad set out his new, hard-line policy in the negotiations with the EU3, in which he made it clear that he was not interested in reaching a deal with Europe whereby the Europeans offered technical assistance with helping Iran to complete its nuclear power programme. 'We will not agree to outside diktats that are illegal and violate the rights of Iran,' he declared. A few weeks later, in September, Ahmadinejad attended his first session of the United Nations General Assembly in New York, where he made a veiled threat to develop nuclear weapons if the Western powers persisted with their policy of what he called 'nuclear apartheid'. Whilst stressing that Iran's nuclear intentions were peaceful, Ahmadinejad warned that 'if some try to impose their will on the Iranian people through resort to a language of force and threat with Iran, we will reconsider our entire approach to the nuclear issue'.[7]

Ahmadinejad had a deeply held personal conviction that he

had been divinely appointed for the task of governing Iran, which he believed had been confirmed during his address to the UN. When he got back to Tehran he told friends that he had experienced a mystical, out of body experience while addressing the assembly. 'One of our group told me that when I started to say, "In the name of the God, the almighty and merciful", he saw a light around me and I was placed inside this aura.' Ahmadinejad was convinced the audience had experienced the same feeling. 'I felt the atmosphere suddenly change and for those 27 or 28 minutes the leaders of the world did not blink . . . they were rapt. It seemed as if a hand was holding them there and had opened their eyes to receive the message from the Islamic republic.'[8]

Attempts to persuade Iran to observe the agreement it had signed with the EU3 to halt work on uranium enrichment got nowhere, not least because Russian President Vladimir Putin refused to back the West's attempts to have Iran referred to the Security Council for non-compliance. By the end of 2005 Putin, who had initially given his support to America's war on terror campaign, had started to distance himself from Washington. One of the reasons for this rift was the Bush administration's insistence on locating key parts of its new national missile defence system in former Warsaw Pact countries such as Poland and the Czech Republic. Washington wanted to put the early radar warning systems and interceptor missiles in central Europe to protect the West from the potential risk of being the target of nuclear weapons fired by rogue states such as Iran. But Moscow violently objected to the missile defence system being located so close to Russia's borders, and Putin sought to persuade Bush to change his mind by frustrating Washington's attempts to impose wide-ranging sanctions against Iran at the UN.

Tehran skilfully exploited the divisions within the Security Council to its advantage and, sensing the West was reluctant to act, continued work on the nuclear programme regardless of the international hostility it attracted. In January 2006, Ahmadinejad ordered Iran's nuclear scientists to remove the IAEA's seals at the uranium enrichment plant at Natanz to enable them to resume work on assembling the centrifuges needed for uranium enrichment. Tehran brushed aside a deadline imposed by the UN Security Council to halt its nuclear enrichment programme by the end of May. 'The enrichment matter is not reversible,' declared a government official. Although the Security Council had taken months to reach agreement on imposing the deadline, Iran was well aware that it only had lukewarm support from Russia and China, countries that had lucrative trading ties with Tehran. But all the while new details continued to emerge about important aspects of Iran's nuclear programme that had not been declared to the IAEA's nuclear inspectors. For example, a number of nuclear scientists and researchers were found to be conducting secret nuclear research work at Tehran's Imam Hossein University which had not been declared to the IAEA.[9]

In April Ahmadinejad excitedly announced that Iran had joined the 'nuclear club' after scientists working at Natanz claimed they had succeeded in enriching a small quantity of uranium. 'This is the result of the Iranian nation's resistance,' Ahmadinejad proudly declared on Iranian television. 'We will continue our path until we achieve production of industrial-scale uranium.' A few weeks later the IAEA produced its latest progress report on Iran's nuclear programme, which confirmed small quantities of uranium had indeed been enriched at Natanz, and that the Iranians were making good progress in assembling the centrifuges used for enrichment. Iran's actions persuaded the normally neutral Mohammed ElBaradei, the head of the IAEA, to state publicly for the first time that the nuclear watchdog could no longer judge whether Iran's nuclear programme was 'entirely peaceful'.

A few days later the Iranian president did little to reassure international opinion about Iran's ultimate objectives by predicting that the 'Zionist regime' of Israel would soon be annihilated. Attending a conference in Tehran on the future of Palestine, he declared that Israel was 'heading towards annihilation', questioned whether the Holocaust had ever happened, and predicted that the Middle East would soon be 'liberated'. Iran's growing isolation from the outside world was not helped by its belligerent response every time the Western powers sought to have Iran's nuclear programme referred to the Security Council. In February Tehran warned that it would use 'all means' at its disposal to repel any attempts to force it to halt the nuclear programme, and in August the regime threatened to block oil exports to the West from the Gulf if sanctions were imposed against Tehran.

For all the international opprobrium Ahmadinejad's nuclear policy attracted, it nevertheless strengthened his domestic position, where he came to be regarded as the champion of Iran's quest for nuclear technology. When he returned from addressing his first UN session, thousands of supporters holding posters of the Iranian president turned out at Tehran airport to welcome him home. His unqualified support for Iran's nuclear programme certainly helped its development. By the end of 2006 technicians at Natanz had made enormous progress in assembling the centrifuges and were close to achieving Ahmadinejad's goal of enriching uranium on an industrial scale. But the West refused to be intimidated by Tehran's threats and bullying, and on Christmas Eve 2006 the UN Security Council finally passed the first of its resolutions, 1737, imposing economic sanctions against Tehran to persuade the regime to halt its nuclear programme. Although the measures themselves were relatively mild, it served as a warning shot across the bows of Ahmadinejad's regime that the West would not stand idly by while Tehran pursued its nuclear programme in defiance of the UN. The sanctions included a ban on the sale of any material to Iran that could be used for nuclear or missile programmes, and imposed a travel ban on the movement across international borders for twelve individuals, including Rahim Safavi, the commander of the Revolutionary Guards. The assets of companies and banks believed to be involved in the nuclear and missile programmes were frozen, and the resolution called for Iran to suspend its uranium enrichment activities and the development of the heavy-water plant at Arak. In typically combative mood, Ahmadinejad denounced the imposition of sanctions, remarking, 'Whether the West likes it or not, Iran is a nuclear country and it is in their interests to live alongside Iran.'

*

Iran's relentless pursuit of nuclear technology was just one of several factors that led to yet another dramatic escalation in tension between Tehran and the West. Another was the Revolutionary Guards' continued support for radical Islamist groups, particularly in Iraq. Iran's defiance of world opinion over its nuclear programme, which increased significantly after Ahmadinejad came to power, was to a large extent encouraged by the belief in Tehran that, with most of Washington's military resources tied up in Iraq, the United States was in no position to confront Tehran over its nuclear programme. It was consequently very much in Iran's interests to sustain the violent insurgency which by 2004 had fully engulfed post-Saddam Iraq, and the Revolutionary Guards and the Quds force were active on a number of fronts making sure there was no let-up in the violence. For the most part the Iranians focused their attention on supporting the main Shia militias, such as Muqtada al-Sadr's Mahdi Army and the Badr Corps, which owed their allegiance to SCIRI.

Muqtada, or 'Mad Max' as he became known in the Western media, was particularly troublesome, taking it upon himself to do everything in his power to undermine coalition efforts to establish security in Iraq. In August 2004 Sadr came close to declaring all-out war against the US when he seized control of the holy Shia shrine at Najaf and attempted to set up a power base to rival that of the newly installed Iraqi provisional government of the secular Shia leader Ayad Allawi. Thanks to the training facilities provided by the Quds force across the border in Iran, the Mahdi Army had been transformed into a highly effective, 5,000-strong force that was more than a match for the other militias fighting in the area.[10] The Mahdi Army also controlled the 1.5 million Iraqi Shia who lived in the Sadr city slums of east Baghdad and, at Muqtada's insistence, they had launched their own insurgency against US forces responsible for securing Iraq's capital.

The stand-off at Najaf was finally ended following the intervention of Iraq's Grand Ayatollah Ali Sistani, who ordered the Mahdi Army to lay down its arms and vacate the Najaf mosque. Sistani was a firm adherent to the Shia clerical tradition of quietism, in which the religious establishment refrained from involvement in the grubby world of day-to-day politics. It was a tradition that had once been observed in Iran before the Islamic revolution, and Sistani's dramatic intervention to force Muqtada to end the siege in Najaf served as a reminder to the Guards and their backers in Tehran that a sizeable majority of Shia Muslims in Iraq did not necessarily subscribe to Khomeini's revolutionary Islamic agenda.

But the Iranians were not to be discouraged, and after Ahmadinejad came to power there was a dramatic intensification in Iran's efforts to destabilize Iraq. British and American commanders identified a noticeable rise in Iranian activity in Iraq from July 2005, the month Ahmadinejad became president. In the British area of operations in southern Iraq, which was closest to Iran's main smuggling routes into Iraq, there were at least a dozen Islamic groups operating in the sector that were funded by Tehran. Muqtada al-Sadr's Mahdi Army remained the militia most closely associated with Iran, and many of Muqtada al-Sadr's senior advisers liaised directly with the Quds force, which provided the Mahdi Army with financial support, modern weapons and good communication systems. Among the equipment provided by the Revolutionary Guards to the militias were advanced 'infra-red' roadside bombs of the type used by Hizbollah in southern Lebanon against the Israelis.

Iraqi militiamen were offered up to $800 by Iran to carry out attacks against the American military or assassinate leading Iraqis. The Badr corps, the other main Shia militia operating in southern Iraq, also took its orders directly from Tehran, even though it was competing with the Mahdi Army for influence over Iraq's Shia population. Intelligence officials estimated that throughout the country there were at least 30,000 Iraqis who were receiving monthly salaries from Iran, ranging from $300 to $1,000 per month.[11] Hazim Shalan, a former Iraqi defence minister who served in Iraq's first provisional government, even claimed that parts of the Iraqi government were being directly controlled by Tehran, such was the influence Iran had already established throughout Iraq.[12]

Some Iraqi ministers and government officials were convinced that Tehran was trying to drive the coalition out of Iraq so that it could establish an Islamic theocracy. The rise in Iranian activity coincided with the Iraqi government's plans to hold a referendum on the proposed new constitution. Iraqis were expected to vote for the establishment of a secular Shia government in Baghdad, which Iran's hardliners feared might raise serious questions about the legitimacy of the authoritarian theocracy that had seized power across the border in Tehran. There were serious concerns in Baghdad that the Revolutionary Guards might replicate the vote-fixing activities in Iraq that had been so successful in getting Ahmadinejad elected.

Coalition officials, meanwhile, identified what they believed was a direct correlation between increased Iranian activity in Iraq and international pressure being applied to Tehran over its nuclear programme. In September 2005, when the UN first began to consider imposing sanctions against Iran, British commanders, responsible for security in southern Iraq, openly accused Iran of supplying the explosives used in attacks against British patrols. In particular they accused Iran of responsibility for a number of roadside bombs that had killed eight British soldiers. Britain, along with the United States, was at the forefront of attempts to persuade the Security Council to impose sanctions against Iran, and by attacking British forces Tehran was sending a signal to the British government to drop its support for sanctions. As one senior British commander in Basra remarked, 'This was Iran's way of telling the British government, "If you want to confront us over our nuclear programme, then we have every right to blow up British soldiers."'[13] Meanwhile, in Baghdad, Muqtada's Mahdi Army had such a grip over the Iraqi capital that senior Iraqi politicians found themselves regularly travelling to Iran just to find out what was going on in their own country.[14]

The British and American governments responded by lodging formal complaints with Tehran over its continued interference in Iraq. Donald Rumsfeld, the US Defense Secretary, said Iran was 'interested, involved and not helpful' in Iraq, while Tony Blair, the British prime minister, went even further, warning Tehran that it could face military action if it did not change its attitude to the West. Blair was particularly incensed by Ahmadinejad's remark that Israel should be 'wiped off the face of the earth'. 'If they carry on like this,' said Blair, 'the question people are going to ask me is, "When are you going to do something about this?"' He also warned that Tehran was making a very big mistake if it believed its involvement in Iraq would distract US and European leaders from confronting it over its nuclear programme.

Iran's confrontational attitude towards the West over its nuclear programme and its increased support for Islamist terror groups, both in Iraq and elsewhere, raised the stakes considerably between the West and Tehran. The EU3 continued with their attempts to persuade Tehran to suspend the nuclear programme, and great care was taken not to provoke the mullahs, even when they were effectively waging a clandestine war against coalition troops in Iraq. Jack Straw, the British Foreign Secretary, summed up the attitude of most Europeans when he stated in early January 2006 that the dispute 'can only be resolved by peaceful means . . . Nobody is talking about invading Iran or taking military action against Iran . . . Iran is not Iraq.' Tehran responded to Mr Straw's emollient words by warning that Iran would use its long-range missiles to strike Israel or Western forces stationed in the Gulf if it was attacked.

But the Bush administration took a different view to the Europeans, and was not prepared to mince its words with regard to Tehran. Rumsfeld accused the Revolutionary Guards of dispatching units to Iraq 'to do things that are harmful to the future of Iraq', while in April Bush bluntly contradicted Straw's claim that military action against Iran was 'inconceivable' when he insisted that all options, including the use of military force, remained very firmly on the table at the White House. By the spring of 2006 war fever was raging in both Washington and Tehran, where both countries were said to be preparing for the possibility of military action. In Washington, Bush's aides briefed heavily that the issue of Iran's nuclear programme 'is not one this president is likely to leave to a successor'.[15] Seymour Hersh, the veteran American investigative reporter, revealed in the *New Yorker* that the US military had drawn up plans to use bunker-buster tactical weapons to destroy the thick protective concrete shield the Iranians had built to protect the Natanz facility.[16]

The Revolutionary Guards, meanwhile, responded by announcing that they had successfully test-fired a new high-speed underwater missile which travelled at three times the speed of a conventional torpedo and had the capability to destroy warships and submarines. The tests were carried out as the Guards conducted war games codenamed 'Great Prophet' in the Gulf which also involved a flying boat equipped with radar-avoiding stealth technology. While the crisis between Washington and Tehran deepened the US State Department issued its annual summary on state-sponsored terrorism which concluded that Iran was the country most active in sponsoring international terrorism. It stated unequivocally that the Revolutionary Guards and the Ministry of Intelligence and Security were directly involved in the planning and support of terrorist acts in Iraq and elsewhere, supporting militant Islamist groups in Lebanon, the West Bank and Gaza, and continued 'to fail to control' the activities of al-Qaeda fugitives that had sought refuge in Iran after the fall of the Taliban.[17]

As if to confirm the State Department's findings, Iran's overseas support for radical Islamist groups was graphically illustrated in the summer of 2006 when Hizbollah provoked an all-out war with Israel. The Revolutionary Guards had been supporting the south Lebanon-based militia for more than two decades, and most Western observers believed Tehran had given Hizbollah a green light to provoke the conflict, which started when the militia staged an ambush and kidnapped two Israeli soldiers. The ambush took place the day after a meeting on Iran's nuclear programme between Ali Larijani, Iran's chief negotiator, and the EU3 in Brussels, which broke up without agreement. Larijani flew straight from Brussels to Damascus, where he met with Hizbollah officials. The following day Hizbollah staged its ambush in southern Lebanon, prompting suspicions that Iran had deliberately started the war to distract attention from the stalled nuclear talks.[18]

The attack began when Hizbollah succeeded in destroying an Israeli Merkava tank – reputed to be the best protected in the world – with the same type of armour-piercing explosive device that had been used so effectively against British and American forces in Iraq. When Israel responded by attacking Hizbollah positions in Lebanon, the Shia militia fired volleys of missiles at towns and villages in northern Israel, many of which had either been supplied or manufactured by Tehran. Scores of Revolutionary Guards commanders were dispatched to southern Lebanon to oversee Hizbollah's military strategy, including Imad Mughniyeh who, apart from his many other duties, was the militia's head of security. When the fighting finished many Lebanese families of those killed or injured in the fighting received payments of $1,000 by way of compensation from Iran's Foundation of the Oppressed, the charity run by the Revolutionary Guards.[19]

Undeterred by the international criticism of the role Iran had played in what became known as the Second Lebanon War, Ahmadinejad further increased Iran's isolation when the fighting stopped by ignoring a deadline set by the UN to suspend the nuclear enrichment activities at Natanz. Despite the threat of increased UN sanctions, Tehran saw no reason to suspend its nuclear programme when the West was too weak and divided to take any effective action to force Iran to comply. While the Security Council sporadically achieved a consensus on taking punitive measures against Tehran, they were nothing like as strong as Washington wanted them to be, and the Russians and Chinese showed little interest in taking a confrontational approach towards Tehran.

From Ahmadinejad's perspective, by late 2006 Iran could argue with some conviction that it was in its strongest position since the 1979 Revolution. Hizbollah was deemed to have triumphed in the war against Israel, a fact that was acknowledged by the political turmoil that afflicted Israel after the war, which was hit by a series of high-level military resignations over the tactical errors committed by Israel's armed forces and a lengthy political inquiry – the Winograd Commission – into where the politicians had gone wrong. Meanwhile by late 2006 the involvement of the American military and its allies in Iraq had reached such a low ebb that the Iraq Study Group that Bush had asked to study America's options in Iraq recommended withdrawing the coalition forces as soon as it was practicable. Tehran was well aware that Iran's enemies were in no position to dictate terms over its nuclear activities.

With little prospect of a resolution to the stand-off between Iran and the West, there was no effective impediment to Iran maintaining progress on the development of its nuclear programme. By the spring of 2007 – exactly a year after Iran had first succeeded in enriching small quantities of uranium at Natanz – Ahmadinejad was able to claim that Iran had acquired the capability to enrich uranium 'on an industrial scale'. The Iranian president made the historic announcement amid much fanfare, and assembled a group of foreign diplomats and journalists for the announcement in the vast, underground hall at Natanz where Iran planned eventually to set up more than 50,000 centrifuges. The event was clearly an emotional moment for the Iranian president, who was caught by Iranian television cameras shedding an emotional tear shortly before he made the announcement.[20]

While international nuclear experts tried to play down the significance of this technological breakthrough, pointing out that Iran had only succeeded in enriching modest quantities of uranium, and still faced significant technological difficulties in achieving its desired goal, there was no doubt that this was nevertheless a watershed moment in Iran's attempts to become a self-contained nuclear power. While the previous year Iran had only a few hundred centrifuges operational at Natanz, Larijani claimed there were 3,000 fully operational centrifuges, although this was disputed by international experts. What was not in dispute, though, was that Iran had now acquired full mastery of the nuclear fuel cycle. It could take uranium ore from its indigenous mines, convert it to UF_6 at Isfahan, and then enrich UF_6 at Natanz for either commercial or military use. Iran had made a giant leap forward in its ambitious programme to become a nuclear power. And Ahmadinejad marked the occasion by issuing another veiled warning to the

West that Tehran would develop nuclear weapons if the UN maintained its confrontational approach. While his supporters chanted their customary 'Death to America', 'Death to Britain' and 'Death to Israel', Ahmadinejad advised the West 'to observe the legal rights of different nations and stop monopolising, because that will not be to their benefit'.[21]

*

However much Washington and its allies wanted to take effective action to force Iran to suspend its nuclear programme, the Bush administration found itself sidetracked by other, no less important, security issues. At the end of 2006, after the Republicans had lost control of Congress in the mid-term elections, Bush decided to make important changes to America's approach to the war effort in Iraq. Robert Gates, a former CIA director, was appointed the new Defense Secretary to replace Donald Rumsfeld. Bush wanted what he described as a 'fresh perspective' on Iraq and, rather than accepting the recommendations of the Iraq Study Group, Bush took the bold decision to undertake a military 'surge' in Iraq, where extra American forces would be deployed in a last-ditch effort to tackle the insurgency. Both Gates and General David Petraeus, the newly appointed commander of coalition forces in Iraq, were fully committed to the surge strategy, whereby Washington committed an extra 30,000 troops to Iraq. The new strategy, a reversal of Rumsfeld's insistence on keeping manning levels to a minimum, was seen as the Bush administration's last chance to make a success out of America's involvement in Iraq. Consequently, the Bush administration's energy was now almost entirely focused on Iraq, not Iran.

The only reason the United States was likely to attack Iran during this period was over the Revolutionary Guards' continued meddling in Iraq, not Iran's nuclear programme. But rather than being intimidated by the presence of extra American troops in Iraq, Tehran took the view that its own strategy of fuelling the insurgency by all means at its disposal was working. The longer the United States and its allies were bogged down in Iraq, the less likely they were to act over Iran's nuclear programme. In January 2007 a group of five Iranian diplomats – who later turned out to be members of the Revolutionary Guards' elite Quds force – were caught red-handed by US forces supplying Shia militias in northern Iraq with cash, weapons and training facilities. Washington responded by ordering American special forces to conduct covert operations against Iranian assets in Iraq. By the spring of 2007 coalition forces were receiving intelligence reports that the Revolutionary Guards were once more linking up with al-Qaeda and other radical Sunni groups in Iraq. Senior American commanders working for Petraeus accused Iran of fighting a 'proxy war' against American and British forces in Iraq, and accused Iranian forces of 'committing acts of war'.[22]

British forces in southern Iraq suffered their own humiliating encounter with Iranian forces when fifteen Royal Navy crew members patrolling the Shatt al-Arab waterway were taken hostage by a group of Revolutionary Guards in fast motor patrol boats. The crew members were eventually released on Khamenei's orders, but the once-mighty Royal Navy had been humiliated by a group of Iranians equipped with rocket-propelled grenades. The incident inflicted a deep psychological blow on the morale of British forces serving in Iraq, and British commanders started to give serious consideration to withdrawing their forces. After Gordon Brown replaced Tony Blair as British prime minister at the end of June 2007, it soon became clear the new British government was seeking to withdraw forces from Iraq at the earliest available opportunity, despite the objections of American commanders. In September British forces were ordered to withdraw from the centre of Basra to their heavily fortified air base on the city outskirts, abandoning control of Iraq's second city to the control of lawless, Iranian-controlled militias.

Nor were the Revolutionary Guards' activities at this time confined to Iraq. From the summer of 2006 tens of thousands of NATO forces had been deployed to Afghanistan as part of a belated international effort to help with the Afghan government's reconstruction effort following the overthrow of the Taliban. But the Taliban had been allowed to regroup and become an effective fighting force in the period since the US-led coalition had overthrown the Taliban government in 2001, and by the spring of 2007 senior NATO commanders found compelling evidence that the Revolutionary Guards had set aside their traditional antipathy towards the Taliban and were supplying them with roadside bombs and rockets to attack NATO positions, particularly British forces deployed in southern Afghanistan. The Taliban demonstrated their new-found technical capability by firing a Russian-made anti-aircraft missile at an American F-18 fighter, although the aircraft managed to take evasive action. NATO commanders were convinced that the Taliban had received the technology from Iran, which had negotiated a number of lucrative arms deals with Moscow.[23]

At the same time Iran maintained its campaign of intimidation against Israel by increasing its support for the radical Palestinian Islamic group Hamas. Following Hamas' victory in the 2006 Palestinian elections, Iran became the group's main financial backer after most of the main Western aid donors to the Palestinians withdrew their support in protest at Hamas' uncompromising stance towards Israel. By the summer of 2007 Iran had signed a memo of understanding with Hamas to fund the militant group to the tune of $800 million a year. In addition senior Hamas officials regularly travelled to Iran for training at Quds force camps. When Hamas decided to launch a military operation in June to seize control of the Gaza Strip from its main political rival, the secularist Fatah group of Yasser Arafat, Revolutionary Guards officers were on hand to assist Hamas achieve its objective of creating the new Palestinian territory of what became known as Hamas-stan.[24]

With the West stymied in its confrontation with Iran –
both with regard to the progress of Tehran's nuclear programme and its support for radical Islamist groups – the only
country that seemed prepared to act was Israel, which saw
itself as the ultimate target of Iran's nuclear ambitions. While
the West's intelligence agencies continued to debate whether
or not there was significant evidence to prove Iran had a
clandestine nuclear weapons programme, the Israeli government was in no doubt as to Tehran's objective, and regarded
the possibility of Iran acquiring nuclear weapons as a threat to
its own survival. In early 2007 Ehud Olmert, the Israeli prime
minister, declared that, 'The Jewish people, with the scars of
the Holocaust fresh on its body, cannot afford to allow itself
to face threats of annihilation once again.' Fearful that the
West would not intervene to prevent Iran acquiring nuclear
weapons, Olmert ordered his military chiefs to ensure Israel
had the capability to carry out unilateral air strikes against
Iran's nuclear facilities if the need arose.[25]

Israeli fears about the direction in which Iran's nuclear
programme was heading appeared to be confirmed in September when Israeli warplanes bombed a secret nuclear installation
in Syria in September 2007. The Israelis launched their attack
after discovering North Korea was helping the Syrians to build
a nuclear reactor similar to the one North Korea had used to
conduct its controversial test of an atomic device in late 2006.
The North Koreans were known to have shared the results of
that test with Iranian nuclear scientists, and the Israelis suspected that Iran had encouraged Syria to embark upon its own
nuclear programme as a fall-back option in case the Iranian
programme came under attack by the West.[26] Evidence of the
deepening cooperation between Iran and Syria on weapons of
mass destruction projects had been uncovered the previous
year when a number of Iranian missile engineers were killed in
Syria while trying to fit a chemical warhead to a missile. The
Israeli air strike demonstrated its ability to conduct bombing

raids against suspected nuclear targets with pinpoint accuracy. But it also did nothing to allay Israeli fears that Iran itself was working on a clandestine nuclear weapons programme. With Saddam Hussein's Iraq no longer posing a threat to global security, it seemed a new axis of evil was taking shape in the form of North Korea, Iran and Syria.

Washington's frustration with Iran's continuing involvement in terrorism and nuclear proliferation, and the West's failure to take effective measures to curtail these activities, finally boiled over in the autumn of 2007 when the Bush administration unilaterally designated the Revolutionary Guards' Quds force a terrorist group, and imposed wide-ranging punitive measures against the organization. While Washington stopped short of imposing sanctions against the entire Revolutionary Guards infrastructure, it nevertheless accused the Guards of involvement in a clandestine nuclear weapons programme and developing ballistic missiles. The sanctions imposed by Washington were the toughest measures taken against Tehran since the American embassy siege in 1979, and it was the first time the American government had ever taken action against the armed forces of an independent government.

The Revolutionary Guards had developed far beyond the motley collection of Islamic fanatics that had originally been brought together to defend Khomeini's 1979 Revolution. The three decades following the Iranian revolution had seen the Guards become almost a state within a state, an organization that rivalled the official government in terms of the day-to-day power and influence it exerted throughout the country. The primary responsibility of the 125,000 men who formed the main body of the Guards remained taking care of the regime's defence, security and intelligence operations. Apart from having its own navy, air force and army, the Guards had control over significant areas of weapons development, including Iran's nuclear and ballistic missile programmes. The Quds force helped to set up an estimated fifty-one separate smuggling routes into Iraq and ran more than a dozen training camps in Iraq for militant groups that included Iraqi insurgent groups, Hizbollah and Hamas. The elite unit, whose strength was estimated at several thousand, also had exclusive responsibility for exporting the Iranian revolution, which meant financing sympathetic Islamic groups in places such as Lebanon, Gaza, Iraq and Afghanistan. In 2008 it was calculated that 80 per cent of Hizbollah's funding came directly from Iran, while in Iraq pro-Iranian fighters were said to be paid ten times more than local Iraqi police officers.[27]

The reason the Guards could afford to distribute such largesse was that they controlled many key sectors of the Iranian economy. Their pre-eminent role in defending the principles of the Iranian revolution – as enshrined in the constitution drawn up by Khomeini – enabled them to extend their influence through all aspects of Iranian life. They had their own university which allowed them to develop their skills over a wide range of subjects, from engineering to economic development. As the young firebrands of the 1979 Revolution, such as Ahmadinejad, moved into middle age, so they diversified their range of interests and activities, primarily in the economic sphere. The Guards acquired a voracious appetite for taking on ambitious – and potentially lucrative – economic projects. In 2007 the Guards acquired a $2.09 billion contract to develop one of the country's largest gas fields, a $1.3 billion gas pipeline construction contract and another deal worth $2 billion to renovate and extend the Tehran metro. Apart from their constitutional role of defending and exporting the Islamic revolution, the Guards had transformed themselves into a self-contained economic empire. In 2008 an estimated 30 per cent of the Guards' personnel were involved solely in economic activity which, apart from making senior officers very wealthy, provided the organization with the funds to support their wide range of activities, from financing the nuclear programme and the development of ballistic missiles to funding radical Islamist groups around the world.[28]

The Bush administration's decision to target the Revolutionary Guards, then, was a deliberate attempt to apply pressure to the regime's political and economic powerhouse, and provoked an immediate response from General Mohammad Ali Jafari, the newly appointed Guards commander, who declared, 'The corps is ready to defend the ideals of the revolution more than ever before.' Condoleezza Rice, the US Secretary of State, said the measures had been taken 'to confront the threatening behaviour of the Iranians', which suggested the action had been taken more in response to Iran's unwelcome intervention in Iraq rather than its persistent defiance of the UN over the nuclear issue. But the fact that Washington was forced to act alone demonstrated the deep divisions within the UN over how to deal with the continuing threat Iran's Islamic revolution posed to world security. Russia and China, which both had lucrative trade and military ties to Tehran, were unwilling to support the wide-ranging economic sanctions regime Washington demanded, while most European governments – with the exception of Britain – were also lukewarm about taking further action against Iran. Germany in particular was concerned about the huge economic stake it had in Iran which was worth $5.7 billion in exports.

Even the Bush administration appeared to be divided over how to deal with Tehran following the publication of a National Intelligence Estimate in December that stated that Iran had halted its military nuclear programme in 2003 after the US-led invasion of Iraq. The estimate was based on the latest intelligence available to the various American agencies responsible for monitoring Iran, and appeared to undermine completely Bush's position that Iran's nuclear programme posed the greatest threat to world peace. The hawks in the administration immediately pointed out that the assessment was the first time an official document had confirmed that Iran had set up a clandestine nuclear weapons programme, even if it had been put into cold storage in 2003. The more moderate voices, on the other hand, argued the assessment suggested that Iran was still a long way from acquiring the capability to develop nuclear weapons, should it decide to resume the military programme. The Israelis, meanwhile, dismissed the report and said Iran would be able to make an atom bomb by 2009.

Ahmadinejad did not appear unduly concerned about the mounting international pressure when he made his annual trip to New York to address the UN that year. He sought to reassure the delegates by insisting that Iran did not have a weapons programme, but then called into question his own credibility by insisting Iran had no gay people either. He also provided a rare insight into his devotion to the Twelfth Imam when he gave the delegates a lecture on how he believed a Muslim saviour would relieve the world's suffering. The era of Western dominance, he said, was drawing to a close and would soon be replaced by a 'bright future' which would be ushered in by the Twelfth Imam's return. Later on in his visit he was met by angry crowds of jeering demonstrators when he arrived to address a meeting at New York's Columbia University, where he called for more research to be undertaken into the Holocaust.

The policies and personal philosophy of Ahmadinejad continued to cause consternation abroad, but at home there appeared to be little prospect of his regime loosening its grip on power. When demonstrators took to the streets in the summer of 2007 to protest at the introduction of petrol rationing – a belated effect of the UN sanctions implemented the previous year – Ahmadinejad's security forces brutally suppressed the disturbances. To deter further outbursts of unrest, the regime introduced public executions as the regime launched one of the most brutal purges witnessed since the 1979 Revolution. The regime even devised a special device, a miniature version of the French guillotine, to amputate the limbs of those convicted of offences under Sharia law.

Ahmadinejad sought to consolidate his domestic position by replacing the long-standing Revolutionary Guards commander Rahim Safavi with the more hard-line Mohammed Ali Jafari, an ultra-conservative who had been in charge of anti-American activities in Iraq. In a speech delivered shortly before he took up his new post Jafari demonstrated his commitment to the cause of the Islamic revolution when he declared, 'If America were to make a mistake and carry out an attack against the sacred state of the Islamic Republic of Iran, we will set fire to its interests all over the world and will not leave any escape route.'[29] Apart from developing its ballistic missile capability, the regime was said to have a number of sleeper terrorist cells planted in all the major European capitals ready to launch operations if Iran came under attack.

The Majlis elections in the spring of 2008 provided the hardliners with yet another opportunity to fix the result in their favour. Nearly all of the estimated 2,000 candidates contesting the 290 parliamentary seats first had to be vetted by committees of the Revolutionary Guards, who took great care to exclude anyone with a history of supporting the reformist agenda of former president Khatami. As a consequence the hardliners repeated their 2004 success and achieved a clear majority, making Ahmadinejad's position even more secure. Occasional protest voices were heard in the run-up to the election, with critics of the regime blaming the government, as they had done so often, for economic mismanagement and increasing Iran's isolation from the rest of the world. But without the ability to challenge the supremacy of the Revolutionary Guards, the opposition was easily side-lined, leaving the regime free to pursue its confrontational policy with the West.

Not that Washington and its allies had completely given up on their attempts to contain Iran's various activities. In April, Admiral Mike Mullen, chairman of the joint chiefs of staff, publicly blamed the Iranian government and the Quds force for its 'increasingly lethal and malign influence' in Iraq, while General Petraeus briefed Congress about the 'nefarious activities' of the Quds force in stirring violence in Iraq. Mullen, who was known to oppose launching military action against Iran over its nuclear programme, admitted the level of America's commitment to Iraq made it difficult for the United States to confront Iran over its support for the insurgency. But he warned, 'It would be a mistake to think we are out of combat capability.'

Washington became more forthright in condemning the Quds force's role in providing what it described as 'lethal support' for the Taliban in Afghanistan. The US Treasury Department, as part of its justification for imposing sanctions against the elite Revolutionary Guards unit, described the Quds force as the 'Iranian regime's primary instrument for providing lethal support to the Taliban.' The Treasury claimed that since 2006 Iran had arranged the shipments of small arms and ammunition, rocket-propelled grenades, mortar rounds, short-range rockets, and the technology for making roadside bombs to the Taliban for use against American and NATO forces fighting in Afghanistan.[30] As if to confirm the Treasury Department's assessment, a senior Taliban commander credited his successful operations against coalition forces in Afghanistan to weapons supplied by Iran. 'There's a kind of landmine called a dragon. Iran's sending it,' the Taliban commander boasted. 'It's directional and it causes heavy casualties. We're ambushing the Americans and planting roadside bombs. We never let them relax.'[31] As one senior Bush administration official remarked, 'Even by the standards of Central Asian duplicity Iran's involvement in Afghanistan is mind-blowing.'[32]

The Israelis also achieved a significant breakthrough in their attempts to limit Iran's glowering presence on their borders when Mossad agents assassinated the terrorist mastermind Imad Mughniyeh in Damascus. The master terrorist had first come to prominence with the attack on American and

French forces in Beirut in 1983 and, after Osama bin Laden, was at the top of Washington's list of most wanted terrorists. For twenty-five years, while managing to evade capture, he had continued his involvement in plotting some of the world's most deadly terrorist attacks, from the Buenos Aires bombings in the 1990s to training Shia insurgents in Iraq. From his base in Iran he travelled frequently on false passports, with the Syrian capital his favourite stopping-off point. It was here that Mossad staged a classic honey trap, taking advantage of an illicit liaison Mughniyeh was having with a female Syrian intelligence officer while away from his family in Iran. For once Mughniyeh broke with his strict practice of moving to a different location each night, and stayed frequently at the same Damascus hotel so that he could be with his mistress. This gave Mossad the opportunity it had been seeking for decades, and in February Mughniyeh was killed by a car bomb as he made his way to the hotel.[33] As one Israeli security official commented after the attack, 'He who lives by the car bomb, dies by the car bomb.'

Mughniyeh's assassination was a major coup for the Israelis, not least because it seriously disrupted Hizbollah's attempts to regroup after the 2006 war with Israel. As the militia's head of security, Mughniyeh had been central to Hizbollah's successful resistance to Israel's assault on its infrastructure, and his participation was regarded by Sheikh Hassan Nasrallah, Hizbollah's leader, as vital to rebuilding the organization's military capability. Following the 2006 war Hizbollah significantly increased its arsenal of missiles from 10,000 to 30,000 – most of them shipped from Iran, via Damascus – in anticipation of renewed hostilities with Israel. But Mughniyeh's death was a significant setback both for Hizbollah and Iran's attempts to provide training and support for Islamist terror groups.

The Iraqis, too, started their own fightback against Iran's pernicious influence in their affairs during the course of 2008 as the government of Nouri al-Maliki became more confident in its ability to assert its authority. The previous year former Iraqi Prime Minister Ayad Allawi, who had narrowly escaped several assassination attempts at the hands of Iranian agents, had decried the fact that Iran had extended its influence throughout Iraq to the extent that it was virtually running the country. 'The Iranians are running Iraq, not the Iraqis,' Allawi lamented. 'They have taken us over completely.'[34] But the execution of Saddam Hussein and other members of the Baathist regime eventually helped Maliki's government to become more self-confident and determined to resist Iranian interference.

A state visit by Ahmadinejad to Baghdad in March – the first by an Iranian president since the 1979 Revolution – helped to ease the tensions between the two countries. But while Ahmadinejad hailed a new era in relations between the two countries, the more significant event came the following month when Maliki ordered Iraqi forces to seize control of Basra from the Iranian-controlled militias. It was the first time the coalition-trained Iraqi forces had been tested in action, and while they required support from the United States, they succeeded in forcing the Shia militias out of the city and bringing Iraq's second city firmly under the government's control. The success of Maliki's military offensive served to demonstrate that Iraq's Shia population wanted to be governed by an Iraqi government, not an Iranian one, and the manner in which the local Shia supported government forces suggested the Iranians had overplayed their hand in trying to foment instability among the local population. Muqtada al-Sadr, the Iranian-backed cleric who had worked so hard to undermine the coalition, retreated to the safety of Qom to further his religious education at the spiritual headquarters of Khomeini's revolution.[35]

The American-led military surge made similar progress in stabilizing the overall security situation throughout Iraq. The surge tactics succeeded in achieving a dramatic fall in the level of violence: by the summer of 2008 there was an average of

20 daily attacks on coalition forces, compared with 180 the previous year. But General Petraeus was under no illusions as to the greatest threat to Iraq's future progress. Addressing the US Senate, Petraeus warned that the Iranian-backed militias continued to pose 'the greatest long-term threat to the viability of a democratic Iraq', while Ryan Crocker, the US Ambassador to Iraq who had previously served in Lebanon during the 1983 embassy bombing, said the Quds force was pursuing the same 'Lebanization strategy' that the Revolutionary Guards had successfully implemented in Lebanon in the 1980s.[36]

But the intractable issue of Iran's nuclear programme remained the greatest source of concern for the Western powers, particularly as Ahmadinejad steadfastly refused to cooperate with the UN's various attempts to break the deadlock. In June the United States deliberately took a back seat as a group of the world's other leading powers – Russia, China, Britain, France and Germany – offered to help Iran build civilian nuclear power stations if Tehran obeyed the UN and suspended its uranium enrichment activities at Natanz. But the Iranian government rejected the offer out of hand, declaring that the uranium enrichment issue was 'not debatable'. The United States then agreed to hold its first direct talks with Iran over the nuclear issue, sending William Burns, the State Department's undersecretary for political affairs, to meet Tehran's chief negotiator in Geneva. But that meeting also drew a blank, and by September UN officials admitted they had reached a 'dead end' in their attempts to negotiate a resolution with Iran.[37]

The stalemate over the UN-sponsored negotiations enabled Iran to continue unhindered with its uranium enrichment activities, which many Western governments still believed were aimed at producing nuclear weapons. The basis upon which the CIA's 2007 National Intelligence Estimate (NIE) concluded Iran had halted work on its military programme in 2003 was hotly disputed by rival agencies in Washington as well as by other intelligence services, such as Britain's Secret

Intelligence Service, which sent a team of Iran experts to the CIA's headquarters to dispute the findings. The NIE's credibility was further undermined when Western intelligence agencies uncovered new evidence to suggest Tehran had resumed work on its military programme.

In the summer of 2008, US spy satellites detected several installations in Iran that intelligence officials believed were being used by Iran for a nuclear project that had not been declared to the teams of UN nuclear inspectors. Intelligence experts were particularly concerned about the work being carried out at the Amir Abid residential district of Tehran, where experiments were being conducted with the sophisticated P2 gas centrifuge provided by Pakistani scientist A.Q. Khan's nuclear smuggling ring. Another facility that aroused suspicion was the planned nuclear installation at Darkhovin in south-west Iran, located 200 miles from the Bushehr plant. The Iranians announced they were planning to build a light water reactor at the site, which would use the uranium enriched at Natanz, but there were intelligence reports that Iran was undertaking undeclared nuclear research at the site that could have a military use. In September there were reports that between 50 and 60 tons of uranium hexafluoride, or UF_6, the basic feeder material for making enriched uranium, had been 'diverted' from the Isfahan Uranium Conversion Facility. The Iranians had severely curtailed the IAEA's ability to monitor their operations at Isfahan two years previously, and nuclear experts estimated the missing UF_6 would be sufficient to make between five to six nuclear bombs. These revelations further deepened suspicions that Iran had a well-advanced clandestine nuclear weapons programme concealed from teams of nuclear inspectors sent regularly to check on Iranian facilities. At the very least, IAEA nuclear experts estimated that, if Iran maintained its ability to enrich uranium at Natanz, it would have the ability to produce sufficient quantities of highly enriched uranium to build one nuclear weapon by 2009.

In the past both Iraq and Libya had managed to set up nuclear weapons programmes despite being subjected to regular inspections by the IAEA and, as Iran continued with its defiant stance towards the West, it appeared that the ayatollahs were doing the same. The fact that Iran continued work on developing long-range ballistic missiles capable of carrying nuclear warheads also suggested that Iran's nuclear intentions were not entirely benign. Washington was concerned that Iran's nuclear technology might fall into the wrong hands, particularly terrorist groups such as bin Laden's al-Qaeda organization, which made no secret of its desire to acquire weapons of mass destruction. The only two countries where a group like al-Qaeda could obtain such technology were Pakistan and Iran. Pakistan's nuclear arsenal was subjected to various safeguards negotiated between Washington and former Pakistani President Pervez Musharraf, but the possibility of Iran sharing its technology with Islamist extremists caused deep concern throughout the West's intelligence agencies. 'Iran does not have to develop an atom bomb to constitute a threat to global security,' said a senior Western intelligence official. 'The mere fact that it possesses the means to do so is enough to give us all sleepless nights.'[38] The prospect of Iran acquiring nuclear weapons would also have a calamitous effect on nuclear proliferation, as other states in the Middle East sought to match Iran's nuclear capability. Saudi Arabia, Egypt and Syria, to name but a few, had given strong hints that they would seek nuclear parity with Iran if the Islamic revolution succeeded in arming itself with a nuclear bomb.

As Bush entered the twilight of his presidency, he reiterated his view that Iran's nuclear programme constituted a grave threat to world peace. In his final address to the UN General Assembly, he urged the UN to make tougher sanctions against Iran. But with Moscow effectively withdrawing its cooperation from the negotiations over Iran, the Bush administration was obliged to resort once more to taking unilateral action, with the US Treasury announcing a new set of sanctions against Iran and Iranian officials. Although the Bush administration's room for manoeuvre on Iran was limited, nevertheless the nuclear issue was a dominant issue in the presidential election campaign, with both candidates promising to take a firm line with Tehran. John McCain, the Republican candidate, revealed his deep antipathy to the Iranian regime by singing 'Bomb Iran' to the tune of the Beach Boys' classic 'Barbara Ann', while Barack Obama, the Democrat contender, told a pro-Israel lobby in Washington that he would do 'everything in my power to prevent Iran from obtaining a nuclear weapon'.

With Barack Obama's convincing election victory in November 2008 there was a widespread expectation in Washington that the new American president would attempt to enter into direct negotiations with Tehran over the future of its nuclear programme, and attempt to distance the US from the confrontational approach adopted by the Bush administration. The Iranian president certainly anticipated a sea-change in relations between Washington and Tehran following Obama's victory, and Ahmadinejad offered his personal congratulations to the new president on his win; the first time Iran has issued an official goodwill message to an American leader since the 1979 revolution. 'As you know the opportunities provided by the Almighty God, which can be used for elevation of nations, or God forbid, their collapse, are transient,' said Ahmadinejad in a statement carried by the state-owned new agency IRNA.[39] But Iran's real attitude towards the change of government in Washington was made clear in an editorial in another government-owned media publication, the daily *Kayhan* newspaper, which stated that the 'Great Satan's' face had changed colour, but no more. 'Obama's view on talks with Iran is not strategic, it is a hostile tactic,' the newspaper warned in an editorial marking the anniversary of the storming of the American embassy in Tehran in 1979. 'He does not regard talks as a means to reach a solution, but as a way to increase pressures on Iran.'[40]

12
The Clenched Fist

When President Barack Obama took office in January 2009, the issue that featured most prominently in his White House in-tray was the deepening crisis over Iran's nuclear programme. And the new president was determined to break the impasse that had hindered the efforts of previous administrations to establish a constructive dialogue with Tehran. A few days before his inauguration Obama gave an unequivocal signal that he wanted to adopt a new approach to America's historically difficult relationship with Tehran. He readily admitted that Iran was going to be one of the biggest challenges his adminis-tration faced, and was particularly critical of Tehran's policy 'of exporting terrorism through Hamas and Hizbollah'. Obama feared that Iran's pursuit of an atomic weapon could trigger a nuclear arms race in the Middle East. To prevent that from happening he wanted America to try another approach by establishing a dialogue with Tehran, a feat that had evaded previous US administrations dating back to the 1979 Islamic Revolution. But Obama retained great faith in his ability to change not only the landscape of American politics, but America's relations with the outside world. 'We respect the aspirations of the Iranian people,' he said in a pre-inaugural television interview. 'But we also have certain expectations of how an international actor behaves.'[1]

Obama reiterated his desire for change in his inaugural speech on 20 January when he said he sought a 'new start' in Washington's relations with the Muslim world, one based on 'mutual interest and mutual respect'. Although he did not mention Iran by name, he gave an interview to the Arabic television station al-Arabiya the following week in which he made a direct appeal to Tehran to end its diplomatic isolation. Paraphrasing the sentiments set out in his inaugural address, Obama said that 'if countries like Iran are willing to unclench their fist they will find an extended hand from us'.[2]

Obama's appeal represented a radical change in diplomatic direction from that pursued by his predecessor, who had famously described Iran as forming part of an 'Axis of Evil'. Obama hoped the rhetorical change would reap benefits in Tehran, where he believed the regime could be persuaded to abandon its decades-old hostility to America. Prior to the al-Arabiya interview, Obama's advisers had been working hard behind the scenes to inform Tehran of their good intentions. The State Department drafted a letter providing Iran with assurances that it would not attempt to topple the Iranian government, which had been the policy of the Bush adminis-tration. In 2008 Bush had authorized a covert operations programme designed to undermine any attempt by Iran to build a nuclear weapon. The operation aimed to break the supply chain of essential parts and equipment from overseas that were essential to the development of Iran's nuclear pro-gramme, as well as applying experimental techniques to disrupt essential computer and electrical systems.[3]

The new administration invested much energy in its attempts to re-calibrate Washington's relations with Tehran, but the initial response from Iran was hardly encouraging. The government-owned state television studiously avoided showing a single frame of Obama's inaugural address, and the only mention of Obama's arrival at the White House came in an item about America's economic crisis. On the streets of Tehran the reception was openly hostile. Crowds of pro-government supporters set fire to pictures of Obama alongside those of Bush, while chanting 'Death to Obama'. Echoing the language

Khomeini had often used to denounce American policy, the official spokesman for Ayatollah Ali Khamenei, Khomeini's successor, announced, 'Obama's is the hand of Satan in a new sleeve. The Great Satan now has a black face.'[4] The country's president, Mahmoud Ahmadinejad, was more circumspect. He told visiting journalists that he would be patient and analyse Obama's words for signs of real change. 'If it's like the past and America is bullying us, then there will be no new era between us,' he said. 'The language of sticks and carrots is dead.'[5]

Tackling the Iran issue was a key element in the Obama administration's ambitious overhaul of American policy objectives. At home the main priorities were tackling the impact of the global financial crisis and implementing a radical reform of the health care programme. Further afield Obama's appetite for reshaping the dynamics of America's relations with the outside world knew no bounds. During the Democratic primaries Obama had attracted fierce criticism for saying he would hold direct talks with hostile states, particularly from Hillary Clinton, his main rival for the nomination. But once in office he appointed Clinton his Secretary of State and immediately set about fulfilling his campaign pledge. His aim was to reverse the political unilateralism that had characterized the Bush administration and usher in a new era in which Washington sought to establish a dialogue with those states that had previously been deemed hostile to American interests. Overtures were made to Moscow, where the recently elected president, Dmitry Medvedev, was regarded as being less confrontational towards the West than Putin. Similar initiatives were directed towards neighbouring states, such as Cuba and Venezuela, to overcome the feelings of mutual antipathy that had existed for many years.

By far the most challenging feature of the new administration's agenda was its ambitious plans for the Middle East. While Iran took centre stage, Obama was committed to undertaking a radical restructuring of US involvement in the region.

He was keen to keep to his campaign commitment to withdraw the bulk of American forces from Iraq at the earliest opportunity, allowing the war against al-Qaeda and other Islamist militants based in Afghanistan and Pakistan to be the main focus of America's military strategy. He was also determined to resurrect the negotiating process between Israel and the Palestinians. This had become a pressing priority in the wake of the military offensive Israel had launched against Hamas militants based in Gaza at the start of the year.

The White House regarded the resolution of the Israel–Palestinian issue as being integral to solving the Iran crisis. If the Israelis and Arabs could be persuaded to sign a peace deal, much of the anti-Israeli rhetoric used by Ahmadinejad to justify his opposition to the West would be removed. Forging a close bond with the Israelis would also enable Washington to use its influence to persuade Israel not to launch unilateral military action to destroy Iran's nuclear infrastructure. Shortly before Obama's inauguration it was revealed that the Israeli government had seriously considered attacking Iran's uranium enrichment plant at Natanz in the spring of 2008, and had approached the Bush administration for its support. The Israelis were still incensed by the CIA's National Intelligence Estimate that Iran had stopped work on its military nuclear programme in 2003, and were minded to take matters into their own hands.[6] But to do so they needed Washington's help, particularly the specialized bunker-busting bombs that could penetrate the deep protective layers that covered the Natanz facility. Israel also needed permission to fly over American-controlled Iraqi air space. But Bush denied the request outright. 'We said, "Hell no" to the overflights,' a senior Bush aide later recalled.[7] Bush was persuaded by his senior officials, led by Defence Secretary Robert M. Gates, that any military strike against Iran would most probably prove ineffective, lead to the expulsion of international inspectors and drive Iran's nuclear programme further out of view. There was a distinct possibility that an attack would ignite a broader Middle East war in which America's 140,000 troops in Iraq would inevitably become involved.[8] The NATO mission in Afghanistan was also likely to be destabilized. As a consolation to the Israelis, Washington agreed to sell Israel 1,000 bunker-busting bombs, and to step up the covert operation to disrupt Iran's nuclear programme.

The first signal that Iran might be prepared to respond positively to Obama's appeal to the regime to 'unclench its fist' came in mid-February during the celebrations to mark the 30th anniversary of the Islamic revolution. Ten days of nation-wide festivities – *Daheh-ye Fajr*, the 'Ten Days of Dawn' – were arranged to celebrate Khomeini's triumphant return from exile in February 1979. The regime used the anniversary as an opportunity to educate the country's predominantly youthful population – 70 per cent of Iranians were born after the 1979 Revolution – about Khomeini's legacy. Crowds of visitors thronged Tehran's Martyrs Museum, located opposite the old American embassy compound, to learn how the Shah's opponents had been tortured and murdered by SAVAK, and of the Revolutionary Guards' heroic exploits during the eight-year war with Iraq. The Imam Khomeini mausoleum, a sprawling complex next to the Behesht-e Zahra cemetery where the revolution's founder had given his first speech after returning from exile, was also busy with those coming to pay their respects. 'The revolution came from the people,' explained one middle-aged rice merchant. 'They believed Imam Khomeini was saying the words of God so they followed him.'[9] Both Khamenei and Ahmadinejad attended a ceremony at the mausoleum to commemorate Khomeini's return, during which Ahmadinejad made a speech promising to 'renew allegiance to the late Imam's aspirations'. He said Khomeini's revolution was 'alive and well', and hailed it as 'a new chapter in the life of world communities'.

By way of demonstrating the revolution's enduring strength, the regime launched its first home-made satellite, the

Omid (Hope), into orbit. While the satellite launch drew pro-tests from Washington and London, which claimed it would increase tensions between Iran and the West, the celebra-tions ended with Ahmadinejad making his first public response to the Obama offer. He used the final rally of the festivities to declare his readiness for talks with America 'based on mutual respect and in a fair atmosphere'.[10] Washington responded to the overture by appointing Dennis Ross, the veteran Middle East negotiator who had served under President Clinton, as Obama's special envoy on Iran. At the same time the serious-ness of the crisis surrounding Iran's nuclear programme was underlined by the release of an IAEA report at the end of February that confirmed Iran had already succeeded in stock-piling enough enriched uranium to build an atom bomb.

Obama maintained his pro-Iran charm offensive by record-ing a video appeal to the Iranian people which was broadcast on the Internet website YouTube to mark the beginning of *Nowruz*, the Persian New Year, which coincides with the Western spring equinox. It was a bold initiative, as the Ameri-can president was appealing over the heads of the country's leadership and directly addressing the nation's citizens. The carefully worded video, which contained Farsi subtitles, wished the Iranian people a Happy New Year and expressed the hope that the United States and Iran could settle their differences. He invited Iran to 'take its rightful place in the community of nations', and ended with a few words of Farsi declaring, 'This process will not be advanced by threats. We seek instead engagement that is honest and grounded in mutual respect.' But buried within the text there was also a warning that Iran needed to mend its ways for proper reconciliation to take place. Peace 'cannot be reached through terror or arms, but rather through peaceful actions that demonstrate the true greatness of the Iranian people and civilization.'[11]

Nor did the Obama administration pin all its hopes on a diplomatic breakthrough with Tehran. While Obama drafted his appeal to the Iranian people the administration worked hard to repair relations with Moscow, which had become decidedly frayed towards the end of the Bush and Putin administrations. The main source of Russian grievance remained Washington's plan to establish a missile shield in eastern Europe to protect the West from the possibility of a future Iranian nuclear attack. In March Obama wrote to Medvedev offering to cancel the missile shield in return for Moscow's help in resolving the Iran crisis.[12] Moscow's support for Tehran had been a major stumbling block to the West's attempts at the UN Security Council to impose effective sanctions against Iran. Obama hoped that if the Russians could be persuaded to be more supportive of Western policy, Iran would be placed under greater pressure to comply with the West's demands.

As far as Iran was concerned, there were two major obstacles standing in the way of Tehran giving a positive response to Obama's overtures. The first concerned the perennial problem of who had the ultimate say in the direction of Iranian policy, the Supreme Leader or the democratically elected President? The historic friction between Khamenei, whose fundamental duty was to safeguard the principles of Khomeini's revolution, and the president, who was elected by the people to run the country, meant that Western policymakers were forever trying to fathom how best to tackle Iran's complex power structure. Should Washington make a direct approach to Khamenei's office, or deal solely with Ahmadinejad? And if Ahmadinejad were minded to make a deal with the West on the nuclear issue, would Khamenei have the final say over whether or not to implement it?

The other factor that hampered Obama's initiative was the preparations for June's presidential election, in which Ahmadinejad sought a second four-year term in office. In view of the decades of hostility that had characterized US–Iran relations since 1979, a rapprochement with Washington would be a dangerous electoral card to play for any of the candidates, particularly as, under the terms of Khomeini's constitution, the victor required Khamenei's approval before being allowed to take office. This made it particularly difficult to interpret the different messages coming out of Tehran in response to Obama's initiative.

The signals from Khamenei, whose deeply held opposition to America had been a constant feature of his twenty-year tenure, were not encouraging. In his speech to mark the Persian New Year he insisted 'the path of Iran's nuclear progress could not be blocked'. And he was dismissive of Obama's video broadcast, which he said was nothing more than a 'slogan'. 'They [the Americans] give the slogan of change but in practice no change is seen,' he said in his own televised address to the Iranian people. 'We haven't seen any change . . . If the extended hand is covered with a velvet glove but underneath it the hand is made of cast iron, this does not have a good meaning at all.' As he made his speech at the north-eastern city of Mashhad, thousands of supporters chanted their familiar refrain of 'Death to America'.[13] Ahmadinejad's public comments were similarly discouraging. When Hillary Clinton announced in early April that Washington would henceforward participate directly in talks to persuade Iran to cooperate with the West on its nuclear programme, Ahmadinejad responded by boasting about the country's latest nuclear advances. He reiterated that Iran was ready to take part in talks over its nuclear programme, but only if the negotiations were based on 'justice and respecting rights', a reference to Iran's long-standing demand for the right to develop its home-grown nuclear capability. And in a repeat of the classic Iranian intimidation tactic, Tehran announced it would proceed with the trial of Roxana Saberi, a journalist with dual American and Iranian citizenship, who stood accused of spying for Washington.[14] She was jailed for three years on three counts of espionage, but released a month later as a goodwill gesture. But the regime had nevertheless sent a message to the outside world that it would not tolerate any interference in its domestic affairs.

*

As with previous Iranian elections, the powerful conservative forces established by Khomeini to protect the Islamic revolution moved with quiet efficiency to ensure that their preferred candidate won. Expectations were certainly running high in Washington and throughout much of the West that the election, which was scheduled for 12 June, would finally allow Iran's oppressed masses to give vent to their mounting frustration at the way the country was run. Apart from international isolation caused by the regime's confrontational approach to the West, the country was suffering severe hardship as a result of Ahmadinejad's disastrous mismanagement of the economy. With both unemployment and inflation running in double figures, there were widespread allegations, particularly from Tehran's prosperous *bazaari* middle class, that Ahmadinejad had squandered Iran's vast oil wealth through his obsession with developing Iran's nuclear infrastructure. There was also general disquiet about the extensive use of the death penalty, the strict application of Sharia law which resulted in adulterers being publicly stoned to death and the regime's discrimination against women.

Not surprisingly there was no shortage of candidates wishing to put their names forward for the presidential ballot. In all a total of 475 candidates applied to become the country's seventh post-revolutionary president. But by the time the Guardian Council, which reported directly to Khamenei, had finished examining each of the candidates' revolutionary credentials, a total of four remained. All the candidates, including the 52-year-old Ahmadinejad, were veterans of Iran's revolutionary establishment. Mohsen Rezai, fifty-five, the infamous Revolutionary Guards commander who was still the subject of an international arrest warrant for his alleged role in the 1994

Buenos Aires bombings of Jewish targets that killed eighty-five people, was allowed to stand. So too was Mahdi Karroubi, the 72-year-old former speaker of the Majlis who enjoyed the distinction of having been a close confidant of both Khomeini and Khamenei. Finally there was Mir Hossein Musavi, the 67-year-old conservative hardliner who had served as Khomeini's last prime minister, until the position was abolished on Khomeini's death.

In many quarters Musavi was regarded as the pro-reform candidate, not least because he had a long history of clashing with Khamenei going back to the days when the Supreme Leader was a mere president. But Musavi's supporters seemed happy to turn a blind eye to his involvement in one of the darker episodes in the revolution's history, when thousands of political prisoners were purged in mass executions that took place in Iran's prisons in the final year of Khomeini's life (see pages 240–241). Musavi had the advantage of receiving the backing of former president Mohammed Khatami who, having initially signalled his willingness to run, withdrew his candidacy in favour of Musavi, whom he believed had the best chance of defeating the incumbent. 'The most important goal is to prevent Mr Ahmadinejad from winning re-election,' a Khatami aide explained.[15] From the outset, Khamenei indicated that, as in 2005, Ahmadinejad was the regime's preferred candidate. Consequently Revolutionary Guard commanders and the other security forces responsible for safeguarding the revolution were ordered to ensure the president was re-elected to serve a second term.[16]

The Obama administration's only significant intervention when campaigning began in earnest in early June was the president's ground-breaking speech on his new approach to the Middle East that he delivered at Cairo University. Echoing the message he had been sending out to Iran, Obama directed his appeal to the entire Muslim world. 'I have come here to seek a new beginning between the United States and Muslims around the world, one based upon mutual interest and mutual respect.' He called for the 'cycle of suspicion and discord' between the United States and the Muslim world to end. While he conceded that there had been 'years of distrust', he urged both sides to make a 'sustained effort . . . to respect one another and seek common ground.' Just before Obama delivered his address, Khamenei delivered a speech of his own at Khomeini's mausoleum in Tehran to mark the twentieth anniversary of his death. Khamenei insisted that America remained 'deeply hated' throughout the region, and no amount of 'beautiful and sweet words' from the new American president was going to change that view. 'If the new president of America wants a change of face, America should change this behaviour. Words and talk will not result in change.'[17]

Obama's words did, however, have a galvanizing effect on the outcome of Lebanon's general election which took place a few days after the Cairo speech. In the run-up to the poll it had been widely predicted that Hizbollah, which continued to receive most of its funding from Iran, would emerge victorious, enabling it to take the first steps towards establishing an Iran-style Islamic republic on the eastern shores of the Mediterranean. But Hizbollah's hopes were dashed by a last-minute revival in the fortunes of the pro-Western coalition, which won a narrow majority. The surprise result was attributed in many quarters to the 'Obama effect', and hopes were raised that the American president's desire for change in the Middle East might have a similar impact on Iran's elections.

For the most part Iran's election campaign concentrated on domestic issues, in particular the country's dire economic plight. From an early stage Musavi emerged as Ahmadinejad's leading opponent. Backed by a powerful clique of like-minded pro-reform campaigners, which included former presidents Khatami and Rafsanjani, Musavi was vociferous in his criticism of Ahmadinejad's presidency, particularly in the live televised debates that provided Iranians with an entirely new and exciting dimension to the country's normally drab political discourse. The sharp exchanges between the rival candidates produced the liveliest presidential contest in Iran's post-revolutionary history, and the election really came to life when Musavi went head-to-head with Ahmadinejad. Musavi denounced Ahmadinejad's presidency as 'disgraceful', and highlighted the unnecessarily bellicose policies he had pursued during his first term. 'In your foreign policy you have brought shame upon Iran,' said Musavi. 'You have created tension with other countries and heavy costs have been brought on this country in recent years.'[18]

To boost his appeal, Musavi took the unconventional step of inviting his spouse, Zahra Rahnavard, to appear alongside him. A grandmother, painter, and former law university chancellor, Rahnavard, who dressed in an all-black chador, proved an unlikely champion of women's rights. At a rally she held in Tabriz, she stole the show from her husband by demanding, 'Why are there no women presidential candidates or cabinet ministers? Getting rid of discrimination and demanding equal rights with men is the number one priority for women in Iran.'[19]

As the campaign entered its final week Musavi's pro-reform movement succeeded in drawing large crowds of protesters onto the streets, who wore green ribbons and waved green banners in support of their candidate. Green is the colour of hope and of Islam, and Musavi's skilful exploitation of modern communication methods such as text messaging, email and Facebook succeeded in mobilizing thousands of young protesters, both male and female, who mixed freely in defiance of the morality police. In Tehran's leafy northern suburbs the gleeful chant 'Ahmadi bye bye' echoed through the streets. Young women, inspired by Rahnavard's outspoken opposition to sex discrimination, were particularly prominent, and in many cases covered their faces in green paint as a sign of solidarity with Musavi's campaign. Ahmadinejad was openly taunted by the green protesters, a rare public manifestation of anti-regime sentiment in post-revolutionary Iran. 'Go open a grocery' was one of the slogans they chanted, ridiculing the president's decision to distribute 400,000 tonnes of free potatoes to allevi-ate the economic hardship of the unemployed.[20] A newspaper controlled by Musavi mocked Ahmadinejad's claim that he had been exposed to a celestial light during his first address to the UN General Assembly. Every night, as the campaign reached its climax, the atmosphere in downtown Tehran was electrified as the city's youth let their hair down in nightly rallies with cars and bikes roaring up and down the main thoroughfares, blaring their horns in support of Musavi. When Musavi's supporters attempted to form a human chain of protesters through the centre of Tehran, as Khomeini's supporters had done on the eve of his return from exile, comparisons were inevitably drawn between Musavi's anti-government protest and the build-up to the 1979 Revolution.

Ahmadinejad and his conservative backers were deeply shaken by the strength of the opposition movement that materialized out of nowhere in the week before the election. For weeks the opinion polls had predicted a comfortable majority for the incumbent, but as polling day approached supporters feared that Ahmadinejad might fail to secure the 50 per cent majority required to avoid a run-off vote, which would be held between the two candidates who secured the most votes in the first round. The president's security appara-tus tried hard to restrict Musavi's activities. Several rallies were cancelled at the last minute because the authorities withdrew permission, giving no explanation. A rally planned at Karaj, a residential district outside Tehran, was cancelled because the electricity to the public address system mysteriously failed. Ahmadinejad himself went onto the offensive, launching per-sonal attacks against Musavi, accusing him of associating with former presidents Rafsanjani and Khatami, whom he accused of corruption. The president's accusations drew a sharp response from Rafsanjani, who wrote an open letter to Khamenei urging him to rein in his president. 'I am expecting you to resolve this position in order to extinguish the fire, and to foil dangerous plots,' wrote Rafsanjani.[21]

As in the 2005 campaign, Ahmadinejad remained massively popular in conservative rural areas and villages, where his credentials as a Khomeini loyalist, and as a religious man of humble origins, guaranteed a high level of support. While Musavi brought tens of thousands of supporters out onto the streets of Tehran to stage 'mass action' night and day demonstrations, Ahmadinejad staged mass rallies of his own, where he was supported by crowds of frenzied, flag-saving supporters. In his final pre-election rally in Tehran Ahmadinejad remained defiant. 'Ahmadi, we love you,' the crowd roared, as Ahmadinejad accused his opponent of deliberately spreading lies about him. 'The foreign powers wanted to break us with sanctions . . . They said Iran's economy was finished,' he said. But production had soared and construction had doubled during his presidency. It was his opponents who were responsible for pillaging the nation's wealth. 'Musavi, liar,' and 'Musavi go,' the crowd chanted. 'We don't want an American sympathizer.' Ahmadinejad ended the rally with a prayer. 'Oh Great and Compassionate God, sit the Iranian nation on the roof of the world.'[22]

Less than twenty-four hours after Iranians had finished voting in their tenth post-revolution poll, Ahmadinejad was declared the outright victor, with 62.6 per cent of the vote, compared with Musavi, who came second with just 33.7 per cent. The size of Ahmadinejad's victory meant there was no need for a run-off, but the atmosphere immediately turned ugly when Musavi claimed he had been the victim of 'fraud' and 'manipulation'. In Tehran the carnival-like atmosphere among Musavi's supporters abruptly turned violent, with thousands of angry and frustrated voters congregating in the city centre, where they clashed with riot police in some of the most violent scenes witnessed in Tehran since the student protests of 1999. The protesters defied official orders to stay off the streets, shouting 'Death to the dictator' while hurling rocks at riot squads. The Islamic regime's well-documented track record of fixing previous Iranian elections, both for the Majlis and the office of president, led many anti-Ahmadinejad supporters to conclude the 2009 result had been fixed by the regime. Musavi, who had taken the precaution of going into hiding, encouraged the protesters by issuing a statement on his website claiming the official result was an outright fraud. 'I'm warning that I won't surrender to this manipulation. People won't respect those who take power through fraud.'[23] But the regime refused to back down. Khamenei urged Iranians to accept the result, calling it a 'divine assessment', and the authorities moved quickly to clamp down on the dissent. Within hours of the result being declared, the country's text messaging system was shut down, thereby denying Musavi's supporters their favoured method of communication. The Interior Ministry issued a warning to citizens not to join 'unauthorized gatherings', while police units dispersed crowds, beating up both male and female demonstrators.

Musavi maintained his defiance, and issued a direct appeal to the Guardian Council to cancel the result. 'I urge you, the Iranian nation, to continue your nationwide protests in a peaceful and legal way,' a statement issued by his office declared. As the council reported directly to Khamenei, who had the final say over the council's membership, it was unlikely the request would be granted. Ahmadinejad insisted the contest had been 'clean', and dismissed the demonstrations in Tehran as 'the passions after a football match'. But the unrest continued to spread. Pro-Musavi demonstrators broke the windows of city buses, burned banks, rubbish bins and used tyres as flaming barricades. Others tried to maintain a peaceful protest in Tehran's Azadi Square. Several members of the national football team entered the spirit of the anti-government protest when they wore green armbands during a fixture against South Korea.

The regime responded by arresting the ringleaders, and made their customary raids on student dormitories at Tehran university. Hundreds of protesters were arrested, and scores killed and injured as the regime's security officials responded to the challenge to their authority. Western journalists who had been invited to cover the elections were suddenly ordered not to leave their offices or report on the protests. At night militias loyal to the regime opened fire from rooftops on the unarmed demonstrators gathered in Azadi Square. The brutality meted out to the pro-reform movement forced its leaders to warn its supporters to avoid death or serious injury. 'Don't protest today – you must protect your lives,' they were told. In an attempt to take the sting out of the protests, the Guardian Council announced that it was prepared to undertake a recount of 10 per cent of the votes. In some provinces it found that the number of votes counted exceeded the number of registered voters. But the council refused to annul the vote. Musavi rejected the recount offer, and bitterly criticized the regime's heavy-handed response. 'They have attacked dormitories and brutally broken legs, heads, arms and thrown some of the students out of the windows and arrested lots of people.'[24]

The disturbances continued for a full week as the regime struggled to come to grips with the unprecedented challenge to its authority. The government was convinced that the pro-reform protests had, in part, been inspired by Obama's new approach to Iran, and suspected that the West was helping to foment the unrest. In times of crisis successive Iranian regimes have exploited the nation's visceral paranoia about foreign plots to shore up their own position. The BBC Persian Service, funded by the Foreign Office, was accused of encouraging Iranians to protest. Tehran responded by expelling the BBC correspondent John Leyne, who had done nothing more than report that the election result was in dispute. Iran's foreign minister, Manouchehr Mottaki, accused the British government of sending planeloads of spies to destabilize the election, which was rigorously denied by London.

American officials countered by accusing the regime of deliberately rigging the result because they were concerned about the impact of Obama's Cairo speech on the Muslim world, particularly in the wake of the surprise election result in Lebanon. It seemed as if the revolution's entire raison d'être was in question when the leading Shia clerics at Qom, where Khomeini had first conceived his radical Islamic ideology, were openly critical of the result. Iran's leading ayatollahs had always entertained reservations about the clerical takeover of the country, and had little regard for Khamenei, whom they regarded as a theocratic lightweight who owed his elevated position solely to his slavish devotion to Khomeini's cause. The Association of Combatant Clerics, a fifty-strong group of leading ayatollahs based at Qom, joined forces with Musavi in denouncing the result as invalid.

To take the heat out of the crisis Khamenei ordered an inquest into how the presidential election contest had been allowed to develop into a grave national crisis. Khamenei was particularly critical of Ayatollah Ahmad Jannati, the head of the Guardian Council, who had initially been instructed to draw up the list of suitable presidential candidates. Khamenei accused Jannati of seriously underestimating Musavi's populist appeal. He ordered Jannati to prepare a report on what had gone wrong.[25] It was Khamenei's way of exerting his authority over the Guardian Council and making sure it complied with his wishes, which were to confirm Ahmadinejad's victory. Next he summoned the leaders of the Revolutionary Guards to determine how best to respond to the challenge from the pro-reform protests. Khamenei resolved to deploy the Guards and the volunteer Basij militia to bring the protests under control, while at the same time making a direct, personal appeal to the Iranian people to halt the disturbances.

A week after the elections, on 19 June, Khamenei tried to regain the initiative by addressing a special Friday prayer service at Tehran University, which was turned into a make-shift mosque for the occasion. The university was a known hotbed of opposition to the regime, and by choosing it to be the venue for his first post-election address Khamenei sought to send an unequivocal message that the regime remained in complete control of the entire country. Khamenei attempted to persuade his audience that no deep divisions existed within the regime. 'Differences of opinion do exist between officials, which is natural,' he said. 'But it does not mean there is a rift in the system.' But he gave a firm warning that no further anti-government protests would be tolerated.

Ahmadinejad, meanwhile, was ordered to keep a low profile while the ultimate source of political power in the country, the Supreme Leader, set about resolving the crisis. Ahmadinejad was dispatched to attend a security conference in Moscow, where Putin, who, as prime minister, still retained significant influence over foreign policy, pledged to send a number of Russian security officials to help Tehran suppress the anti-government protests.[26] Soon after his sermon at Tehran University Khamenei declared Ahmadinejad the winner of the presidential election. At the same time he ordered the Basij and Revolutionary Guards to close down the protests once and for all. When, the following day, pro-Musavi demonstrators appeared in central Tehran, the regime reacted forcibly to drive them back. Students at Tehran University who chanted 'Death to the dictator' were met with water cannon, baton charges and tear gas. In the city centre Basij militiamen opened fire on demonstrators, in one case killing Neda Agha-Soltan, a 26-year-old student, whose death was filmed, blood streaming from her chest, on a digital camera which was then posted on the web, provoking an international outcry.

As the post-election turmoil unfolded, Barack Obama and other Western leaders were uncertain how best to react to the risis. If they were too critical of the regime's tactics, they might be accused of openly supporting the protesters, which would undermine their claim to neutrality. But if they failed to register any protest, then the demonstrators might feel justified in thinking the West was not serious about confronting the ayatollahs. Obama finally broke his silence after the harrowing images of the dying, blood-soaked Neda Agha-Soltan had been broadcast throughout the world. He described Neda's death as a 'searing image', and claimed the protesters would ultimately be seen to have been 'on the right side of history'. But Obama's intervention, a media-driven response to Neda's murder, lacked conviction, and gave the impression that he was more concerned with protecting his own attempts to establish a dialogue with the Iranian regime than caring for the victims of its brutal repression. The British government, meanwhile, became more deeply embroiled in a row over accusations that it had sent spies to provoke unrest. Iran expelled two British diplomats, and Britain responded by sending home two Iranian officials. The Iranians then responded by detaining a number of embassy employees, a deliberate act of intimidation designed to stop any further British interference in the election aftermath.

But it was the absence of an effective, organized opposition within Iran that ultimately meant the protesters' sacrifice was doomed to failure. Musavi had fought a good election campaign, and succeeded in mobilizing tens of thousands of young Iranians who had never previously had the opportunity to engage in Iranian politics. But Musavi, a self-effacing, bespectacled academic, neither had the charisma nor the organizational structure to mount any serious challenge against the deeply entrenched security apparatus controlled by Khamenei, whose fundamental duty was to protect Khomeini's Islamic revolution. The longer the protests continued, the more brutal the regime's response became.

The relatives of prominent politicians who had supported

Musavi's campaign were arrested, including Rafsanjani's daughter Faezeh. Under the constitution, as head of the Assembly of Experts, Rafsanjani technically had the authority to depose Khamenei as Supreme Leader. But he was unlikely to do so while his daughter was effectively being held as the regime's hostage. And even though the protests continued for several more weeks, with anti-government protesters taking to their rooftops at night to chant 'Death to the dictator', the regime gradually succeeded in closing ranks, and crushing the dissent. Scores of journalists and bloggers were jailed without charge, anti-government journals were closed and foreign journalists banned from the country. On the rare occasions, such as the anniversary of the 1999 students protest in early July, that groups of demonstrators took to the streets in Tehran, they were met by an overwhelming show of force by the state's security forces. The small group of protesters that gathered in central Tehran were overwhelmed by an army of riot police and Basij militiamen who beat them mercilessly. By mid-July the regime felt confident enough, through the government-owned *Kayhan* newspaper, to accuse Musavi of 'acting as America's fifth column', and of being responsible for 'terrible crimes', including 'murdering innocent people'. When Rafsanjani, flanked by Musavi, appeared in public to demand the release of the thousands of political prisoners rounded up by the security forces, Khamenei issued a tough rebuke. 'Anybody who drives society towards insecurity and disorder is a hated person in the view of the Iranian nation, whoever he is.'[27]

By August the regime had succeeded in crushing the pro-reform protests, just as it had done in 1999 and 2003. The most public display of dissent witnessed since the revolution of 1979 had severely rattled the clique of conservative hardliners who controlled the regime, but had ultimately failed in its attempt to effect a radical change in the way the country was run. The protests revealed the deep schism that existed between the hardliners, such as Khamenei and Ahmadinejad, and the more pragmatic figures such as Rafsanjani, Khatami and Musavi. But the dispute never seriously jeopardized the survival of Khomeini's legacy. The struggle between the hardliners and the pragmatists had, after all, been one of the defining features of the Islamic revolution for three decades. On this occasion it had revealed the full extent of the bitter rivalry that existed between the different factions. But at no time did the unrest of the summer of 2009 seriously challenge the survival of the Islamic republic. For all the political excitement the 2009 election campaign generated, none of the pro-reform demonstrators had campaigned for an end to Islamic government and a return to the more secular, democratic form of government that had existed during the 1950s under Mossadeq. Not even the so-called moderates would have tolerated that. The dispute was essentially the manifestation of a long-running dispute between the original architects of the Islamic revolution over how best to implement Khomeini's legacy. The argument was about who ran Iran, not how Iran should be run.

Those who supported the pro-reform movement paid a heavy price for their courage. With the Western media banned from covering events in Iran, it was difficult to establish an accurate picture of the casualties, but Iranian human rights groups claimed that at least 200 demonstrators were killed in Tehran, another 56 were unaccounted for and another 173 were killed in other cities, which was several times higher than the official figures. An estimated half of those killed died on the streets during anti-government protests, while the rest died in custody. The regime established a chain of unofficial, makeshift prisons to deal with the protesters, where torture and rape were said to be commonplace. In Tehran alone it was reported that 37 young Iranian men and women were raped by their captors, and doctors' reports smuggled out to the West said that two males, aged 17 and 22, died as a result of severe internal bleeding after being raped.[28]

A series of show trials were held for those who survived

the brutality of the regime's prisons. In early August more than a hundred opposition figures were presented to Tehran's Revolutionary Court to stand trial for conspiring with foreign powers to stage a revolution. The concept of the Revolutionary Court had first been conceived by Khomeini to conduct summary trials of those deemed to be enemies of his Islamic revolution, and their revival in August 2009 was an indication of the seriousness with which the regime regarded the latest challenge to its authority.

The accused, many of whom had held senior positions in the Rafsanjani and Khatami administrations, were dressed in grey prison uniforms, had lost weight and were denied access to lawyers. The proceedings were held in camera, with the exception of the state-controlled media, which later broadcast selected highlights. They showed various defendants making rambling 'confessions', including Mohammed Ali Abtahi, a former vice president who served under Khatami, who apologized for his previous claims that Ahmadinejad's election victory was fraudulent, and accused Musavi of conspiring with former presidents Khatami and Rafsanjani. Musavi denounced the show trials, claiming the defendants' confessions 'bore the hallmarks of medieval-era torture', and argued that the victims were those who had given 'great services to Iran in the past'. Undeterred by the hardliners' crackdown, Musavi mocked the whole notion of the Revolutionary Courts. The regime, he said, was expecting 'a court, which itself is fraudulent, to prove there was no fraud committed in the election.' He still held out the prospect that the reformers would one day triumph over the conservatives. 'Soon we will see the trials of those who committed these crimes, the torturers and the interrogators.'[29]

By now the regime had regained its confidence sufficiently to proceed with the formal confirmation of Ahmadinejad's appointment to serve a second term as Iran's president. Ahmadinejad took the oath of office on 3 August in a brief ceremony conducted by Khamenei. The deep divisions within the regime's senior echelons were evident in the fact that it was boycotted by two previous presidents, Rafsanjani and Khatami, and by two of the defeated candidates, Musavi and Kharroubi. Relations even appeared strained between Khamenei and Ahmadinejad. When the president sought to embrace the country's Supreme Leader, his advance was brushed aside, and instead of kissing Khamenei on the cheek, as is the Iranian custom, Ahmadinejad ended up planting an awkward kiss on his shoulder. The body language might not have been reassuring, but both men had got precisely what they wanted when the presidential election process had been set in train the previous spring. In his speech Khamenei described his protégé's victory as 'a golden page' in Iran's history and, a couple of days later when Ahmadinejad made his inaugural address to the Majlis, he described his victory as an 'unprecedented epic'. But the reality of Ahmadinejad's victory was reflected in the massive security operation that was mounted outside the parliament building as he spoke. An estimated 5,000 police and Basij militiamen ringed the parliament building to protect it from the anti-government protesters. But the increased security presence was of little concern to Ahmadinejad and his followers. After the convulsions of the summer they had emerged victorious and the guardians of Khomeini's revolution remained as deeply entrenched as at any time in its thirty-year history.

*

Ahmadinejad's election victory was a serious setback to President Obama's attempts to establish a constructive dialogue with Tehran. For all the Obama administration's peaceful overtures to Tehran, Washington found itself still having to deal with a regime that was committed to maintaining its confrontational stance towards the West. The massive support the pro-reform protests had attracted suggested that the Khamenei/Ahmadinejad axis was not as secure as it might have liked, but it still maintained a stranglehold over the levers of power in Tehran, and the prospects of the opposition making any serious challenge against the regime appeared remote.

After his re-election was confirmed Ahmadinejad moved quickly to strengthen his political power base. One of his first acts was to order the arrest of the pro-Musavi newspaper editor responsible for publishing the article that mocked his 'mystical' UN experience. And with the new appointments to his cabinet, which were announced in early September, Ahmadinejad indicated the regime was in no mood to tolerate dissent. The new cabinet was filled with hard-line conservatives, such as Ahmad Vahidi, the founder of the Revolutionary Guards Quds force, who was promoted to defence minister, even though he was still subject to an international arrest warrant for his alleged involvement in the 1994 Argentina bombings. Ahmadinejad's choice for interior minister, Mostafa Mohammad-Najjar, was also a Guards veteran while Heyder Moslehi, the new intelligence minister, was closely associated with the Basij militia that had been so effective in crushing the pro-reform protests. Ahmadinejad also made significant changes to the team of officials responsible for the nuclear negotiations. Gholam Reza Aghazadeh, the head of Iran's Atomic Energy Organization, was forced to resign after he was accused of being too closely associated with Musavi. He was replaced by Ali Akbar Salehi, although it was made clear that ultimate responsibility for conducting the nuclear talks would reside with Saeed Jalili, the secretary of the Supreme National Security Council, and a close ally of the president. The new government indicated that there was unlikely to be any softening of the regime's position, either in dealing with domestic opposition or Iran's relations with the outside world. On the day he announced his new cabinet, Ahmadinejad maintained his customary defiance. 'No one can impose sanctions against Iran any more,' he said. 'We welcome sanctions. We can manage ourselves.'[30]

Ahmadinejad was equally uncompromising in his first press conference after the election, in which he insisted Iran would persist with the development of its nuclear programme. The meeting was arranged to coincide with the quarterly board meeting of the IAEA in Vienna, at which the subject of Iran's continued non-cooperation with nuclear inspection teams topped the agenda. 'From our point of view, Iran's nuclear issue is over,' Ahmadinejad emphatically declared. As if to underline the regime's determination to resist foreign interference in its affairs, Tehran pressed ahead with the trial of a 44-year-old political analyst employed by the British embassy in Tehran. Hossein Rassam, who had originally appeared in court during the show trials that began in early August, made a public confession in which he admitted recruiting a network of fifty agents on behalf of the embassy, and attending pro-democracy demonstrations and fomenting unrest. In late October Rassam was jailed for four years at a closed session of the Revolutionary Court.

The domestic tumult over Ahmadinejad's re-election caused a great deal of soul-searching in Washington over how best to respond to the regime's repressive tactics. As Ahmadinejad and his supporters acted to crush the pro-reform movement, there was nothing to indicate the regime was about to unclench its fist. On the contrary, seldom had a fist been clenched more tightly, as the forces of reactionary Islam that had held power for thirty years closed ranks with ruthless efficiency. After the 12th of June vote both Secretary of State Hillary Clinton and Vice President Joe Biden, the more hawkish members of the administration, pushed for Washington to take a harder line with Tehran. But although Obama was eventually persuaded to issue a public denunciation of the regime's clampdown, he remained determined to persist with his policy of engagement, which many of his advisers believed had proved more unsettling to Tehran than the threatening posture adopted by the previous Bush administration. 'Given the profoundly serious consequences of an Iranian regime that acquires a nuclear weapons capability, the judgement in the end was that it was important to follow through on the offer of direct engagement,' explained a senior Obama aide.[31]

The White House nevertheless decided to take a more robust approach to Iran if the regime continued to prevaricate on the nuclear issue. In mid-September Obama announced that he was cancelling the controversial missile defence for eastern Europe. While the decision caused much consternation among those countries that had previously formed part of the Soviet Union, the announcement provoked widespread rejoicing in Moscow, which had been bitterly opposed to the deployment of the missiles so close to its borders. Obama gambled that this unilateral gesture of goodwill might persuade the Russians to take a more robust approach to Iran at the UN Security Council. A few days later, at the start of the G20 summit in Pittsburg, Obama showed there was another side to his policy of direct engagement when he caused Ahmadinejad immense embarrass-ment by publicly revealing details of a hitherto secret uranium enrichment facility under mountains close to the holy city of Qom. Fearing that the existence of the facility was about to be made public, Tehran had hastily sent a letter to the IAEA that did no more than suggest that such a programme might exist. But Obama was not prepared to let the Iranians off the hook so easily. Since becoming president he had received detailed intelligence briefings that suggested Iran had a number of nuclear installations not declared to the IAEA, and further evidence that Iran was working on a clandestine weapons project. In all, there were about a dozen nuclear estab-lishments that had not been declared to the IAEA, including the Qom facility.[32] In addition, a secret report drawn up the IAEA, which was leaked in mid-September, concluded that Iran's scientists had 'sufficient information' to make a nuclear weapon, and had 'probably tested' a key component.[33]

Obama believed the discovery of the secret uranium enrich-ment plant at Qom was a good opportunity to demonstrate to Tehran that he was determined, one way or another, to resolve the nuclear crisis. Flanked by Gordon Brown, the British prime minister, and Nicolas Sarkozy, the French president, Obama held a press conference on the opening morning of the Pittsburg summit at which he revealed the existence of the Qom facility, and accused Iran of deliberately misleading the UN inspectors. Work on the Qom plant had begun a year into Ahmadinejad's first term as president, and the fact that Iran felt it necessary to build a second enrichment facility did not square with Iran's repeated claims that its nuclear intentions were peaceful. The revelation was designed as much to embarrass Ahmadinejad, who was still in New York following his attendance at the UN General Assembly, as to persuade Russia and China that the issue of Iran's nuclear programme was too serious to be ignored. It was also designed to increase the pressure on Tehran to give a positive response to the peace offer due to be discussed at a special meeting in Geneva on 1 October.

At first, Ahmadinejad appeared deeply flustered by Obama's revelation, but by the time he gave a press conference at his New York hotel he had recovered his composure. He insisted the Qom site was perfectly legal, and claimed that Iran was to be congratulated on revealing its existence to the IAEA. UN inspectors would be allowed to inspect the plant, and he made a point of saying that he would 'refrain from acting strongly to what happened this morning'. But no sooner had he returned to Tehran than the regime was once more indulging in the bellicose rhetoric that made the prospect of any meaningful rapprochement with the West appear remote. After test-firing a number of missiles capable of hitting Israel, Vahidi, the new defence minister, warned that Iran would destroy Israel if it launched an attack against its nuclear installations.

Hopes that Iran might be prepared to cooperate fully at Geneva also diminished when Tehran said it needed more time to respond to the offer made by the six powers – Russia, Britain, France, Germany, China and the United States – which had supplanted the EU3 negotiating team. Under the 'freeze-for-freeze' formula, Iran would halt its uranium enrichment programme in return for the UN freezing the sanctions on Iran. As a first step towards defusing the crisis, the six powers suggested Iran hand over 75 per cent of its enriched uranium to be processed by Russia and France. This would be a significant confidence-building measure, as it would remove most of Iran's stockpile of fissile material, thereby preventing Iran from going ahead with development of an atom bomb, and creating a climate in which more detailed negotiations could take place. Iran was given until the end of the month to respond to the offer. But when Tehran finally replied in late October, the regime's answer fell well short of what the six powers – backed by the IAEA – were demanding. Rather than hand over 75 per cent of its enriched uranium stocks as requested, Tehran said it would only give smaller amounts, and that in return for so doing Iran expected the West to provide technical assistance on other aspects of its nuclear programme. As it had done for the previous six years, Iran was playing for time in the hope that it could maintain the development of its nuclear programme while giving the pretence that it was cooperating with the UN. The deep sense of frustration felt by the negotiators over Tehran's tactics was summed up by Hillary Clinton, who said the offer put forward by the six powers in Geneva was non-negotiable. Iran should accept in full the proposal that had been made, she said, 'because we are not altering it'.

The underlying hostility of the regime's attitude towards the West resurfaced when five senior Revolutionary Guard commanders were killed in a suicide bomb attack in Baluchistan, close to the border with Pakistan, in early October. Ahmadinejad accused Britain of training the terrorists responsible for the attack and vowed revenge. The regime was in a similarly uncompromising mood when pro-reform demonstators took to the streets on the day Iranians were supposed to mark the 30th anniversary of the storming of the American embassy with nationwide anti-American demonstrations. Instead the tens of thousands of protesters chanted 'Death to the dictator'. The crowds were eventually dispersed by the Basij and riot police, but their reappearance showed that the spirit of resistance to Ahmadinejad's repressive regime refused to be cowed.

But that was of little consequence for Obama and all the other world powers that were concerned about Iran's determination to proceed with its nuclear programme. For all the effort Obama had made to build a new relationship with Tehran, none of the key figures in power showed much inclination to make the concessions necessary to break the impasse. In early November Khamenei provided an insight into the regime's post-election approach when he declared that he saw no sign of Obama bringing 'change' to Washington's policy on Iran. 'On the one hand, Americans talk of negotiations. On the other hand, they continue to threaten and say the negotiations must have our desired results or we will take punitive measures.' Quoting Khomeini, he compared the relationship between the America and Iran as being like that between 'the sheep and the wolf, which the late Imam Khomeini said we do not want'.[34]

Khamenei knew he could count on the support of Ahmadinejad, another dedicated adherent to Khomeini's radical ideology. While the hard-line conservatives remained in power in Tehran, they would maintain their commitment to the principles of the Islamic revolution and fulfilling Khomeini's legacy, whether it concerned becoming a nuclear power or exporting Khomeini's revolution. By doing so they were implementing the policies that had come to define the Iranian revolution for the three decades since its inception. From Khomeini through to Ahmadinejad, Iran's leaders had pursued their uncompromising doctrine of fundamentalist Islam. And so long as the heirs to Khomeini's revolution retained their iron grip on power, the Islamic Republic of Iran would raise the banner of radical Islam and proclaim its defiance to the rest of the world.

Notes

1: Stealing the Revolution

1 Ruhollah Khomeini, *Islam and Revolution: Writings and Declarations*, trans. by Hamid Algar, London 1981, p. 55
2 Private interview
3 *Iranian*, 5 June 2000
4 Private source
5 Private interview
6 *Le Monde*, 6 May 1978
7 Abol Hassan Bani-Sadr, *L'Esperance Trahie* (Papyrus, Paris, 1982), p. 40
8 Quoted in Baqer Moin, *Khomeini: Life of the Ayatollah* (I.B. Tauris: London, 1999), p. 191
9 Private interview
10 Private interview
11 Quoted in Amir Taheri, *The Spirit of Allah* (Hutchinson Ltd.: London, 1985), p. 242
12 Ibid., p. 243
13 *Time*, 12 February 1979
14 Quoted in Moin, p. 200
15 BBC, 1 February 1979
16 Taheri, p. 253
17 Private interview

2: Child of the Revolution

1 Dilip Hiro, *Iran Today* (Nation Books: New York, 2005), p. 116
2 Taheri, p. 24
3 Ibid., p. 23

4 Most of the details concerning Ayatollah Khomeini's family background have been provided by his son Ahmad Khomeini in a series of interviews with the ayatollah's Iranian biographer, Hamid Algar.

5 Moin, p. 7

6 Quoted in Moin, p. 8

7 A report of the events surrounding the execution appeared in the Iranian newspaper *Adab* on 15 May 1905.

8 Private interview

9 Taheri, p. 37

10 Chris Paine and Erica Schoenberger, 'Iranian Nationalism and the Great Powers, 1872–1954', MERIP reports (May 1975), p. 4

11 Ervand Abrahamian, *Iran Between Two Revolutions* (Princeton, N.J.: Princeton University Press, 1988), pp. 53–4

12 Ibid., p. 81

13 Amir Arjomand, *The Turban and the Crown* (Oxford University Press: 1988), p. 33

14 *American Journal of Sociology*, January 2004, p. 937

15 Verses written in prison by Mirza Aqa Khan of Kirman shortly before he suffered death in 1896.

16 Edward G. Browne, *The Persian Revolution of 1905–1909* (Cambridge University Press: Cambridge 1910), p. 365

17 Ibid., pp. 374–8

18 Taheri, p. 44

19 Vanessa Martin, *Islam and Modernism: The Iranian Revolution of 1906* (London, 1989), p. 97

20 Taheri, p. 44

21 Ibid., p. 45

22 Interview with Ayatollah Jalal Ganjei

23 Quoted in Moin, p. 13

3: To Be a Mullah

1 James A. Bill, *The Eagle and the Lion* (Yale University Press: 1988), p. 57

2 Ibid., p58

3 Quoted in Moin, p. 24

4 Taheri, p. 43

5 Ibid., p. 48

6 After 1925, when Western-style surnames were introduced to Iran,

he changed his name to Ruhollah Mostafavi – the name chosen for him by his brother.

7 Moin, p. 28

8 *Resalat* (Tehran), 1 February 1994

9 Quoted in Moin, p. 37

10 *Resalat* (Tehran), 11 July 1979

11 The word Pahlavi, meaning 'heroic', comes from ancient Persian.

12 A detailed account of Reza Khan's rise to power is provided by the late Professor Laurence Elwell-Sutton's *Reza Shah the Great: Founder of the Pahlavi Dynasty* in *Iran Under the Pahlavis*, ed., George Lenczowski (Hoover Institution Press: Stanford, California, 1978).

13 Robert Byron, *The Road to Oxiana* (Macmillan: London, 1937), p. 54

14 Mark Gasiorowski, *U.S. Foreign Policy and the Shah: Building a Client State in Iran* (Cornell University Press, 1991), p. 39

15 Said Amir Arjomand, *The Turban for the Crown* (Oxford University Press: 1988), p. 82

16 Ruhollah Khomeini, *Kashf al-Asrar (The Discovery of Secrets)*, (Qom, 1961), p. 69

17 Quoted in Taheri, p. 77

18 Ibid., p. 81

19 Quoted in Moin, p. 52

20 *Zan-e-Ruz* (Tehran), 6 February 1982

21 Moin, p. 54

22 Khomeini, p. 9

23 Ibid., pp. 9–10

24 Ibid., p. 132

25 Quoted in Taheri, p. 108

26 James Bill, *The Eagle and the Lion: The Tragedy of American–Iranian Relations* (Yale University Press: 1988), pp. 100–1

27 Ruhollah Khomeini, *Sahifeh-ye Nur* (Tehran, 1982), vol. 3, p. 36

4: Living in Exile

1 SAVAK – *Sazman-iIttili'at va Amniyat-I Kishvar*

2 Ali Ansari, *Modern Iran Since 1921: the Pahlavis and After* (Longman: London, 2003), p. 136

3 Bill, p. 107–9

4 Taheri, p. 111

5   Moin, p. 67

6   Mohammad Razi, *Athar al-Hojjat* (Qom, 1953), vol.2, pp. 11–13

7   Private interview

8   Private interview

9   Private interview

10   Taheri, p. 112

11   Quoted in Moin, p. 75

12   Quoted in Shaul Bakhash, *The Reign of the Ayatollahs* (Basic Books: New York, 1984), p. 26

13   Ruhollah Khomeini, *The Life of Imam Khomeini* (Moharram Publications: Tehran, 1978), vol I, p. 157

14   Ibid., p. 104

15   Private interview

16   Khomeini, p. 99

17   Ali Ansari, *Modern Iran* (Longman, London, 2007), p. 187

18   Henry Kissinger, *The White House Years* (Little, Brown: Boston, 1979), p. 1259

19   Moin, p. 80

20   Khomeini, pp. 157–8

21   Moin, p. 89

22   Khomeini, p. 173

23   Ibid., p. 173

24   Ibid., p. 142

25   Private interview

26   Quoted in Bakhash, p. 31

27   Khomeini, *Islam and Revolution*, pp. 181–8

28   Moin, p. 128

29   Taheri, p. 153

30   Private interview

31   Private interview

5: The Ayatollah Returns

1   Moin, p. 143

2   Bakhash, p. 34

3   Ibid., p. 36

4   Hossein Musavian, *Imam Khomeini: His Life and Leadership* (Saffron Books: Tehran), p. 117

5   Private interviews

6 Lady Bell, ed., *The Letters of Gertrude Bell* (Ernest Benn: London, 1927), p. 484

7 Mir Ali Asghar Montazam, *The Life and Times of Ayatollah Khomeini* (Anglo-European Publishing Ltd., London, 1994), p. 161

8 Ervand Abrahamian, *A Modern History of Iran* (Cambridge University Press: 2008), p. 146

9 Ibid., p. 148

10 Private interview

11 Anthony Parsons, *The Pride and the Fall: Iran 1974–1979* (Jonathan Cape: London, 1984), p. 19

12 *Time*, 10 December 1979

13 Kissinger, p. 1261

14 Cynthia Helms, *An Ambassador's Wife in Iran* (Dodd, Mead: New York, 1981), p. 61

15 *Le Monde*, 16 October 1971

16 Helms, p. 61

17 Parsons, p. 20

18 William H. Sullivan, *Mission to Iran* (W.W. Norton: 1981), p. 84

19 *Time*, 1 April 1974

20 Resurgence Party, *The Philosophy of Iran's Revolution* (Tehran, 1976)

21 Oriana Fallaci, *Interviews with History* (Houghton Mifflin: 1976), pp. 262–87

22 *Harper's Magazine*, November 1974, p. 81

23 Abrahamian, p. 152

24 Quoted in Bakhash, p. 44

25 Fouad Ajami, *The Vanished Imam: Musa al Sadr and the Shia of Lebanon* (Cornell University Press: 1986), p. 194

26 Ibid., p. 195

27 *Le Monde*, 23 August 1978

28 Taheri, p. 166

29 *Time*, 10 December 1979

30 Private interview

31 Quoted in Taheri, p. 170

32 Private interview

33 Sullivan, pp. 167–8

34 Mohammed Reza Shah Pahlavi, *Answer to History* (Stein and Day: New York, 1980), p. 165

35 Moin, p. 184

36 Private interviews

37 Parsons, p. 71

38 Ibid., p. 71

6: The Revolution Unveiled

1 BBC Persian Section, *The Story of the Revolution*
2 Bakhash, p. 53
3 Mehdi Bazargan, *Difficulties and Problems of the First Year of the Revolution* (Iran Freedom Movement: Tehran, 1982), p. 74
4 Ibid., p. 27
5 Bakhash, p. 49
6 Ansari, p. 269
7 Arjomand, p. 135
8 BBC, 13 February 1979
9 Sadeq Khalkhali interview with BBC, Qom, May 1997
10 *Tehran Radio*, 16 February 1979
11 Moin, p. 211
12 Private interview
13 Address to Islamic Revolutionary Guards Corps, Qom, 20 August 1979
14 *Guardian*, 2 March 1979
15 Mohamed Heikal, *The Return of the Ayatollah* (Andre Deutsch: London, 1981), p. 181
16 *New York Times*, 21 October 1979
17 Private interview
18 Private interview
19 *New York Times*, 7 October 1979
20 *Time*, 22 October 1979
21 *Ettela'at*, 19 September 1979
22 Moin, p. 216
23 Ibid., p. 219
24 Bakhash, p. 62
25 Bakhash, p. 67
26 *Ettela'at*, 8 March 1980
27 Ansari, p. 284
28 Mark Bowden, *Guests of the Ayatollah: The First Battle in the West's War with Militant Islam* (Grove/Atlantic Ltd.: 2006), pp. 615–16
29 John Simpson, BBC, 31 August 2005
30 Private source
31 Bowden, pp. 93–4
32 Moin, p. 226
33 Bowden, p. 291

34 Moin, p. 227
35 Abrahamian, p. 169

7: Taking On the World

1   Personal interview
2   Dilip Hiro, *The Longest War* (Palladin, London, 1990), p. 34
3   Patrick Cockburn, *Muqtada al-Sadr and the Fall of Iraq* (Faber and Faber: London, 2008), p. 52
4   *Washington Post*, 18 April 1980
5   Con Coughlin, *Saddam: The Secret Life* (Macmillan: 2002), p. 185
6   Moin, p. 236
7   *Le Monde*, 27 January 1980
8   Bakhash, p. 98
9   Ibid., p. 112
10 Private source
11 *Financial Times*, 17 March 1981
12 Private source
13 Masud Rajavi, *The World Made Manifest* (Muslim Students Society, Long Beach, Calif., 1980), vol.2, p. 16
14 *Kayhan*, 19 April 1980
15 *Kayhan*, 9 June 1981
16 *Le Monde*, 14 June 1981
17 *Kayhan*, 16 June 1981
18 *Kayhan*, 22 June 1981
19 *New York Times*, 22 June 1981
20 Ervand Abrahamian, *Radical Islam: The Iranian Mujahideen* (Tauris: London, 1989), p. 220
21 Marian Rajavi, the wife of Masud Rajavi, the leader of the National Council of Resistance of Iran, the main opposition group to the mullahs, is based in Paris while her husband's Mujahideen organization is based in Iraq.
22 Abrahamian, p. 175
23 Ian Brown, *Khomeini's Forgotten Sons: The Story of Iran's Boy Soldiers* (London, 1990), p. 84
24 Moin, p. 249
25 *Kayhan*, 22 June 1982
26 BBC Summary of World Broadcasts, ME 6992/I, 31 March 1982
27 *Kayhan*, 31 August 1983
28 Moin, p. 251

29 Ahmad Khomeini, *Yadegar-e Imam* (Tehran, 1996), vol.1, p. 718
30 *Kayhan*, 24 August 1983

8: The Legacy Defined

1 Although the Libyan government has always insisted Sadr left the country on a flight to Italy, it is generally believed he died during his stay in Libya.
2 Fouad Ajami, *The Vanished Imam: Musa al Sadr and the Shia of Lebanon* (Cornell University Press: 1986), p. 196
3 Hala Jaber, *Hizbollah* (Fourth Estate: London, 1997), p. 112
4 Ibid., p. 112
5 Private interview
6 Con Coughlin, *Hostage* (Little Brown: London, 1992), p. 114
7 *The Times*, 3 November 1983
8 Robin Wright, *Sacred Rage* (Touchstone: New York, 1985), p. 83
9 *Asharq Al-Awsat* (London), 11 August 2006
10 Jaber, p. 116
11 George P. Shultz, *Turmoil and Triumph* (Charles Scribner's Sons: 1993), pp. 653–67
12 Abrahamian, p. 175
13 Ibid., 178
14 Moin, p. 254
15 Kasra Naji, *Ahmadinejad: The Secret History of Iran's Radical Leader* (I.B. Tauris: New York, 2008), p. 116
16 Private source
17 *Washington Post*, 12 April 1987
18 Leonard S. Spector, *Going Nuclear: The Spread of Nuclear Weapons 1986–1987* (Ballinger: Cambridge, Mass., 1987), p. 45
19 Alireza Jafarzadeh, *The Iran Threat: President Ahmadinejad and the Coming Nuclear Crisis* (Palgrave Macmillan: New York, 2007), p. 126
20 Ibid., p. 127
21 Private source
22 'Implementation of the NPT Safeguards Agreement in the Islamic Republic of Iran' (Vienna), 10 November 2003
23 Private source
24 Coughlin, *Hostage*, pp. 298–9
25 *Associated Press*, 23 November 1986
26 Hiro, *The Longest War*, pp. 181–4

27 Bakhash, p. 273
28 Tehran Radio, 20 July 1988
29 Ahmad Khomeini, *Yadegar-e Imam* (Tehran, 1996), vol.6, p. 468

9: The Global Brand

1 Amnesty International, *Iran: Violations of Human Rights* (Amnesty Press: London, 1991), p. 12
2 Abrahamian, p. 182
3 BBC, 29 September 2006 – http://news.bbc.co.uk/1/hi/world/middle_east/5392584.stm
4 Patrick Seale, *Abu Nidal: A Gun for Hire* (Random House: London, 1992), p. 280
5 Private source
6 *Glasgow Herald* (Scotland), 28 May 2000
7 *Der Spiegel*, 17 July 1997
8 Moin, p. 299
9 Nikki R. Keddie, *Modern Iran: Roots and Results of Revolution* (Yale University Press: 2003), p. 262
10 Abrahamian, p. 182
11 Private interview
12 Quds (Jerusalem) Force, Federation of American Scientists Intelligence Resource, 1 October 2006
13 *The 9/11 Commission Report* (W.W. Norton and Company: New York, 2004), p. 57
14 *New York Times*, 31 October 1991
15 BBC, 11 February 1995
16 Private source
17 *Sunday Telegraph*, 3 November 1991
18 *Washington Post*, 31 October 1991
19 *Daily Telegraph*, 23 November 1993
20 IRNA News Agency, Tehran, 18 December 1991
21 Peter L. Bergen, *Holy War Inc* (Weidenfeld and Nicolson: London, 2001), p. 31
22 Ann M. Lecht, *Osama bin Laden's 'Business' in Sudan*, Current History (January 2002)
23 Shaul Shay, *The Axis of Evil: Iran, Hizbollah and the Palestinian Terror* (Transaction Publishers: New York, 2005), p. 54
24 *Sunday Telegraph*, London, 10 October 1993
25 *Sunday Telegraph*, London, 8 November 1992

26 U.S. Department of State, *Patterns of Global Terrorism 1993*
27 Warren Christopher, *In the Stream of History* (Stanford University Press: 1998), p. 201
28 National Public Radio, 15 March 1995
29 Christopher, p. 448
30 *Sunday Telegraph*, London, 7 July 1996
31 Richard A. Clarke, *Against All Enemies* (Simon and Schuster: 2004) p. 112
32 Private source
33 Moin, p. 305
34 Clarke, p. 113
35 Shay, p. 55
36 Peter L. Bergen, *The Osama bin Laden I Know* (Free Press: New York, 2006), p. 143
37 Quoted in Bergen, *Holy War Inc.*, p. 95
38 *The 9/11 Commission Report*, p. 60
39 Clarke, p. 114
40 Clarke, p. 118

10: Rogue Regime

1 BBC, 29 May 1997
2 CNN, 7 January 1998
3 Kenneth Pollack, *The Persian Puzzle: The Conflict Between America and Iran* (Random House: New York, 2004), p. 317
4 *Sunday Telegraph*, London, 18 July 1999
5 *The 9/11 Commission Report*, p. 68
6 George Tenet, *At the Centre of the Storm: My Years at the CIA* (HarperCollins: 2007), p. 129
7 *The Times*, London, 23 July 1999
8 *Sunday Times*, London, 5 August 2000
9 Tehran Radio, 20 October 2000
10 IRNA, 24 October 2000
11 *Sunday Telegraph*, London, 9 January 2000
12 *Patterns of Global Terrorism* (US State Department: 2001), p. 62
13 Central Intelligence Agency, *Unclassified Report to Congress January–June 2001*
14 *Daily Telegraph*, London, 28 September 2001
15 *Daily Telegraph*, London, 29 September 2001
16 Pollack, pp. 346–7

17 *Guardian*, London, 4 September 2002

18 Bob Woodward, *Plan of Attack* (Simon and Schuster: New York, 2004), p. 87

19 *New York Times*, 12 January 2002

20 *The 9/11 Commission Report*, pp. 240–1

21 Tehran Radio, 30 January 2002

22 *Sunday Times*, London, 14 April 2002

23 http://www.globalsecurity.org/wmd/world/iran/nuke2003.htm

24 *Daily Telegraph*, London, 6 March 2006

25 *The Times*, London, 24 February 2003

26 US State Department Briefing, 13 December 2002

27 Patrick Cockburn, *Muqtada al-Sadr and the Fall of Iraq* (Faber and Faber: London, 2008), p. 168

28 L. Paul Bremer III, *My Year in Iraq* (Simon and Schuster: New York, 2006), pp. 121–2

29 Ibid., p. 71

30 Cockburn, p. 167

31 BBC Worldwide Monitoring, 12 August 2004, 'Iranian Guards Leader Reportedly Admits Helping a-Zarqawi'

32 *Sunday Telegraph*, London, 24 April 2004

11: In Search of the Apocalypse

1 Kasra Naji, *Ahmadinejad: The Secret History of Iran's Radical Leader* (I.B. Tauris: New York, 2008), p. 16

2 *New York Times*, 23 February 2004

3 Naji, p. 79

4 Ibid., p. 93

5 John Bolton, Speech to Hudson Institute, 17 August 2004

6 Private interview with Western intelligence source

7 *Iranian News Agency*, 17 September 2005

8 *Sunday Times*, London, 15 January 2006

9 *Sunday Telegraph*, London, 16 April 2006

10 'Understanding Muqtada al-Sadr', *Middle East Quarterly*, Fall 2004

11 Private interview with Iraqi government official

12 *Sunday Times*, London, 25 September 2005

13 Private interview with British military official

14 Private interview with Iraqi government official

15 Private interview

16 *The New Yorker*, 17 April 2006

17 US State Department, *Country Reports on Terrorism*, 30 April 2006, chapter three

18 *Daily Telegraph*, London, 16 July 2006

19 *Daily Telegraph*, 4 August 2006

20 Naji, p. 135

21 *The Times*, London, 10 April 2007

22 *Guardian*, London, 22 May 2007

23 *Daily Telegraph*, London, 22 May 2007

24 *Daily Telegraph*, 15 June 2007

25 *Daily Telegraph*, 24 February 2007

26 Private interview with Israeli officials

27 Private interview with coalition officials

28 *Daily Telegraph*, London, 7 March 2008

29 *Sunday Times*, London, 2 September 2007

30 US Treasury Department, *Fact Sheet: Designation of Iranian Entities and Individuals for Proliferation Activities and Support for Terrorism*, 25 October 2007

31 *Daily Telegraph*, London, 15 September 2005

32 Private interview with US government official, July 2008

33 Private source

34 Interview with Ayad Allawi, August 2007

35 Private source

36 Testimony of General David Petraeus and Ambassador Ryan Crocket to US Senate Committee on Armed Services, 8–9 April 2008

37 *Washington Post*, 16 September 2008

38 Private interview

39 *IRNA*, 6 November 2008

40 *Kayhan*, Iran, 7 November 2008

12: The Clenched Fist

1 ABC News, interview by George Stephanopoulos, 'This Week', 11 January 2009

2 Interview with al-Arabiya, 27 January 2009

3 *New York Times*, 10 January 2009

4 *Daily Telegraph*, London, 22 January 2009

5 Ibid.

6 Private interview

7 *Guardian*, London, 12 January 2009

8 *New York Times*, 11 January 2009
9 *Guardian*, London, 7 February 2009
10 *Guardian*, London, 11 February 2009
11 YouTube, 'A Nowruz Message from President Obama', 3 min. 36 sec., 19 March 2009
12 *New York Times*, 2 March 2009
13 *Sunday Telegraph*, London, 22 March 2009
14 *Independent*, London, 10 April 2009
15 *New York Times*, 16 March 2009
16 Private interview
17 BBC News, 4 June 2009
18 *Sunday Telegraph*, London, 7 June 2009
19 Ibid.
20 *Guardian*, London, 11 June 2009
21 *Independent*, London, 10 June 2009
22 *The Times*, London, 11 June 2009
23 *Sunday Telegraph*, London, 14 June 2009
24 *Evening Standard*, London, 16 June 2009
25 Private source
26 Private source
27 *Independent*, London, 21 July 2009
28 *The Times*, London, 18 September 2009
29 *The Times*, London, 3 August 2009
30 *The Times*, London, 4 September 2009
31 *New York Times*, 2 August 2009
32 Private source
33 Associated Press, 17 September 2009
34 Press TV, Tehran, 3 November 2009

Select Bibliography

Abrahamian, Ervand, *Iran Between Two Revolutions*. Princeton University Press: Princeton, 1982.
——— *A History of Modern Iran*. Cambridge University Press: Cambridge, 2008
Albright, Madeleine, *Madam Secretary*. Miramax Books: New York, 2003.
Ajami, Fouad, *The Vanished Imam: Musa al Sadr and the Shia of Lebanon*. Cornell University Press: Ithaca NY, 1986.
Algar, Hamid, *Religion and State in Iran, 1785–1906: The Role of the Ulama in the Qajar Period*. University of California Press: Berkeley and Los Angeles, 1969.
Amnesty International, *Iran: Documents Sent by Amnesty International to the Government of the Islamic Republic of Iran*. London, 1987.
——— *Iran: Violations of Human Rights*. Amnesty Press: London, 1991.
Ansari, Ali, *Modern Iran Since 1921: The Pahlavis and After*. Longman: London, 2007.
Arberry, A.J., *The Legacy of Persia*. Oxford University Press: Oxford, 1953.
Arjomand, Said Amir, *The Turban for the Crown*. Oxford University Press: Oxford, 1988.
——— *The Shadow of God and the Hidden Imam*. University of Chicago Press: Chicago, 1984.
Avery, P., Hambly, G.R.G., and Melville, C., *The Cambridge History of Iran*, 6 vols. Cambridge University Press: Cambridge, 1968–86.
Baker, James A., *The Politics of Diplomacy*. G.P. Putnam's Sons: New York, 1995.
Bakhash, Shaul, *The Reign of the Ayatollahs: Iran and the Islamic Revolution* (2nd ed.). Basic Books: New York, 1990.
Bani-Sadr, Abol Hassan, *L'Esperance Trahie*. Papyrus: Paris, 1982.

Bazargan, Mehdi, *Difficulties and Problems of the First Year of the Revolution*. Iran Freedom Movement: Tehran, 1982.

Bell, Gertrude, ed., *The Letters of Gertrude Bell*. Ernest Benn: London, 1927.

Bergen, Peter L., *Holy War Inc.*. Weidenfeld and Nicolson: London, 2001.

——— *The Osama bin Laden I Know*. Free Press: New York, 2006.

Bill, James A., *The Eagle and the Lion*. Yale University Press: New Haven, 1988.

Bolton, John, *Surrender Is Not An Option*. Simon and Schuster: New York, 2007.

Bowden, Mark, *Guests of the Ayatollah: The First Battle in the West's War with Militant Islam*. Grove/Atlantic: London, 2006.

Bremer, Paul, *My Year in Iraq*. Simon and Schuster: New York, 2006.

Brown, Ian, *Khomeini's Forgotten Sons: The Story of Iran's Boy Soldiers*. Grey Seal Books: London, 1990.

Browne, E.G., *The Persian Revolution of 1905–1909*. Cambridge University Press: London, 1910.

Bulloch, John, and Morris, Harvey, *The Gulf War*. Methuen: London, 1989.

Byman, Daniel, *Deadly Connections: States that Sponsor Terrorism*. Cambridge University Press: Cambridge, 2005.

Byron, Robert, *The Road to Oxiana*. Macmillan: London, 1937.

Carter, Jimmy, *Keeping Faith: Memoirs of a President*. University of Arkansas Press: Fayetteville, Ark., 1995.

Christopher, Warren (ed.), *American Hostages in Iran*. Yale University Press: New Haven, 1985.

——— *In the Stream of History*. Stanford University Press: Stanford, 1998.

Chubin, Shahram, and Tripp, Charles, *Iran and Iraq at War*. I.B. Tauris: London, 1988.

Clarke, Richard A., *Against All Enemies*. Simon and Schuster: London, 2004.

Cockburn, Patrick, *Muqtada al-Sadr and the Fall of Iraq*. Faber and Faber: London, 2008.

Cordesman, Anthony H., *The Iran–Iraq War and Western Security, 1984–87*. Jane's Publishing: London, 1987.

Coughlin, Con, *Saddam: The Secret Life*. Macmillan: London, 2002.

Curzon, George, *Persia and the Persian Question*, 2 vols. Frank Cass: London, 1966.

Ebadi, Shirin, *Iran Awakening*. Random House: London, 2006.

Elwell-Sutton, L.P., *Modern Iran*. Gordon Press: New York, 1976.
———— 'Reza Shah the Great: Founder of the Pahlavi Dynasty' in *Iran Under the Pahlavis*, ed., George Lenczowski. Hoover Institution Press: Stanford, California, 1978.
Fallaci, Oriana, *Interview with History*. Houghton Mifflin: Boston, 1976.
Freedman, Lawrence, and Karsh, Efraim, *The Gulf Conflict 1990–91*. Faber and Faber: London, 1993.
Frum, David, *The Right Man*. Random House: New York, 2003.
Gasiorowski, Mark, *U.S. Foreign Policy and the Shah: Building a Client State in Iran*. Cornell University Press: Ithaca NY, 1991
Gates, Robert M., *From the Shadows*. Simon and Schuster: New York, 1996
Graham, Robert, *Iran: The Illusion of Power*. Croom Helm: London, 1978.
Halliday, Fred, *Iran: Dictatorship and Development*. Penguin Books: Harmondsworth, New York, 1978.
Heikal, Mohamed, *The Return of the Ayatollah*. Andre Deutsch: London, 1981.
Helms, Cynthia, *An Ambassador's Wife in Iran*. Dodd, Mead: New York, 1981.
Hiro, Dilip, *Iran Today*. Nation Books: New York, 2005.
———— *The Longest War*. Paladin: London, 1990.
Hoveyda, Fereydoun, *The Fall of the Shah*. Weidenfeld and Nicolson: London, 1980.
Huyser, Robert E., *Mission to Tehran*. Harper and Row: New York, 1986.
Jaber, Hala, *Hizbollah*. Fourth Estate: London, 1997.
Jafarzadeh, Alireza, *The Iran Threat: President Ahmadinejad and the Coming Nuclear Crisis*. Palgrave Macmillan: New York, 2007.
Karsh, Efraim, *The Iran–Iraq War 1980–1988*. Osprey: London, 2002.
Katzman, Kenneth, *The Warriors of Islam: Iran's Revolutionary Guard*. Westview: Boulder, Colorado, 1993
Keddie, Nikki R., *Iran: Religion, Politics and Society*. Frank Cass: London, 1980.
———— *Modern Iran: Roots and Results of Revolution*. Yale University Press: New Haven, 2003.
Kelly, J.B., *Britain and the Persian Gulf*. Oxford University Press: Oxford, 1968.
Khomeini, Ruhollah, *Islam and Revolution: Writings and Declarations of Imam Khomeini*, trans. and annotated by Hamid Algar. Mizan Press: Berkeley, 1981.

—— *Kashf al-Asrar (The Discovery of Secrets)*. Qom, 1961.

Kinzer, Stephen, *All the Shah's Men*. John Wiley and Sons: Hoboken NJ, 2003.

Kissinger, Henry, *The White House Years*. Little, Brown: Boston, 1979.

Ledeen, Michael, and Lewis, William, *Debacle: The American Failure in Iran*. Random House: New York, 1981.

Malcolm, Sir John, *The History of Persia*, 2 vols. John Murray: London, 1815.

Martin, Vanessa, *Islam and Modernism: The Persian Revolution of 1906*. I.B. Tauris: London, 1989.

Menashri, David, Iran: *A Decade of War and Revolution*. Holmes and Meier: New York, 1990.

Moin, Baqer, *Khomeini: Life of the Ayatollah*. I.B. Tauris: London, 1999.

Montazam, Mir Ali Asghar, *The Life and Times of Ayatollah Khomeini*. Anglo-European Publishing Ltd: London, 1994.

Musavian, Hossein, *Imam Khomeini: His Life and Leadership*. Saffron Books: Tehran, 1990.

Naji, Kasra, *Ahmadinejad: The Secret History of Iran's Radical Leader*. I.B. Tauris: New York, 2008.

O'Balance, Edgar, *The Gulf War*. Brassey's: London, 1988.

Pahlavi, Mohammad Reza Shah, *Answer to History*. Stein and Day: New York, 1980.

—— *Mission for My Country*. Hutchinson: London, 1961.

Parsons, Anthony, *The Pride and the Fall: Iran 1974–1979*. Jonathan Cape: London, 1984.

Pollack, Kenneth, *The Persian Puzzle: The Conflict Between America and Iran*. Random House: New York, 2004.

Ricks, Thomas E., *Fiasco: The American Military Adventure in Iraq*. Penguin: London, 2006.

Ritter, Scott, *Target Iran*. Nation Books: New York, 2007.

Roosevelt, Kermit, *Countercoup: The Struggle for the Control of Iran*. McGraw-Hill: New York, 1979.

Rubin, Barry, *Paved with Good Intentions: The American Experience and Iran*. Oxford University Press: Oxford, 1982.

Sciolino, Elaine, *Persian Mirrors: The Elusive Face of Iran*. Free Press: New York, 2000.

Seale, Patrick, *Abu Nidal: A Gun for Hire*. Random House: London, 1992.

Shawcross, William, *The Shah's Last Ride*. Chatto and Windus: London, 1989.

Shay, Shaul, *The Axis of Evil: Iran, Hizbollah and the Palestinian Terror*. Transaction Publishers: New York, 2005.

Shultz, George P., *Turmoil and Triumph*. Charles Scribner's Sons: New York, 1993.

Spector, Leonard S., *Going Nuclear: The Spread of Nuclear Weapons 1986–87*. Ballinger: Cambridge, Mass., 1987.

Stempel, John D., *Inside the Iranian Revolution*. University Press: Bloomington, Indiana, 1981.

Sullivan, William H., *Mission to Iran*. W.W. Norton: New York, 1981.

Synnott, Hilary, *Bad Days in Basra*. I.B. Tauris: London, 2008.

Taheri, Amir, *The Spirit of Allah*. Hutchinson: London, 1985.

Tenet, George, *At the Centre of the Storm: My Years at the CIA*. HarperCollins: New York, 2007.

The 9/11 Commission Report. W.W. Norton: New York, 2004.

Tripp, Charles, *A History of Iraq*. Cambridge University Press: Cambridge, 2000.

Weinberger, Casper, *Fighting for Peace*. Warner Books: New York, 2000.

Woodward, Bob, *Bush at War*. Simon and Schuster: New York, 2002.

—— *Plan of Attack*. Simon and Schuster: London, 2004.

Wright, Robin, *Sacred Rage*. Touchstone: New York, 1985.

—— *In the Name of God: The Khomeini Decade*. Simon and Schuster: New York, 1989.

Zonis, Marvin, *Political Elite in Iran*. Princeton University Press: Princeton, 1971.

—— *Majestic Failure: Fall of the Shah*. University of Chicago Press: Chicago, 1991.

Index

Index